Pursuing a Divine Life

A Study of the New Nature

J. W. Phillips

Cover design by Shayna Kusumoto (www.9thavestudio.com)
Cover photo: bbourdages

PURSUING A DIVINE LIFE: A STUDY OF THE NEW NATURE

Printed in the United States of America.
HCC Publishing, Honolulu, Hawaii 96701

ISBN: 978-0-9890020-0-4

Comments about the Book

A major contribution ... a remarkable book ... I am exceptionally impressed with all the resources you found. A great job of research ... You have provided God's people with an excellent tool for coming to grips with the marvelous truth of regeneration—the new creation.

David C. Needham, author of the Christian classic, *Birthright*

This book is dedicated to my children, all grown and married with children of their own:

Dr. Amy Elizabeth Gonzalez

Michael Sean Phillips

Christopher Mark Phillips

Table of Contents

Chapter 1

The Greatest Treasure

Of all the biblical teachings describing the life of a believer, none is more important—and none is less understood—than the doctrine of the new nature. What the Bible says about the new nature is so elevating in vision, so widespread in application, and so profound in impact, one can hardly stack enough superlatives to describe its importance. Commenting on this importance, Paul Tillich, a former professor of theology at the University of Chicago, said this: "If I were asked to sum up the Christian message for our time in two words, I would say with Paul: It is the message of a 'New Creation' ...." It is true that other biblical themes could compete for this acclaim, but with justifiable insistence Tillich stressed that at its heart "Christianity is the message of the New Creation, the New Being ...."[1]

On the other end of the theological spectrum, Professor John Murray, the Reformed theologian, spoke of the new nature and our union with Christ as "being the central truth of the whole doctrine of salvation."[2] Strongly agreeing with this conclusion, Dr. A. J. Gordon, the Baptist pastor and hymn writer, declared that the new nature is one of the most profound proclamations of divine revelation:

> God taking upon himself humanity, and yet remaining God, is hardly more inexplicable to human thought than man's becoming "a partaker of the divine nature," and yet remaining man. Both are those secret things that belong wholly to God. Yet, great as is the mystery of these words,

> they are the key to the whole system of doctrinal mysteries.[3]

F. J. Huegel—professor, missionary, and author of many deeper life books—also affirmed the paramount value of the new nature by calling it "a central sun in the galaxy of the church's doctrine."[4]

The quintessential significance of the new nature is acknowledged across a wide theological spectrum. Virtually every major doctrine converges on this one, and apart from new nature truth diminishes considerably in purpose and meaning. But if the divine nature, the new creation, is this central to our faith, and if it is a core truth around which so much of Scripture revolves, why do we hear so little about it?[5]

Most of us routinely quote the verse that says we are a new creation, but have almost no idea what is being asserted. We know something profound is being said, although we find it hard to believe that at the time of our conversion a radical change actually took place inside us. We experienced the joy of having our sins forgiven and the thrill of beginning a new relationship with Jesus, but we also experienced, soon enough, the return of our old sinful ways.

So, based on this continued and unwanted sin-struggle, we had to conclude that whatever happened at that moment we became a Christian must not have meant becoming a totally different person.

And yet, II Corinthians 5:17 does seem to be wide-sweeping in its scope when it asserts that not only have we become a new creation but that old things have passed away and that all things have become new. So what passed away—and what became new?

The church hasn't answered these questions very well, and this is largely due to the erection of certain theological constructs into which II Corinthians 5:17 simply doesn't fit. Faced with this dilemma, some people have resorted to rationalizing their definition of the new nature so it will better correspond with their theological presuppositions. Typically, this rationalization avoids the view the new nature is real. For example, R. Maculay and J. Barrs wrote:

> Some claim that something inside us as believers actually changes or a part of our person, "the spirit," which before was dead, is made alive, and so we can look inside ourselves and see a new life there. Paul does say that we are a new creation, that we have new life, but he does not mean by this that a dramatic change, observable internally, has taken place in some part of us. He is referring primarily to our new status before God.[6]

A new creation isn't actual, it's only a new status? But saying this hardly squares with the obvious meaning of a new creation, which is a new nature or, to use Tillich's words, a new being. More recently, David Needham has taken to task this minimalist view of the new nature by insisting that something did happen inside us at that moment we became a Christian, something very wonderful and dramatic.

According to Needham, we were supernaturally birthed into a new nature. And while we may not be able to inspect this new nature as one might inspect some specimen under a microscope, this new nature is present within every child of God. This is a fact Scripture amply documents when it states that we were "quickened" (Ephesians 2:5), "born of God" (I John 5:1) and given a new life that is none other than the life of Jesus (Colossians 3:4). These biblical declarations, Needham says, are talking about actual truth, not positional truth—something imparted, not imputed; something experienced and not just explained.

So where is this new life? The obvious answer is that it is inside us—but then again so are some other qualities that are less than desirable. So does this mean that we have two natures? No, as we shall see, and as many evangelicals do see, the Bible never says anything like that. The born-again believer has only one nature. I Corinthians 6:17 states: "He that is joined to the Lord is one spirit." The connection between his Spirit and our spirit goes beyond standing and state, beyond function and formality, as the very words of this verse indicate. The reality referenced in this verse surpasses fellowship, intimacy, and even the concept of enmeshing[7] (see Appendix A).

Exactly how God gave us a nature so completely imbued with divine life will be explained with much detail in this book. But to put a suitable frame on this picture we need to reflect on how God responded to that great rebellion in heaven which resulted in Satan and a third of the angels being cast out. Did God, by fiat decree, create more angels to replace the ones he just lost? No, what God did was far better. He devised a plan that would bring "many sons to glory" (Hebrews 2:10).

Reflecting on this fact, Martyn Lloyd-Jones proclaimed, "Human nature has been raised to surpassing height of glory."[8] According to Scripture, there will come that day when these "sons," once welcomed into consummate glory, will be more highly exalted than the highest-ranking angel in heaven! Indeed, redeemed humanity will one day be married to Jesus (Revelation 19:7-9)!

The significance of this thought elevates prior thinking about the new nature far beyond what we have ever imagined! Moreover, the trajectory of these thoughts, stimulated as they are by Scripture, do serve to redirect us away from minimizing the new nature, as we have been prone to do.

The new nature, as set forth in Scripture, is an internal reality and not some judicial reckoning in the record-keeping of God. In the words of Paul Billheimer:

> Through the new birth we become bona fide members of the original cosmic family (Ephesians 3:15), actual generated sons of God, (I John 3:2), "partakers of the divine nature" (II Peter 1:4), begotten by him, impregnated with his "genes," called the seed or "sperma" of God (I John 5:1, 18 and I Peter 1:3, 23), and bearing his heredity.[9]

The practical significance of our new nature may very well be forfeited, though, unless at some point we translate abstract theory into daily-life reality. Much that is written about our union with God is more theoretical than practical, more mystical than concrete. And this deficiency is not without consequence. Multiplied millions have never discovered what God actually did inside them and are therefore forgoing the extraordinary benefits the new nature most assuredly affords. Among these benefits the new nature provides are remarkable remedies for such plaguing problems as:

- The sin problem—must there always be another inning of sinning?
- The identity problem—are we part good and part bad, a composite of past acts and attitudes?
- The relationship problem—can there be oneness between people who ooze acidic hatred toward each other?
- The worship problem—why are we often stranded in the outer court of protocol and so seldom break through to an inner court intimacy?
- The ministry problem—why do we do what we do with dedication and consecration but see so little change?

Many Christians would admit that the life they are now living doesn't come anywhere close to what four thousand years of redemption history should have produced. It is not until the new nature is released that the world will see, what it so seldom sees, a life that gusto and gumption could never generate. This releasing of the new nature, with all of its practical benefits, isn't likely to occur, though, so long as the new nature continues to be widely ignored.

The inability to define the new nature has caused theologians and pastors to neglect what may very well be the most astonishing doctrine in Scripture. A. W. Tozer declared: "The eternal plan was not to bring God down to man's level, but for the Son to take humanity up into God. Thus we are to be joined in the beauty and wonder of the theoanthropic union—God and man in one."[10] Such stunning words! Words that Andrew Murray, the great devotional writer, strongly supported when he similarly observed, "... God's one object was to dwell in man, making him a partaker of his goodness and glory."[11]

In her book, *Rivers of Living Water*, Ruth Paxson said, "When the Holy Spirit begat in the believer a new nature, he opened the door to a living organic union between the Christian and Christ."[12] Not just a relationship, but something profoundly more intimate than that. In the words of Ruth Paxson, "It is to have the glorified Christ in us in actual presence and power."[13] According to A. B. Simpson, "This is not the old man improved, but it is the Christ man, the Lord Jesus himself becoming our new life."[14] From the very center of our life to the circumference, his life can replace what would have been our life had not the new nature been given to us and then released.

We've long known that Jesus wants to come into our hearts. What hasn't been made clear is the fact Jesus wants to replace our hearts with his heart. A. B. Simpson wrote, "It is not only that we have a new heart but we have the Almighty God residing in that heart."[15] Think of it! We mortals, tragically flawed since Adam's fall, now having the very nature of God! This heart transplant has to be among the most amazing truths ever uttered, so one wonders how a truth like this can go unheralded from the pulpit.

A. W. Pink, another evangelical, offered this insight regarding the theoanthropic union's virtual neglect.

> The present writer has not the least doubt in his mind that the subject of spiritual union is the most important, the most profound, and the most blessed of any that is set forth in Scripture; and yet sad to say, there is hardly any which is more generally neglected.[16]

The new nature has an optimum importance that is difficult to overestimate, so it is almost past comprehension that this doctrine has been so summarily ignored. But it has, despite the fact that the new nature is so central to the gospel.[17] According to William Law, "Everything in the gospel is for the sake of the new creature, this new man in Christ Jesus, and nothing is regarded without it."[18] Martyn Lloyd-Jones offered exuberant and even effusive praise about our union with Christ when he wrote:

> ... it is one of the most glorious aspects of the Christian truth, one of the most profound, one of the most stimulating, one of the most comforting—indeed, I rather like to use the word exhilarating. There is nothing, perhaps, in the whole range and realm of doctrine which, if properly grasped and understood, gives greater assurance, greater comfort and greater hope than this doctrine of our union with Christ.[19]

Stressing further the importance of this doctrine, A. W. Tozer once asked this most intriguing question: "What is the supreme benefaction, the gift and treasure above all others which even God can give?" In response, Tozer replied, "Not the pearly gates, not the golden streets, not heaven, not even the forgiveness of sins, although these are God's gifts, too. Not a dozen, or two dozen, or a thousand [other] ... gifts God lays before his happy people."[20] God's supreme and final gift, Tozer says, is this: "He makes us the repository of the nature and person of the Lord Jesus."[21]

This is an amazing truth, the implications of which are enormous in their very practical import. But in order to overcome the neglect this "supreme gift" has suffered, we will need to identify exactly what the new nature is, how it was created, how it is received, how it can be released, how its release can be sustained, and how the new nature can transform all those qualities of the soul (our mind, will, and emotions) that have long been influenced by an alien force, what the Bible calls the flesh.

In undertaking this task, we will first focus on the glorious fact of our new nature. And in doing so, we will attempt to use easy-to-understand language and not abstract theological terminology.

Providing further incentive to study the new nature, Andrew Murray said, "One of the greatest hindrances in the spiritual life is that we do not know—we do not see—what God wants us to be."[22] Indeed, what God has fully enabled us to be!

Any journey without a destination, any project without a goal, is hindered by a lack of vision. Knowing this truth, A. H. Strong's words stress the need for this vision:

> Couldest thou in vision see
> Thyself the man God meant,
> Thou never more couldest be
> The man thou art—content

We must see, we must know, exactly what God meant for us to be! For without this knowledge, every spiritual discipline we undertake will fall far short, in purpose and outcome, from that which the Lord designed for us to receive.

In his book, *He is There and He is Not Silent*, Francis Schaeffer articulated yet another reason for learning about the new nature, one which extends beyond its benefits for the individual believer. Schaeffer writes: "Evangelicals have made a horrible mistake by often equating the fact that man is lost and under judgment with the idea that man is nothing—a zero. This is not what the Bible says ... it is the Bible which explains *why* man is great."[23] The opportunity for evangelism would be strengthened, Schaeffer contended, if we embraced this truth, and then fully explained it.

Offering a more biblical perspective of man than what some churches do, A. B. Simpson noted:

> When the New Testament talks about the natural man it does not mean a gross, sordid, sensual, brutal wretch, groveling in swinish lusts; but it means a man with all the graces and gifts of the highest genius and the most refined culture. He may be a poet like Shakespeare, a composer like Mozart, a sculptor like Phidias, a painter like Raphael, an architect like Wren, an orator like Cicero, or a man with a face as beautiful as an angel.[24]

Though these qualities are insufficient for fellowship with God, they do testify of the creative work of God and the great value he gave to man. Upon seeing this greatness in man, at least potentially, G. D. Watson invited further inquiry along these lines.

> Have we ever thought for five minutes of the grandeur of being created with a unique, individual personality all to ourselves, with a private nature, a great soul world in ourselves, a distinct orb of conscious immortal existence? We are walled in from all other creatures, with a deep privacy of nature into which no one in all the universe can enter except the Lord our God, our loving Creator. Probably this is the greatest glory of our creation, that each of us has in our personality a sacred sanctuary in the ocean depths of his soul, with a door that never opens except to the touch of that eternal, blessed One, who created us out of his love.[25]

From the vantage point of creation, this *is* man's greatness. From the vantage point of history, however, man's greatness diminished disastrously when he became the perpetrator of so much misery and ruin. Nevertheless, Pascal had it right when he said these "miseries prove man's greatness. They are the miseries of a great lord, of a deposed king."[26] And so it is that from the vantage point of redemption that man, through the cross, is restored to greatness and is able to function increasingly in it even now. Jessie Penn-Lewis observed: "Few people get even a glimpse of the huge dimensions of their destiny, or the solemn grandeur of existence."[27]

To better understand the greatness of man, we must contemplate the very essence of redeemed humanity with a more steadied and studied focus than what we have been accustomed to give. In riveting our attention on this subject, our primary intent is to learn from the Word of God what it means to be a son of God.

Reflection Questions

1. Which quotation in this chapter do you most appreciate?

2. What most surprises you about this introduction to the new nature?

3. Why do you think the new nature has been neglected?

Chapter 2

A Higher Order

It happened at the end of World War I. American soldiers, amnesia victims, were paraded on stage before a large French audience, whereupon each soldier was instructed to inquire, "Do you know who I am?" What a sad scene that must have been! Each man was looking for a clue, any clue, that would reveal his true identity. In a larger sense, though, our world is just like that stage—in that it too is crowded with people who are asking this question.

The question—"Who am I?"—skewed by the scientist and obscured by the philosopher, can be approached in several ways. The philosopher Bertrand Russell called man "a curious accident in a backwater," and the cynic H. L. Mencken considered man "a local disease of the cosmos."[1] Nietzsche classified man as "vermin on the crust of the earth." Sir Arthur Doyle referred to man as "poor silly half-brained things peering out at the infinite with the aspirations of angels and the instincts of beasts." William James declared, "Our civilization is founded on shambles, and every individual existence goes out in a lonely spasm of helpless agony." Shakespeare summed up what he deemed the pathetic history of man as "a tale told by an idiot, full of sound and fury, signifying nothing." At the very least, perspectives like these would certainly insist that the savagery and selfishness of man are far more reliable descriptors than the ones man himself more frequently cites when eulogizing his own industry and ingenuity.

Fortunately, this negativism has only a small appeal—which can be latched onto in a trendy way by the college freshman, or it can be embraced with greater comprehension by the existentialist, or it can embed more deeply still in the gloomy disposition of the nihilist. Sadly, all those plagued by this mindset are disillusioned to think that man is a chance collocation of atoms whose genius and nobility will be consumed like the weekly garbage. Gather, isolate, dump, burn—to them, man has no more significance than that.

A more common approach can be found in those less philosophical ones among us—those who stay busy and don't bother to think, at least in any abstract, searching-for-significance sort of a way. Their projects are many, their calendars are full; and so for them there isn't much time to reflect on the grand scheme of things. Instead, they rush from deadline to deadline, much like that airplane pilot who radioed back, "We're lost, but we're making record time."

Victor Frankyl, the father of logotherapy, once observed that for these people Sunday is the saddest day of the week. For it is on this day, he said, when all those racing through life without purpose are compelled to face their meaninglessness. While the race is on and the commotion is distracting, their minds can be taken off the situation. But come Sunday, when everything stops, they've got to make peace with a hollow humanity. That—or just take a nap. This preference for motion instead of meaning prompted the philosopher Pascal to remark, "Most of man's troubles come from him not being able to sit quietly in his chamber."[2] Sensing a disturbance of a deeper sort, Helmut Thielicke observed, "The unredeemed man fears solitude."[3]

Some of those who keep themselves busy, busy, busy, do so in pursuit of self-worth. The knowledge they get, the money they earn, the positions they hold—all this was their goal! And while pursuing it, their cheeks were flushed with excitement, even as their will was steeled in determination. But once they got to the top of that very high mountain, the fulfillment wasn't what they had thought it would be. It was good, but it wasn't that good. Consequently, they began to ask the question Peggy Lee made musically famous, "Is That All There Is?"

It is in this regard that we can recall the testimony of Ian Fleming, the author and creator of James Bond. There can be little doubt that Ian Fleming enjoyed more than his share of this world's success. Nevertheless, when he came to die, he said, "I'm now, my God, ashes, just ashes. You have no idea how bored one gets with the whole silly business of life."[4]

Even for those who haven't experienced this despair (and perhaps don't think they ever will), the question "Who am I?" isn't easy to answer. Attempting to answer it, the adolescent may seek self-esteem in popularity. But how will this need be met after graduation? Similarly, the athlete may seek self-esteem on the ball field. But how high will his stock be once his playing days are over? A young lady may seek self-esteem in her beauty. But how will she feel about herself once her beauty begins to diminish? A mother may seek self-esteem in her parenting. But how will she feel about herself after her children leave home?

Furthermore, what are we to say to those people who weren't popular in school, or outstanding in their talents, or attractive in their appearance, or effective in their life's work? Voicing the view of many, Edna St. Vincent Millay once said, "Life must go on, but I forgot why." Is this why drug use is such an appealing option? People who can't feel good in any other way will try to do so chemically?

The place—a commuter train; the time—midnight. Loren Eisely, an anthropologist, recounts the episode. He boarded the train in New York City and upon taking a seat in the smoking compartment his eyes fell on a gaunt, shabbily dressed man. The man, eyes closed, head thrown back on the seat, appeared to be drowsy either from exhaustion or liquor. Momentarily, the conductor came into the car asking for tickets. Opening his eyes slowly, the derelict fumbled around in his pocket, then, pulling out a roll of bills, he said in a death-like croak, "Give me a ticket to wherever it is."

The conductor recited the list of stations, but the man—his eyes closed once more—said nothing. The conductor then deducted the price of a fare to Philadelphia and put the rest of the money back in the man's pocket.

"Give me a ticket to wherever it is." In a single, poignant phrase, this bummed-out man on a midnight express personalized the emptiness of all those people who don't know (that is, from God's perspective) who they are, what they've got, where they're going, or how to get there.

True enough, the question—"Who am I?"—has not gone without a reply. Actually, there have been many responses to this question, from the carefully crafted theories of psychology to the less sophisticated notions of popular culture. It certainly would have been helpful, though, had the church weighed in with a word from eternity. But, for the most part, both pulpit and pew have been equally unaware of God's answer to this question.

Nice People or New Men

In his book, *Mere Christianity*, C. S. Lewis contended that God didn't come to this world to make us nice; instead, pursuing a much more radical objective, he came to make us new! Addressing this point further, Lewis wrote:

> God became man to turn creatures into sons: Not simply to produce better men of the old kind but to produce a new kind of man. It is not like teaching a horse to jump better and better but like turning a horse into a winged creature. Of course, once it has got its wings, it will soar over fences which could never have been jumped and thus beat the natural horse at its own game.[5]

This image of a flying horse, intended by Lewis to be an "extreme example,"[6] conveys the very point people in the church need to hear. The change made in a believer is so radical that A. W. Tozer declared, "When God infuses eternal life into the spirit of a man, the man becomes a member of a new and higher order of being."[7] Spurgeon noted that the word "new," when used to describe our new nature, "does not signify something *recent*, but something altogether different from that which previously existed."[8]

The infusion of this new nature transacts not in heaven someday where all is glorious and perfect—but right here, right now, at that precise moment when the Lord Jesus enters a person's heart. The change is far more profound than what may be known at the time. The corrupted heart is totally and eternally changed into a being whose hidden glory will one day outshine the sun.

In making this same observation about our higher order of being, the Apostle John could hardly control his excitement! He said, "What manner of love the Father has bestowed upon us that we should be called the children of God!" (I John 3:1). In the Greek, that word "manner" means foreign. What God did was so unique this wasn't just foreign in the sense of one country versus another—it's foreign to the whole world! In fact, in all of human history this is a miracle without precedent or parallel! For some reason, though, whenever we come across a verse like this, we will read right on to the next verse—with no quickening of pulse, no tearing of eyes, and no gulping in amazement. It seems as though, sedated by all the religious verbiage, we have no idea what's being said. So let's slow down and seek with understanding to enter into John's excitement.

Perhaps this illustration will help. Let's say that one day while taking a walk, you saw—right before your eyes—a tree turn into a dog. That's right, at one moment it was a nice little tree with trunk and limbs and leaves; and the next moment—in but a millisecond of time—it became a playful, tail-wagging, four-legged dog. In response, you blinked your eyes, you shook your head, and then, trying to make sure this wasn't a dream, you pinched yourself. But, just as you already knew, you were awake, all right. Therefore, as absurd as all this appeared, you had to accept the impossible—a tree had just become a dog!

Later that week as you took your walk down that same road, you saw this barking, flea-swatting, running-after-the-mailman dog turn—in just a moment's time—into a well-dressed, sophisticated man who was reading the *Wall Street Journal*. What would you think? That you are going crazy? That you should never walk down this road again?

The point, though, is this: The gaps between a tree and a dog, and a dog and a man, are not nearly as great as the gap between a sinner and a son of the living God.[9] Just as Lewis and Tozer implied, what Scripture is talking about is a new species.[10] To use the language of the scientist, it isn't microevolution (the old species refining, progressing) but macroevolution (something coming into existence that never existed before). But as with the original creation, there wasn't any evolving; it all happened suddenly.

Stephen Charnock, the seventeenth-century Puritan writer, concluded correctly, "Nothing in the world can raise itself to a higher rank of being than that which nature has placed it in; a spark cannot make itself a star, though it mount a little up to heaven ..."[11] Similarly, a speck cannot become a planet, although each may have in common certain properties from the Periodic Table of Elements. And further: A human being cannot become a son of God, though each has characteristics of personality. Indeed, there is no elevation of thinking, refinement of taste, improvement of behavior, or alteration of temperament that can transport a human being into the domain of God's family. All progress of this sort will fail to alter human nature sufficiently. Impressive though our achievements may be, the ennobled will and the tutored mind can never propel a trajectory of progress that will elevate one from the human species to the spiritual status of a son of God.

At this point in our study, as we simply introduce this subject, you may not understand how God gave man a new nature. That the Lord did precisely this is what caused the Apostle John to marvel in such an eye-popping, jaw-dropping way.

The Divine Masterpiece

While we may gulp and gawk at such vision-lifting truth, there is this to remember: Our transformation into sons isn't going to take place when we cross the threshold of heaven. Instead, it is an already accomplished fact, true this very moment! Expounding this truth, the Apostle John wrote, "But as many as received him, to them gave him the right to become the children of God, to those who believe in his name: who were born, not of blood, nor of the will of the flesh, nor of the will of man, but of God" (John 1:12, 13). In his book, *The Christ Life*, A. B. Simpson helps us understand the significance of John's declaration.

> Two words are used in the New Testament to describe sonship. One word means a born son. But the other word means much more. The second word for sonship is almost always applied to Christ's sonship, and is rarely used of anybody else but Jesus; but it is also used to denote those who enter into union with Christ. Not only are they born the children of God, but they are accepted in the same sense Christ is; that is, they have not only the sonship of the new birth, but the place of Christ himself.[12]

John's testimony, then, is this: Someone becomes a child of God at that precise moment he believes and receives Jesus. This isn't a matter of biology, as the Jews had thought (according to them, all Israelites are children of God). And it isn't a matter of humanity, as the world still thinks (their consensus being we are all God's children by virtue of creation). Moreover, becoming a child of God isn't a matter of performance or self-improvement, as those of other religions and no religion commonly suppose (they believe that just being good will merit eternal reward). Nor is this a decision that can be made for us by somebody else—not Constantine centuries ago when he declared the Roman Empire Christian, and not Father and Mother today when they declare their family Christian.

"Narrow is the way?" inquired the provocative Kierkegaard, "Why, the way is as broad as all Denmark!" He said that because in his day everyone born in Denmark was automatically placed on the church's roll—namely, the Lutheran Church, the official church of Denmark. However, the born-again experience isn't a matter of heredity, our willpower, or someone else's decision on our behalf. Each of us must on our own believe and receive.

Yet, it is not entirely on our own. Scripture says that this born-again experience is "of God." This implies not only that God is the initiator, provider, and sustainer of this experience, but also, to use Scripture's birth analogy, that our nature will be just like the One who produced us.[13] Consider the logic of this: When lions procreate, they have lions. When bears procreate, they have bears. And when one is born "of God," that one will have a nature just like God's.[14] Samuel Chadwick wrote, "As the father's very being lives in the being of his child, so is the being of God in the being of man."[15] According to Chadwick, "Parentage determines nature."[16]

Just now your defenses may be shooting up as you suspect something akin to Mormonism or New Age thinking being introduced. But be aware that the Enemy counterfeits virtually everything God does; and therefore if we're going to keep our distance from everything that has been contemptibly counterfeited by the Enemy, there isn't going to be much truth left for us to embrace.

We can be certain about this: To say that the born-again Christian is a god very much exceeds the claims of Scripture. In and of ourselves, we are nothing. Furthermore, any good that we have—no matter how godly and glorious—is altogether derivative. Nevertheless, Scripture has the most awesome things to say about our new nature—truths that are not hidden in obscure verses, nor are they the dubious conclusions of deductive reasoning. What Scripture sets forth on this issue is indisputably clear.

For example, Ephesians 4:24 says of the new man, or the new nature, that it "was created according to God, in true righteousness and holiness." This holiness, it should be noted, is not one of mere resemblance or faint similarity; it is much higher than that. A. B. Simpson observed:

> The holiness to which we are called and into which we are introduced by the Holy Spirit is not the restoration of Adamic perfection or the recovery of what we lost by the Fall. It is a higher holiness, even the very nature of God himself and the indwelling of Jesus Christ ....[17]

Ephesians 4:24 says this new nature wasn't the result of our efforts—it was "created." Furthermore, it was created by none other than the altogether Pure One! Therefore, just as one might expect, what God created is perfect. Its essence is one of "true righteousness and holiness."

This quite obviously does not describe what we, as successors to Adam, were born with; for the Bible characterizes that nature in an absolutely, diametrically opposite way, saying not only that it is desperately wicked (Jeremiah 17:9) but also that its so-called righteousness is as filthy rags (Isaiah 64:6). The righteousness Ephesians associates with our new nature is in a decidedly different category, not in any way achievable, even by the most rigorous religionist on earth.

In his book, *The King of the Earth*, the German scholar Erich Sauer explained man's need for a new nature by commenting first on the extent of his guilt.

> It is not only his life history that makes the sinner guilty but also his whole nature, not only the desires of his will but also all that he is spiritually. Therefore, he must become a "new man" (Ephesians 4:22-24; Colossians 3:9, 10) and be "born again" (John 3:3, 5). It is not merely canceling the old guilt, or guiding the will in a new direction, but bringing the spiritually dead to life (Ephesians 2:5, 6), being born "of God" (I John 3:9; Titus 3:5), i.e. a *creative renewal* of the whole man himself (II Corinthians 5:17). God alone has the power to create. Hence no creature, not man or angel, but only a Person of the Godhead could bring this work of the new creation to pass.[18]

According to Scripture, so bad was our old nature (in terms of its immersion into evil), and so hopeless its condition, it could not be *repaired*; instead, a more radical procedure was needed: It had to be *replaced*. Nineteenth-century writer, Horatius Bonar, commented on this replacement in his thoughtful book, *God's Way of Holiness*.

> The old man is slain; the new man lives. It is not merely the old life touched and made more comely, defects struck out, roughnesses smoothed down, graces stuck on here and there. It is not a

broken column repaired, a soiled picture cleaned, a defaced inscription filled up, an unswept temple whitewashed. It is more than all this or else God would not call it a new creation.[19]

Only the miracle of a new creation could give man the ability he needed to please God, worship God, and live for God. This new nature changed everything from the inside out.

Understanding Who We Are

Second Corinthians 5:17 declares, "Therefore, if anyone is in Christ, he is a new creation; old things have passed away; behold, all things have become new."[20] According to this verse, our true identity is singularly bound up in this new nature. We are not, it must be emphasized, part this and part something else. The spiritual schizophrenia that says we have two natures is, as we shall later see, unbiblical. No such hybrid humanity is taught in the Scripture. We are a new creation—period! The old, Scripture says (and we'll expound this later) is gone! The new is completely new.

There are two Greek words which are translated "new" in the Bible. The first, *neos*, refers to something of recent construction but already in existence (such as a car on day one-hundred of an assembly line production). The word translated "new" in this verse, though, is the word *kainos*, which means something just made that is unlike anything else in existence. What Jesus fashioned for us, and then made available to us, had never been on earth before—not in Adam, not in Abraham, and not in any prophet or priest.

When Colossians 3:4 speaks of "... Christ who is our life," it isn't just saying that Jesus is number one in our life. He may be, but that isn't what this verse is saying. This verse is saying that all that constitutes the inner life of Jesus is in us right now. Our new nature is composed of all those character qualities that exist in his heart. And even better they exist in our heart in full measure! John 1:16 says, "And of his fullness we have all received ...." We know that when it comes to beautifying our hair, the old commercial may well have it right, "a little dab will do you." But when it comes to our spirit, God isn't in the business of portioning out little dabs.

Ephesians 3:19 speaks of being "filled with all the fullness of God."[21] Now, who would think that anything like this is possible? Many of us, when reading a verse like this, don't even have the good sense to be startled. Instead of letting our minds engage what is being said, we just put the label of "mystery" on it and immediately proceed to the next verse.

To illustrate what is indeed a mystery (but not one without some explanation), let's imagine a circle as big as this page. We will let that circle represent the inner life of God. Then let's imagine a barely visible dot, located, let's say, in the upper right-hand corner of the page. That dot, we will agree, represents the individual Christian. Now, when Scripture says that you are "in Christ"—which it does say 132 times—this you can easily envision. "Your life," Colossians 3:3 says, "is hidden with God in Christ." Consequently, what we have here is the little dot in the big circle. But when Scripture speaks of the fullness of God in you, that doesn't seem to be comprehensible at all, for this would mean putting the big circle in the little dot.

To partially explain how this is possible, it must be pointed out that the fullness of God, as Scripture speaks of it here, doesn't equate with all of God's attributes—his omniscience, omnipotence, and omnipresence, for example. Donald Grey Barnhouse is correct in his observation that the preferred rendering of Ephesians 3:19 ("... that you may be filled with all the fullness of God") substitutes the word "unto" for the preposition "with," thus avoiding the thought of exactness or equivalency, which would obviously be an impossible transaction.[22] John Tauler, the fourteenth-century German teacher, said this of God: "His essence is incomprehensible, unspeakable and without a name."[23] Of course, the ineffable in God will never be replicated in man.

Still, Scripture bids us to consider a stunning proposition, a filling that doesn't involve all the capacities of God, certainly, but one that involves qualities of his spirit—such as love, joy, peace, and patience. These qualities, the essence of divine life, are put inside the believer in full measure—and not just some believers, but every believer, because referring to this infusion of God's fullness, John said "We have *all* received." So this isn't reserved for only a rare few super, duper saints.[24]

A. T. Pierson's observation about this mystery is helpful. Pierson said of Jesus, "He is filled with God, and in him we also are filled with God."[25] Just as Jesus possessed all the Father's life, the redeemed inherit not just fragments and portions but share all of his life as well.[26] G. D. Watson said that "the life of God in the soul, even in its earliest stage, possesses all the attributes and inherent graces, both in number and quality which it ever will possess through eternal ages."[27] Walter Marshall, the seventeenth-century Puritan, maintained, "... all spiritual life and holiness are treasured up in the fullness of Christ and communicated to us by union with Him."[28] Spurgeon said, "The babe in grace who is just now born to God, hath every part of the spiritual man ...."[29] And Dr. Dale Yocum remarked, "It may appear unthinkable that divine fullness should dwell within human capacity. But God is able to do exceeding abundantly above what we can think ...."[30]

Of course, it would strain anyone's belief to say that these qualities *manifest* in a believer to the same extent they manifest in our most holy God.[31] However, the fullness of God can be understood in the sense of a divine seed being placed in the believer (I Peter 1:23; Galatians 4:16). While a seed may not yet be a tall and mighty oak tree, nevertheless within that seed are all the elements necessary for the seed to become just that.[32]

It must be quickly pointed out that we can become a victim of this metaphor if we think it's going to take decades for the new nature inside us to rise up and flow out with a magnificence that reminds others of the Messiah. True, for many believers the divine seed planted within remains inconspicuous for a long time. But it doesn't have to be that way. And it shouldn't be that way. For unlike the way the oak tree grows, the divine seed in us could manifest its marvelous and glorious reality a lot sooner than we think. For example, Paul commended the believers at Thessalonica for their great faith and labor which had spread its influence throughout Macedonia and other cities in Northern Greece (I Thessalonians 1:5-9). Yet, these people had been Christians less than two years.

Exhibiting the Lord's life in such a powerful way isn't limited to only a few Christians, on a few continents, during but a few centuries. Jesus made this very point in the most awesome way. In Matthew chapter 11, verse 11, he said, "Assuredly, I say to you, among those born of women" (this I think includes most of us) "there has not risen one greater than John the Baptist." According to Jesus, then, when evaluating all the spiritual giants of history—Moses, David, Elijah, and Jeremiah—John the Baptist stands the tallest. In fact, he (except for Jesus himself) was (up until the time of these words) the most spiritual person who had ever lived!

In thinking about that, imagine how you would feel if you could meet the greatest prophet of all time, the man who was closer to God than any other man. Wouldn't that meeting make you a little more than awe-struck? And in retrospect, wouldn't you regard such a meeting as one of the most memorable experiences in your whole life?

With that thought in mind, consider next what Jesus had to say in the last part of this verse: "... but he who is least in the kingdom of heaven is greater than he." Do you understand what Jesus is saying? Jesus is saying that that druggie who got saved five minutes ago, he who has a criminal record longer than your arm, has right now an even higher standing before God than John the Baptist did. How could this be true, you ask? It is true because that druggie has within him what John the Baptist never had, a brand-new nature. A. B. Simpson declared, "The feeblest saint is a new order of being, in the eyes of the angels as marvelous as when Adam stepped out upon the theater of Eden ...."[33]

Oswald Chambers said, "God made man a mixture of dust and deity ...."[34] But, again, the born-again man is even higher than Adam! For this reason, A. B. Simpson said that the 17th chapter of John "was the highest utterance of Christ in this world; and these last three words, 'I in them,' are the most precious of all."[35] A. T. Pierson wrote, "Those three short words, 'in Christ Jesus,' are, without doubt, the most important ever written, even by an inspired pen, to express the mutual relation of the believer and Christ."[36]

Making a similar point, Paul Billheimer said, "The highest ranking angel hovering over the throne of the Most High is outranked—wonder of wonders—by the most insignificant human being who has been born again ...."[37] The basis for this assertion rests in the amazing qualities of our new nature. Commenting further, Billheimer wrote, "Only man has a nature in which God can become incarnate ... By this he dignified the human race and elevated redeemed humanity beyond the highest ranking angelic star in the radiant canopy of the firmament."[38]

In his book, *The Attributes of God* (Volume One), A. W. Tozer also offers a useful comparison with angels.

> ... if it were possible to put an ape and an angel in the same room, there would be no comparability, no communion, no understanding, no friendship; there would only be distance. The shining angel and the slobbering, gibberish ape would be far, far removed from each other.[39]

When contemplating the ineffable qualities of God, certainly—qualities that are indescribable, unutterable, incapable of expression—one might think an even greater distance exists between God and man. Angels and apes are both created beings, after all, despite their enormous differences. But the immensity and infinity of the creator God would seem to remove him entirely from any comparisons with that which he created.[40]

One might also think that the difference between God's nature and man's nature is too vast for Jesus to take on one nature without contradicting the other.[41] But E. J. Carnell accurately observed, "Human nature is a fit receptacle for the divine being. Though Christ *humbled* himself by taking on flesh, he did not *degrade* himself."[42] There was no smear spoiling divine essence, no corruption compromising his holy character. He was as pure on earth as he was in heaven. Of course, the humility Jesus exhibited should never be overlooked or reduced to a mere mention, either.

Therefore, helping us to appreciate such humility, F. B. Meyer wrote:

> The profoundest stoop of his humility was that he became man at all. He was infinite in his unstinted blessedness; rich with the wealth that has flowered out into the universe; radiant in the dazzling beauty of perfect moral excellence. What agony, therefore, must have been his to breathe our tainted air, to live in daily contact with sinners, and to be perpetually surrounded by the most miserable and perpetually plague-stricken of the race![43]

The transition from the God of Glory to earthly man was wide in its mystery and deep in its profundity. But not so wide and deep it must be denied or set aside by assumptions declaring its contemplation useless. The intersecting of humanity in divinity and divinity in humanity has been sufficiently cast in revelation's light to yield valid information. Jesus invested humanity with a measure of his glory so that men today could have a new nature imbued with divine life.

This new nature wasn't available to anybody in the Old Testament; nor was it available to anyone who died before Jesus did. However, when this new nature enters even the vilest person on earth today, that person has just been elevated to a spirituality significantly higher than that attained by any of the Old Testament prophets. What makes this true is the fact that the new nature is perfect.

Ephesians 2:10 says that we are God's workmanship—quite literally his poem, his masterpiece, his work of art. All that it took to produce our new nature, and all that is true about its makeup, far exceeds whatever suffering, sacrifice, and steadfastness the most noble prophet ever endured. As we recall Jeremiah's pathos and all that he did for an unappreciative people; and as we consider, too, the faith of Elijah, the worship of David, the martyrdom of Isaiah, and all the commendable qualities of other notable greats—the uncompromising spirit of Moses, the fearlessness of Daniel, and the submissiveness of Joseph—not even a composite of all that goodness could possibly compare with the new nature put inside us by God.

In one of his sermons, Phillips Brooks pictures the great Michelangelo standing outside a home while peering through a window where he sees all the tools an artist uses: brushes and paint, canvas and easel, the glow of light and the privacy of space. Upon seeing the opportunity existing there, the great artist then says, "If only I were inside, what a beautiful picture I could paint."

Today, Jesus, the Master Artist is looking into human hearts filled and felled with mistakes and neglect, and he says, "If only I were inside, what a beautiful life I could create—a life greater than all the best qualities of all the best people who ever lived."

It is instructive that God refers to this new nature as a new creation. For as we think about the original creation: galaxies and galaxies of planets, full of suns and moons and stars—dazzling lights, vast oceans, magnificent mountains, and many scenes of luxuriant beauty—we are bound to ask ourselves: Which creation has the greater value—the first one, the universe; or the second one, our new nature?

The answer to this question can be discovered in these observations: 1) Whereas the universe was created by a few spoken words, our new nature is the product of God's unspeakable suffering; and 2) whereas the universe displays the excellence of God's hand; the new nature displays the excellence of God's heart; and 3) whereas the universe is likened to a footstool when compared to heaven; the new nature belongs to those who will outrank even the highest angels of heaven. The bottom line is this: The first creation God enjoys; however, it is the second creation that God will one day marry.

For the Christian, then, there's no reason to be confused about one's identity. We are a child of God, the Lord's brethren and bride, possessors of a divine nature, inheritors of the very qualities that are pulsating in the heart of Jesus. We are a brand-new species, something that for many millenniums never existed. We are, in one sense, greater than the greatest prophet, pure and perfect as God intended us to be. What was created in Bethlehem, tested in Jerusalem, raised up near Golgotha, and approved in heaven has now been incarnated in us—the very life of Jesus!

This and this alone is who we are.

Reflection Questions

1. Briefly describe how you have tried to feel good about yourself in the past. Identify the obstacles you've encountered in these various attempts?

2. After reading the first two chapters, how has your view about your true identity begun to change?

Chapter 3

The Ultimate Makeover

Makeovers have become quite the rage these days. The transformation of a formerly dowdy looking person into a strikingly attractive individual is frequently viewed on TV.

To accomplish one of these makeovers, a team of professionals will be assembled, often with no expenses spared—massage therapists, hair beauticians, facial beauticians, manicurists, clothiers, dentists, physical fitness specialists, and maybe even plastic surgeons. Their task? To change physical features that obviously detract, and also enhance other features until their positive potential is fully realized.

Finally, after considerable labor from these experts, the makeover recipient will walk on stage, exquisitely dressed and beaming from ear to ear as an appreciative audience marvels at the outcome.

Of course, a makeover like that is partial at best, in that it deals only with the physical. But wouldn't it be good if there could be a *supernatural* makeover, a makeover *on the inside,* a makeover that was so thorough it actually elevated us to a place that was even better than where Adam was before the fall? Such a makeover is exactly what God had in mind! Not a "heaven someday" makeover, or some gradual, day-by-day makeover that we scarcely notice, but a sudden and dramatic makeover that is available in this life.

But saying this is getting a little bit ahead of our story. Before explaining how God made this ultimate makeover available, let's first identify what the makeovers we see on TV are intended to produce. There are physical imperfections in most people—some of these quite obvious, others that are less noticeable—and people want these flaws changed! Or, if these flaws can't be changed, people want them hidden, masked, covered up.

Even more troublesome than these physical flaws, however, are certain character flaws so humiliating and degrading that we will do whatever we have to do to hide them. Instead of being perpetually targeted by the shame these faults generate, what we far prefer is a sure and certain knowledge that we are significant, that we have value, that there is something in us worthy of love.

Most of us aren't demanding center stage attention for ourselves, yet we do want a certain measure of respect. Therefore, it would be gratifying if family, friends, and others in the community favorably regarded us.

Despite this deep down desire, and despite attaining a certain measure of success, most people still have "not okay" feelings about themselves. In his book, *I'm Okay; You're Okay*, Thomas Harris estimated that 93% of our population have what Alfred Adler first called inferiority feelings. That these feelings are so widespread shouldn't really surprise us, though, since we were all born inferior!

In the beginning, we were completely helpless—without knowledge, without skills, and without much of an ability to communicate. The earliest memory for most of us is that of a small person living in a "big people's" world. Why, our parents, teachers, and relatives could do all sorts of things we couldn't do!

This perception of ourself didn't change when we began school, for we soon discovered that there were others in our class who were either smarter than we, or, if not that, more athletic, more popular, or better looking. Accordingly, the opportunity was present, almost from day one, to question our self-worth.

Putting forth a somewhat different slant on this, G. D. Watson wrote: "There is hardly an animal, or bird, or insect, that cannot in some particular excel me, either in speed of motion, or beauty of song, or hardiness, or docility, or some trait which makes me as a creature feel my inferiority."[1] It should be obvious, then, that this sense of inferiority is one to be reckoned with.

Strategies for Not Okay Feelings

Our own observation informs us that people will respond to feelings of inferiority in various ways. There are some who will find themselves *so* criticized, *so* rejected, that their hearts get bruised, if not totally and devastatingly crushed! Consequently, their ability to relate to others becomes severely impaired, prompting them to withdraw, to drop out, or to identify only with those people who, like themselves, have been shunned by society.

Then there are others among us who will become "people pleasers," "approval addicts"—each of these desperately craving acceptance or love. This desire for acceptance may translate into sexual promiscuity, gang membership, or a series of "clinging vine" relationships that always have a way of bearing rotten fruit. Tragically, the very acceptance these people want, they never seem to get—from lovers, from their children, or from society at large.

Of concern, too, is the collateral damage that results from pursuing society's approval in the wrong way. T. S. Eliot wrote, "Half the harm that is done in this world is due to people who want to feel important." The full impact of this damage scarcely registers with the people who caused it, Eliot said, "because they are absorbed in the endless struggle to think well of themselves."

Many others in our midst will fall into what is sometimes called "the performance trap." Of these, a rare few will become "overachievers," attempting through grit and guile to prove early failures an exception and those predictions about their future in error. And, yes, before it's all over, they may even exceed the most optimistic projection of their most positive friend, achieving a success that astonishes everyone. Having done so, we would conclude that they are no longer a part of that 93%—because, good golly, Miss Molly, they have everything going for them now!

Nevertheless, if we could see into their hearts and retrieve a printout from their brains, we would discover that all those "not okay" feelings from earlier years are driving them harder than ever. For no sooner do they reach the top of one mountain, when suddenly there is another one in view to climb—each mountain presenting keener competition, a greater risk of failure, and a climate with many more hostility factors. Therefore, what others may envy isn't nearly as satisfying as it may appear.

If a person were to seek counseling for self-worth concerns, almost every counselor would make one of two mistakes. Either the counselor would try to affirm that person's value on the basis that this person possesses innate worth, as every human being does. Or the counselor would try to enhance the counselee's self-esteem by telling him to get back in the game and improve his performance.

The performance trap will claim many victims, thus generating many disappointments; because big bucks, notable achievements, and advanced college degrees just won't meet our need in the way many people suppose. Even if one has a Ph.D. behind his name, that still sounds like Fudd, as in Elmer! Besides, God says that our flesh—that is, our self-life with all of its native abilities—produces nothing! So how are we going to get much esteem from that?

The first idea—we have value simply because we exist—is only partially true. Yes, we have potential value in that we might come into a right relationship with God.[2] But this value is very tentative. Contrary to the misty-eyed blather of sentimental humanists, this value is not the self-evident truth as is commonly supposed. In fact, if one were to die in this condition, he or she would be utterly banished from the presence of God, and his or her value would be certified by the flaming fires of hell.

Value, it must be remembered, cannot be determined solipsistically (by what *we* think, feel, or wish). The study of value (in philosophy this is called axiology) makes us aware of the need for absolutes. There must be One outside the flux of space and time, and outside the ebb and flow of human opinion, by whom all values are measured. Hence, only his revealed standard (which may very well refute natural thinking) can be the final arbiter of anyone's value or worth. Therefore, essential to one's quest for significance is this all-important discovery of how one can have real worth in the eyes of God. Taking counsel with ourself, or accepting the views of tradition or culture, are too high-risk for this issue.

The Search for Significance

It has been said that the most important question any of us can ask is indeed the question Job asked, "How can a man be right with God?" The other issues that preoccupy us—the welfare of our families, the progress of our careers, and our ongoing pursuit for inner fulfillment—can scarcely compare with this issue, the salvation of our souls.

Furthermore, the only opinion that matters in this, the most ultimate question we'll ever face, is God's. This means if others lightly regard us when God highly treasures us, then they're wrong and he's right. And conversely, if the world fawns all over us—adoring us and even honoring us with its acclaim of legendary status—but all the while God resists us, and in the end rejects us, then again we know which view is right and which one isn't.

In his book, *Soul Food*, G. D. Watson declared, "What we are in the sight of God, that we are, no more and no less, regardless of what men or saints or angels think of us, and regardless of what we think of ourselves."[3] That being true, this should put us on a search to discover God's criteria for value.

The critical question to ask is: What makes a person worthy to God? Are we valuable because of what we can do? For example, if we give the Lord a lot of money—or better still, if we give our lives to a ministry on foreign fields, does that in his eyes enhance our value? No, because to say that would "Christian coat" the performance trap.

In his book, *A Pot of Oil*, G. D. Watson maintained, "The ruin of spirituality among modern Christians is in putting the fussy doing of religion ahead of the deep, divine inward being like Jesus."[4] Although "doing" does have a legitimate place in our Christian walk, it is never by itself the basis of our worth. This was precisely Paul's point in I Corinthians 13 when he pointed out that one could have mountain-moving faith and even die as a Christian martyr, but if there wasn't love (which finds its deeper roots in being, not in doing), it would amount to nothing.

In checking out what the Bible has to say about essence, being, our inner core, what Martin Luther King called "the content of our character," we discover some very polarizing views. For example, Romans chapter 3 says that there are "none righteous, no not one." These are words which, even as we read them, seem very emphatic—and all the more so when we discover that just two verses later God repeats them! Moreover, when the Bible says that our righteousness is as filthy rags, we pretty quickly get the idea that God isn't much impressed with our attempts to be good.

Interestingly, the filthy rags to which God refers are menstrual cloths used by a woman. The flow of her blood is an indication of death on the scene, since during this time in her cycle there can be no giving of life. Similarly, the so-called righteousness of natural man is what the Bible calls "dead fruit" (Romans 7:5). And what good is such smelly, disease-producing, insect-gathering fruit?

Commenting on the nature we were born with and its incapacity to produce good fruit, Oswald Chambers wrote, "... human nature cannot come anywhere near what Jesus Christ demands, and any rational being facing his demands, honestly, says, 'It can't be done apart from a miracle.' Exactly."[5] Natural man cannot live a life like that!

Cyprian, Bishop of Carthage during the third century, expounded this point in his *Letter to Donatus*:

> How ... is such a conversion possible, that we can suddenly and speedily strip off all those things that are innate in us and have become hardened in the corruption of our material nature and all those things that we have acquired and have become deep-rooted by lengthy habit? These things are deeply and radically ingrained within us ... It is inevitable, as it has always been, that the love of wine should entice, pride inflate, anger inflame, covetousness disturb, cruelty stimulate, ambition delight, lust hasten to ruin with fascinations that will not let go their grip.[6]

Conversion is indeed a miracle; it takes precisely that to change all these qualities of the old nature.[7] A. W. Tozer declared, "God can give every one of us a whole new set of instincts, a new set of moral desires, a new moral bent so that we will do right because we are right."[8] Diligence and discipline can never produce this radical revamping of the inner life. The miracle of the new birth is required.[9]

Not recognizing the need for the born-again miracle, the Pharisees taught a different way. And how successful was this way? Well, Jesus said of the Pharisees, men whose sense of duty and devotion had earned them the high respect of their countrymen, that these religious leaders were nothing but a white-coated sepulcher—that is, a good paint job on the outside, with nothing but death on the inside!

Attempts to renovate self through diligence and desire didn't work for the Pharisees then and it will never work for anyone today. With forceful clarity, Jesus repeatedly repudiated all such attempts.

Although Jesus rejected any form of performance-based righteousness, he did not say that performance was a lost cause and that all desires for a radically changed life should be set aside. To the contrary, Jesus actually raised expectations along these lines, envisioning an outcome for those who would follow him that extended far beyond what the Pharisees could ever hope for.

We need only examine a brief passage of Scripture, words Jesus prayed just before he went to the cross, to see this vision cast. These words are found in the 17th chapter of John's Gospel.

Our attention first will be given to verse 22, where Jesus said, "And the glory which you gave me I have given them, that they may be one just as we are one." Does this shock you? Here, Jesus speaks of his glory being conferred upon these disciples. But who in his right mind would dare to think that anything like this is possible? Not only was it possible, but according to the biblical record it had been God's plan from all eternity to bring "many sons to glory."

In contrast with the Sinai way proposed by the Pharisees, Donald Barnhouse wrote that "this glory is for every believer, not for the face of one man. Moses alone had the shining face at the giving of the law but we all are to know the glory that is ours since Pentecost."[10]

But what exactly is this glory? In his book, *Jesus, Our Man in Glory*, A. W. Tozer addressed the misconceptions that exist about this word.

> Glory is one of those beautiful, awesome words that have been dragged down until they have lost much of their meaning. The old artists may have had something to do with it, depicting the glory of Jesus Christ as a luminous halo—a shining neon loop around his head. But the glory of Jesus Christ was never a luminous ring around the head. It was never a misty, yellow light.[11]

Significantly, the Greek word for "glory" in this passage has two primary meanings. It can mean to splendidly shine—a light so bright it reveals, it discloses, it shows what is true about God. And, of course, this is precisely what Jesus, "the light of the world," had come to do: He came to reveal the Father to a world that desperately needed to know him. Additionally, this word "glory" can mean a "weight," signifying substance, value, importance—as opposed to something light and insignificant, such as a mist that can easily be blown away.[12]

So God is saying that a believer can have what Jesus has: a life within that has a supernatural glow, a life that is substantively the same as what Jesus has right now. In his book, *Destined for the Throne*, Paul Billheimer declared that redeemed humanity has been "elevated above all other created beings to the most sublime height possible short of becoming members of the Trinity itself. Although Christ is the unique and only begotten eternal Son, yet he does not retain his glory for himself alone."[13]

In II Thessalonians 2:14 this truth is reaffirmed as the Apostle Paul declared that one of the reasons we are saved is "for the obtaining of the glory of the Lord Jesus Christ." We might want to say, "Yes, this glory could be ours in *kind*, but not to the same *degree* our Lord had." In saying this, however, we may be retreating too far. Yes, the glory belonging to the Lord Jesus is like none other; for a thousand reasons we can all readily affirm that. Nevertheless, the glory referred to here is the very presence of God, the essence of our new nature. And as this new nature is increasingly released from within us, we will find ourselves moving from "glory to glory" in our daily living (II Corinthians 3:18). Isn't that a wonderful way to live? To transcend hum-drum existence into that sphere where the glory abides is an intrinsic dynamic of abundant life.

Let's read further. In John 17:23 Jesus proceeds to pray, "I in them and you in me," words very much like those he prayed in the previous verse. Martyn Lloyd-Jones declared, "That is one of the most staggering statements in the whole of the Bible."[14] Just as the life of the Father perfectly intersected and saturated the life of Jesus—wherein both were mysteriously the same and yet somehow distinct—so this same phenomenon is now at work in believers. Believers are recipients of a new nature, its essence being the very life of God. Although our individuality is certainly and permanently retained, our nature, nevertheless, is exactly like his. In his book, *The Christ Life*, A. B. Simpson wrote that we are "not merely called and legally declared the sons of God, but [we are] actually the sons of God by receiving the life and nature of God ...."[15]

While distinctions between Christ and his creation are real and permanent, the nature shared between the Lord and those who will be his bride is remarkably the same. To better explain this point, Paul Billheimer writes:

> Those who have worked on an assembly line know that a prototype is first designed, handcrafted, and tested before it is committed to the assembly line. They also know that the purpose of the assembly line is to produce exact duplicates, perfect copies of the original. This is God's purpose in the plan of redemption—to produce by means of the new birth, an entirely new and unique species, exact replicas of his Son with whom he will share his glory and his dominion, and who will constitute a royal

progeny and form the governing and administrative staff of his eternal kingdom.[16]

This is not a novel notion of contemporary origin, for Thomas Goodwin, the seventeenth-century Puritan scholar, said much the same thing when he wrote, "God did set up Christ as the prototype and principal masterpiece, and made us as little models and copies of him."[17]

It is quite clear that something is set forth in this John 17 prayer that is far more amazing than anything our sluggish brains have ever contemplated. Jesus continued his prayer by saying, "... that the whole world may know that you have sent me, and have loved them as you have loved me." What? God loves you like he loves Jesus? This can't be! Indeed, reason wants to protest—and for once orthodoxy has become its ally! We are *very* uncomfortable with words like these. First, because no one in the church we attend talks this way, at least no one we can respect. Furthermore, too much has been engrained in us from both our fragile past and the Accuser himself to allow us to step right up and bask in the truth of this verse. Quite frankly, we feel embarrassed ... almost as if the Lord had made some mistake. But there these words stand, forever inscribed in Scripture!

At the very least we can agree that if the life of Jesus is indeed in us and, as we shall see, completely defines who we are; and if we have the very glory Jesus has and are recipients of the same love he got, that has to blow every vestige of personal inferiority right out of the water! And further: It also meets our need for value such as nothing else can!

The Securing of Significance

What would further enable us to appreciate this new nature is to understand better how we got it. Most believers think the new nature is something that gradually emerges after a lot of learning and diligence during their daily walk with God. However, Scripture tells us this new nature was "created" (Ephesians 4:24). This means it is something God already provided for us. It is not something we can do, or should even attempt to do, for ourselves.

One of the most important truths we can ever learn is this: We can never provide our own "makeover" through Scripture, prayer, fellowship, and service. This business of "being made conformable to the image of Christ" does not and cannot mean that the Christian life is essentially a partnership with God, wherein we labor together to construct a life that in the end resembles his. The reason such a notion isn't true is because the life we got when we were born again was already perfect, in every way! It can never be made to look more like him, or to become more pleasing in his sight, than it was the split-second we first received it.

There is a progressive aspect to spiritual growth, to be sure, but it's not the one most believers have been pursuing. They've been pursuing a step-by-step, principle-by-principle "makeover" that wrongly asks God to do what he has already done. But to undertake something like this is really a complete waste of time!

Randolph Hearst, the late California newspaper publisher, decided one day that he wanted to buy a particular painting; so he sent one of his employees to check out the famous art galleries in America. When this painting didn't turn up anywhere, the search then became worldwide, including the aristocratic attics of Europe. Despite these exhaustive efforts, this painting was nowhere to be found. Or so it seemed.

Then one day one of Mr. Hearst's employees came rushing into his office to say, "We found it!" "You did?" Mr. Hearst replied. "Where was it?" "In one of your old warehouses," the employee said. "You bought that painting years ago!"

Upon hearing this story, one has to wonder whether Christians today, just like Mr. Hearst, are also unaware of what we've got. If so, we will repeatedly go through cycles of wanting, seeking, but doing without, when in fact the very thing we're looking for already belongs to us. Commenting on this dilemma, Miles J. Stanford, in his book, *The Complete Green Letters*, offered these two quotations:

> William R. Newell said, "Satan's great device is to drive earnest souls back to beseeching God for what God says has already been done" .... "In our private prayers and in our public services," A. W. Tozer writes, "we are forever asking God to do things that he has either already done or cannot do because of our unbelief ...."[18]

When it comes to experiencing the life of God, our new nature, we need to quit chasing what we've already got! Splendid preaching, intense prayer, effective discipleship are commanded and commended in Scripture, but they cannot produce that which God already created for us. If we trust these and other worthwhile activities to transform us into this kind of life, we will actually move further away from what we are seeking.[19]

In seeking to understand how God created this new nature, we must again keep in mind that the reason he did so was because this was something impossible for us to do—though many of us have spent many futile years trying. With a hope that your futility will soon end, and that your confusion will soon give way to clarity, let's now set forth the six steps that needed to occur for the new nature to come into existence.

Centuries ago, God told two of his prophets, Jeremiah and Ezekiel, that he was going to give men a new heart, a heart that already had his laws written within. The background to this pledge was a history of covenant-making and covenant-breaking. The purpose of these covenants was to establish a closer, more blessed relationship between God and his people. These covenants, representing the highest jurisprudence in the universe, were designed to boost faith and release blessing. However, man, in the all too plain language of Scripture, had the heart of a whore. For no matter how good God was to him—irrationally, insanely—man repeatedly violated these sacred covenants. Therefore, God made it known what history had already amply confirmed: *The heart of the human problem is the problem with the human heart*. Man didn't have what it takes to keep a covenant—hence, God's pledge to give man a new heart.

The question that can be easily anticipated is this: If God declared that in Jeremiah's day, why didn't he proceed at once to give man this new heart? Many years earlier David had cried, "Create in me a new heart, O God" (Psalm 51:10a). So even back then, hundreds of years before Bethlehem, man knew what God knew: that there were going to be many more innings of sinning so long as the old heart remained. Why, then, didn't God simply speak the word, give the zap, and put within his people this brand-new heart?

The reason he didn't was because he couldn't—this new heart wasn't in existence yet; nor could it come into being by some fiat decree. While God could achieve the first creation by standing on the portals of heaven and letting loose his booming voice commands, he could never accomplish the "new creation" that way. Think about it: The only heart that could live above sin was *God's* heart. But God couldn't just put his heart inside us, simply because he was of one order and realm and we were of another. So the only way God could give us this new heart was if somehow he entered our order—which is exactly what he did at Bethlehem.[20]

Years ago J. B. Phillips wrote a book entitled *When God Became Man*. One day, while cleaning the office of a pastor, an employee saw this book on the shelf and, instantly shocked, she ran out of the office to ask the pastor, "Is this true?" Her face, flushed in excitement, communicated the enthusiasm of her words. She was determined to know if the title of this book was accurate!

For most people, such awesome truth hardly captures their imagination. They may watch Christmas plays, attend nativity scenes, sing the carols of the season—and never once be stunned or astonished by what is being celebrated. Can you fathom it? The high and holy God, whose eyes are too pure to even look upon sin, becoming what he had created—man! This is simply amazing! Much more amazing than a professor becoming a petunia, or a king becoming a worm! A. B. Simpson once observed:

> If a king should stoop to become a worm it would still be one creature becoming another, a lower gradation of the same class of being. But when

> Christ became a man and took upon him the form of a created being, he stepped out of his class completely and plunged to a depth of condescension which is absolutely without any standard of comparison.[21]

Yet, this is precisely what had to happen first if man was going to get what he so desperately needed, a new heart.

It is in the Gospel of John that we read these words about Jesus, "He came unto his own ...." Commenting on this verse, Tozer writes, "All the pity God is capable of feeling, all the mercy he is capable of showing and all the redeeming grace he could pour out of his heart are at least suggested here in two simple words, 'He came.'"[22]

When contemplating the far-reaching implications of these words, Tozer offered this uplifting conclusion, "Gather together in one place all the great philosophy of every culture from the beginning of time, and none of it remotely approaches the wonder and profundity of these words, 'He came.'"[23]

The second thing that had to happen was that Jesus had to be fully tested, a fact that the book of Hebrews expounds. Jesus couldn't just descend upon a mountaintop one weekend and then airlift to glory. He had to enter fully into the human experience, which means he had to become a baby. And then, as his life, like ours, took on new dimensions, new responsibilities, and new challenges, he had to respond to each dimension, responsibility, and challenge without compromise. The necessity of this criterion was attributable to the fact that if men were ever going to get a perfect heart, that heart had to undergo first the most stringent tests. Consequently, just one sin, however slight and seemingly insignificant, would have brought this whole redemption project into terminal failure.

Third, Jesus had to die, the reason for this being: He had identified himself with the human race, and by the will of the Father found himself facing the curse of sin that had been brought upon the whole race—death. This curse of death, obviously, had to be removed, if the new heart was to have its intended future.

In order to remove the curse, the requirement was a perfect sacrifice—to use the symbolism of the Old Testament, an unblemished lamb. Anything less than that would have meant dying a victim's death or, better still, a hero's death, or maybe even a martyr's death, but not a Savior's death. Now, since Jesus was tempted in every respect but never sinned, he alone qualified to die a death that would satisfy God's justice.

Do understand that God could never sweep sin under the rug and let bygones be bygones. This is because his justice—far from being trivial or excessively compulsive—was the very foundation upon which his own character rested. When analyzed more fully, this justice can be seen as that which preserves the safety and sanctity of heaven.

Fourth, Jesus had to be raised from the dead. After all, if death were to have the final word, how would we ever get that new heart? It is certainly significant that Revelation 1:5 says that Jesus was "the first born from the dead." But doesn't this raise the question: How could Jesus be the first born from the dead? Wasn't Lazarus raised from the dead just a couple of weeks before? And weren't there many others raised from the dead when, just days later, that earthquake opened all those graves? Moreover, didn't Jesus himself raise people from the dead while ministering in Israel? And, even as far back as the Old Testament, didn't Elijah raise that little boy from the dead?

Some have tried to explain this verse by pointing out that Jesus wasn't the "first born" in the sense of sequence or chronology; he was the "first born" in the sense of supremacy and priority of purpose. Which is true, but it doesn't go far enough. Actually, Jesus was the "first born" in the sense that he inaugurated a humanity that never existed before—sin free, debt free, and beyond any reproaches from the devil that have merit. Quite literally, Jesus was "born again." Andrew Murray writes, "Jesus was born twice. The first time he was born in Bethlehem ... But the second time he was born from the grave."[24]

Consequently, this does stand in sharp contrast to Lazarus and all those others who came back from the dead. Because when they came back, they came back just as they had been before. However, when Jesus came back, he came back as the originator of a new heart, the superior successor to Adam, the confirmed head of a new race. In the words of Francis Schaeffer, Jesus was "the second founder of the human race."[25]

Theology and psychology haven't duly considered this remarkable fact, the implications of which are far-reaching. In his book, *Making All Things New*, Oswald Chambers stated what really happened at the resurrection:

> Our Lord rose to an absolutely new life, to a life he did not live before he was incarnate; he rose to a life that had never been before. There had been resurrections before the resurrection of Jesus Christ, but they were all resuscitations to the same life that had been lived heretofore. Jesus rose to a totally new life ....[26]

In his book, *A Man in Christ*, James S. Stewart wrote, "When Jesus rose, the new age broke in. A new humanity came into being. A new moral and spiritual order was established."[27] Likewise, C. S. Lewis observed: "The New Testament writers speak as if Christ's achievement in rising from the dead was the first event of its kind in the whole history of the universe ... This is the beginning of the New Creation: a new chapter in cosmic history has been opened."[28] Yet, additional steps were required before this new heart could become ours.

The next step involved Jesus appearing before the Father. John 7:39 says "... for the Holy Spirit was not yet given because Jesus was not yet glorified." Since Jesus had lived his entire earthly life submissive to the Father and totally dependent upon the Father, he of necessity, but with gladness of heart, would need to present this new heart for the Father's approval.

Then—once the Father approved it, credentialed it, and glorified it—something else of great significance happened: The Holy Spirit entered into that new life. Do you remember how God had told the prophets that he would give man a new heart *and a new spirit*? As a fulfillment of that pledge, the

Holy Spirit cocooned his presence inside that new heart that Jesus had fashioned. This is why Paul speaks of "the Spirit of life in Christ Jesus" (Romans 8:2). This is the essence of our new nature: The Holy Spirit indwelling a life that was miraculously created at Bethlehem, fully tested during those thirty-three years, offered as a saving sacrifice, born again in resurrection triumph, and approved by the Father in Glory.

Thus, as early as the second century we find the Church Father Irenaeus declaring, "Jesus Christ our Lord who, because of his immeasurable love, became what we are in order to make us what he is."[29] In his book, *Love Abounding*, G. D. Watson wrote: "Every part of Jesus' life—the various traits of his life, the various instincts of that life, the various longings of that life—is implanted in the life that is born again, that is regenerated by the Holy Ghost."[30]

Curiously, the book of Acts opens by speaking "of all that Jesus began both to do and to teach"—the implication being: He began it, but we are to continue it. To those people who have their brains in gear, this thought will appear to be more than incredible, prompting the obvious question: Do you actually mean that we're to do what Jesus did? If so, there's just no way! That would be like Michelangelo, after a year's labor in the Sistine Chapel, turning to some novice who happened to be walking by and saying, "I want you to finish it."

Finish it? Why, once this pedestrian viewed the brilliance of Michelangelo's work, he would have found this suggestion to be nothing short of Looney Tunes ludicrous! "What! Am I to draw my little stick men alongside Michelangelo's magnificent depiction of creation? That's absurd! Because anything I'd do would only ruin what he already did!" But, if somehow the genius of Michelangelo could miraculously come inside that man, then what followed would be a far different story, right? For now there *could* be continuity with what had gone on before.

This, by analogy, is exactly what God promised to the prophets, performed by Jesus, and is now offered to us today. The very heart of Jesus—who came into our order so that we could go into his—has been put inside every believer. Therefore, anyone even halfway aware of what this new heart is—pure, perfect, and incapable of sin—isn't likely to feel inferior. Not anymore! Because the born-again believer has an inestimable value, one so precious and priceless that nothing on this earth can even begin to compare with it. In his book *Destined for the Throne*, Paul Billheimer declared, "God has exalted redeemed humanity to such a sublime height that it is impossible for him to exalt them further without breaching the Godhead."[31] A. W. Tozer announced, "The truly regenerated man is a new creature; he belongs to another order of being; he has another kind of life, another origin, another destiny."[32]

Illustrating the dramatic difference the new nature can make, James S. Stewart wrote this:

> Henry Drummond, at one of his great student meetings in Edinburgh, read a letter he had received from a man who had made shipwreck of life, a letter full of hopelessness and bitterness, a terrible revelation of a sunk and ruined soul. It was anonymous, signed with one word, "Thanatos"—Death. And Drummond (as he afterwards confessed) felt then that if there was ever a man who was irretrievably lost it was the writer of that letter. But there was another night, a year or two later, when Drummond was facing a student gathering again. He reminded them of the story he had told of the man who was a moral, social and spiritual wreck; and then went on, "Gentlemen, I have in my pocket tonight a letter from "Thanatos," which he sent me this week, and he says he is at last a changed man—a new creature in Christ Jesus."[33]

Talk about the ultimate makeover! There's nothing our world has to offer that can even begin to compare with this! A modern day Nicodemus may ask the question, "How can these things be?" But before answering this question—which we will do with much detail in subsequent chapters—what must be set forth next is exactly what the new nature is, in terms of its components and its characteristics.

Reflection Questions

1. How have you tried to defense some of the "not okay" feelings you have had about yourself?

2. Have you accepted the judgment God made about the nature you had when you came into this world?

3. Have you been trying to experience the life God wants you to live by diligence and dedication, only to discover that something is missing?

4. Upon reviewing the six-step procedure that Jesus undertook to give us a new nature, what did you learn? What did you come to particularly appreciate?

Chapter 4

Introducing the New You

In his book, *Created in God's Image*, Anthony Hoekema wrote, "The Christian life involves not just believing something about Christ but also believing something about ourselves. We must believe that we are indeed a part of Christ's new creation. Our faith in Christ must include believing that we are exactly what the Bible says we are."[1] But can we be this exact? When the Bible uses the terms the "new man," the "new heart," the "new spirit" and the "new creation," does it clarify what these terms mean, or are these intangibles that defy description?

In his book, *The God Players*, Earl Jabay contended that "man is quite as indefinable and as descriptively illusive as God himself. The most the word 'spirit' can do is tell us that we really cannot be seen."[2] Is this true: Our spirit is invisible, and that's all we know about it?

Having humility about what we know can be healthy, especially if our attempts to define are like trying to bottle a sunbeam. Yet, Scripture was given to reveal. So are we to believe that on a topic as important as this Scripture said next to nothing? Actually, we need not believe this, for Galatians furnishes a nine-point profile of the new nature, a comprehensive overview of the driving dynamics of divine life. In terms that are very specific, very concrete, we are given a functional understanding of the components constituting our new nature. Galatians 5:22 and 23 state: "But the fruit of the Spirit is love, joy, peace, longsuffering, kindness, goodness, faithfulness, gentleness, self-control."

Before examining this passage, observations of an introductory nature ought to be surfaced. First, it should be noted that the term "fruit" is singular in form, not plural. This is because the divine life within, like that priestly robe Jesus wore, has a seamless integrity—these nine qualities are interwoven! For example, one can't possess the fruit of love but at the same time lack the fruit of patience. Nor can one possess the fruit of peace but at the same time lack the fruit of faithfulness. Similarly, there can be no joy without goodness and no gentleness without temperance. Therefore, because all nine parts of the fruit are essential to divine life, the omission of any one part would describe something other than divine life.

Second, it should be acknowledged that the capitalizing of the word "Spirit" is itself an interpretation, given the fact that capitalization isn't provided by the Greek language. Moreover, the context of this passage suggests an ongoing civil war between two somewhat parallel capacities: our phantom self (the flesh) versus our real self, our born-again spirit (the new nature). Now, because the Holy Spirit indwells the recreated spirit (our new nature), John Calvin interpreted the word "spirit" in this passage as being both the "Spirit of God" and "the renewed nature, or the grace of regeneration."[3] This means: What God wants behaviorally manifested by us is not something we crank out by ourselves; it's in our new nature already. As a proponent of this truth, G. D. Watson wrote, "When we are regenerated, the life of Christ is imparted to our human spirits ...."[4] Friedrich Schleiermacher said, "The fruits of the Spirit are nothing but the virtues of Christ."[5] These nine qualities, descriptive of divine life, are the very essence of our new nature.[6]

Third, when comparing the two lists—what the flesh produces (verses 19-21) with what the spirit produces (verses 22 and 23)—we see that the first list concludes with the words "and the like," suggesting that this list is not comprehensive. What the flesh can and does produce has more ruin and rot than even what this lengthy listing has enumerated. However, no such words conclude the second list. Why? Because this list *is* comprehensive. In a brief, all-inclusive way, God has helped us to see—in terms that are very definable—what the new nature is. Other virtues may come to mind as possible additions; but, when examined, we'll see these are embedded in the qualities of this list.

This profile of the new nature is a remarkable teaching, quite unlike anything the world has to offer. Will Durant, the twentieth-century century philosopher, wrote voluminously about the human condition, acknowledging in one place "... psychology has not yet put together the human nature it has taken apart; and it is still easier to describe man than to say what he should be, and how he may be changed."[7]

But what psychology and all the human disciplines cannot do, God accomplished more than two thousand years ago. For the new nature describes exactly what man should be. Moreover, the Bible describes precisely how this change in man can be made.

Fourth, the words following this listing—"against such there is no law"—are very radical indeed! What is really being said here is that every demand of the law, whether conveyed in an imperative or embedded in a principle, is completely satisfied by new nature living. God said he would write his laws on our heart—and in time he did! The new nature achieves what one's well-intentioned flesh could never achieve, a life that is totally pleasing to God! Hence, Andrew Murray declared that "the new man we have put on is created in true holiness. We are not only counted holy, we are holy."[8]

While religion summons us to ideals that cannot be reached, and philosophy studies evil that cannot be remedied, the Bible surpasses every religion, every philosophy, by exhibiting a life that realizes its ideals and effectively remedies all that contradicts it. This life, at its core and in its essence, is divine life, a life scarcely understood by many in the church. Addressing this point, A. B. Simpson asked:

> What is the highest Christian life? What is the life that God is trying to reproduce in the lives of his saints? Is it the repair of wrecked humanity? Is it simply the restoration of Adamic purity? Is it only the bringing back of the human soul to the

> condition in which it was before the fall? This would be a poor result for such tremendous cost as the death of the Lord Jesus Christ. And what guarantee have we that, if this were accomplished tomorrow, the wreck would not be repeated the next day, and the race as lost as ever?
>
> No, God has accomplished something very much higher; nothing less, in fact, than the creation of a new race, patterned not after the human, but the divine.[9]

When James S. Stewart described our new life "in Christ," he said it was nothing less than being "filled with the pulse and power of the Spirit" and being "penetrated by the love that moves the sun and all the stars." According to Stewart:

> This is the secret of the life of the redeemed, life eternal here and now in the midst of time. This is the inbreaking into history of the kingdom of heaven. This is the darkness routed and the night gone, and the glory of God risen upon us.[10]

To appreciate the essence of our new nature more fully, it is now incumbent upon us to examine each part of the spirit's fruit. Mindful, of course, that there are many counterfeits for each authentic virtue, it is important to offer only those definitions that will set forth the biblical distinctions.[11] We will begin with the greatest virtue of all, love.

The Limits of Love

Can anyone love? In his book, *Practical Religion*, J. C. Ryle insists, "The heart in which love grows is a heart changed, renewed, and transformed by the Holy Spirit." Yet, because our world is oblivious of this fact, A. B. Simpson acknowledged, "No word has been so prominent in song and story all through the history of human life and literature as this old word, 'love.'"[12] Popularly used in poems, conspicuous on many cards, crooned through loud speakers everywhere, proclaimed from a thousand pulpits, love has been extolled and exhorted until the word itself has almost lost meaning. The very real danger, then, is this: By overly elasticizing a word, we skew and distort it, until finally what we elasticized snaps, and all that is left is something tattered and worthless.

Love, which is not only the first of the fruit but also sums up its content, can be counterfeited in several ways. First, there is a glandular love that only responds to physical attractiveness. If a man is tall, dark, and handsome; or if a woman is slender, smart, and seductive, perhaps then the sparks will fly—which, according to these counterfeit criteria, is a sure sign of love! The tabloids frequently feature this kind of love in their weekly publications. Scientists are attempting to explain it by chemicals in the brain or by the predictable patterns of animal mating behaviors.

Second, there is an existential love that comes and goes according to the chemistry of certain intangibles, measured for the most part by emotion. If someone is "turned on," then love will be released; but if that person is "turned off," love will then disappear. This kind of love rises and falls on the fickle, flighty testimony of feelings. And while one could wish that only soap operas engaged in this type of love, there's enough evidence to indicate that the suburbs of Middle-America have succumbed to it as well.

There can be little doubt that Satan's most popular counterfeit of God's love is that love which loves only the lovable—fun, affable, generous people: people who think like you think, like what you like, and do what you do. This is the marketplace kind of love, a love that scrounges for advantages, benefits, and compensating rewards. Needless to say, all the counterfeits just mentioned are extensively evident in today's world but are obviously contrary to the love resident in the new nature.

Perhaps this truth can be more clearly seen by examining the following passage from the pen of Paul. In Ephesians, chapter 3, the apostle writes: "... that you, being rooted and grounded in love, may be able to comprehend with all the saints what is the width and length and depth and height—to know the love of Christ which surpasses knowledge" (Ephesians 3:17b-19a). The words "rooted" and “grounded” are encouraging words, as is the word “know,” because they suggest a reality that is constant and attainable, as opposed to something that is fleeting and elusive.

The Broadway musical “Oliver” features a wistful little song entitled, “Where Is Love?” This song about an orphan boy living among unsavory characters on the streets of London has become the plaintive heart-cry for many people. The reason people can identify with this song is because they too have been moving in and out of relationships that never offered love. But Scripture says that every believer can be both rooted in love (that is, constantly absorbing its blessings) and grounded in love (that is, forever established in its benefits).

When Scripture also says that we can “comprehend” this love, it doesn’t mean we can intellectually define it. The word “comprehend,” in the Greek, literally means to seize, possess, or grasp. And similarly the word “know”—instead of referring to cognitive awareness or to conceptual constructs that need to be mastered—refers to an experiential knowing, something meaningful and practical and real.

So what exactly is this love which the world at best can only counterfeit? To better understand what it is, let’s explore its four dimensions, all cited in this same letter to the Ephesians. First, we are told of the width of this love. This speaks of an enormously inclusive love, the kind of love that would bring together both the Jew and the Gentile (Ephesians 2:14).

Had we been alive during Jesus’ day, and had we witnessed firsthand the entrenched hostility between these two groups, we would have put their relationship at the very top of our “impossibility list.” And due to our awareness that the Jews were “God’s people,” perhaps we would have also thought (in error) that the Gentiles weren’t candidates for God’s love but were the eventual targets of his wrath.

Contrary to Jewish thought (and, for that matter, common opinion), God’s love isn’t limited to one’s family, country, or race, because his love reaches across all kinds of boundaries—demolishing walls, opening doors, and even melting the hardest of hearts. While the homogeneous principle may appeal to certain marketers of church growth, it isn't to be found in the heart of God. What God offers, by contrast, is a fervent, stretched-out love, intent on blessing people whom many of us, carelessly or deliberately, would have excluded.[13]

Victor Hugo once said, "The supreme happiness of life is the conviction that we are loved." This is a truth we can easily warm up to as we think about our inner circle, and perhaps a little ways beyond. But when it comes to those unknown, unlovely people we'd just as soon not think about, we find ourselves digging in our heels and looking at the Savior with much consternation as he marches right past us, ever intent to reach these people, too. The width of God's love!

Then, according to Scripture, there is the length of God's love (Ephesians 1:4)—a love that chose us before the foundations of the world (this refers to eternity past) so that we should be holy and without blame before him (this extends to eternity future). So how long is God's love? Its length can be characterized in this way: Before we were even born, he loved us. While we were wallowing in sin, he still loved us. Now that we are his, he particularly loves us. And throughout eternity he will ravishingly love us. So you tell me: Is there any other love as sure and steadfast as God's love?

The length of human love is not so easily documented, and maybe that's just as well. Because as we look back over our lives and remember the various circles of friends to which we've belonged, we have to wonder: What happened to all those relationships? These were people we liked, some of whom were very close friends! And yet most of these people don't even get a Christmas card from us. So how do we account for this—out of sight, out of mind?

One reason we become fickle in our friendships is because of our propensity to frame situations in too small a way. Someone says something to irritate, and we do an inward burn. Instead of exhibiting resilience in our relationships, too often the immediate is everything and everything else is but a blur. This helps to account for why it is that our love fades; whereas God's love glows with an undimmed brightness.

The third dimension of divine love is referred to in Scripture as "depth." So how deep is God's love? As with these other dimensions of love, Ephesians explains this one as well: It is so deep that it reached way down to rescue lust-driven sons of disobedience, men who were not only in bed with the world but who were also in lock-step with Satan. According to Scripture, the Prince of the Power of the Air was pulling their strings (Ephesians 2:1-4)!

Celsus, the Greek critic, once said, "Everybody knows from long experience with actual life that once a man has gone a certain length in sin and folly, there is no smallest prospect of reclaiming him, because inevitably man is carried downhill faster and faster by his own impetus." Should we agree with Celsus? Is there a place on sin's great decline too far from the arms that save?

C. S. Lewis answered that question by describing Jesus as the Divine Diver. In his book, *Miracles*, Lewis wrote:

> ... one may think of a diver, first reducing himself to nakedness, then glancing in mid-air, then gone with a splash, vanished, rushing down through the warm and green water into black and cold water, down through increasing pressure into the deathlike region of ooze and slime and old decay; then up again, back to color and light, his lungs almost bursting, till suddenly he breaks surface again, holding in his hand the dripping, precious thing he went down to recover.[14]

This is what Jesus did for us! In his incarnation and in his subsequent death, he went all the way to the bottom, to the lowest of the low, on a mission to recover what must have seemed a worthless thing—fallen man: the defiant defiler, the rebellious reviler.[15] And just think: When love paid its highest price, those for whom it was intended only mocked and jeered. So can anyone deny that the love of God is unsurpassed in its depth?

The fourth dimension of God's love, hence the love of our new nature, is height. How high is God's love? So high, that according to Ephesians 2:6 he has enabled us to sit together in heavenly places! In clarifying this truth F. J. Huegel pointed out:

> We do well to look at the tenses of the verbs which the Holy Spirit employs ... It is ours now! "He *has blessed us* with every spiritual blessing in the heavenly places in Christ." It is not death (physical dissolution) that will bring us into our heritage in Christ. It is faith. We may *now* sit with him in the heavenlies because God has already made us to sit there in the person of Christ, the head of the church.[16]

How little we have believed God, though, for the throne life which is ours to utilize on earth! Such ascendancy not only speaks of our exalted relationship with God but also speaks of certain privileges delegated by him—such as dominion, power, capacity, and control! Tozer writes, "To regain her lost power the church must see heaven opened and have a transforming vision of God."[17] Such a vision will depict heaven and earth operating in sync as God releases his power through those who lay hold of it by faith.

During a time of great financial difficulty in our country, a Philadelphia pastor was walking the streets of his city when he came upon one of the elders of his church. "How are you doing?" the pastor asked as he extended his hand to this elder. "Oh, all right ... I guess," came the feeble reply. And then—following a punctuated pause and a doleful, downcast look—the elder added the words, "under the circumstances." "Under the circumstances?" the pastor probed. "What are you doing under there?"

Good question! Why should the believer become a hapless victim in life? For doesn't the Bible say that we're "more than conquerors," abundantly resourced for whatever challenges us? Mindful of this perspective, people will sometimes say, "Keep looking up"—these words of encouragement that remind us of God's willingness to help! But there may be even more faith in the words "Keep looking down." For these words envision throne life, our current seating in heavenly places (Ephesians 2:6), whereby we access *his* mind and *his* might to transform for *his* glory each trial into a triumph. Throne life exercises the astounding authority God has given the believer.

The four dimensions of love![18] For the believer (to put this succinctly) *love means to will another's good.* And in assessing this definition you will notice first that feelings aren't even mentioned.[19] This is because feelings follow behavior. If, in God's strength, you exercise your will in loving behaviors, your feelings will catch up soon enough.

There's a big difference, however, between wishing and willing. Wishes come and go and demand nothing of us; whereas willingness calls for personal sacrifice, and sometimes in extraordinary measures. This may mean giving yourself to someone who at first may repel and repulse, to someone who isn't particularly grateful about your efforts and therefore offers not the first hint of reciprocation.

Also important to note is that the "good" we purpose is defined by God, and therefore may not resemble what the world thinks is good.[20] So are you beginning to see how this definition of love charts a different course than the one your initial ideas of love would have pursued?

Most of us have never related the new nature to love, even though it is through the new nature that we are able to love like God (our flesh will never do this), purposing to see his character exhibited in the lives of others. Yet, whenever people give their views about an ideal mate, or an ideal friend, those views tend to be considerably less than what the new nature offers.

For a Christian, the new nature should immediately spring to mind in considerations like these. Because who wouldn't want to see love and joy, peace and patience, gentleness and kindness, in the life of a family member or friend?

In this respect Dostoyevsky is right, "To love a person means to see him as God intended him to be." But without the new nature, the new heart, true love is impossible. According to Richard Sibbes, "They seek for heaven in hell that seek for spiritual love in an unchanged heart."[21]

Now, as we think of these four dimensions of love, it becomes clear that this love isn't at all like the world's love.

However, the more honest assessment would acknowledge that these four dimensions aren't consistently obvious in our love, either. So how are we to account for this absence of godly love even among believers?

In his book, *The Spirit of Christ,* Andrew Murray writes:

> Many have sought in vain to follow Jesus in his life of love and could not, because they neglected what was essential—denying self. When self is not denied, but follows Jesus [anyway], it always fails. It cannot love as he loves.[22]

In fact, even after Scripture-stipulated steps have been taken (such as those involved with the crucified life), there still may not be a big gush of love brimming over the reservoir of our heart, ever ready to flow if not flood. Instead, as Galatians puts it, we'll need to love by faith—a faith that trusts God for both the resources and the outcome. Andrew Murray explains:

> The way by which the Spirit works any virtue in believers is by stirring us to do it. The Spirit of God does not effectually work love, or give strength to love, until we act upon it. We cannot see or feel any such thing as love for God or man in our hearts before we act with love. We do not know our spiritual strength unless we use and exercise it.[23]

Hudson Taylor added a confirming word when he declared, "God does not give us overcoming life. He gives us life as we overcome."[24] This means that if we wait to be smitten by sentiment or fired up by feelings, we'll end up waiting a long time!

But since the Word tells us the love of God has already been shed abroad in our hearts (Romans 5:5), we should trust that it's there, no matter what mood or contrary thought may be cycling through at the moment. Challenging us to act in this way, A. B. Simpson wrote:

> Do we want more love? When we come up to some hard place where we are wronged, we are not to struggle to work up love in ourselves. We are not to be discouraged when we do not find love there ... Go to God and take the love from him."[25]

And just think: How much nearer could this love be? It already resides within us, as does the Lord who indwells us.

A Jubilant Joy

The next part of the Spirit's fruit to be examined is joy. Like love, joy has been counterfeited in many ways. For example, there are those who will associate joy with pleasure. It may be the pleasure of some daredevil stunt—pursuing a speed or height or distance no one else has ever experienced. Or it may be the pleasure of gaining some long sought-after possession, or attaining a very difficult-to-achieve position. J. H. Jowett spoke of "the rush to be rich, the race to be happy, the craving for sensation."[26] It may even be what the Bible calls "the pleasures of sin" (Hebrews 11:25)—for example, the "buzz" that comes from a few drinks, or the "hormonal high" that comes from a sexual escapade. But as G. D. Watson observed, "There is a difference between pleasure and joy. Pleasure is that happiness which is on the outside, and in connection with the various senses of the body or soul, whereas joy is ... from the state of the inner spirit."[27] Joy is "not a scintillating, transient happiness," Dr. Jowett said.[28] Of course, what all these counterfeits to joy have in common is the idea that pleasure leads to fulfillment. But is this true?

A young man once approached a renowned doctor in Paris, saying that he was despondent over the emptiness of life. In reply, the doctor, speaking with a trace of envy, pictured the happy life of Grimaldi, a young man-about-town in Paris nightclubs. "Go to him," said the doctor. "Let him show you how to have a good time." The downcast patient then looked up and with a sardonic smile said, "But I'm Grimaldi." This story illustrates the point J. H. Jowett made: "Sin puts out the light of joy. I am persuaded that there is not a man or woman in God's wide world, who persists in deliberate sin, in whose life we could find the light of joy."[29]

The carefree life isn't all that it is cracked up to be! Proverbs 15:21 says, "Folly is joy to him who is destitute of discernment ...." In other words, if we don't have any sense, we'll settle for something so much less than what God has to offer. What we must remember is that when the Bible talked about "the pleasures of sin," it added an ominous phrase, "for a season." The intended implication being: This is a gratification that won't last very long. What once satisfied, incrementally loses its appeal, until eventually the appeal is gone. J. I. Packer added historical commentary to this point when he lamented:

> Poor pathetic Marie Antoinette had everything a queen could ask for and ended up bored stiff: her final complaint was, "*Nothing tastes.*" Pleasure-seeking, of whatever kind and at whatever level, is subject to the law of diminishing returns.[30]

But while the thrill won't last, its dominion over you probably will![31] You will discover that you can't get free and, to the chagrin of your frustrated soul, you can't get satisfaction.

To avoid this dilemma, Oswald Chambers offered this criterion for our consideration:

> With regard to all the pleasures, sciences, and interests in this world, push this simple consideration, "Is this the kind of thing the Son of God is doing in the world, or is this what the prince of this world is doing?" ... If you only give up wrong things for Jesus Christ, don't talk about being in love with him.[32]

Many of us, it seems, gravitate toward pleasure, instinctively and almost mindlessly, without any assessment given about how the Lord wants us to use our time.[33] But had we given more thought to this area of our life we might have seen how a certain preferred pleasure takes seriousness out of living and the eternal out of time. A. B. Simpson warned, "There is nothing that so relaxes the cords of spiritual earnestness as the life of the world, the life of ease and pleasure."[34] Because unnoticed, but complicit with this agenda, is a willingness to neglect one's spirit and enthrone oneself.

Whenever we sequester self in an environment that entices with entertainment and pampers with pleasure, we invariably idle our spiritual growth—this due to brain-numbing, soul-shriveling amusement.[35] Besides, Alexander Maclaren remarked, "There is nothing more wearying than the pursuit of pleasure."[36]

The possibility that some pleasure is evil is an obvious concern, but so is the possibility that this pleasure is utterly and uselessly trivial. Quite often, the joy counterfeit some people settle for is much less sinister than outright evil. They just want to be happy, to have a good time, to enjoy a few laughs. For them, therefore: the less the encumbrances, the lighter the burdens, the fewer the obligations—the better! Or so they think. But is this laidback view of life scripturally sanctioned? And does it really gratify?

The playwright William Saroyan said it well, "Only the pigs are happy." These rotund creatures of ridicule can slosh around in the mud, enjoying the sun and the breeze and their carefree environment. But not to be forgotten is the close connection between swine and sludge, and the connection between boars and bilge.

Whether we frolic in filth or something less demeaning, such is hardly worthy of us. Hence, Saroyan observed, "The greatest happiness is knowing that you don't have to be happy." Alexander Maclaren declared, "God has larger and nobler designs for us than merely to make us happy."[37] This perhaps explains why Jesus was never frantic to perk people up, intent that they should be exuberant with intoxicating glee. Jesus' most characteristic greeting, "Be of good cheer," was never one of a revved-up euphoria.

The idea that joy is first an emotion—a breezy, effervescent spirit that enables one to go through life grinning—must be directly challenged. It is true that Jesus talked about a joy no one could take away, but it was only a few hours later that he faced Gethsemane with blood-sweating dread.[38] And had you and I been present that night, we wouldn't have seen anything in his countenance that looked like joy. For instead of skipping into the garden, Jesus entered with slow, measured steps and the most sobered, almost ashen look on his face. So where, it may be fairly asked, was his joy? His joy—the biblical record shows—existed in his confidence in God. In fact, repeatedly encouraged by this confidence, Jesus yielded his life to the Father yet again, despite the fierce assault of hell that warred against his soul.

Then came the moment of drama! Horse hooves intruded on the silence of the scene, even as torch lights turned the night into noon. When the soldiers arrived to arrest this preacher at midnight—more than six hundred of them, mind you, armed to the teeth!—Jesus exhibited a remarkable composure—mastering first them, then the disciples, and most of all his own soul. How did he do it? To answer in a word—joy! For, just as the Old Testament had declared it, the joy of the Lord provides strength (Nehemiah 8:10). Yet, not only in Gethsemane was this joy important, but also at Golgotha, since Scripture very clearly tells us that Jesus endured the suffering of the cross because of the joy that was set before him (Hebrews 11:2).

Joy is this belief in the unfailing faithfulness of God and in the complete sufficiency of his resources. But as was the case for Jesus that night in the garden, the froth of delighted feelings may be absent from us as well. This need not mean that joy is absent or in any way diminished.

Did you know that when the Bible tells us to rejoice, it quite literally means to "re-joy"? This means to draw from our reservoir of belief the very confidence in God that will see us through the trial. Fullness of joy is in that reservoir (our new nature); and drawing it out in faith releases its strength. This dynamic produces, then, what Scripture calls gladness of heart. But although this gladness is produced by joy, it doesn't equate with joy (see Appendix E), since the real nature of joy is found in the controlling conviction and the unbendable belief that God is willing and able to meet every need!

The biblical record documents the lack of joy in the disciples' hearts. In the sixteenth chapter of John's Gospel, where we find the disciples to be anything but joyful (this due to the Lord's imminent death on the cross), we read that the Lord Jesus taught them how their joy could be "full," and, further, how that joy could "remain." So let's contemplate the prospect Jesus was putting forth that day by asking: What would constitute fullness of joy?

To answer this question with accuracy, we must first see how the Bible uses the word "filled."

In this same chapter, Jesus said, "... sorrow has filled your heart" (John 16:6)—sorrow to such a degree that they were completely controlled by it! In Luke 5:3 we read of those who "were filled with fear"—a fear so strong nothing could coexist with it! In Luke 6:11 we find the phrase "filled with rage"—a rage so intense it resulted in deicide, the killing of God! In Acts 5:3 Peter accuses Ananias of being filled with Satan—a governance so drastic it resulted in Ananias' instant death! And in Ephesians 5:18 we are told to be filled with the Spirit—a filling so total it permeates, possesses, and actually drives us!

So the word "filled" is obviously a comprehensive word, dictating a dominance that is virtually unrivaled. Hence, with this background benefiting us, we can now ask: What would it be like to be filled with joy?

On a scale of one-to-ten it would mean we would be all the way over to a ten! There would be no ambivalence, no ambiguity, and no restraint on our emotions. In its deepest state, we would be enthralled by God, compelled within to give our hearts to exuberant worship.

While most Christians agree there are occasional moments of bliss like this, they would quickly remind us that we can't stay on the mountaintop forever. For in this life, they would lecture (probably with punitive parent tones), we're going to have to acclimate to the valley. And in so saying, history would appear to be on their side. But if Jesus said that our joy can "remain," then there must be a way to bring the mountaintop into the valley! Moreover, if his words are true, we won't have to be profoundly confused in our thinking or severely damaged in our emotions. Instead, joy—

for every situation, relationship, or challenge—can keep us looking to our ever willing and able God for another demonstration of his greatness. This is why, whenever problems come, our first assignment is one of attitude: "... count it all joy ...." (James 1:2) "Rejoice in the Lord always ...." (Philippians 4:4). That first, because this pleases God, protects us, and then releases the needed provision.

The basis of this joy, as John 16 makes clear, is heaven backing us up, the Lord answering our prayers. "Ask," Jesus said, "and you will receive" (notice: not might, could, or perhaps), but "you *will* receive, that your joy may be full" (John 16:24b).

So, if you knew that every prayer request would end in either rescue, reversal, or a restoration from God, wouldn't that boost your confidence? And if you also knew that every promise was already extended to you by a willing God who was saying an emphatic "Yes!" and a hearty "Amen!" (II Corinthians 1:20), wouldn't that further boost your confidence?

Just know: We are not having to persuade a reluctant God, and we are not facing problems that in any way tax his resources. The will, the ability, the motive, the method—all of it is already there! This, then, is the basis of our joy.

The joy we seek exists entirely and eternally in the nature of God. In 1677 Henry Scougal made a similar observation in his remarkable book, *The Life of God in the Soul of Man*.

> It should delight beyond all expression that the beloved of our souls is infinitely happy in himself and that all his enemies cannot shake or unsettle his throne, "that our God is in the heavens and doth whatsoever he pleaseth."[39]

This ability to live with purity and power, to accomplish what you purpose to do with unrivaled wisdom and unequaled resources, is a source of joy that we can tap into when we learn to pray.

I Peter 1:8 uses the phrase "joy inexpressible"—because even when we point out how prayer enhances our joy (Isaiah

56:7), as does ministry (II Corinthians 1:24), fellowship (I Thessalonians 2:20), the Word, (I John 1:4), daily problems (II Corinthians 7:4), and even the Holy Spirit himself (I Thessalonians 1:6)—that still doesn't say it all. For this joy touches us in ways nothing else can, enabling us to worship and experience God so even our present joy will become all the more inexhaustible.

Commenting on I Peter 1:8, R. A. Torrey said, "The Greek word translated 'joy' is a very strong word, describing extreme joy or jubilant joy. The word 'inexpressible' declares that this jubilant joy is of such a character that we cannot, by any possibility, explain it adequately to others."[40] Andrew Murray wrote, "There is nothing as attractive as joy, there is nothing that can help a man endure and bear as much as joy."[41]

This sounds good, and is good, yet it isn't much on display in today's church.[42] John Hunter observed, "One of the present tragedies in the Church is the absence of joy in so many lives."[43] Hunter exclaimed—not brutally, but bluntly—"A joyless Christian is an ineffective Christian."[44]

Actually, it doesn't matter how developed one's theology may be, how splendid one's gifts, or how committed one's will, it remains true nevertheless that a life without joy isn't going to impress anyone.

One man who did impress people with his joy was the thirteenth-century century Portuguese priest, St. Anthony, of whom it was said, "He seemed to bear on his face ... a gladness from heaven that came from no human source."[45] This look from the Lord is one the Lord intends for us to have, too, which is why Andrew Murray said, "One is not living right if he is living a sighing, doubting, trembling life."[46]

Network newscaster, David Brinkley, once quoted one of the Moorish kings who after fifty years of reign declared, "I have enjoyed total power, the affection of my friends, the respect of my enemies, every earthly pleasure at the clapping of my hands, and in fifty years my days of happiness number about fourteen." David Brinkley was then asked how many days of happiness he had known. His eyes narrowed, a tight smile appeared on his lips, and in characteristic candor he answered, "about fourteen." This is always the way—fame, fortune, friendships, and fun can never reward us like the joy of God can.[47] This is why hymn writer John Newton said that God has to break all our "schemes of earthly joy."

But in sharp contrast to David Brinkley's testimony, is that remarkable breakthrough Hudson Taylor experienced once the Spirit of God finally filled him. "Unspeakable joy all day long and everyday was my happy experience," he wrote. "God, even my God, was a living bright reality, and all I had to do was joyful service."[48]

How gratifying to know that the "new you" created by God already has within this abounding love and exceeding joy, each ready for release, no matter how difficult your circumstances, or what your natural temperament is.

Reflection Questions

1. Which counterfeit of God's love has surfaced the most in your life?

2. Of the four dimensions of love discussed in this chapter, which one needs the most strengthening in your life?

3. Which counterfeit of God's joy has exhibited the most in your life?

4. How did this chapter's discussion of joy help you the most? And how did it challenge you the most?

Chapter 5

Seeing the Picture

High in the dome of the Palace Rospigliosi in Rome is a classic painting by Guido Reni entitled, "The Aurora." But because the viewing of this picture required that long upward look, thus straining the neck and eyes of anyone making the attempt, its beauty was somewhat difficult to appreciate. Attempting to mitigate this problem, a man of caring, if not cleverness, placed a high-powered mirror on the floor; and so, by magnifying the masterpiece in this way, the genius of Reni's painting became more accessible to people.[1] Should not this example be one that we all ought to follow: becoming a reflector of our most high God?

Aspiring to such a goal would be audacious indeed, if it weren't for the fact God had already put his nature inside us. "By their fruit you shall know them," Jesus said, thus conveying confidence in the ability of this fruit to reveal God (Matthew 7:18). Jesus even gave the world the right to inspect your life and mine and on that basis to decide whether or not he was the Messiah (John 17:21-23). Does this not astound you? He has put the burden of proof on you and me, on your character and mine.

You are writing a gospel
    a chapter each day
By the things that you do
    and the words that you say.
Men read what you write
    whether faithless or true

Say, what is the Gospel
according to you?

There *can* be a good-news story in our lives, one that is not only respected by others but is also worthy of God! To that end, we are exploring in these pages the very qualities that reflect the nature of God. And with this agenda in view, we'll turn our attention next to that fruit of the spirit called peace.

The Peace Path

For hundreds and thousands of years, from his days in the jungle to his days in the city, men and nations have been on a search for peace—peace for themselves, peace for their children, and peace for all mankind. The peace they've been searching for, though, they have scarcely ever found—despite all the self-help books! They have thronged the offices of psychiatrists by the multiplied millions, gulping down Prozac, Paxil, and what is much more difficult to swallow—Freud! But all to no avail.

The search for personal peace didn't have its genesis in the modern West, as some have postulated. Documenting this fact, University of Glasgow Professor William Barclay wrote: "Justyn Martyr, one of the greatest of the second-century fathers, tells how he wandered from philosophy to philosophy until he finally found the elusive secret of peace in Christianity."[2] Apparently, even for those in the ancient, pre-industrial, pre-technological world, the longings for peace, and the arduous search to find it, were both personal and painful.

The Bible actually speaks of three types of peace. First, there is what Romans 5:1 calls "peace with God." This is the most important peace of all, salvation peace, because prior to our salvation we were on a collision course with God. It was not until the Holy Spirit appealed to our hearts that we did a spiritual U-turn, which is exactly what the word "repent" means: to turn around, to reverse our course, to go the opposite way. This repentance enabled the Lord's salvation peace to become irrevocably ours.

Second, there is the "peace of God," spoken of in Philippians 4:7. This refers to that inner serenity of soul, that elevating elation of spirit, which—even in the midst of challenge, chaos, or corruption—infuses us with its tranquil composure. Although this isn't the most important kind of peace, this is the peace that the world has been so desperate to find.

Third, there is what Ephesians 2:14 describes, peace with one another. This is the peace that unites former enemies—not in an uneasy truce, but in a camaraderie that is only possible through Christ. Because relationships are as important as they are to our happiness, and because these relationships can be very difficult to sustain in a satisfactory way, this particular peace is of extraordinary value.

The peace we will focus on in this chapter is the second one mentioned, the peace that only a Christian can know (although most of them don't), the peace *of* God. Like the eye of a hurricane—still, calm, and restful even while the whirling winds of destruction are blowing with devastating force—this rare and wonderful peace, supernatural in its source, showed itself in Jesus.

In his book, *The Gates of New Life,* Scottish professor James Stewart described this peace so frequently seen in the life of our Lord but so often absent from the lives of his disciples.

> There was a Samaritan village that was rude and inhospitable. "Lord," they cried exasperated, "let us call down fire from heaven. Let us teach these boorish folks a lesson." But Jesus? "Ye know not what manner of spirit you are of." Always that strong serenity!
>
> The frail boat was being tossed one night on the murderous sea. "Master," they shouted, all self-control flung to the winds. "Master, carest thou not that we perish?" "Peace, be still," Jesus said. And I think he was speaking to those panic stricken hearts as much as to the angry waves. Always that inner calm.

A crowd of five thousand followed them one day out to their secret retreat in the wilderness. "Send them away," said the disciples, "for heaven's sake, let us have a holiday for once!" "They need not depart," said Jesus. "They are sheep without a shepherd and I love them." Always that heart at leisure from itself.

Then came the end; and things went terribly wrong, or so it seemed. "Don't go to Jerusalem," they implored him. "There is danger in the air—don't go!" And when he went and the enemy struck, their strained nerves snapped completely; they all turned and fled. But Jesus? "Father, into thy hands I commend my spirit" ... Is it not marvelous? All the way from Bethlehem to Nazareth to Calvary—"My peace," My strong, untroubled peace![3]

This peace, which isn't at all like the catatonic, zombie-like behaviors tranquilizers produce, has many counterfeits. There is, for example, the peace of stoicism, a peace no other generation has opted for as much as our generation has. Rollo May once observed that we live in a schizoid culture, in that we often defend ourselves by refusing to feel.[4] Intent on avoiding hurt, we decide to become detached, to deliberately keep our distance, to thrust a stiff arm into any relationship that might result in intimacy. This type of peace, the peace of stoicism, will throw cold water on the fires of feeling, attempting to extinguish all emotions, even positive emotions; because to desire anything, we reason, is to risk the pain of loss.[5]

Another counterfeit peace is the peace of optimism. This peace minimizes the coming winter and, by design, knows nothing of scandal, or terror, or tragedy, but only knows a sugarcoated positivism dripping with sweetness and fun. "Divert yourself," says the gospel of optimism. "Escape, relax, take your ease. Why weigh yourself down with the problems of heaven and hell when you can block the negative, seek the positive, and as the song says, 'put on a happy face'?" But by indulging ease, Dr. Jowett warned, "our couch has almost become our tomb."[6] The American theologian Dr. Lewis Sperry said, "Much of our religious activity is nothing more than a cheap anesthetic to deaden the pain of an empty life."[7]

The optimism that lulls people into a false sense of security and drugs them into a dreadful slumber is really an enemy to the gospel. Jesus warned against this type of optimism when he said, "Remember the days of Noah." Interestingly, the words that followed said nothing about the evil of that day—only that they ate, they drank, they worked, they married, all the good and routine things of day-to-day life. But then one day—and, oh, what a day!—a swift and terrifying judgment came, consuming everyone in their spiritual neglect. It all happened so suddenly, too! Why, just moments before the disaster there were broad smiles, words of cheer, and the kindest sentiments expressed about some transaction of the day.

A third counterfeit of peace is a little stranger than the rest—we may call this the peace of pessimism. The pessimist sees the reigns of the universe flying in the wind. To the pessimist, life is but a blind game of dice, an aimless journey into the unknown. If today is good, tomorrow will be worse! If happiness comes, trouble will chase it away! Now, one might think there's no peace possible with this mindset, but there is. By expecting the worst, these people won't even bother to raise their puny defenses against it. Hence, no struggle is required, only the nursing of pity, the caressing of despair, and that resulting numbness that comes once stronger emotions have played themselves out.

It's warped! It's wacky! But more than a few are familiar with it—the peace of pessimism.

Some have erroneously viewed peace as the absence of trouble. To them, if the road is smooth and the circumstances are pleasant, then (for a brief while anyway) there can be some semblance of peace. Biblical peace, however, isn't based on circumstance; it's based on "inner-stance." Jesus said, "In the world, you shall have tribulation" (John 16:33). Similarly, Paul reminded Timothy that "the godly shall be persecuted" (II Timothy 3:12). The mistaken thinking which assumes persecution was true only for that day is premised on the notion that the world has changed! But the world hasn't changed. All one has to do to incur the world's wrath today is simply to speak like Jesus, act like Jesus, and love like Jesus—and once again this world will erupt into a vituperative rage (Psalms 2:1).

You must dismiss the delusion that Jesus was killed by some unusually brutal men, a remnant of barbarism that has long since passed away. To the contrary, Jesus was killed by the highest expression of culture and religion known in that day. While the poet Tennyson envisioned man "moving forward and upward, letting ape and tiger die," history proves that the tiger in man has refused to die, for he is as much a warmonger today as he ever was. What this combination of guided missiles and misguided men is leading us to is an alarming thought to consider! But this much is sure: The warpath will benefit far less than the peace path will.

So how can this peace path be found? One scripture that has much to say on this topic is Isaiah 26:3. Referring to God in this verse—who obviously is the only source of true peace—the prophet declared, "You will keep him in perfect peace whose mind is stayed upon you ...." This is a verse we should meditate upon, drawing different meanings from different words as we do so.[8]

For example, the word "you." Where does peace come from? It comes only from God. "*You* will keep him in perfect peace ...." Scripture says. This is why in I Thessalonians 5:23 and Romans 16:20 the Lord is called "the God of peace." And similarly Jesus is called "the Prince of Peace" (Isaiah 9:6), because, like no other, "He is our peace" (Ephesians 2:14). Therefore, since the Lord is our source and supply, only he can bind troubled hearts fractured by worry and woe—which, by the way, etymologically, is what the Greek word for "peace" means: to bind, to hold together.

To find added meaning in this verse from Isaiah, we will stress the next word for purposes of meditation. "You *will* keep him in perfect peace ...." In other words, this isn't a hit-and-miss proposition for the believer, wherein peace becomes a fleeting commodity, in that sometimes we seem to have it and sometimes we don't. To the contrary, no matter how challenging the situation and how great the stress, we can take comfort in the absoluteness of this word—a word without caveats, contingencies, or escape clauses—God *will*!

The certainty of his faithfulness is further confirmed by the fact this is really a matter of his legal will. Shortly before his death, Jesus left his last will and testament, in which he bequeathed his spirit to the Father, his mother to John, his clothes to the soldiers, his body to Joseph of Arimathea, and to his disciples, both then and now, he gave his strong and wonderful peace (John 14:27).

Notice next from this verse in Isaiah the word "keep." The prophet declared, "You will *keep* him in perfect peace ...." This suggests permanence, steadfastness, and uninterrupted protection. Reinforcing this image, Philippians 4:7 pictures God as a sentry, a soldier, standing outside the believer's heart in order to keep the peace. Can you imagine the Almighty decked out in military apparel, ever ready to deal with any intruder who surreptitiously comes on the scene? Better watch it! There aren't any Barney Fife weaknesses in him!

Those who like watching TV westerns perhaps remember the old codger who guarded the bank. This guy would have his hat pulled down over his eyes and, with one leg stretched out on another chair, he would doze away an entire afternoon. But God neither slumbers nor sleeps! Absolutely nothing will get by him! Hudson Taylor once acknowledged, "I used to try to keep my own heart right, but it would keep going wrong. So at last I had to give up trying myself, and to accept the Lord's offer to keep it for me. Don't you think that is the best way?"[9]

Of course, it is! What a strong assurance can be ours by knowing that the Lord's keeping watch—and more importantly still, he's keeping *us*. This means that while the slightest change in barometric pressure can put a violin out of tune, the believer need not find himself out of tune so easily, since the believer's peace is being preserved and protected by Almighty God.

To contemplate further Isaiah's message, we will read on, giving emphasis to yet another word. "You will keep him *in* perfect peace ...." Isn't that good? Not just close to it—having sufficient proximity for viewing, although too far away to actually experience—for God will put the believer right in the middle of this enviable environment that Philippians says "passes all understanding." Therefore, as the center and circumference of a believer's life, this peace will both emanate calm and eliminate chaos, thereby helping the believer function with greater godliness.

As you think back on certain decisions you've made—decisions that you later regretted, decisions that didn't exactly exhibit a whole lot of grace under pressure—can you imagine how much better those decisions would have been (and also how much more blessed others would have been) had you enjoyed the advantage of being "in" peace? And not just a partial peace, mind you, because that will never get the job done; Isaiah says it will be a *perfect* peace—a peace that calms every raw nerve, sedates every destructive emotion, making clear the mind and steady the will so that life can now be faced with an unswerving confidence in God.

Notice next how Isaiah puts it: "You will keep him in perfect peace whose *mind* is stayed on you." This is always God's way. He appeals to the mind first, the will second, and the emotions last; whereas Satan, salesmen, and politicians prefer another order. They appeal first to the emotions, then to the will, and quite often bypass the mind altogether—unless they schmooze or scam with a lie.

Notice further how Isaiah pointed out that our minds should be *stayed* on God? This reflects an implied caution against double-mindedness, wherein there is a vacillation between a promise-consciousness and a problem-consciousness—between faith and feelings, between revelation and reason.

Too often, instead of aggressively applying the Word of God to our problems, we sometimes lack the stamina for this, preferring what Eric Berne calls, "Yes, but games." To those trying to help us we say, "I know you're right, but ...." "I should take your advice, but ...." However, instead of rationalizing and thereby distancing ourselves from the truth, we should turn on whatever disturbs, destroys, and dislodges our peace by rearranging whatever mental furniture is out of place and refuse Satan's devious strategies to pull us down.[10]

Intellectual honesty isn't the only issue, though, for Scripture also says of God, "You will keep him in perfect peace whose mind is stayed on *you*." Notice: The mind should be fixed not just on Bible verses, or on the encouragement of Christian friends, or on the resolve of our own will. All that is good, but when our gaze is fixed on the Lord, the happier result will be an infusion of God's presence in us before we see his working in our circumstances.

This sequence makes a lot of sense, especially when recalling that it is none other than our dear, darling self which moves in constant opposition to the very peace we desire. Addressing this issue, G. D. Watson wrote:

> If a mysterious yet mighty voice should piece the heart of every Christian on earth and propound the question, "Why are you not cheerful and peaceful and content in spirit?" ... not one in ten thousand but what would begin instantly to lay the blame on somebody, or something, or some circumstance outside of their own hearts.[11]

However, the more ominous obstacle to our peace exists within us, which is why F. J. Huegel declared, "... unless Christ works in you an inner crucifixion which will cut you off from self-infatuation and unite you to God in a deep union of love, a thousand heavens could not give you peace."[12] Say what we will about the waywardness of the world, the stealth of Satan, and those fierce factions that exist even among friends, our biggest enemy (the carnal) has established headquarters within our own soul. Hence, peace isn't possible until this fortress is sealed off.

In his book, *The Higher Christian Life*, W. E. Boardman, writing at a time the Civil War was about to subject America to bloodbath anguish, made this observation: "Too many learn to live just when they come to die. The great principles that give men peace in the hour of death would have given them power, had they known them throughout their lives."[13] Whenever danger is near, or when death itself is immanent, it seems that a focus is finally achieved which casts aside worldly distractions. Finally, there is this ability to see beyond the familiar, the foreboding, or the fascinating, and allow a rest of soul—so coveted and so elusive for so long—become an abiding reality. But all that produced these happy outcomes was actually available long before danger arose, and could have been used to live a more noble, godly life.

A Patent for Patience

Before considering the next part of the spirit's fruit, we would do well to acknowledge the wisdom in this sequencing Galatians provides. First, according to this passage, we must allow ourselves to receive and return God's love. The by-product of this love, then, will be joy—inasmuch as our God is a Savior still, willing and able to deliver us, no matter what. In turn, this factor will establish our emotions in an environment of peace, about which we have just commented. Subsequently, this environment of peace will encourage what may very well be the difference between victory and defeat—patience. While love, joy, and peace provide the climate that nurtures patience, every other part of the fruit is dependent upon patience being exercised.

Ask most people to identify an obvious weakness in their character and it will be this one, the one about patience, that will be cited most frequently. By contrast, the seventeenth-century writer William Gurnall marveled at the patience found in God, and thus wrote: "When I consider how the goodness of God is abused by the greatest part in mankind, I cannot but be of the mind that said, 'The greatest miracle in the world is God's patience and bounty to an ungrateful world.'"

Undeniably true, you would agree, is the fact patience finds its deepest roots in the heart of God, and therefore must be gained from him if it is going to manifest authentically in our lives.

Like all the other parts of the spirit's fruit, patience does have its share of counterfeits. One example of counterfeited patience is seen in the Old Testament story of

Joseph. Had you been an outsider to Jacob's family, you might have thought that the brothers were patient with Joseph when he bragged how all of them would one day bow down to him. As Joseph announced his one-day rise to prominence—and did so with adolescent airs that hardly invited rejoicing—the brothers said little to him. Beyond a brief hint of protest, they seemed to exhibit remarkable restraint. Appearances can be deceiving, though, for as the story unfolds we come to see these brothers in a very different light. Instead of patience prevailing in their hearts, a more sinister reality was actually on the scene. The brothers were just biding their time, waiting with calculated coolness their opportunity for revenge.

Then came that day when Joseph, on a mission from his father, was sent to the far country. Even from a long way off the brothers could tell from that contemptible swagger that it was Joseph—child of favor, young man of destiny! Violently (and certainly not religiously) they soon laid their hands on him, ripping away that brightly colored coat that announced his favorite son status. Then, with vehement forcefulness, they threw dear brother into the pit! Oh, my! With a shriek and a thud, the deed was done. Then, peering into that pit with fists-on-hips satisfaction, the brothers shared a smirk of congratulations for such a well-executed plot. So much, then, for *his* destiny!

A little later, it is true, they did retrieve Joseph from the pit. But not because of mercy; they did it because of money! Scheming to make a few bucks off baby brother, they soon sold Joseph to Midianite slave traders who marched him off into bondage.

See with your imagination the brothers standing there in happy unison—minus one! Waving bye-bye to the dreamer, it is mock sorrow that replaces pretended grief. The biting of the upper lip and the drying of the eye is only a joke at this point, as their shrewd scheming is finally unmasked to reveal sheer envy. G. D. Watson wrote, "It was envy that sold Joseph, that made Saul persecute David, that made the princes try to kill Daniel, that sold Jesus, and that has been the passion producing murder in all generations."[14] Envy, lying low for a season while counterfeiting itself as patience.

Another counterfeit of patience can be seen in those people who seem to be calm all the time, people who take everything in stride and allow nothing to bother them. What may appear to be a virtue is really nothing more than a reduced capacity for life. The true reason nothing bothers these people is because there is nothing they particularly want. Hence, they sleepwalk through life, waiting for the grave to confirm what others have long known—they are dead! The mere fact that someone's emotions don't roller-coaster, or that their reactions are always even-keeled, isn't a valid proof of patience. Because while people with thick skin and hard hearts may appear patient, what actually accounts for their lack of impulsive or compulsive reacting is insensitivity—a decided detachment from life itself.

Henry David Thoreau said that, "Most men live out their lives in quiet desperation." By resigning themselves to their supposed fate, and then reducing their expectations of what life has to offer, they do little more than exist. Patience, however, isn't a mild form of despair. Authentic patience has a "know-so" hope in it that the God of many promises and unrivaled power is going to come through!

Abraham Kuyper said, "Patience does not sparkle in the sunlight of the day. It glows in the darkness with an inner light. It glows in the night of suffering—of physical suffering, but especially of spiritual suffering, when the soul wrestles in deepest distress."[15]

According to the Bible, patience can take two forms. The active form of patience is steadfastness; the passive form of patience is waiting—and both are surely needed by Christians today! There will be those times when we will want to call a halt to our efforts; and there will be other times when we will want to cease our waiting. That which we've been working hard for, that which we've waited so long for, seems nowhere in sight. Given the fact that no Christian goes through life without having his or her patience tried, James S. Stewart wrote:

> We all get our share of this: the cutting edge of sorrow; the wear and tear of tasks beyond our strength; the discipline of adversity, of

> frustration, of hopes indefinitely deferred; the discipline of fierce temptation. Many a time, under such experience, faith flinches and endurance breaks.[16]

This is especially bound to occur if the patience exercised is natural and not supernatural in its origin and operation.[17]

Patience actually means to rely on the divine supply. It is the decision to keep faith on the job. To better grasp this picture, patience can be depicted in this way. Picture over yonder the stacked up blessings of God, each with your name on it. This, we shall say, represents grace, the realm of God's promises. Now picture your present circumstances—each situation, each relationship, each achievement as things currently stand. Is there anything lacking? No doubt, there is! The gap between your present life and God's promised life is huge! Now, even though God said that he will do exceedingly, abundantly, above all you ask or think, there is so much you have wished for that hasn't yet come true.

There is a reason for this. According to Romans 4:16 and Romans 5:2, the only way to access grace is by the bridge of faith. Indeed, no other bridge—the bridge of brilliance, the bridge of hard work, the bridges of fortune and favor, the bridge of networking—can possibly get you there.

The biggest problem with faith is that sense and sight so thoroughly disagree with it! And these two surveyors of reality can be so convincing! Therefore, you're tempted to pursue what is reasonable, and not what is biblical, casting away what Hebrews 10:35 calls your confidence in God. But don't do that, this verse counsels, for it is only this continuing confidence in God that will pay off!

You should know that in every situation, you're going to cast away something—either your confidence in God (Hebrews 10:35) or your problems upon God (I Peter 5:7). There may be, at different times along the way, several opportunities to take matters into your own hands, to pursue a course of your own choosing, whereby you tune out the voice of God and tune in the voice of expediency. But whenever a decision like that is made the very opposite of patience has just gained control.

Patience, if we were to attempt to depict it graphically, can be represented by all those pillars under the faith bridge. Now, while it is true that only faith can lay hold of grace, it is also true that nothing is going to be gained unless patience holds up faith. For if the pillars of patience give way, the bridge of faith will quickly crumble—and therefore grace will remain out of reach.

Tertullian used a different metaphor to show the connection between faith and patience. Writing in the third century, Tertullian said, "Faith is patience with the lamp lit." The particular message this metaphor conveys is that patience doesn't require us to stand against the dark with determination but no revelation; for God has shed his light, the truths of which must now prevail.

Thomas Watson, the great Puritan preacher, said, "Faith argues the soul into patience."[18] Often the journey to God's grace supply takes time, during which sentiments unhealthy to our faith will begin to surface. At such times as these, there is a need to cut off the soul's complaints and to tune into God for direction. It was in this context that Watson said, "Patience opens the ear but shuts the mouth."[19] Needing to be shut down is the "get-it-now-anyhow" message. Needing to be heard is the "if-you-wait-it-will-be-great" message.

Perhaps you're one of those people who *is* able to see the good life as Scripture describes it, and yet it doesn't seem to be turning out that way for you. Why is this? Could it be because you were often impatient and that time and again, when it came to choosing God's way or your way, you chose your way? In choosing their own way, many people will elevate what they call "common sense" over the revealed will of God, while other people will rely on their own abilities, or perhaps on the resources of others to see them through. What must be remembered, though, is that yielding to these alternative approaches will never secure what God is offering.

James 1:4 describes what God, through our patience, *can* contribute when it says: "But let patience have its perfect work that you may be perfect and complete lacking nothing." The emphasis in this verse, you will notice, is *first* on our inner life and *then* on our circumstances. There is wisdom in this sequence, because circumstantially people may have everything lining up right, while on the inside there is so much upheaval and unrest! Knowing that it can be this way, God designed his blessings to first meet our innermost needs to an extent he called "perfect."

This idea of being perfect isn't the hype of heaven or some mistake in translation that now must be explained away, inasmuch as Jesus himself said (Matthew 5:48), "... be perfect"—and he meant it! More timid ones will quickly assert that the word "perfect" really means mature, but this is a doubtful interpretation in this instance, given what Jesus said next in this verse: "... be perfect, just as your Father in heaven is perfect." The example, then, is God himself! Perfect means perfect! According to Tozer, "In the original Greek, exactly the same word that applies to God applies to people, too."[20]

It is common for this idea of perfection to die the death of a thousand qualifications in the hands of its interpreters, thereby causing perfection to disappear from our lives as a meaningful, strategic goal. While perfection, in context, often refers to purity and not maturity, and to how the race is being run and not the end of the race,[21] this biblical word must not be redacted from the lexicon of faith.

Yet, we seemed to have done this, and in so doing have developed this penchant for talking out of both sides of our mouth. At one time we will wax eloquent, saying with Paul, "I can do all things through Christ who strengthens me." And then, not too much later, we will talk about daily sin in our lives, as if Christ's strengthening grace couldn't possibly stop that. In this same vein of duplicitous thinking, we'll rattle off verses such as: "Christ is able to save them to the uttermost ...." and God is "able to do exceeding abundantly above all that we ask or think ...." But then we'll compartmentalize these verses far from our moral struggle so that indwelling sin remains in place, intact: its assaults so formidable that Christ's ability to save to the utmost and to do exceeding abundantly is deemed inadequate.

When Paul prayed for the Thessalonian believers that God "sanctify you wholly" (I Thessalonians 5:23), did Paul only mean that God would keep on forgiving them, and perhaps help them to do a little better in their ongoing battle with sin?

Asa Mahan, at one time the president of Oberlin College while Charles Finney served as a professor there, disputed such a suggestion when he wrote, "The original word rendered 'wholly,' I would observe, is one of the strongest words known in the Greek or any other language. It is made up of two words, *olos*, or all, and *telos*, everywhere in the New Testament translated perfect."[22] The force of language here is made more impressive when noting that the action in view is not reserved for the believer's eventual entrance into heaven, because Paul prayed that "your whole spirit and soul and body be *preserved* blameless ...." Notice: not suddenly made that way at the end of life, but *sustained* in that condition during these days on earth. Asa Mahan concluded, "The passage might be literally rendered thus, the very God of peace sanctify you in all respects to perfection."[23]

Too easily, we resign ourselves to a life far beneath perfection, because aspiration and motivation simply do not exist for the higher life.[24] Rote, stoic commentary about moral failure being "just the way it is" in our world clearly discloses how shallow in manner, and seldom in frequency, perfection is even considered.

A wrong view of Romans 7 has no doubt contributed to the theft of these desires (see Appendix F)—as well to the cover-up that followed! To us, perfection seems so far way, so unreachable, so contrary to the life we've always known, that getting anywhere near it never crosses our mind. Indeed, whenever this subject is mentioned, perfection is dismissed immediately, and almost unanimously, as something that occurs only upon our arrival in heaven. But until then, forget it.

Could it be, though, that we have overreacted?[25] True enough, perfection in its consummate form does transact in heaven, but what is also true is that what the law demands, the new nature fulfills.[26] Moreover, these nine qualities, given in fullness to every believer, represent a perfection in us right now. It is only when we begin to experience these qualities, if ever we do, that our desire for the higher life won't be relegated to the status of blocked thinking and vacant emotion—instead it will stir us! And not in a manner that excites expectations bound to fail, or only depresses us once the need for further progress is made clear. No, it will stir us in the same way hunger and thirst stir us—with an intent to supply that which satisfies.

People may say that this higher life will bind us to legalism, or trigger a harsh treatment of others, or result in judgmental condescension. Yet, none of this needs to occur. This criticism really represents the devil's designed detour away from new nature living.

So what if someone were to say to you, "I have a key that will unlock the door to all your dreams, a key that will unlock all those doors that have kept you from the satisfaction you've been seeking." Would you want that key?

Surely, you would! But maybe you'd draw back, thinking that this is one of those get-rich-quick schemes. Well, patience, by definition, isn't very quick. Nevertheless, this *is* the key that will unlock the door to a treasure house of stupendous blessings. And it is precisely because patience is the one key that works, casting this key away makes no sense! What does make sense is exercising a steadfast reliance upon God—because when we wait, he works! But if we decide to take matters into our own hands, then he'll wait and we'll work—hard! Hellishly hard! And for what? For something much less than what God gives!

Impatience is likely when we don't see things right. To fail to see what we need to see—about the peace of God and the patience he supplies—will indeed hurt us. But more than Reni's painting, what the world really needs to see is a reflection of God so stunning in its view that reliance on him makes total sense, although the peace he provides can't be captured by sense—since it still surpasses, even to us, all understanding!

Reflection Questions

1. Which one of the counterfeits of peace have you experienced the most?

2. In what specific way did this discussion on peace help you, or challenge you?

3. After reviewing the counterfeits of patience and the characteristics of patience, how would you assess the quality of your patience?

4. Identify one area of your life where you want to see God's patience more in evidence. Then, giving reference to the material you read, explain how you will increase your patience in this area.

Chapter 6

There Must Be a Difference

The hour had come! Having left the Upper Room, Jesus and his disciples were on their way to Gethsemane. But before going down into the Kidron Valley, Jesus stopped at a vineyard located just outside Jerusalem to make a point uppermost in his mind.

This is often true of a man who's about to die: He will talk only of those things that are of consummate importance. So, while holding a vine in his hand, Jesus interrupted his departure from the city that night to say, "I am the true vine." And by true vine, Jesus meant that what he had in his hand was only a copy, nature's illustration of a far greater truth. The real vine, Jesus said, the vine from which all spiritual life will be received for ages to come, is me!

The purpose of a vine isn't for mere show; the vine is planted so it might bring forth fruit. Hence, as Jesus walked to his appointment with death, the passion of his heart flows right here. He is concerned that his character (represented by that fruit) would be reproduced in the lives of those who love him. This passion for fruit was clearly evident throughout Jesus' ministry. Do you remember what happened to the fig tree? It was cursed—and not in an irrational tantrum, as some have supposed. The real reason for this tree cursing is because it didn't bear fruit. This acted out parable on the road to Bethany demonstrates for all time what God thinks about those who don't bear fruit.

Like Israel, this fig tree, from a distance, looked good—the showy religion of a lot of leaves. But upon a closer examination it was seen to be barren. And is this not the way it is with the church today? According to church growth statistics, more people attend church in a given weekend than attend all the professional football, baseball, and basketball games combined for a whole year! And yet, according to many studies, most of these church attendees (in terms of ministry, fellowship, and other spiritual disciplines) are functionally unchurched. Which is to say that just like the fig tree, they may look good—*but* there isn't any fruit! They profess what they don't possess. They want to be counted in, but they don't want to be counted on!

Do you realize that twenty-four of the twenty-seven New Testament books talk about the fruit? According to Psalm 1, this fruit distinguishes the godly from the ungodly (Psalm1:3, 4). And from the Sermon on the Mount we learn something even more sobering: Those without fruit are going to be cast into the fire (Matthew 7:19). This was a warning so serious that the Lord restated while on his way to Gethsemane (John 15:6), and it was stated yet again by the writer of the book of Hebrews (Hebrews 6:8).

G. D. Watson said, "There are two kinds of burning—either sin must be burned out of the soul, or the soul itself must burn forever."[1] The point of all this being: There must be a difference, a real and noticeable difference—one so unique in its kind and so utterly beyond human capacity that people will draw the only conclusion possible: We have been with Jesus (Acts 4:13).

So is this difference manifesting? In reply, Hannah Whitall Smith said, "... the followers of the Lord Jesus Christ are satisfied with a life so conformed to the world, and so like it in almost every respect, that, to the casual observer, no difference is discernible."[2]

Abraham Maslow once characterized the church as "non-peakers talking to non-peakers about peak experience." Phenomenology of religion studies document a tremendous gap between our talk and our walk, between our creed and our deed, between what we know and what we grow. Talk about the dangers of inflation! What about the dangers of deflation? How sad it is when the high language of Scripture is used to label lives that simply don't measure up.

One reason for this discrediting discrepancy is the fact many on the church's rolls aren't really born-again. Hitler, Mussolini, and Stalin were all baptized into the church. Karl Marx even wrote a dissertation on John 15, where Jesus talked about the vine and its fruit. Still, neither baptism nor correct doctrine will make a man a Christian. There must be a corresponding internal reality, supernatural in its origin, for one to be a child of God. Going to church doesn't mean going to heaven. One can attend a service, yet never give soul-saving attention to the Word of God.

Another reason for the defeat in church member's lives was identified by Dr. Lloyd Ogilvie, the former Chaplain of the United States Senate. Dr. Ogilvie remarked: "There is seldom a week in my ministry that goes by without talking to many people whose basic problem is that they have tried to integrate the lordship of Christ into an old life."[3] As millions of people can testify, this is altogether impossible! Remnants of the old life will trigger a civil war, provoking complaints such as the one Fredrich Buechner conveyed.

> Lust is the ape that gibbers in our loins. Tame him as we will by day, he rages all the wilder in our dreams by night. Just when we think we are safe from him, he raises up his ugly head and smirks, and there is no river in the world which flows cold and strong enough to strike him down. Almighty God, why dost thou deck men out with such a loathsome toy?[4]

Whatever form lust may take (sexual, financial, or egotistical), it can never be conquered by mere knowledge or sheer willpower. What is needed is something supernatural—the infusion of divine life!

Consider Jesus' word about the vine and its fruit. Does the grape strive and strain in order to attain grapehood? Does it read horticultural manuals, or lapse into a deep trance chanting the mantra: "grape" ... "grape" ... "grape"? Hardly! The only reason it becomes a grape is by virtue of its connection to the vine; apart from this connection it could never become a grape.

This is precisely what Jesus does for us as well. The very fruit that makes a difference—what by our own self we could never achieve—he produces! E. Stanley Jones, the great devotional writer and former missionary to India, once said:

> I laid at Christ's feet a self of which I was ashamed, couldn't control and couldn't live with; and to my glad astonishment he took that self, remade it, consecrated it to kingdom purposes and gave it back to me, a self I can now live with gladly and joyously and comfortably.[5]

Being that this is the desire of every growing Christian and, for that matter, the red-hot passion of God himself, we will continue our study of the fruit of the spirit, focusing next on the disposition and deeds of kindness.

A New Kind of Kindness

In this increasingly uncivil world where our unmannered discourse is harsh and what we do to each other suggests a rampant narcissism let loose on society, this word about being kind appears to be too tame and tardy to make a difference. The call for kindness poses a very real problem in this respect, because, on the one hand, God wants a difference in our lives so decisive and dramatic that the glory would have to go to him. But, on the other hand, kindness appears to be so bland, so banal, that no such glory is possible.

Think about it. Everyone believes in kindness. You do, I do; there isn't a respectable religion or philosophy around that denies it. Kindness is a virtue casually and commonly commended from the Boy Scouts on up!

So, again, when contemplating our crude and coarse culture, one has to wonder, what difference can kindness make? Can kindness rise above the level of the innocuous and the inconsequential? If so, something much more than the puff of piety and the sloganeering of sanctimony is needed. Stories meant to inspire aren't enough, either.

What's required is insightful defining from the Word of God. Before distinguishing conventional kindness from biblical kindness, though, we would do well to reflect on the queries George MacDonald posed:

> Can a man become strong in righteousness without learning to perform ordinary acts of kindness for his neighbor? Will a man climb the last flight of the stair when he has never set foot on the lowest step? Could it be that the Lord, who demands high virtue of us, tests us first in little tasks before he entrusts to us bigger ones?[6]

Other parts of the Holy Spirit's fruit may be more impressive upon inspection, but simple acts of kindness, set aside and ignored, predict that these other dimensions of Holy Spirit living will be forever forfeited. It matters not how deep the love, how exhilarating the joy, how sweet the peace, and how indomitable the patience, all this will have a hollow ring if one refuses to render small acts of kindness.

The universal sentiment, "try a little kindness," is not without its appeal, though, even on the simple level in which it is offered. Nevertheless, this conventional view of kindness severely skews the radically robust vision Scripture sets forth on this subject. One way to see the tremendous difference between these two perspectives is to expose some of their counterfeits.

Mother Teresa is known all over the world for her charitable work in India. As the founder of the religious order, The Missionaries of Charity, she devoted decades of her life to helping the poor. But as commendable as her contributions are, they do stand in contrast with biblical kindness.

Following the teachings of universalism (espoused by Pope John Paul II), Mother Teresa did not by her own admission relate evangelism to her work. This icon of humanitarianism targeted the physical needs of the people, but not their spiritual needs. Mother Teresa believed that Hindus should pray to their gods, that Buddhists and people of other religions should pray to their gods, and that none of these people were, on that basis, lost and in need of conversion.[7]

But what did Jesus say? To give the cup of water *in his Name*! We minister to only part of a person when we give just the cup of cold water (and even that part is only temporary). However, when we give to others "in his name"—holding up Jesus as the Living Water who forever satisfies—that produces something, which, if received, is not only permanent but also eternal. Food, clothes, shelter, medicine—all these are fine, but there is an opportunity present, which, if sensitively pursued, shouldn't be overlooked.

One of the reasons Romans 2:4 connects kindness with repentance is because at the point of an unmet need, the heart can become especially tender and teachable. Just then it may be more receptive than ever before—not just to gifts, but to the Giver himself! So a right relationship with God is foundational to the kindness God wants to give.

A. B. Simpson pointed out that kindness is founded on the word *kin*. For the eternal purpose of bestowing great kindness upon us, it was necessary, Scripture states, for God to make us his kindred. "In order to do this," Simpson writes, "he makes us his kindred first by giving us his own nature, making us his children; then by taking human nature into his own person through the incarnate Son of God; and then by wedding us to the Lord Jesus and making us the Bride of the Lamb."[8]

Given the divine strategy, it becomes clear that the failure to even mention Jesus, or to encourage a right relationship with him, demonstrates a deficit of kindness that is too critical to overlook.

By contrast, there is a kindness that degenerates into a crass grabbing of attention, a philanthropy that doles out its goods in a mechanical, if not self-serving way. Witness all the corporate executives as they hold up their check on some national do-good telethon! Biblical kindness doesn't require all those drum rolls, fanfares, and ingratiating words by a fawning emcee! You will recall that Jesus talked about giving in secret and not letting the left hand know what the right hand is doing. But doesn't parceling out our gift so we can get on the same show four times fly in the face of our Lord's call to secret giving? One man, thinking he understood this principle, stood to his feet and announced proudly, "I want give five hundred dollars to the church—anonymously!" Well, it was a little too late for that!

Others will employ kindness in a very manipulative way. They will court favor for their own ends, using flattery, gifts, and whatever else might work—because to them, it's all part of the game. Believing they are on their way to the top, they'll do whatever they've got to do to get there! But surely the boss isn't that much of a fool. Wouldn't he, or she, see right through this? Why on earth would such pampering ever be regarded as a positive thing?

William Thackeray, the nineteenth-century British novelist, didn't regard it that way. "Kindness is very indigestible," he wrote with quaint British indignity. Especially that kindness attached to a pompous condescension or a huckster's scheme.[9]

Talk about kindness with malevolent intent! What about "the Angel of Light" himself? Recall how he approached Jesus sounding ever so humane and kind. "Jesus, you're hungry," he said, his voice oozing all the pretended concern of a funeral director. "You've been without food for so long! So why don't you turn these stones into bread?" Satan suggested, with sympathetic eyes and contrived concern. And while this suggestion seemed reasonable enough, in fact it came straight out of the pit!

What Lucifer really wanted was for Jesus to distrust the guardianship of the Father to the extent Jesus would now receive counsel from his adversary. What Lucifer also wanted was for Jesus to reject this idea of being a suffering servant messiah. Take a short-cut! Make it easier on yourself! Meet your own need! This was the real message so cleverly hidden in the Trojan horse of his kindness.

The "kiss-up" kindness that has only its own selfish motives, or the partial kindness that elevates the physical over the spiritual, stand in sharp contrast with the kindness of our God. We see this contrast crystallized in Titus, chapter 3, verse 5, where we read the words "... but when the goodness and the loving kindness of our God appeared, he saved us ....” Contemplate for a moment the enormous implications of these words. Is not “salvation” kindness the greatest kindness of all?

Think of it: the forgiveness of sins, a brand-new nature, thousands of promises pledged, a new destiny offered, a new power to rely upon, an ongoing intimacy with God, and the blessed assurance of an eternity in heaven—there’s simply no way that the world’s kindness can ever compare with this!

In the Bible kindness has the heartbeat of evangelism. Thus, we read in Colossians 3, verses 11 and 12, “... but Christ is all and in all. Put on therefore ... kindness ....” In other words, because Jesus is either in or near every human heart, either indwelling or inviting, this is our motive for kindness. And as such, it also suggests our goal for extending kindness: to encourage by word, deed, gift, or some other form of help, a closer relationship with God.

So kindness isn’t just an innocent, innocuous term that means to be polite or to do a good deed. The scope of Christian kindness extends far beyond the world’s efforts, since it encourages through practical, daily love a desire to woo others to the Lover himself.

There are those who will give money, provide do-good help, and extend kindness to others from time to time through polite, cordial words. But such, for them, doesn’t exactly represent a lifestyle.

They’ll write their check, stick it in the mail, and that’s that! Or they’ll bag up old clothes, set aside used furniture, put in the call to Goodwill—and soon enough the truck arrives to cart it all away. But this type of kindness doesn’t exactly put their lives on a stretch. Why, such a small portion of time and abundance hardly touches their lives at all.

The kindness of God’s Spirit will mean doing what Jesus did—going out of our way to get close to certain people who may not be all that thrilled to see us. Then, upon achieving this access, kindness requires a willingness to lay down one’s life on their behalf—not because they are worth it at that point, but because the Father is—and he loves them! Therefore, for his sake, so will we.

In his classic, *The Problem of Pain*, C. S. Lewis offers this shrewd insight:

> ... "kindness" is a quality fatally easy to attribute to ourselves on quite inadequate grounds. Everyone feels benevolent if nothing happens to be annoying him at the moment. Thus a man easily comes to console himself for all his other vices by a conviction that "his heart's in the right place" and "he wouldn't hurt a fly," though in fact he has never made the slightest sacrifice for a fellow creature. We think we are kind when we are only happy.[10]

What happens if the person we're kind to is mean, spiteful, or obnoxious? And how will we respond if our kindness is met with ingratitude, with a "take-it-and-run" selfishness? Do we look for a new recipient? We may do exactly that, unless something supernatural from our spirit is at work.

In the Greek Old Testament, and in other parts of Scripture as well, the words "gentleness" and "kindness" are nearly synonymous. Therefore, when James 3:17 says that the wisdom which is from above is gentle it addresses an issue very much related to kindness.

Commenting on this issue, G. D. Watson wrote, "To have a real gentle spirit there must not be the least secret feeling of anything bitter, or sour, or severe, or combative, or dictatorial, or a sitting in judgment ...."[11] And yet how easily one or more of these feelings can surface if our kindness doesn't secure the desired response. The kindness we are more familiar with is mood-generated and mood-terminated.

But biblical kindness originates in a higher order, G. D. Watson explained: "To be filled with the gentleness of Jesus we must put it above everything else; that is, set a price on it in our hearts, above all Christian activity, above all preaching, or evangelistic work, or Scripture exegesis, or building of churches ...." Mr. Watson asked this critical question, "Who will believe this and comply with it?"[12] And the answer may be, not many.

We could rattle off ten reasons why a particular person doesn't deserve our kindness. If we seek God's wisdom, however (which so very often refutes our own), a kindness will be generated that wouldn't have otherwise come. Case in point—Stephen! While his enemies hurled rocks at him, Stephen "looked up steadfastly into heaven." And *that* made the difference! It was this upward look, this fixed and stunning view revealing Jesus, that changed everything. Stephen died like our Lord, praying for his murderers' forgiveness, because he got this vision of our Lord.

How easy it would have been for Stephen to die a bitter man! What curses he could have uttered! What vitriol he could have vented! What bitterness he could have unleashed as he fixated on the injustice of it all! But what averted all this is the fact Stephen didn't just look up; but he looked up *steadfastly*, the Bible says. You see, there are times when the trials we face can be so severe that a quick glance, a faint request, isn't going to be enough. If godly kindness is going to manifest, we're going to have to get much closer to God.

Are you beginning to sense the scope of this? God's kindness—not just for the body, but for the soul. Not just for here, but for hereafter. Not just provisions, but the Provider himself! Not just when it's easy, but even when it seems impossible. And further: not just in a token way, but in a way that requires our life. Lacordaire, the nineteenth-century French priest, wrote: "Above all other things be kind. Kindness is the one thing through which we can most resemble God and ... most disarm men."[13] Esteeming kindness as one of the principal charms of life, Scottish theologian John Watson said it well, "Let us be kind to one another for most of us are fighting a hard battle."[14]

Growing In Goodness

The next fruit, so close in character with this one, is goodness. Significantly, as with the fruit of kindness, goodness is also a much-counterfeited fruit, if not a fruit that is totally misunderstood! Many people think that anyone can do a good deed and that religion has nothing to do with it. They would even say that people will be rewarded in the life to come, if the good in them outweighs the bad. But is this true? No, it isn't. There won't be any scales at the Pearl Gate of heaven, for those refused admission won't have anything good to weigh. Does this surprise you?

In the seventh chapter of Matthew, Jesus said something that to me, for a long time, made no sense at all. He said that a bad tree couldn't bear good fruit, and that a good tree couldn't bear bad fruit. Now, had Jesus said the world could produce some good—maybe not as much as the church—I could have understood that. But he said a lost person couldn't do anything good! This assessment will shock most people, especially those who are depending on their good works to reward them with eternal favor.

According to Scripture, "there are none good; no, not one" (Romans 3:10, 12). And yet, in utter naiveté, many today are just like that rich young ruler who came asking Jesus the question, "What lack I yet?" Anyone conversant with the high standards of God, and the feeble attempts of man to measure up, would be flabbergasted to hear such a statement, "What lack I yet? You mean, you don't know? Are you thinking you've arrived? Are you really so grandiose in your thinking that you believe you have achieved what Sinai required? But instead of launching this scorching rhetoric of prosecutorial aggression, Jesus took a different approach. With sage wisdom and a calm, loving demeanor, Jesus simply remarked, "You still lack one thing."

In his splendid book, *The Holiness of God*, R. C. Sproul said this about Jesus' response:

> If ever Jesus spoke with tongue in cheek, it was here. If we take Jesus' words literally, we would be forced to conclude that the conversation took place between the two most righteous men in history: ... between the Lamb without blemish and a lamb with only one blemish.[15]

True, while most people may not claim for themselves what the rich young ruler did, they do think they'll go to heaven one day, and that when they arrive the sandpapering of soul prior to admission shouldn't take very long. Such an assessment, though, is most astounding! Kierkegaard once remarked, "... it is horrible to see a man rush toward his own destruction. It is horrible to see him dance on the rim of the abyss without any intimation of it."[16]

But because of blind, unwarranted optimism many people regard the status of their soul and their safety on judgment day as issues of no great concern. A recent poll in the United States disclosed that only one-half of one percent of the population believes they are going to hell. This indicates the extent the blinders are on when it comes to assessing one's own goodness. The decline in America's morality is too obvious to deny. Yet, those who are living compromised lives doubt its damage to them?

Tozer challenged such thinking, saying, "Let me tell you what a moral man really is: He is good enough to deceive himself and bad enough to damn himself."[17] Just like the rich young ruler, he imagines a goodness that doesn't exist while remaining ignorant about a righteousness that does.

In his book, *Revival at Midnight*, Angel Martinez acknowledged, "I am like old Ben Johnson, who said, 'I know that men are bad because I am supposed to be a good man, and I know how bad I am.'"[18]

Perhaps you will recall from your study of American literature that Sinclair Lewis was the first American to win the Nobel Prize for Literature. In assessing the brilliance of Lewis' writing, the striking feature that draws the most attention is his uncanny insight into the perversities of human nature. Sinclair Lewis wrote *Babbitt*, exposing the corruption of the business world; *Arrowsmith*, exposing the corruption of the medical world; and *Elmer Gantry*, exposing the corruption of the religious world.

When the day finally arrived for Sinclair Lewis to receive his Nobel Prize, an Italian journalist inquired, "Mr. Lewis, having set forth the seriousness of man's problems, I wonder if you have any answers." "Sir," this man of genius replied, "not only do I not have any answers; I don't even care about answers." Don't even care, Mr. Lewis? How evil is that?

The evil in all of us is extensive: In the words of Scripture, "There is none that does good." Not just *enough* good, you will notice, because what Scripture affirms is more extreme than that—*any* good! When C. E. M. Joad, the militant, agnostic philosopher came to Christ, he said that what most convinced him was the Bible's doctrine of original sin. To him, Scripture's analysis of what is wrong with mankind made a lot of sense.[19] Pascal came to the same conclusion several centuries earlier, thus he wrote:

> I confess that so soon the Christian religion reveals the human principle that human nature is corrupt and fallen from God, that opens my mind everywhere to see the mark of this truth: for nature is such that she testifies everywhere, both within man and without him, to a lost God and corrupt nature.[20]

Who does not see this—a doting mother? No, she sees this. While caressing the sleeping head of her child at night, she has not forgotten the sinful deeds of the day. In 1926 the Minnesota Crime Commission published a report that said:

> Every baby starts life as a little savage. He is completely selfish and self-centered. He wants what he wants when he wants it—his bottle, his mother's attention, his playmate's toy, his uncle's watch. Deny him this once and he seethes with rage and aggressiveness which would be murderous were he not so helpless. He is dirty, he has no morals, no knowledge, no skills. This means that all children—not just certain children, all children—are born delinquent. If permitted to continue in the self-centered world of his infancy, given free reign to his impulse actions to satisfy his wants, every child would grow up a criminal, a thief, a killer, or a rapist.[21]

G. D. Watson observed, "There is in every baby's heart a miniature world, and every baby is a miniature Alexander. There is a desire for wealth, renown, a desire to boss people, and to be supreme, and to have your own way."[22]

Entrenched evil is universal and, as far as human initiative is concerned, irreversible. Moral training, whether undertaken at home or at school, just won't accomplish what society supposes it will. By inculcating principles and incentivizing good, there can be some success, it is true. Nevertheless, the heart we are born with is too perverse to be transformed by mere assent to moral principles.

Modifying behaviors is not now, nor can it ever be, the same thing as changing hearts. For the heart to undergo real change—not cosmetically, but at its core—God's salvation grace is indispensably vital. "To make a man a saint," Pascal said, "grace is absolutely necessary, and whoever doubts it, does not know what a saint is or what a man is."[23]

In our attempt to believe the best about humanity, we want to think that at the very least man will lay hold of this grace soon after hearing about it. However, not even this assumption is true; for while grace may sound like a lovely word, the dark side of grace implies that we're so bad off we can't be fixed through our efforts toward improvement. For this reason, then, man doesn't want grace; he wants approval. In support of this fact, Charles Spurgeon the famous London pastor who spoke each week to thousands, gave this account of his pre-conversion experience:

> I must confess that I never would have been saved if I could have helped it. As long as ever I could, I rebelled, and revolted, and struggled against God. When he would have me pray, I would not pray, and when he would have me listen to the sound of the ministry, I would not. And when I heard, and the tear rolled down my cheek, I wiped it away and defied him to melt my soul.[24]

How insanely grace-resistant we can be! Even though the grace of God could change everything! And it can do so, no matter how evil we are!

We all know the story of John Newton who went to Africa for the express purpose of sinning without having to endure the reproaches of society. There he sank to the lowest of the low, becoming, if you can imagine, a slave to an African slave. But just when it seemed as if he were going to die, God saved him—first, physically, in the middle of a storm, and then spiritually, when he entered his corrupted heart. As a memorial to this greater salvation, John Newton wrote the words to what is now one of the most beloved hymns, "Amazing Grace how sweet the sound, that saved a wretch like me ...."

What manifested in John Newton may be dormant in others, but it isn't absent. And therefore anyone who has seen their old self with Scripture's light can identify with these words.

But for many people, grace isn't all that amazing; because to their way of thinking, their sins aren't all that bad. So, taking eternity for granted, they have the attitude of the man who said, "God will forgive; that's his job."[25] These words, spoken not in confidence but in cynicism, convey a hardness of heart not melted by grace. Yet, how stunning the contrast that exists between people like these with those sinners whose hearts grace did melt!

More than a century ago there was a man who took the rent money, the food money, and virtually every penny he earned and spent it all at the liquor store. As a result of this unconscionable neglect, this man's daughter—right here in America—literally starved to death! In fact, so impoverished was this man at the time of her death, he couldn't even buy a dress for his daughter to be buried in; so a friend had to do it. But here's the most shocking part of this story. Instead of being overcome with the grief, as any normal man would have been, this sorry excuse-of-a-man snuck into the funeral home one night, stole the dress off his dead daughter's body, sold it, bought another bottle of liquor, and got roaring drunk.

It's almost comprehensible—that a man could seek *this* low! And yet, before it was all over, this scum of our species got gloriously saved, and under the Spirit's power so turned his life around that he later became a wonderful minister of the gospel, just as John Newton had done many years before. I tell you, this restoring of a near wasted life, a life that everyone else would have given up on, is something *only* the grace of God can do.

In the Christian classic, *The Power-Filled Christian*, there is an account of another man who was so contemptible, so deplorable, no one had any hope for him. The author wrote:

> There died in America two summers ago, a man whose record was so despicable that he was probably one of the greatest criminals in the United States. After years of vice and crime, during which time he had been expelled from the city of his birth and forbidden never to return; twice turned out of the Army and once out of the Navy as too vile a man to be in the ranks, a boon companion laughingly taunted him with being afraid to attend a mission service! He went to scoff and to mock! God met him there, convicted him of sin and drew him to the cross of Christ for pardon and deliverance. He quickly became one of the saintliest men in America.
>
> For years he—the Rev. William Jacoby—was assistant to the [internationally known] Dr. Torrey in Chicago. Dr. Torrey [the revered companion of D. L. Moody] ... had traveled all over the world and had come in contact with the leading Christian men of all continents, said that, without exception Jacoby was the most holy and most loved man he had ever met![26]

What are we to make of this? In the Old Testament the question is asked, "Can the Ethiopian change his skin or the leopard his spots? Then may you also do well who are accustomed to do evil?" (Jeremiah 13:23).

The likelihood of an unsaved man doing good is said to be the same as a black man turning white or a leopard having his spots removed.[27] It was in this regard that Judson Cornwall wrote:

> It has been well said that living the Christian life is not difficult, it is impossible! Only Christ can live the Christian life. One of the most miserable ways to live is to embrace Christian principles

> without receiving the life of Christ to implement those principles in day-to-day living.[28]

This assertion requires some explanation, perhaps, for while the Bible regards good as an out-of-reach attainment for the non-Christian, the non-Christian doesn't have this view at all. He actually thinks there are many commendable qualities in his life! And although he isn't as smug as the Pharisees—who practically dared the judgment to come, thinking they could pass inspection with flying colors—yet, not for one night does this man toss and turn in his bed, convulsed with moral anguish. Oh, no! He sleeps like a baby! And actually thinks like one, too—because he doesn't have a clue about how God defines good. So, absent this knowledge, he greets the next day with confidence and cheer.

In his book, *Truths that Transform*, Dr. James Kennedy helps us understand the three criteria for goodness. First, he says, the deed itself must be consistent with the ethics of Scripture. Usually, this is the only criterion most people will think of. If they work, or give, or try to help another person in some tangible way, in their own minds, that puts a wrap on it: What they just did was good. Biblically, however, two other criteria apply.

The second thing necessary for a biblically constituted good work is that it must be done from a posture of faith. Hebrews 11:6 says, "... without faith it is impossible to please him ...." This means that if we did what we did in our own power, what we did is not good. In fact, the biblical assessment of this is much worse. Romans 14:23 goes so far as to say, "... whatever is not from faith is sin."

To illustrate this point, the Bible makes a statement that really upsets natural man thinking. In Proverbs 21:4 we read, "The plowing of the wicked is sin." Now, picture good old Silent Sam—sturdy, solid, steadfast—getting up before the sun rises, laboring long and hard while the sun beats down on him with its heat, then finally coming home long after the sun goes down in order to drift off into the arms of sleep. This is his routine, day after day, and year after year! He takes care of his family, he helps his neighbors; and of course the work he does is certainly commended in

Scripture. So why would Scripture call it sin? Because by continuing to live independently of God, this man is really fueling his rebellion. He is simply sustaining a life that excludes God.

The third prerequisite for a good work is that it must be done for the glory of God. I Corinthians 10:31 says, "... whatever you do, do all to the glory of God." To help us better understand this command, the Danish theologian Abraham Kuyper offered this illustration. Imagine, he said, two yachts of equal value—splendid, magnificent, sea-worthy vessels. However, if the rudder of one of them is wrongly directed, that yacht will smash on the rocks. Similarly, it is true that if that wonderful work (at least in our own eyes) wasn't done for God's glory, it, too, will smash on the rock of God's judgment. Only a Bible-consistent, faith-energized, God-honoring work will avoid this fate.

The dilemma of millions, then, is this: They are hoping that if the good in their life outweighs the bad, that the God of mercy will welcome them into his heaven; when in fact, they don't have one good work to their name—not one!

Not to oversimplify this subject, we must also point out that being good isn't automatically overcome by becoming a Christian. Brother Lawrence, in his book *The Practice of the Presence of God*, offered this helpful advice.

> The greatest glory one can give to God is to entirely mistrust one's own strength, relying completely on God's protection. This constitutes a sincere recognition of one's weakness and a true confession of the omnipotence of the Creator.[29]

Speaking in a similar vein, Watchman Nee said:

> It is not that I have strength through him to seek humility, meekness, holiness. He is all that in me; for he is my Life. The Christian has not a lot of odds and ends of virtue; indeed, he has no virtues; he just has Christ. The question is again, do we believe God's Word? Do we believe I Corinthians 1:30?[30]

I Corinthians 1:30 says that Jesus became for us righteousness and sanctification. According to this verse, the good we seek is already ours; it's a part of our new nature. Therefore, achieving victories of our own is not our assignment; our assignment is to walk in the Lord's already accomplished victory. And we do this as we look confidently to God to release in our present circumstances that which he already put inside us. Each day we are to act with expectancy that God will release the goodness so graciously deposited in us when we were born again.

To apprehend this truth with utter realism and not with a theory-floating postulating that sometimes borders on fiction or fantasy, we would do well to focus our attention on the goodness of Jesus, now replicated in our life. In his book, *Christianity: The Witness of History*, J. N. D. Anderson says this about the goodness of Jesus.

> There is in all his talk no trace of regret or hint of compunction, or suggestion of sorrow for shortcoming or slightest vestige of remorse. He taught other men to think of themselves as sinners, he asserted plainly that the human heart is evil, he told his disciples that every time they prayed they were to pray to be forgiven, but he never speaks or acts as though he himself has the slightest consciousness of having ever done anything other than what was pleasing to God.[31]

How would you like to start living a life which resembled that? The confidence of every Christian is that it is this life—the only one that was ever perfect—which is inside them right now. And once released, it will make a real and radical difference—the very difference Jesus desired when he walked first to Gethsemane and then to Golgotha.

Reflection Questions

1. As you compared the counterfeits of kindness with God's kind of kindness, what personal conclusions did you draw? And in that context, what decisions are you prepared to make?

2. How did the defining of goodness offered in this chapter change your thinking on this subject?

3. How would you evaluate your current struggle against sin: Are you in a pre-Romans 7 state, in that you are not all that upset about your lapses into sin? Or are you in the throes of a Romans 7 conflict, in that you are intensely desiring to obey God but you're experiencing consistent defeat? Or are you in Romans 8 victory, in that there are long intervals of time when you do not sin?

Chapter 7

Multiplying the Life of Jesus

Ever since God pronounced that curse in the garden, saying that one from the human race would crush Satan's head, Satan was on high alert to find that one. So as soon as Satan saw the worshipping heart of Able, he put a spirit of murder into the heart of his brother. But, as it turned out, Able wasn't the deliverer.

Not one to take chances, though, Satan kept his watch during the centuries that followed, suspiciously eyeing any man of purity who took up the Lord's cause. And whenever Satan found such a man, he would seek to remove his rival at once—preferably by death. But, as it turned out, none of the martyred prophets proved to be the deliverer.

At that time in Israel's history when expectation of the coming Messiah was noised throughout the land, Satan, that murderer and destroyer, conspired to kill every male baby in the region! And perhaps he thought he had succeeded, for a more tranquil time returned to the land. In fact, during the thirty years that followed Bethlehem, there was no sign of the Messiah on the scene. But then one day a humble, Galilean Jew walked down to the River Jordan and, upon being baptized, none other than God Almighty spoke, saying: "This is my beloved Son in whom I am well pleased." And it was then, for the very first time, Satan knew!

It is significant that immediately after the baptism, Jesus went straight to the wilderness to confront—face to face, in a high noon showdown—the Evil One himself. This dramatic encounter in that place called "the Devastation" showed the old Serpent to be as subtle as he was sinister. Nevertheless, round one went convincingly to Jesus—so much so that the "Shining One" was in danger of having his lights put out!

Taking on the roles of sympathizer and philanthropist, Lucifer put forth the most subtle deceptions. However, when Jesus detected and rejected each deception, Satan decided to change his strategy. Discarding the approaches that didn't work—the supposed confidante or the slick negotiator—Lucifer elected to go for the jugular.

Indeed, this single-minded goal to kill Jesus looked like it would be a mission accomplished much earlier than it was. There was that time, for example, when Jesus declared himself the long-awaited Messiah in his hometown synagogue, setting off a rage that resulted in an immediate attempt to stone him. But for some reason Jesus walked right through the middle of that crowd—and nothing happened! Needless to say, when it turned out this way, Satan sweated, swore, and seethed.

Then there was also that time when soldiers from Fortress Antonia, a contingent assigned to the religious leaders in Jerusalem, were told to arrest Jesus and to bring him in for what would have resulted in certain death. As instructed, the soldiers went and found Jesus preaching in public. They listened ... and watched ... and for reasons that could only be regarded as extraordinary, they chose not to carry out their orders.

Well! To their infuriated superiors, these soldiers were worse than empty-headed for having returned empty-handed! Thwarted yet again, Satan churned and burned in incendiary rage as only this malevolent being could do.

When, at last, it happened—when Jesus was put on that center cross on top of the town's garbage heap—the Devil and all his demons danced in glee, thinking that, finally, their Rival had been eliminated and that the world was now theirs for keeps.

What followed, though, the underworld never anticipated; because not only did Jesus break the bands of death, but he also became "the first born among many brethren" (Romans 8:29).

Would you consider the implications of this? If Jesus was the first born, as this verse claims, this would imply a second born, a third born, and who knows when the numbering would stop. What actually happened was this: The earth began to be populated with thousands of people who had a nature just like Jesus!

Exalting in this accomplishment, the Bible says Jesus "is not ashamed to call them brethren" (Hebrews 2:11, 17). So, instead of one Jesus to contend with, the Enemy now had the impossible task of conquering the Lord's life multiplied in many. And interestingly, Romans 16:20 declares it will be under *their* feet that Satan will be crushed.

So, as brothers to our Lord—members of his family, the possessors of his life—we are examining with scrutiny exactly what constitutes this new life within us. The three qualities that will claim our attention in this chapter—faithfulness, gentleness, and temperance—all have the common denominator of a determined dependency on God. Let's examine next how each of these qualities is manifested. We'll focus first on faithfulness.

The Dependency That Produces

In his classic, *Our Own God*, G. D. Watson wrote, "Our blessed Creator refers to his faithfulness more frequently in his Word than to any other of his attributes because it is faithfulness that his creatures have to deal with more constantly, and more universally, than any other one attribute of his nature."[1] Given all these biblical references, and the obvious importance they have, it is predictable that what God declares to be true of himself is going to be required of us.

The fruit of the spirit called faithfulness speaks not of an episode, but of a lifestyle, emphasizing not just outcomes, but the means by which these outcomes are attained. When the Bible declares the just are to live by faith—which it expressly declares in four passages—it stresses the fact that faith is the only channel through which God's blessings will flow. Romans 1:17 speaks of moving from "faith to faith"—that is, from one experience of depending on God to another.

John 1:16 speaks of "grace for grace"—that is, securing one divine solution after another. And II Corinthians 3:18 speaks of moving "from glory to glory"—that is, experiencing one God-honoring testimony after another. What a wonderful way to live life: from faith to faith (a constant dependence on God), from grace to grace (a constant deliverance by God), and from glory to glory (a constant reflection of God)!

As with all the fruit, faithfulness can be very subtly counterfeited in several ways. There is, for example, the counterfeit of appearance. Back in the day when Amos preached, some seven hundred years before Christ, the people of God *appeared* to offer authentic worship. They sang loudly, gave generously, but lived unethically throughout the week. Eventually, God had enough of this and told his people, "I don't want anything to do with your staged worship services. I don't really care about your rising membership rolls, your increased offerings, or even your music that sounds so professional. What I want is justice—and not this pretense of piety" (Amos 5:21-24).

Someone has cryptically observed, "Scratch a Christian and you'll find a pagan," for under a thin veneer of niceness—which quickly dissipates whenever self is frustrated or in some way disadvantaged—this is the same life these people lived before they came to the Lord. One megachurch pastor confessed, "We are many, but we are not much!" Another pastor complained, "We are two miles wide and two inches deep!"

In truth, institutional successes often mask individual failures. George Gallop wrote, "Religion is growing in importance among Americans but morality is losing ground ..." According to Gallop, "There is very little difference in behavior between the churched and the unchurched on a wide range of items including lying, cheating and pilferage."[2] But how can this be? Simple! What looks like faithfulness may not really be that. T. S. Eliot once said that doing the right thing for the wrong reason is "the greatest treason." And in saying this, he couldn't be more right, because to offer the externals of faithfulness while masking the unaffected internals has to be a stench in the nostrils of God.

A second counterfeit of faithfulness has to do with method, and more particularly with a zeal that exceeds passion by becoming obsessive. Whenever the faithful becomes fanatical, something has gone wrong! Devoting eagle-eye attention to detail and bulldog tenacity for getting it done is not the inordinacy that constitutes fanaticism; and, conversely, lukewarmness isn't its cure. The major failing of fanaticism is its insistence on blind loyalty and (as a correlate of this demand) on uncritical thinking.

Once fanaticism adopts its stated views, it dismisses outright any factors that may amend it and any truths that may altogether refute it. Hence, there's no checking for contamination, no updating to refine thought, no dialectic that pursues precision. Instead, the mind is dismissed, the will is overworked, so every issue but its own is marginalized. And because, also, every contrary voice is demonized, fanaticism will end up doing not only the wrong thing but atrocious things, things a backward pagan would never do, things no one in his right mind would ever do.[3] Fanaticism is capable of great blindness and, as history informs us, of grievous harm.

A third counterfeit of faithfulness has to do with the wrong power. Peter, you'll recall, had vowed such great heroism when the end seemed to be drawing near. Jesus prophesied that all the disciples would fall away, and Peter granted that the Lord's assessment of the others was probably true. As for himself, though, Peter expressed unwavering confidence that his courage was on a higher level. If needs be, Peter announced, he would even die for the Lord. In response, Jesus answered, "Peter, before the cock crows three times you'll deny me that many times."

Have you ever considered the symbol Jesus used? A cock (from which we get our words "cocky" and "cocksure") is a rooster that struts around the barnyard as if he owns the place. So to the disciple strutting all this self-confidence, Jesus said, "Peter, you're not even going to make it through the night. In mere hours, you're going to renounce all that you hold dear." And according to the biblical record, this is exactly what happened! The blustery bravado of the flesh proved to be no match at all for that one who wanted to sift the apostle like wheat. Big, brave Peter saw his courage shriveled and his faith shredded.

This fruit of faithfulness can also be counterfeited in a less sensational way; for instead of the blustery bravado of Peter there can be the fatalistic resignation of Thomas. Do you remember what Thomas said when the time drew near for the apostles to join Jesus in Jerusalem? His exact words were these, "Let us go with him that we may die with him."

And was this faith? No, this was grim determination, at best, and morose melancholy, at worst. But in no way did these glum, gloomy words exhibit faith. Yet, many believers plod through life just like this—fully expecting to be targeted by Satan, attacked by the world, and tested by God. They may not posture as Peter did, betray as Judas did, or flee as the other disciples did. They simply take one duty-bound step after another (in the words of Stephen Vincent Benet) "day by dragging day," heading straight for the dead-end of doubt and depression.

Is this faith? No, this is joyless resignation. Although resignation may look like faith, at least in the beginning, in the end its truer colors reveal that it never was faith. For faith believes that the path ahead, though difficult, is much better than what it may seem. As the book *God Calling* puts it, "... dreary as that Path must look to those who view it from afar, it has tender lights and restful shades that no other walk in life can give." Moreover, after passing through the dark valley, what awaits is the Shepherd's prepared table, bestowed blessings, and overflowing cup.

I submit that *the* major problem of the Christian life is attempting faithfulness without faith. Had God said, "According to your dedication be unto you," a lot of people would be in the fast lane with God. But because God established faith as the decisive factor, many, if not most, are none too anxious to respond. Of course, the real reason they're not isn't difficult to discern. It's because faith can only operate from a place of utter weakness—which is exactly where they don't want to be! They don't want to be so far out on a limb that their only hope for success is God. Of greater appeal to them are those alternative schemes they conceive, whereby the same goal can be achieved in a much easier way.

But they would never concoct such schemes if they saw how shockingly high God's standard is, and if they saw also how supernatural his promises are. Andrew Murray writes, "Every glance at my own impotence or sin, every glance at the promise of God and his power to fulfill it, must arouse me to the gladness of faith that God is able to work all."[4]

The fallback options of our own invention never work, and that's why those native abilities we rely on must yield to the worthier capacities of our new nature. In his book, *The Spirit of Christ,* Andrew Murray writes, "Faith is the instinct of the new nature by which it recognizes and receives its divine food and drink."[5] But again: *Only* faith can secure the divine blessing. Hence, every task and goal we undertake requires a biblically informed transaction of faith that knows how to activate the Lord's strong arm on our behalf. In this regard, J. E. Conant wrote:

> Christian living is not our living with Christ's help, it is Christ living his life in us. Therefore that portion of our lives that is not his living is not Christian living; and that portion of our service which is not his doing is not Christian service: For all such life and service have but a human and natural source, and Christian life and service have a supernatural and spiritual source.[6]

The lifestyle just described is one scarcely contemplated by most Christians today, even though it is uniquely the life the Lord came to give. The life of faith!

The Dependency That Pacifies

The next fruit—referred to in some translations as meekness and in others as gentleness—speaks of a pacifying within that is no easy task. The Greek word for this fruit is a word which means to harness. It speaks of having our will to be wild broken.

Years ago, J. Wallace Hamilton wrote a book entitled, *Ride the Wild Horses.* The "wild horses" in this book is a metaphor used to describe our passions within. But unlike eastern religions which seek to eliminate such passions, Christianity recognizes that passion itself isn't a bad thing. Elton Trueblood declared, "No baby was ever conceived without passion; no great poem was ever written without passion; no great piece of music was ever produced without passion."[7] Why, even the Lord's death was an act of passion! So passion itself isn't the problem; the real problem is the unbridled passion that resists control. As C. S. Lewis once observed: We don't require the fire in the fireplace to be any less hot; we just want it kept in the fireplace.

In the Bible, meekness isn't weakness. Contending otherwise, the musical "Camelot" sings out the words, "It isn't the earth the meek inherit but the dirt." Yet, the Master who called himself meek (Matthew 11:29) also called the influential Pharisees a brood of vipers, children of the devil, a white-coated sepulcher, and a bunch of hypocrites. Twice he stormed the temple, causing hucksters to fall all over themselves in a frantic attempt to escape the fire in his eyes. Not one person on the scene, either day, thought Jesus was weak.

Of interest to note in passing is that the word "gentle" was rarely heard before the time of Christ, and the word "gentleman" was scarcely uttered.[8] It was none other than Jesus of Nazareth who taught the world what it means to be a gentleman. He was gentle, full of sympathy, empathy, and caring—and yet he was a man, with bronzed muscles and a fearless demeanor. Because of *his* example, it is now clear that gentleness and strength are not opposites, as some have supposed, thinking one is from Athens and the other is from Sparta. Jesus exhibited both qualities, and in so doing demonstrated that the gentleness of strength is rightly to be admired.

It must be acknowledged that the idea of a gentle God caught the world completely by surprise. The world could easily accept the idea of God as a lion, or a tiger, or a bear—but a lamb? They just couldn't believe that! Long before the Messiah came as a baby, though, Isaiah declared, "He will not cry, nor lift up, nor cause his voice to be heard in the streets." This emphasizes the unassuming manner the Savior would exhibit and the fact that there would be nothing overbearing or bombastic about him! Yet, had Jesus wanted to, he could have stampeded people into the Kingdom with such a sensational display of supernatural power that even the hardest of hearts would have been stunned into instant submission. This wasn't his way, however. He, the Lamb of God, was as gentle as his namesake.

Even so, there will come that day, the Bible tells us, when the Lamb, so gentle and endearing, will become a sheer terror to his enemies. That One who waited so long and suffered so much will, in the end, cause those who resisted him to become terrorized out of their minds. And Scripture lets it be known that when that time comes, these people will literally beg for the mountains to fall on them—anything, everything, only not the terror of the Lamb!

The gentleness so long displayed by this Lamb was never one of necessity, owing to inferior capacities. His gentleness was of a different type. The effeminate qualities overwhelmed during life's brutal confrontations didn't ever define his meekness. The Greek word for "meekness" actually means "to be in harness." So the truly meek person, the gentle person, is moldable, pliable, teachable. And because his emotions are mastered by the Master, these emotions are not destructive in their designs.

The gentleness of the godly person was well described by George D. Watson, the nineteenth-century American evangelist, who said that being in the company of such gentle souls was like "going to a tropical climate in mid-winter; the very air around them seems mellow; their slow, quiet words are like the gentle ripple of the seas on the sand ...."[9] Completely absent from their lives is the sullen, sour disposition that is ever prone to take up its own causes. Whenever strife stirs, they remain calm.

Years ago, Dr. George A. Gordon, the famous Boston preacher, was taking one of his trips abroad. Upon boarding the ship and going down to his stateroom, he discovered that his roommate was a hunchback, a very ugly man, dwarfish and evil in appearance. After fretting about this for a while, and after returning some icy stares to their original source, Dr. Gordon went to the purser of the ship to say, "I want to leave my valuables with you. I've just been down to my stateroom and, to be honest with you, I don't trust my roommate."

The purser took the valuables, put them in a safe, wrote out a receipt, but then turned around to say, "It may interest you to know, Dr. Gordon, that your roommate was just here a few minutes ago and he said the same thing about you! And it may also interest you to know that your roommate is none other than Dr. Charles Steinmetz, known worldwide as the 'electrical wizard,' employed by the General Electric Company." Well, as it turned out, Dr. Gordon and Dr. Steinmetz later became warm, intimate friends. Yet, their friendship of many years was almost breached at the outset by this needless exhibit of destructive emotions.

So why do we look for the worst in people? Why can't we restrain these feelings that so easily wound? Our penchant for punitive put-downs is taken to task by this little poem:

> Of all the lunacies earth can boast,
> The one that must please the Devil the most,
> Is pride reduced to whimsical terms of
> Causing the slugs to despise the worms.

The self that is less petulant, less absorbed, but more at liberty to see the best in others is a self in harness to the lordship of Jesus. In the book, *The Saving Life of Christ,* Ian Thomas describes what a formidable foe self can be:

> The devil does not mind whether you are an extrovert or an introvert, whether you succeed or whether you fail in the energy of the flesh, whether you are filled with self-pity or self-praise, for he knows that in both cases you will be preoccupied with yourself, and not with Christ. You will be "egocentric"—self-centered—and not "Deo-centric"—God-centered.[10]

In order for self to be harnessed as it should, its destructive propensities must be supernaturally dealt with, as was the case with the demoniac who at last became subdued, properly attired, and in his right mind. This subduing requires a force that is not human in its origin.

Surely, you know how difficult the struggle with self can be if left to your own abilities. Andrew Murray described the problem well:

> Why, after praying and vowing a hundred times, are we still living a mingled, divided, half-hearted life? To those questions there is one answer: Self is the root of the whole trouble. Therefore, if anyone asks me, "How can I get rid of this life of compromise?" the answer would not be, "You must do this or you must do that or the other thing." It would be, "A new life from above, the life of Christ must take the place of the self-life; then alone can we become conquerors."[11]

It is only as his fruit is so effortlessly borne, that these alien hostilities are brought into surrender and the genuine gentleness of our Lord can then exude through our personality.

The Dependency That Protects

Lastly, there is this fruit that most translations call self-control, which is a most unfortunate rendering, because by definition self is the source of the problem, and therefore shouldn't be given control of anything.

Andrew Murray observed, "The accursed self will have its say in everything, and there is no power that can expel that but the power of the presence of Jesus."[12] Expelling the self-life is essential, for Ring Lardner had it right: You can always tell the self-made man— because he's made such a mess of it!

Ian Thomas reports one man boasting, "I'm a self-made man!" only to hear another man say, "That just demonstrates the horrors of unskilled labor!"[13]

Mussolini bragged, "I will make my life a masterpiece." But when reflecting on this assertion many years later, Tozer offered this assessment:

> What a masterpiece he was—that big, bloated arrogant gorilla! And now he lies rotting in the clay and the worms are feasting on the man who used to stand on the balcony and make big, noisy bombastic speeches.
>
> What kind of a masterpiece did he produce, this man who joined forces with Hitler to take over the world and then had his body drug through the streets of his homeland in open disavowal and disgust? The question answers itself.[14]

Yet, it must be acknowledged that there are others who have set themselves on this same course in a more honorable manner, wanting their life to be a masterpiece for good. John Tauler described the temperate man, saying, "He avoids all lukewarmness in discipline and excess of pleasure."[15] Heeding not only the voice of conscience, with its alternate smiles and frowns, but also the Word of God, he has sought to live a righteous life for all to see.

Critiquing this approach, which very often is *our* approach, C. S. Lewis said, "The devil laughs. He is perfectly content to see you becoming chaste and brave and self-controlled provided, if all the while he is setting up in you the dictatorship of pride."[16] Besides, as A. B. Simpson astutely observed, such an approach is bound to fail.

> A man cannot build up a good human character himself and then call it the work of God. It will not stand the strain that is sure to come upon it. Only the house that is founded on the Rock of Ages will abide securely in the wrath of the elements.[17]

Seeing this error, and not at all trusting what well-intended flesh can do, some have chosen to live their lives with different dynamics. Describing this, they use the term "Spirit-control," a term certainly preferable to "self-control." However, this term isn't to be found in the Scripture, David Needham pointed out, and perhaps conveys ideas that aren't exactly biblical. If Spirit-control means only a restraining of what's bad, or if it minimizes the needed exercising of our own will, then this term also lacks the advantages of the more biblical terms "lead," "strengthen," or "filled."[18] Due to all the exegetical difficulties associated with some of these synonyms, perhaps the more old-fashioned word "temperance" is to be preferred.

A. W. Tozer defined temperance this way.

> Temperance is the helmsman in easy control of the powerful ship as it ploughs through the sea with all parts working in harmony. Temperance is that in the Christian man's life which brings every faculty into harmony with every other, and the total personality into accord for God's plan for the whole man.[19]

But Alexander Maclaren worried that "most men's lives are blown about by winds of circumstance, directed by gusts of passion, shaped by accidents ... like some ship at sea with nobody at the helm ...."[20] The temperance needed, obviously, is one that eliminates what should not be and cultivates what should by determining the right authority (self or the Bible), the right goal (temporary pleasure or eternal joy), and the right master (Satan or God).[21]

The meaning of this word "temperance" is often made clearer by the context in which it is found. For example, when Peter came to the end of his life, he told his people how they could live their lives and never stumble (II Peter 1:10). Such an astonishing goal! In explaining how this could be done, Peter talked about temperance (verse 6), which, if examined in isolation, might suggest a reliance on human volition; but, when examined in context, we see faith laying hold of grace after spending time with God to gain revelation knowledge from his Word (verses 1-5). So there was no pull-yourself-up-by-the-bootstraps self-discipline commended in this passage. The willpower of native abilities isn't to be trusted, but the willpower of the new nature is.

The willpower of the new nature is of a different order, having superior qualities to what our natural will possesses.

Describing this will Paul spoke of when he said it is God that wills in you (Philippians 2:13)—A. B. Simpson wrote:

> Our spirit is that which chooses, purposes, determines and thus practically decides the whole question of our action and obedience. In short, it is the region of the will, that mightiest impulse of human nature, that almost divine prerogative that God has shared with man, his child, that very helm of life on whose decisions hang the whole issues of character and destiny.[22]

That part of the spirit that exercises the sanctified will with temperance is a Godsend, without which the other parts of the spirit could not function.

Usually, when we think of temperance, we think of it in terms of keeping certain appetites in check—for example, the drives that result in overeating (Matthew 23:25), drunkenness (Ephesians 5:18a), sexual impurity (I Corinthians 7:5, 9), violent quarreling (I Timothy 3:3), and perhaps the most dangerous rival of God—greed (I Timothy 3:8; Matthew 6:24).

There can be little doubt that Jesus was intensely concerned that our possessions might possess us, since one out of every six verses attributed to him in the New Testament deals with money. Although money is neutral in itself, there is a danger that money can become a ruling passion in our lives. So to keep this from happening, the words of Jesus must be kept in view.

A dramatic example of greed occurred at the time of Charlemagne's death. Court officials dressed this deceased middle-ages emperor in regal clothes, seated him on a marble chair, where they then put a Bible in his lap and placed his dead finger on the words of Jesus "... what shall it profit a man if he gain the world and lose own his soul?" How true it is: that there is no sadder sight in all the world than that of a shrinking, shriveled, sightless soul mocked by the splendors of piled-up wealth.

And as for all these other excesses in need of temperance, they have their dangers, too.

> Arnold Toynbee, the historian, observed that some 26 civilization have risen to their peak; then excelling, they leveled off and plunged down the toboggan slide to the graveyard of nations. He cites that every one of them died, not because of external invasion and destruction by a foe from outside, but because of internal moral decay and social rot.[23]

But the weight of this collapse was individual, familial, and societal before it ever became national. The lesson to be learned from history is that one's lifestyle should never be determined by the spirit of the age but only by the Spirit of God.

You will recall that the prodigal also wanted instant gratification. And what did these ruling passions do for him? They left him in a pigpen! This is just the way it is with self-indulgence; for even from a selfish point of view, self-indulgence just doesn't make sense!

Men like Earnest Hemingway and Jack London seemed to have found the secret for adventurous living, but then, when the full story was known, it became clear that all along there was an inner fainting, an inner losing of heart.[24] The greatest deception of this "grab-for-all-the-gusto-you-can" lifestyle is its insistence on finding satisfaction here and now.

The patriarch Jacob had lived that way also. His name meant supplanter, conniver, cheat. That he would live this way was prophetically pictured at birth, when Jacob was found grabbing the heel of his twin brother, Esau. This seeming attempt to overtake and become first described well Jacob's subsequent life of a manipulator. How he wanted the best this world has to offer!

Much more insightful, though, is the G. K. Chesterton observation, "If you find within your soul a desire that this world cannot satisfy, chances are, you were made for another world." Understand that, and there will be a radical shift in agenda from earth to heaven.

There are two popular counterfeits of temperance. First, there is self-discipline, illustrated well by Bunyan's Mr. Pliable. Mr. Pliable took long strides in his march to the

Celestial City, and was therefore impatient with those who lingered behind. But then one day, after considerable advance, he came against a problem that stopped him dead in his tracks. His own resources proved insufficient. "Help me! Help me!" he cried out; and then, losing heart, he exclaimed. "You can possess the brave country alone. I'm going home." So he ran away—with mud in his hair, mud in his clothes, and mud in his very soul! His retreat was as fast as his defeat was sad.

What happened? Why this sudden failure? The explanation doesn't exactly elude us, because Mr. Pliable had been traveling in his own strength! And this was not unlike the Apostle Paul who finally cried out, "Oh, wretched man that I am, who will deliver me?" All this anguish of soul could have been averted, though, had Paul, Mr. Pliable, and others simply believed Jesus' words, "... without me, you can do nothing."

Another counterfeit of temperance is what Robert Raines calls the "automatic pilot" concept of Christianity. Not too much is required of us once the automatic pilot is allowed to take over. We can sit back, relax, and float into the heavenly city just as easy as we please! The problem with this automatic pilot concept of Christianity is that it leaves everything to God and nothing to self; whereas the Mr. Pliable concept of Christianity leaves nothing to God and everything to self.

Both theories are wrong. Temperance begins with trust, but, we must quickly add that the temperance that trusts also tries! The two go together, trusting and trying, faith and good works.

There is one application of temperance not often discussed. This particular application has nothing to do with making good choices when rival bids compete, or when the torrents of the busy life have to be negotiated. Temperance is certainly needed in circumstances like these, but it is also needed when no choices are offered and life seems to be passing you by. It is when the time of testing goes longer than you ever thought it would, and when all that worked before—expectant faith, righteous living, and fervent prayer—seem not to be working now, it is when heaven doesn't respond but only a stone, cold silence greets you; it is just then that temperance may be needed the most.

The decision to trust God during such a time—and not to separate from him in despondency, or to rebel against him through known evil—is based on the fundamental premise: You belong to him and have no right to take your life back.

For a finite period of time you may be tempted to wallow in bitterness or to seek some substitute gratification. However, you must resist this temptation by trusting the love the Lord clearly revealed when redeeming you.

A. B. Simpson helps us understand what is really going on during such a season in our life when he invites us to think of ourselves as the work of a master artist. Classic art, we know, isn't produced overnight. By investing his treasured time and devoting his undivided attention to what is yet needed, the master artist shows care for his work. With uncanny insight and consummate skill he furnishes that which will later show his greatness.

> ... the artist spends much more time in finishing the details of his picture than in drawing the outline. A few freehand touches will easily sketch the foreground and the perspective, but days and weeks and even months are spent in little touches, faint tints and deepening shades. And it is just these little touches that constitute the differences between the work of genius and the superficial attempts of an amateur. So, too, in the Christian life the finishing touches are the most important and often come near the end. Let us not be weary in the school or easily give up ....[25]

Just know that since the work being done is the work of a genius, it's little wonder that we amateurs think the work is good enough and can't imagine what more needs to be done. But temperance will trust God to do the work worthy of his name. Remember: God deserves to bring glory to himself, and he alone knows how to do it.

Besides, by choosing to be temperate instead of intemperate, our reward will be far larger than anything we would have gained by bailing out and choosing a different direction for our lives.

To sum up, we found in this chapter three types of fruit ... three kinds of dependency ... and three rewarding results! The fruit of faithfulness *produces* (overcoming Satan), the fruit of meekness *pacifies* (overcoming self), and the fruit of temperance *protects* (overcoming sin). Thankfully, this unholy trinity of sin, self, and Satan won't have one more round in our lives—because all will be under our feet, once the Jesus life within us set us free.

Faithfulness, meekness, and temperance—so rare, yet so available to every believer—put on display a God-governed life attractive to the world.

Our review of the fruit of the Spirit is intended to show how the Jesus life, the life of the new nature, conveys qualities that can't be humanly produced. So if we try to produce them, even as a Christian, we will fail. But if we learn the secret of drawing from the Lord's life within us, we will succeed—much more so than we ever thought possible.

Reflection Questions

1. Upon studying these three parts of the Holy Spirit's fruit, which one is the strongest in your life and which one is the weakest?

2. As you reflect on your first answer, identify two specific areas in your life that will benefit from the weakest of these three parts of the fruit getting stronger.

3. After examining this nine-part profile of divine life, are you confident that this is what you are experiencing, or are you thinking that you're on the wrong track? Please explain.

Chapter 8

Getting Rid Of Our Old Man

What happened? This is a question theologians are still asking whenever they contemplate Adam's fall in the garden. All agree that when created by God, Adam entered this world like no one else ever would—not just scientifically, but morally! The blanket indictment that applied to all the rest of us—"There are none good; no not one"—did not apply to Adam, at least not in the beginning.

At the time Adam was created, God said of him that he was "very good" (Genesis 1:31). So, contrary to the depiction of the evolutionists, first man was not some drooling, stooped-shouldered, pea-brained creature who could only utter grunts. Nor did he stumble and bumble along with a fixed, stupid stare, slurping and burping his way across the garden. Adam came from the hand of God physically and morally perfect. In fact, had we been there, we would have looked at Adam in utter awe. And had our opinion been solicited, we would have been more than pleased to have Adam represent us.

But then Adam sinned—a sin that was more irrational than inevitable, because Adam wasn't deceived. He wasn't overmatched.[1] Nevertheless, he did bend his knee to "the Shining One," causing life for himself, his family, and his entire race to degenerate far worse than he could have ever imagined. How quickly the "dust to dominion" journey ended! God had given Adam the resources to kick Satan who knows how far, but instead it was Adam who was kicked out of the garden.

The warning had been given earlier that if Adam ate the forbidden fruit, he would surely die. Given all the destruction that eventually followed, much of it administered firsthand by Satan himself, some have wondered, whimsically, if the history of our world would have been better had God told Adam not to eat the serpent. The more serious point, of course, involves tracking what actually occurred when man first sinned. The earth didn't shake, the animals didn't quake, there were no protests of lightning seen in the sky. Instead of being instantly turned into a little puddle of butter, Adam continued to walk on this earth for more than eight hundred years. So in what sense did he die?

The most important aspect of Adam's death wasn't physical—the stopping of the heart, the ceasing of the brain, the terminating of other bodily functions—but spiritual.[2] At the very moment Adam sinned, his nature instantaneously changed. In her book, *Life in the Spirit,* Jessie Penn-Lewis described this change well:

> ... when Adam was created, the spirit was dominant, the soul was the vessel through which the spirit acted, and the body was the servant to the soul and spirit; but when Adam fell, the spirit sank down into the vessel of the soul, and the soul down into the body—the "flesh"—and he "became flesh" ... these words describe men as they now are when unregenerate.[3]

Although it is difficult to assess the damage, it is obvious that something happened to the inner life of Adam that was disastrous.[4] The actual extent of the damage is an "in house" discussion among Christians even today. Was the image of God destroyed in Adam, as men like Berkouwer, Boice, and Barnhouse contend?[5] Or did this image remain in existence, though badly damaged?

Another way to ask this question is this: Did Adam in his fallen state still have a spirit? Or did his spirit, because of his corruption, suffer extinction? Questions like these were part of the famous Karl Barth/Emil Brunner debate. But with some justification Pascal said:

> We do not understand the glorious state of Adam, nor the nature of his sin, nor the transmission of it to us. These are matters which took place under conditions of a nature altogether different from our own, and which transcend our present understanding.[6]

Offering this observation almost three centuries before Barth and Brunner examined this issue, Pascal recommended due caution in a manner that almost every theologian today would respect.[7] In drawing our conclusions, at the very least we can agree with A. W. Tozer's assessment:

> From man's standpoint the most tragic loss suffered in the fall was the vacating of this inner sanctum by the Spirit of God. There God planned to rest and glow with moral and spiritual fire. Man by his sin forfeited this indescribably wonderful privilege and now must dwell there alone.[8]

Whatever man was left with after the fall, he has had to endure to this day. Henrik Ibsen, the nineteenth-century Norwegian playwright, wrote, "To live is to war with trolls in heart and soul."[9] C. S. Lewis said he found within himself "a zoo of lusts, a bedlam of ambitions, a nursery of fears, a harem of fondled hatreds."[10] And this profile is true of us, potentially, from our first day on earth! When David said, "In sin my mother conceived me" (Psalm 51:5), he wasn't casting aspersions against his mother. He was simply saying that, unlike Adam who had a heart inclined toward righteousness, his own heart was inclined toward evil.

David didn't have to go to school to learn how to be selfish; he had that ability almost from day one.[11] And even today, it isn't a stand-alone truth to assert that society weakens our moral fiber; for also true is the fact that society itself is weakened because of what exists in individual hearts.

How should we describe this heart, what the Bible elsewhere calls "the old man" or "the natural man"? In attempting to describe it, we must keep in mind that this is the heart all of us were born with, the very heart God vowed to replace.

Characteristics of the Old Man

There are two passages in the New Testament that profile the old man. The most extensive one is found in Romans chapter 3, verses 10-18. This passage, drawing heavily from the Old Testament, makes several painful points. It begins by saying that none are righteous, a point we previously explained. It is not that everybody is just as bad as they could possibly be; because, while that sweet, little old lady down the street may never go to church, that certainly doesn't mean that her heart is just like Hitler's. It may be the same in kind, but of course the evil manifested through Hitler was much more heinous than anything she ever did. This is why the Bible teaches that in hell there will be gradations of torment.

The problem that little old lady does have, however, is that no area of her life can be regarded as good; for all is contaminated by sin—more pervasively, no doubt, than what her sweet demeanor would ever suggest. Offering further commentary, A. W. Tozer wrote:

> When a woman sweeps up a house, some of the dirt is black, some is gray, some is light-colored, but it is all dirt, and it all goes before the broom. And when God looks at humanity he sees some that are morally light-colored, some that are morally dark, some that are morally speckled, but it is all dirt, and it all goes before the moral broom.[12]

According to this passage in Romans, another characteristic of the old man is that he doesn't understand (verse 11). It doesn't matter how high his IQ is or how extensive his educational training might be. Whenever the things of God are discussed, his eyes will get glassy, a fog will quickly descend, and hence, for him, meaningful communication will be effectively blocked.

I Corinthians 2:24 describes this condition, saying "But the natural man does not receive the things of the Spirit of God, for they are foolishness to him ...." That is, they are boring, lacking appeal; he has no pegs upon which to hang these thoughts. And since nothing computes, his only desire is for the subject to be changed! This verse continues its description of the unregenerate heart by further stating, "... nor can he know them ...." For the non-Christian, it is impossible to understand the truths of God. Apart from the Holy Spirit illumining the mind, he doesn't have the needed antenna to receive divine truth.

A third characteristic of the old man, also seen in verse 11, is that he doesn't seek God. He may seek the blessings of God, but he doesn't seek God himself! Stephen Charnock explained, "Without a change of nature, we cannot desire communion with God ...."[13] And without the drawing of the Father and the wooing of the Spirit, our nature won't change. For natural man, not even an ember of true spirituality can be found inside—he is totally dead!

Do remember that when determining heaven or hell, this is the decisive criterion: No one will go to hell because of *sins* but rather, the Bible tells us, because of *sin*. To quote Jesus on this point, the only sin that condemns is this: "because they do not believe in me" (John 16:8). In his Sermon on the Mount, Jesus said that men will be told to depart, why? Because they lied, stole, and committed unmentionable immoralities? No, their departure, he said, will be for this one reason, "I never knew you" (Matthew 7:23). Not even for ten minutes out of your entire life!

A fourth characteristic of the old man can be seen in the words, "They have all turned aside" (verse 12). This means they've gotten off track, they've departed the straight and narrow, they've taken a course which puts them in real danger. Speaking a similar message, Isaiah declared, "All we like sheep have gone astray. We have turned every one to his own way ...." (Isaiah 53:6).

Likening us to sheep may seem a positive prospect, since we view sheep as being soft, cuddly, and cute. On a scale of one-to-ten, however, the intelligence of sheep would register somewhere near a minus three! Ask any shepherd and he'll tell you that sheep are double dumb! They are constantly getting lost, frequently going where they should never be going—which is why they are the object of so many search-and-rescue operations. There are even those times when the shepherd has to break the leg of a sheep just to teach a lesson. It is this obtuseness that the Scripture has in mind when it refers to our destructive detours.

The fifth characteristic of the old man is an amazing one, indeed. Verse 12 says, "They have together become unprofitable"—which is a nice way of saying that their choices just don't add up! They make no sense! Frankly, when compared with all the other faults and failings of the old man, this perversity, more than any other, defies description! It was P. T. Barnum who said that there is a sucker born every minute. And there's enough evidence from the Word of God to validate that assertion.

Take Esau, for example. He had gone on one of his game-hunting expeditions, but before he got back his hunger arrived! Upon reaching his destination—depleted in energy, lacking in strength—Esau found his brother Jacob in the kitchen. Well, believing no crisis should ever be wasted, Jacob, known more for his leveraging than for his love, decided to drive a hard bargain. The upshot of it all being that Esau traded away all the favor and fortune of his very sizable inheritance for a bowl of stew!

So what kind of deal was that? To quote from this passage in Romans, a very "unprofitable" one. But to be perfectly clear, the choice Esau made that day doesn't represent an aberration in the human experience. Insane decisions like this occur all the time! Adam, you will remember, had to choose between the forbidden fruit and paradise—and what did he choose? The forbidden fruit! Cain had to choose between a proper worship of God and the attack of a perched, prowling, ready-to-pulverize evil. And you guessed it, he chose the attack by evil! Lot's wife had to choose between a supernatural rescue and sudden, terminal judgment. And she chose—what? Sudden, terminal judgment!

It was to people like this that Moses said, "Life and death are before you. Choose life!" Now, in attempting to understand what this legendary leader was saying, perhaps you remember the old TV game show "Let's Make a Deal." At the end of each show, winning contestants would vie for one of three doors. Behind one door might be a Cadillac, behind another a washing machine, behind a third door a donkey. Of course, no one knew which prize was behind what door. By contrast, Moses not only reduced the doors from three to two, but he also opened both doors for viewing. So the proposition he put before God's people wasn't exactly a brainteaser!

Behind door number one—a soul-satisfying communion with God, the meeting of every need, the fulfillment of every purpose, the sharing in God's supernatural abundance. And behind door number two was death—an alienation from God, a low view of self, a life of constant frustration, and the aggressive attacks by evil. Two choices with such stark contrasts: one gloriously good, the other exceedingly evil. So—duh!—what's there to think about? As G. D. Watson put it, "Sin in every degree and in every form is always and utterly unreasonable."[14]

Amazingly, many people have chosen the door of death. When given the choice between the free gift of salvation and a never-ending death in hell, they (this is so stupid it almost takes your breath away) choose hell! The lineage of this nature goes all the way back to the angels who chose Lucifer over God, and extends to certain ones alive during the millennial kingdom. A. B. Simpson described what it will be like when Jesus rules the earth.

> ... for a thousand years the world is to be without a devil and the human race put on trial to show what really it will do under the fostering influence of divine love and without the instigation and influences of the great seducer. What a world, what an age that will be when Satan will tempt no more and all his deceitful wiles and dreadful power will be withdrawn from human history and the only influence outside of earth and humanity will be the beneficence and holiness of Christ and the heavenly world.[15]

Despite this enviable environment and all the inducements it will offer to woo those not saved to the Lord, the biblical record states many will still rebel against Jesus. Therefore, when Satan returns to the earth, after being bound for a thousand years, these people will align themselves with him! Such obstinacy of heart, even in a perfect environment, should alert us to how stubborn and stout this heart can be, no matter how tender the Lord's appeals.

For some people, having made choices like this throughout their life, there's going to be all that weeping and wailing and gnashing of teeth at the end of history. Not until then, when the sheer insanity of these "unprofitable" decisions finally registers, will these rejecters of Jesus go stark raving mad. Even their own conscience will accuse them on that day—"Lunacy! Idiocy! How could I have been so willingly deceived"? Someone's brain would have had to be fried or scrambled to have made decisions like these!

Verse 13 then talks about how the mouth of the old man will get him into a lot of trouble. The book of James explains that in the same way a rudder controls a ship, and a bit controls a horse, our mouth controls us. Apparently, far more than we realize, our words are destiny-determining! This is why Pentecost featured cloven tongues as of fire. God knew that if he were going to radically change men's lives, he had to do something radical to remedy their tongues. The lies, the hate, the hurt—what incalculable harm has come from the wagging tongue!

The seventh characteristic of the old man is violence. We see such violence in the first family when Cain killed Able. And why did Cain do it? Not once did Able do anything mean-spirited to Cain!

The irrationality of this violence among the brothers became a precursor of the cross—because whatever did Jesus do to deserve that? They plunged those long piercing thorns into a head that perceived more life-giving truths than any other. They drove flesh-ripping nails into those hands that healed hundreds and raised many from the dead. Through those feet that had crisscrossed Palestine in errands of mercy they pounded in the nails. And into his side, where beat the tenderest heart the world would ever know, they flung what they thought was a life-ending spear. And, again, for what purpose did they do all this? For no purpose! As Jesus put it, "They hated me without a cause." But of course the *real* explanation for all this violence is rooted in the fact that the old man, by nature, is vicious and mean!

Verse 16 says that "destruction and misery are in their ways"—and this isn't all physical, by the way. Parents will scar the souls of their kids, friends will betray friends, husbands will cheat on wives—and all this happens where we thought there would be support! It is true that there are worse ways to wound besides those that are caused by fists, guns, and knives. After all, bullets can be extracted and cuts can be sewn up. However, the scars of the soul and the wounds of the heart aren't as easily remedied.

Sometimes the destruction inflicted is self-destruction. In John Milton's work *Samson Agonistes* the beautiful Delilah speaks these words to Sampson, "E'er I to thee, thou to thine own self was cruel." These were words spoken on the other side of death, just moments after Samson had wrestled the pillars from their sockets in the temple and brought down death—upon himself, Delilah, and three thousand others who were in attendance that day. It is true that Delilah betrayed Sampson when she made an alliance with the Philistines to help capture him. Yet, Delilah spoke the truth when she said, "Before I betrayed you, Sampson, you first betrayed yourself." And one wonders to what extent self-betrayal functions today. People are their own worst enemy! The harm they impose upon themselves is often much worse than that imposed by anyone else.

The ninth characteristic of the old man can be any one of more than ninety-six different fears, or any one of more than a hundred ninety psychological problems. Verse 17 says it simply, "the way of peace they have not known." Worry, fear, destructive anger, depression—those without peace have suffered all of these. The angels may have chorused "Peace on earth good will to men," but that isn't exactly what happened. History proves, and daily observation confirms, that God's kind of peace has been experienced by so few! The provision the Lord made has been routinely set aside.

The absence of this peace from the world shouldn't really surprise us, though—not when we think about what the people who are populating our world are really like. Years ago, one of the nation's leading cartoonists, Ralph Barton, took his life. But before committing suicide, he left a note that said, "I have run from wife to wife, from house to house, and from country to country in a ridiculous effort to escape from myself."[16] This self he wanted to escape is described well in Roman's profile of the old man.

The reason that life on this level continues as long as it does is described by the next characteristic of the old man set forth in this profile. Verse 18 says, "There is no fear of God before their eyes." Taking counsel with themselves, they listen to the inner voices of expediency, pleasure, and greed—but not to the voice of God! Like the newcomer who doesn't know the owner is in the room, the old man, buffoon that he is, will say these shockingly stupid things, at times acting in ways that don't just raise eyebrows but cause horrified gasps!

The real reason for such behavior is this absence of awareness that one day he will be summoned before God to give an account for his life. Completely absent, too, is the awareness of a holy God who is observing right now all that he does.

In gathering up all these characteristics of the old man and seeking to understand what each characteristic means, the first question that immediately occurs is this one: What if we had to live our whole lives stuck in this kind of humanity (if we can even call it that)? Given enough time, we would become such detestable people we couldn't stand ourselves! C. S. Lewis speculated that in hell the dammed will live light-years apart, simply because each one so thoroughly hates the other. In Jean Paul Sartre's drama, *No Exit*, a similar perspective is presented, only the inhabitants of hell are compelled to live in close proximity to each other without a chance of escape.

I well understand how this ten-point profile of the old man may seem to be an exaggeration to those this profile describes. That this would be their perspective isn't really surprising, though, given their total lack of self-insight. Sin blinds. Almost as a defense mechanism, it dulls hearing and darkens the mind so no accurate assessment of the soul can be made. The Medieval mystic Francois Fenelon describes what happens when our real condition becomes known:

> As light increases, we see ourselves to be worse than we thought. We are amazed at our former blindness as we see issuing forth from the depths of our heart a whole swarm of shameful feelings, like filthy reptiles, crawling from a hidden cave, we never could have believed that we harbored such things, and we stand aghast as we watch them gradually appear. But we must neither be amazed nor disheartened. We are not worse than we were; on the contrary, we are better. But while our faults diminish, the light by which we see them waxes brighter and we are filled with horror. Bear in mind, for your comfort, that we only see our malady when the cure begins.[17]

Prior to the cure, we see very little.

The Cure for the Old Man

This observation, helpful in its way, prompts another question: What is the cure for the old man lifestyle we just described? Does a cure even exist? Or is man's heart problem, like many medical problems, benefiting from some improvements, none of which are anything close to a cure? To get God's perspective on this issue, let us again receive instruction from that wonderful man of God, the medieval mystic, Fenelon.

> You asked for a remedy, that your problems might be cured. You do not need to be cured; you need to be slain. Quit looking for a remedy and let death come. This is the only way to deal with self.
>
> Kindnesses are a cruelty to one who is being tortured to death. All he longs for is that one fatal

> blow—not food, not sustenance. In fact, if it were possible to weaken him even further and hasten his death, we would be shortening his suffering.[18]

Fenelon is right. Death is God's answer for the old man—not more education, more discipline, and a full regiment of hard work. All forms of self-improvement are bound to fail, because each strategy put forth gives the old man too much credit, thereby sustaining him instead of terminating what needs to die. On this point, the German theologian, Erich Sauer, quoted one of the great geniuses of his era approvingly: "Albert Einstein, the well-known physicist, spoke truly when he said in a lecture held in 1948: 'It is easier to change the composition of plutonium (i.e. to bring about nuclear fission) than to drive the evil spirit out of a man.'"[19] So deeply entrenched is this evil, it will not vacate its occupying control by any means short of death.

Just how this death should occur is good news, though, because Romans 6:6 says, "Knowing this, our old man was crucified with him ...."—that is, with Jesus. Usually when we see a "knowing this" in the Bible, what follows most people don't know; and, unfortunately, this verse isn't any exception! Many Christians today assume that they have an old man and a new man, but this view runs exactly counter to what Romans says. Watchman Nee observed: "God sets us free from the dominion of sin, not by strengthening our old man but by crucifying him; not by helping him to do anything, but by removing him from the scene of action." To be a Christian is to have the old man, in you since birth, totally dead and forever gone.

J. I. Packer writes, "A widespread but misleading line of teaching tells us that Christians have two natures: an old one and a new one."[20] Unwilling to subscribe to the false notion Packer referred to, John MacArthur stated, "If you are a Christian, it's a serious misunderstanding to think of yourself as having both an old and new nature. We do not have a dual personality!"[21] G. D. Watson declared, "The old antinomian idea of dragging two moral natures all through life is not taught in any scripture and is preached from the grossest perversions of Scripture."[22] Theologian John

Murray stated the obvious: It is "no more feasible to call the believer a new man and an old man, than it is to call him a regenerate man and an unregenerate ...."[23]

Yet there are many in the faith who offer theories which blur lines that should be clear, elevated, and pronounced. For example, Miles J. Stanford says, "We are to view the old man as having been crucified: nailed to the cross, helpless but not slain." He even raises the possibility that the old man can be released from the cross to resume his sinful reign.[24] But is this true? In his book, *Birthright*, David C. Needham quoted the Presbyterian theologian John Murray on this subject.

> The term "crucified"... indicates that the old man had been put to death just as decisively as Christ died upon the accursed tree. To suppose that the old man has been crucified and still lives or has been raised again from this death is to contradict the obvious force or the import of crucifixion. And to interject the idea that crucifixion is a slow death and therefore to be conceived of as a process by which the old man is progressively mortified until he is finally put to death is to go flatly counter to Paul's terms ... exegetically speaking, it is no easier to think of the old man as in the process of crucifixion or mortification as it is to think of the resurrected Lord as still being in the process of crucifixion.[25]

When Scripture says, "You are dead," that denotes finality, not process. The idea of progressive dying and progressive resurrection is nothing but unscriptural double-talk. Either someone is dead, or he isn't. And either someone has been raised from the dead, or he hasn't. The idea that both of these occurrences can simultaneously but partially transact is not only false, it actually gives the gospel a hollow ring.[26]

In Martyn Lloyd-Jones' book, *Romans, the New Man*, we are forthrightly instructed to: "Understand that the 'old man' is not there. The only way to stop living as if he were still there is to realize that he is not there ... If we but saw this as we should, we would really begin to live as Christians in this world."[27] Besides, if the old man is still in us, how could the Bible speak of him as being buried, as clearly it does?[28] Furthermore, if he's not dead now, at what point would his demise occur—at the time of our physical death? Many people might think this is what occurs. However, this speculation was effectively addressed by David Needham, who cogently reminded us:

> There is not a single word anywhere implying that at death the believer is finally separated from his "old man" or his "old self." Not a single word. Why? Because that happened when you were saved, not just positionally but actually.[29]

Regrettably, this issue gets confused by certain translations of Scripture that seem to be telling believers that even now they are to be putting off their old man. Grammatically and exegetically, it can be argued that the infinitive "to put off" in Ephesians 4:22 is one of result.[30] Martyn Lloyd-Jones contended, "What we have to put off is the 'conversation' or mode of behavior of the old man, rather than the old man himself."[31] The import of the Apostle's words, as Colossians 3:9 clearly states, is that we're to act as if the old man is gone—because it is! H. G. C. Moule argued that the believer "*has* stepped out of the old position and *has* entered into the new."[32] The putting off in Ephesians 4 is one of memory, habit, and the imprinting of past programming. We are not to allow the residue of past programming, the source of which is now gone, to weasel back into our lives. But we can lapse into this grievous error, Oswald Chambers warns, "If we do not continue to live in the right place, we can get back into 'Adam' sympathies."[33]

Still, A. B. Simpson, one of the ablest communicators of God's truth, rightly said:

> We do not have to fight alone the demon of depravity in our own hearts or slowly build up out of the wreckage of the past a holy character. But we find that the old man as well as the old deeds

> was crucified with him [Christ], and that it is our privilege to lay off the nature of self and sin and put on the nature of the life of Christ ....[34]

Thus, the apostle said in Galatians 2:20: "I have been crucified with Christ ...." Isn't that good news? Finished! Done! It's an accomplished fact! Jesus didn't just die *for* us; he also died *as* us. As our representative, he put an end to what Adam as our representative inaugurated.

Adam actually sinned into existence what God never created. But what Adam produced was so bad off, reform was out of the question; only death would do! Making this very point, Charles Spurgeon wrote: "A man in Christ is not the old man purified, nor the old man improved, nor the old man in a better humor, nor the old man with additions and subtractions, nor the old man dressed in gorgeous robes."[35] None of that! According to Spurgeon, because the old man couldn't be mended he had to be ended! A contemporary of Spurgeon, the nineteenth-century English preacher J. C. Philpot, stated the problem succinctly, "A chained tiger is a tiger still." Therefore, chains aren't the answer; only death is.

The death of Jesus has enormous implications for the individual, certainly, but also for societal systems and world governance. Some have taken note of the fact that Jesus didn't involve himself in a crusade to overturn slavery, so rampant in that day. Unjust wars, political oppression, and other evils that were monstrosities, too, seemed not to have engaged much of his energies. Why is this? It is because by death of the old man every one of these injustices would be dealt with in the most effective way. F. J. Huegel states:

> Jesus did not come to trim the tree of life, to cut off its bitter fruits and make a show of new life by tying on its branches the delicious fruits of social justice. He came to cut the tree down altogether. "And now is the axe laid at the foot of the tree."[36]

Had Jesus devoted himself to stopping slavery, his life would have been consumed by that mission alone, and therefore the outcome of his life would have been so much less than it actually was. But by cutting down the whole tree—and not just the branch of slavery or the rotten fruit of governmental oppression—the old life that produced all this evil in society could then be stopped.

It was the source of evil, the old man, that had to die. And it was on our behalf, the Bible tells us, Jesus died that death. This is why Martin Luther used to say, "When anyone comes and knocks at the door of my heart and asks, 'Who lives here?' I reply, Martin Luther used to do so, but he has moved out, and Jesus Christ lives here now."[37]

Martin Luther's dear friend, Philip Melancthon, spoke imprecisely when he described his sin-struggle as a new Christian, saying, "Old Adam is too strong for young Philip."[38] No, the old Adam, Philip, is already gone! At that precise moment a person receives Jesus into his heart, what was accomplished at Calvary gets retro-activated in him: The old man leaves, the new man arrives. This transaction is quick, not gradual—total, and not partial. Moreover, it deals with the cause, not just with the symptoms. For if abundant life were ever going to be available on earth, there had to be—not accommodation or negotiation, but instead an irreversible termination. And this means getting rid of our old man, once and for all.

Reflection Questions

1. After studying this ten-point profile of the old man, which qualities are you particularly glad to see gone from your life?

2. How does it help you to realize that the old man is no longer alive in you?

Chapter 9

The Enemy Within

D. L. Moody was once asked, "Which person has caused you more problems than any other person?" An interesting question, wouldn't you agree? Because whenever a man has a worldwide impact for God, you can be sure that the bloodhounds of hate are going to be on his trail—especially if that man is an uneducated evangelist! Yet, without any mention of his vocal detractors, the famous evangelist immediately answered, "D. L. Moody."[1]

How can this be—the most famous evangelist of the century, a born-again, Spirit-filled, splendidly gifted man still struggling with "self"? If Mr. Moody's old nature died, and if in its place the very life of God was generated, why should such a problem exist?

It exists because of a formidable force within. This force, destructive in its designs and ingenious in its tactics, has moved with steady stealth against even the choicest saints of God. In fact, in the wide expanse of God's Kingdom there isn't one believer who has successfully avoided this internal opposition. Alfred Lord Tennyson wrote, "Ah, for a new man to arise in me, that the man I am cease to be!" Of course, the old man did cease to be, once Jesus came into our life. But that didn't end the civil war inside us. In one sense, it actually began it.

During those days when our old nature was in control, there wasn't any rival to that nature. Our identity then was old man and nothing but old man. Therefore, whatever aspirations for good existed were initially generated by external influences—our parents, our teachers, respected leaders in society, and maybe even God. Check it out. All the rules that were set forth, all the laws that were declared, all the expectations that were voiced, came from the outside—at least in the beginning.

So, given the fact that the very constitution of the old nature is weak and wicked, this has to mean that—absent an intervention by God—there wasn't much of a struggle going on in anyone. With this context in mind, Robert Browning made a valid point by saying, "When the fight begins within himself, a man's worth something."[2] But to set the record straight, the civil war within begins its fiercest conflict *after* the new man indwells us, and not before.

Thomas Watson said, "The worst civil wars are between a man and his conscience."[3] The cause of this conflict is the new man desiring righteousness while at the same time another force within vehemently resists these aspirations. John Knox, the great sixteenth-century Scottish Reformer, ably described what occurs.

> For as soon as the Spirit of the Lord Jesus, whom God's chosen children receive by faith, takes possession of the heart of any man, so soon does he regenerate and renew him, so that he begins to hate what before he loved and to love what he hated before. Thence comes that continual battle which is between the flesh and Spirit in God's children ... Other men do not share this conflict since they do not have God's Spirit ....[4]

With the new nature comes a new enemy—cunning enough in its deceit, and powerful enough in its resources—to hinder the new man from fulfilling these inbred aspirations.

So what should we do? The first order of business is obvious—find out the name of this enemy! Since an enemy without a name is an enemy not understood, no counter campaign is possible until that enemy has been properly identified. As with any enemy, there are weaknesses to be exploited and strengths to be neutralized. But strategy formulations can't get underway without gaining some basic knowledge of our soul's adversary. Each component and characteristic must be identified.

When undertaking this effort, people soon discover on a personal level what governments discover on a national level: intelligence has prepared them to fight the last war, and not the current one. In this case, the last war involved the old nature, while the current war deals with our flesh—and the two are not the same.[5]

Differences: Flesh and Old Man

Christians often use the terms "the flesh" and the "old man" interchangeably, even though important distinctions exist between these two nemeses. So let's identify some of these distinctions.

The old man, as we saw in the previous chapter, has no desire for God. Those with this nature don't want his fellowship, his rule, his teachings, or his standards for daily life. The flesh, however, may very well desire some or all of these things. In Matthew, chapter 26, verse 41, Jesus said, "the Spirit is willing, but the flesh is weak." Notice: Jesus never said the flesh wasn't willing, because the flesh can be perfectly willing. Ian Thomas said, "The flesh has a perverted bent toward righteousness—but such righteousness as it may achieve is always self-righteousness ...."[6]

Yet, despite a willingness to be righteous, the diligence and desire the flesh produces just can't get the job done. And there are even times when the flesh may bail out altogether and do exactly what the old man did—on purpose!

A second distinction between the old man and the flesh is that the old man totally defines those who have this nature, in that they are singularly bound by old man propensities. The flesh, however, isn't in any way a part of the believer's true identify. This is why, when discussing the flesh's failure in Romans, chapter 7, Paul twice said, " ... yet it is not I ...." We may lament certain behaviors, but Paul had the insight to see what the Accuser doesn't want the rest of the church to see: Moral failure never comes from the believer's real self (see Appendix F). This fact has major implications for our spiritual growth.

A third distinction between the old man and the flesh is that the old man, according to Romans 6:6, was crucified—he's dead, he's buried, and he's not coming back! According to this same verse, though, the flesh (referred to as "the body of sin") can be rendered powerless but it can never be rendered extinct. Even for the most mature of believers, the flesh will always exist within. It can be terminated in its rule, but not eliminated in its existence.

Defining Flesh

In trying to get a more concrete definition of the flesh, we need to contemplate the close association between the flesh and our physical body, an association often mentioned in Scripture. Critical to understanding the role our body has to play requires a prior understanding of the differences between biblical thought and eastern thought on this subject. Eastern thought considers the body evil; biblical thought affirms the body is good. Appreciating the biblical view, A. B. Simpson wrote:

> The human body has been called the microcosm of the universe, a little world of wonders and a monument of divine wisdom and power, sufficient to convince the most incredulous mind of the existence of the Great Designer.[7]

One such mind belonged to Whitaker Chambers, a former member of the Communist Party and a contact man for the notorious Alger Hiss. One day Whitaker Chambers happened to notice the ear of his two-year old daughter—how beautiful the design, almost like a shell; how intricate the design, how effective each part. This incidental observation put Chambers on a search for higher truth, and that search led him straight to Jesus, whereupon Chambers was converted.

The human body is indeed marvelous! And therefore A. B. Simpson was quite right to denounce the diminished esteem accorded the body in eastern thought, and even in some Christian circles.

> One of the gravest errors of all the centuries has been that the body is essentially evil and the great source of temptation and sin, so that the true aim of life in the struggle after sanctity was to get rid of the body, or, at least to reduce it to the lowest possible condition and render it incapable as possible of injuring the soul and spirit.[8]

Voicing a more honorific view of the body, Erich Sauer declared, "The body is like a musical instrument on whose strings, the spirit, as a player, forms and produces its harmonies."[9] According to Herman Bavink, "The body is not a tomb but a wondrous masterpiece of God."[10]

To nail this point down, our bodies are the means and not the source of fleshly activity. It isn't our skin, bones, and vital organs that are the power center for evil. More accurately put, our bodies have been coerced participants of evil, and often even victims of evil, and not the supposed perpetrators we have imagined. With a touch of humor, C. S. Lewis brought clarity to this point with this imaginary conversation between soul and body:

> "You are always dragging me down," said I to my body. "Dragging you down!" replied my Body. "Well, I like that! Who taught me to like tobacco and alcohol? You of course with your idiotic adolescent idea of being 'grown up.' My palate loathed both at first, but you had to have your way. Who put an end to all those angry and revengeful thoughts last night? Me, of course, by insisting on going to sleep. Who does his best to keep you from talking too much and eating too much by giving you dry throats and headaches and indigestion? Eh?"
>
> "And what about sex?" said I. "Yes, what about it," retorted the Body. "If you and your wretched imagination would leave me alone I'd give you no trouble. That's Soul all over; you give me orders and then blame me for carrying them out."[11]

C. S. Lewis' defense of the body has merit, since the body has been unjustifiably blamed. Debbie Rogers noted how this campaign against the body has a centuries-old lineage.

> Even Martin Luther, moving toward the vision the Lord gave him of justification by faith, used to take part in the beating of his flesh. This was a procession common to the Flagellants of 1200 AD. The plague and sin could be driven out of a body ... while men beat or scourged themselves.[12]

After one such regiment of body discipline, Luther was found almost dead, face down in the snow. Incidents like this remind us that, because ideas do have consequences, it is imperative to get our theology right. The real reason Scripture associates the flesh with our body is not because our body is evil, but because our body is earthly and natural, having no moral or spiritual sources of its own to withstand the impositions of evil. Whenever evil mounts one of its campaigns, the body can do little to stop it. Therefore, it is this defenselessness of the body (along with the fact that our bodies become unwitting instruments of evil) that suggests this association of our physical body with what Scripture calls the flesh.

Still, we err if we think the body is the primary source of flesh activity.[13] John MacArthur writes, "Because a man is a new creature in Christ his immortal soul is beyond the reaches of sin. The only remaining beachhead where sin can attack a Christian is in his mortal body."[14]Actually, it is the soul that is the primary source of flesh activity, and not the body.

Dr. Martyn Lloyd-Jones correctly stated, "The 'flesh' means all the faculties of man as influenced by, and perverted by, and controlled by sin. It does not mean the physical body."[15] Providing additional clarification of terms, Lloyd-Jones wrote, "'Body' really means what it says; it literally means our physical body. It does not mean our sinful nature. Even the great John Calvin went astray on this point when he interpreted it as 'sinful nature'; but it does not mean that."[16] The way we think, feel, imagine, and behave (all faculties of the soul) may well be governed by flesh forces within us.[17] Therefore, it is the spirit, and not the soul, which is beyond the reaches of sin.

The flesh is an alien force, a residue of the vanished and vanquished old man. This force can flex or flow in various members of our body, if we act independently of God. Perhaps some life-dominating sin impaired our body before we came to the Lord. The resulting impairment may have left us with physical weaknesses and urges that challenge obedience to God. This is flesh.

Bill Gillham refers to another aspect of flesh as "memory traces." Memory can conjure up contaminated thoughts, stir up destructive feelings, and start us down some well-worn paths that habit helped to create. An example of this, George B. Peck pointed out, is Israel in the wilderness.

> Though they were no longer in Egypt, Egypt was evidently still in them. Freed from Egypt, they at once fell in love with Egypt ... Everything became Egyptianized, even their ostensible worship of Jehovah [the golden calf]. They sighed for the olden flesh-pots, the melons, cucumbers, leeks and garlic, and loathed the manna.[18]

These wilderness wanderers, although saved by God and under the domain of the old life no longer, still carried traces of the old life with them, which well illustrates the flesh.

This imprinting by the old nature will require diligent discovery and purposeful purging. By locating a past imprinting, biblical thought constructs can then be applied, thus isolating that strand of memory that has been perpetrating its harm. A quarantine of thought may not be entirely possible, but recognition and reinterpretation of these thoughts can bring substantial success. We will pursue this point further when we later focus on renewing the mind. Just know in advance, though, that this practice is much more than data shuffling or thought replacement. It arises from the new nature, and cannot be properly taught until we understand how the new nature functions.

A major hindrance to new nature functioning is its minimizing in the minds of many believers. Exporting confusion instead of clarity, many believers say, "I am a sinner saved by grace." This all too frequent comment drew an impassioned protest from David Needham. Needham wrote, "You're casting an undeserved shadow on the greatest miracle God has ever performed concerning you. Don't do it! God has not just justified you and reconciled you, he has also birthed you."[19] And this means you are not a sinner—not even partly so! You are a son! The essence of your true self, the new nature, is vested with his righteousness.

Still, it must be acknowledged that every child of God has been stomping grounds for the Evil One due to an ongoing participation of, and domination by, the flesh. The following illustration may provide some insight as to why this continues to happen.

Not many years ago, we witnessed the official demise of communism in the Soviet Union, at which time the Karl Marx system of government was publicly disavowed. Having collapsed in such a colossal way meant many things, not the least of which was that the heavy hand of the state, aggressively administered by thousands of KGB agents, would no longer come down ruthlessly on its citizens. The days of these intimidating intrusions were finally over!

In its place, a whole new system, opposite in philosophy and far more beneficial to its people, was introduced. The advent of democracy in Russia soon resulted in nation-wide elections, but, surprisingly, there were former communist officials who got elected! These men, who were now repudiating their old government, seemed genuine in their desire to give the new government a chance. Later, however, when some tough decisions had to be made, these former communist officials came down on the side of their older ways of doing—decisions that made it more difficult for the new government to succeed.

This scenario, in some ways, is analogous to our situation. The old nature (communism) is gone; the new nature (democracy) has come to replace it. And just as there was dancing in the streets of Moscow the day Communism ceased to exist, we, too, experienced an indescribable joy the day our old nature ceased to exist. With the dismissal of the old and welcoming of the new, one might have supposed that the prospect for a far greater happiness would now be certain. But as with Russia's government, so also for the believer: There was something on the inside that kept this from happening.

Although these former communist officials seemed sincere about their ideological turnaround (the flesh), they have subsequently acted in ways that are entirely consistent with their past (the old nature). And while these men could never bring the old back (the Soviet Union broke up, and too much has happened to reverse that), they could, in a worst case scenario, discredit the government that replaced it. And should this happen, it would be analogous to the flesh's dominance over the spirit.

Characteristics of the Carnal

Admittedly, analogies have their flaws, and therefore it is all too easy to become a victim of a metaphor. To help remedy this situation, let's set forth concrete, biblical descriptions of how the flesh does and does not function. First, it should be noted that the flesh (just like those former communists elected to serve in the new government) doesn't want to yield control. And so, whether intentionally or instinctively, the flesh will find itself competing with the spirit (Romans 8:5-9; Galatians 5:17). While the flesh can be sincere and well-intentioned, conflict will still ensue because the flesh has no idea about how the spirit's goals should be accomplished.

A perfect example of this would be Peter taking the Lord in hand and telling him ever so forcibly that this (meaning the cross) must never happen. Looking back on this incident, we can easily understand why Peter spoke this way. What Peter said that day seemed so right, when in fact it was so wrong. Today, all the forces of darkness wish Peter had gotten his way; and all the citizens of God's kingdom are eternally glad that he didn't. The main point here is that the flesh can be utterly clueless to the will and ways of God, and therefore will inevitably come into conflict with it.

Sadly, there are a lot of Peters in church leadership today. This enthronement of flesh by a non-discerning congregation can be devastating in its consequences! In his book, *Winning the Invisible War*, E. M. Bounds described those churches which seek decent, moral men, men of high social position who are skilled administrators and impressive leaders. But while likable and capable, they are not men of prayer and spiritual discipline. And precisely for that reason, Mr. Bounds concluded:

> ... an invisible and powerful change has taken place in the church. It has changed from a spiritual church to a worldly one. The change from noonday to mid-night is not more extreme than that.
>
> At this point, Satan is doing his deadliest and most damning work. It is more deadly and damning because it is unnoticed, unseen, producing no shock and exciting no alarm.
>
> It is not by the obvious works of evil that Satan perverts the church, but by quiet displacement and unnoticed substitution. The higher is being retired, the spiritual gives place to the social, and the divine is eliminated because it is made secondary.[20]

How subtle the flesh can be in reasserting its control!

A second characteristic of the flesh is its inability to overcome sin. The same sin that tripped up last month and last year is still doing its damage now, despite red-eyed remorse and the seeking and receiving of God's forgiveness. Demons have been rebuked, Scripture quoted, vows made, accountability established. Yet, what may lie low for a season always comes roaring back to attack. Not even the last revival proves to be the answer!

The Bible calls this phenomenon, "the law of sin." It is called a law because like scientific laws, not legislative ones, it *always* operates. The law of sin, simply stated, is this:

Once we resolve to terminate a certain sin, early successes will be reversed by a resurgence of that sin. One can know the right things, want the right things, and even pursue the right things with impressive determination. But if the flesh is controlling, those in this condition won't understand what they're actually up against. Hence, contrary forces will rebound to trample every vow and to trash every spiritual discipline. Hudson Taylor described his own experience in this way: "Every day brought its register of sin and failure, of lack of power ... I hated myself, I hated my sin, yet gained no strength against it. I felt I was a child of God ... But to rise to my privilege as a son I was utterly powerless."[21]

Multiplied millions could repeat this testimony, for they too have known what it is to desire a life that seems unattainable. Aware of this dilemma, Oswald Chambers remarked, "If Jesus Christ came to be an example only, he is the greatest torturer of the human race."[22] For who could follow his example? Chambers also declared, "If Jesus Christ had come to teach the human race only, he had best stayed away."[23] Why? Because mere teaching will never overcome the flesh! And yet that is exactly what most churches are attempting! Sunday sermons, replete with biblical principles, are sent forth each week with high hopes that entrenched flesh will be forced to relinquish its control. This won't happen, though, and Oswald Chambers discerned the reason it won't. One can never teach the flesh and thereby enable it to live like Jesus.

The flesh is a formidable, multifaceted foe; which is why the "works of the flesh" identified in Galatians, chapter 5, divide into several distinct categories. There are sensual sins: adultery, fornication, uncleanness, and lewdness. There is the sin of making God the means and some other goal the end; the Bible calls this idolatry. Additionally, there is the sin of seeking information through occultist help; the Bible calls this sorcery. There are sins of the frustrated self: contentions, jealousies, and outbursts of wrath. There are sins of the greedy self: selfish ambitions, dissensions, heresies (splitting people up in order to win a following), and envy. And, finally, there are sins of the defeated, dropout self: murders, drunkenness, and revelries.

Whatever sin, or category of sins, the flesh-functioning Christian is succumbing to, this much is sure: Even with a Bible in his hand and a prayer on his lips, this Christian is going down to repeated defeats. The bottom-line explanation for this was actually given by Jesus when he said, "The flesh profits nothing" (John 6:63). But because we haven't believed Jesus on this point, needless and avoidable defeats continually occur.

Contrary to what we've been thinking, neither our brains, nor our willpower, nor even goose bump emotions experienced in church will secure any advance in God's kingdom. Instead, failure with a big "F" will consistently be the outcome. Norman Grubb explained why this is so when he wrote, "... the hidden secret of the Bible is that its commands are to the new man, which is Christ in me ...."[24]

Unless truth targets the spirit, and is accessed by the spirit, truth will not take root and blossom. The "good soil" Jesus spoke of is in our spirit, in our new nature. It is not in our soul, where the flesh likes to roam. Flesh execution of these commands is bound to fail, Thomas Watson said, because "the flesh is a bosom-traitor."[25]

A third characteristic of the flesh is protracted infancy (I Corinthians 3:1-3). Fifteen years after conversion, many Christians are still "goo-gooing" the gospel, acting no wiser or more disciplined than when he or she first became a Christian. Pastors themselves contribute to this situation when they constantly appeal to the lowest common denominator in their preaching. Every service, it seems, is more of the same—pabulum! They'll string stories, tell jokes, seek to work up emotions. And none of this effective.

The Word is being held hostage by preachers who are editing God. One wonders when their preaching is finally going to move to another level, but it never does. Consequently, we have today spiritually-stuck Christians who are unable to meet God in the Word, unable to make a faith transaction with God, unable to enter into a breakthrough worship of God, and unable to prevail in their intercessory prayers for others. Such pathetic results drew the ire of Oswald Chambers who said, "The majority of orthodox ministers are hopelessly useless."[26]

The very last thing the flesh needs is a ministry that accommodates it! This attempt to attract the world by being like the world triggered a corresponding correction from L. E. Maxwell: "O popular Christian and worldly-wise preacher, venture how far you most go with the world in order to win the world; never had the church so much influence over the world as when she had nothing to do with the world."[27]

G. D. Watson declared, "The only religion that looks beautiful to the world is that which is created by the devil."[28] The pragmatic marketing of the church deserves rebuke whenever a pattern develops of paralleling the worldly perspective instead of intersecting it. John Henry Jowett said, "By the methods of the world the Church will never gain her life. Life gained in such conditions is miserably delusive. The vitality is only apparent."[29] John White wrote, "Personally I deplore the pragmatic approach that many church-growth advocates adopt. Christianity may be practical, but it is never pragmatic."[30]

Gospel-lite churches are totally blindsided by the fact that flesh is so entrenched in its ways it won't even begin to change unless it is confronted by the deeper truths of God. Unfortunately, the intractability of the flesh exists in every church. Offering some explanation for this phenomenon, Oswald Chambers wrote:

> The New Testament preacher has to move men to do what they are dead set against doing, viz., giving up the right to themselves to Jesus Christ; consequently the preaching of the gospel awakens a terrific longing, but an equally intense resentment.[31]

This resentment has a subterranean flow that may not be noticed, especially when the atmospherics of a well-staged worship service allows the cosmetic to mask it.

Getting to the core of the issue, Thomas Guthrie, Scotland's famous preacher said, "Where you get the most faithful preaching you get the most hardened sinners."[32] Really? Who would have ever thought that! Yet, Guthrie proved to be correct. For the church in Thomas Guthrie's day (nineteenth-century Europe) constituted more than 70 percent of the world's Christians. But today only 1 percent of the world's Christians reside in Europe.[33] This despite the fact that, historically, the pinnacle of preaching can be located in nineteenth-century Europe.[34]

It is difficult to conceive that supposedly converted hearts can harden to the gospel, but history seems to say otherwise. The church at Corinth, for example, had none other than the Apostle Paul as their teacher. Yet, many of these Christians didn't receive what Paul wanted to give (I Corinthians 3:1-3). This is a problem that was also lamented in the Book of Hebrews (Hebrews 5:12, 13). Many Christians wanted only the shallow or sensational, even though the predictable result of such a limited consumption of God's Word is unbecoming behavior (I Corinthians 3: 3; 4:18; 5:2), a lack of discernment (Hebrews 5:14), and staying utterly clueless when it comes to applying the Bible to daily life (Hebrews 5:13).

A fourth characteristic of the flesh is its inability to effectively serve God. I Corinthians 3:12 identifies two types of works: spiritual works (gold, silver, and precious stones) and fleshly works (wood, hay, and straw). The difference between these two types of work is that one is combustible and the other is not. What God will set to blazes is all that work cranked out by well-intentioned flesh—work that never depended on the energizing of God, and therefore never got it. So, if a ministry wasn't done God's way, with his power, and for his glory, then, despite the accolades of others, it will be totally rejected by God.

In his marvelous book, *The Root of the Righteous*, Tozer addressed this problem of flesh attempting ministry when he reminded us how "the priest of the sanctuary, when they went in to sacrifice were not permitted to wear anything that causeth sweat." Human sweat (the flesh) can add nothing to the work of the Spirit, especially when it is nerve sweat.[35] In this same vein, John Hyde, one of the most advanced prayer-warriors, said, "Self must not only be dead but buried out of sight, for the stench of the unburied self-life will frighten souls away from Jesus."[36] The late Dan DeHaan, in his book, *The God You Can Know*, said it straight out: "Earthbound saints offer little to hell-bound sinners."[37] This would certainly be the case if these saints are operating in the flesh (John 6:63).

Gradations of Flesh

To examine the various types of fleshly activity certainly helps us to more concretely identify what the flesh is. But there are also differing degrees or gradations of each of these types. Bill Gillham does an excellent job of helping us understand this aspect of flesh assessment in his book, *Lifetime Guarantee*, where he speaks of three flesh categories: Yucky Flesh, Plain Vanilla Flesh, and USDA Choice flesh.

Yucky Flesh describes someone whose background is so wretched, or whose present symptoms are so despicable, it would virtually take a miracle to free a person from all of that. Humanly speaking, just getting this person to the same starting line where others routinely begin seems almost impossible. Understandably, such people have a very low view of themselves, and unfortunately this view is also shared by others who know them. Very often, the "yucky flesh" believers are involved in gross sins to such an extent that they're just like those people Peter described: "having eyes full of adultery ... that cannot cease from sin, enticing, unstable souls, they have a heart trained in covetous practices ..." (II Peter 2:14).

Whether their sins are more sensual in nature or they are just psychologically messed up, this degree of flesh activity is so severe that, for them, just getting out of bed in the morning represents something of a victory.

Plain Vanilla Flesh describes those Christians who haven't offended society by becoming a source of scandal or a subject of gossip. Their pictures have never been plastered on some post office wall, and the media has never featured them in a story casting a dark shadow over their reputations. While Christians like these have certainly experienced their share of moral defeats (there are some things in their closets they would never want anyone to know about), still and all, others have a somewhat favorable impression of them.

This well-cultivated impression is only that, however, a mere impression—sustainable only because their sins are more hidden than public; and whenever manifested, are more moderate than extreme, and more occasional than chronic. For example, there may be a succumbing to such sins as anger, envy, covetousness, and pride—sins that are common, sins that trouble us all. Therefore, most people will see these Plain Vanilla Flesh Christians as being neither scoundrels nor saints. The mixture of favorable and not-so favorable qualities in their lives makes them appear normal.

By contrast, the USDA Choice Flesh Christian is clearly seen to be a saint! In the words of Dr. Gillham "he is everyone's candidate for Mr. Christian."[38] He is confident. He is capable. He is conscientious—which is why nearly everyone in the church views him or her in such an appreciative way! An example of such a person from the Bible is Martha. Martha was one of the dearest and closest friends Jesus ever had. Nevertheless, there was one incident in her life worth examining, because in so doing we will see how this "USDA Choice Flesh" Christian completely unraveled one day and thus became the target of Jesus' deserved but gentle rebuke.

Of all the homes in Israel, the home of Mary and Martha was Jesus' favorite "home away from home." One day, while Jesus was there for a visit, Martha was doing all she could to make his visit pleasant. The text makes it clear that in the beginning *both* Mary and Martha were preparing the meal, but such kitchen camaraderie didn't last as long Martha hoped it would—this due to Martha's extravagant agenda. Jesus later said of Martha she was encumbered with "much serving." It seemed not to matter to Martha that the opportunity to hear Jesus speak was being set aside, for uppermost in her mind was her USDA Choice Flesh agenda to serve nothing but the best! So Martha pressed on in her kitchen duties long after Mary took her leave.

As Martha watched her sister sitting in the next room with Jesus, Martha's slicing and stirring became all the more energetic. Stewing and brewing on the inside, she thought to herself—and no doubt with some contempt—"Does that dreary sister of mine think that a meal will cook itself?"

Inwardly, Martha fussed and fumed (all the while crediting her performance while belittling Mary's) until finally, unable to stand it any longer, she burst into the next room, imploring Jesus to send her sister right back to the kitchen where she belonged! What was going on here? Flesh! A flesh that was in constant overdrive to achieve, but a flesh that didn't know what really mattered.

The Marthas in our midst are often greatly respected, for these perfectionist people undertake so many ministries. But could it be that sickness is being baptized as health? Martha's perspective was so distorted she came flying into that living room with her forefinger wagging. To Martha, you see, Sister wasn't the only one who was guilty, for the one who had permitted this rudeness, this inexcusable shirking of one's duty, was guilty, too. Hence, Martha felt herself duty-bound to straighten this situation out!

Can you imagine this? He who was wisdom personified, love supreme, and truth unmatched had seen all three of these virtues fail, according to Martha. So she let this preacher-sent-from-heaven hear one of her sermons! Point one in her sermon: If Jesus had properly assessed the situation, he would have asked Mary to return to the kitchen, pronto! Point two: If Jesus had loved Martha as he should have, he would have commiserated with her predicament *at once*, and quickly relieved her of this suffering. Point three: Truth would have better been served if Jesus had interrupted his teaching that day to upbraid Sister for having shirked her duty.

Well, now! If Martha was right, this would mean that eons of undiluted holiness came to an end that day when the Son of God, who had been perfect in every way, succumbed to not one, not two, but actually three sins! And what do you know? This dear woman, in her Olympian wisdom, was the first to see his stunning fall and to comment upon it with remarkable insight. Although Martha wasn't as strident as this summary suggests, her words (when surfaced and examined) have these very points embedded.

Do you see how misguided and even presumptuous willing flesh can be? Ian Thomas reminds us of how "the flesh loves to be recognized, consulted, honored, admired and obeyed!"[39] And this is exactly what we see in Martha. The Martha legacy lived on, regrettably, long after this incident in Bethany. Consequently, to the Christians at Galatia—who were also attempting a goodness of the flesh—blistering, scorching words from the Apostle Paul deservedly found their target: "Are you so foolish? Having begun in the spirit, are you now made perfect by the flesh?"

What Paul wanted these believers to know is that any effort like theirs is doomed to failure! According to Ian Thomas, "... it was never God's program to improve the flesh, to re-educate or tame it—let alone Christianize it."[40] However, without a discernment like Paul's being voiced, many Christians today will "work so hard for Jesus," without a clue they are on the wrong road.

The double designation, "Martha, Martha," spoken in tones which voiced disappointment and with a motive that urged correction, need not be repeated with our own name inserted. And this is because our flesh, though formidable, is not invincible. So, just as it would be a mistake to think of the devil as a rival who is almost as strong as God, it would also be a mistake to think of the flesh as a rival that is almost as strong as our spirit. It is not. Instead, just as darkness must go once the light shines, and the devil is constrained once the Lord acts, so, too, our flesh is foiled once our spirit manifests. But more on that in the next chapter.

Reflection Questions

1. With regard to the distinctions between the old nature and the flesh, what did you learn that you didn't already know? And how did this help you?

2. Upon reviewing the different types of flesh and some of the characteristics of the flesh, how do you interact with this material? What are points of identification? What are some new talking points between you and the Lord?

3. Why might the following statement be true of some worship services—people frequently confuse interest, laughter, tears, or congregational involvement with spiritual growth?

Chapter 10

The Foiling of Our Flesh

Have you ever watched a movie thriller that showed, with much suspense, the death of a villain? When the climactic scene begins, the music starts to crescendo—at which point all popcorn eating stops! And if it's a really suspenseful movie, so does your heart!

The cause for this mounting tension is the fact that lurking in the shadows, unbeknownst to an unsuspecting population, is evil personified, the very one who is the terror of the countryside!

Meanwhile, young people are innocently enjoying themselves when, suddenly, with axe in hand, this menacing, malevolent being surges from the shadows and *lunges* toward them! Immediately, upon entrance into the light, we are able to see a face so frightening it had to come from hell!

Almost too late, the hero of our story arrives and, upon seeing the danger, rushes into battle. A big mistake! In mere moments, the villain overcomes him. And just when this villain is about to do his worst, a shot rings out ... and then another ... and another. Looking utterly dazed, the villain slumps forward. He then takes a few feeble and perfectly futile steps before falling to the ground, accordion style—dead!

At first, all is silent. Then, in what dramatists call the denouement of the plot, friends embrace each other in grateful relief as the music plays on toward a happy ending. But—oh, no!—a bloody hand surges forward and *grabs* the ankle of our hero! Once again, as the suspense quickly escalates, we gasp for breath, thinking to ourselves, "What's going to happen now?" The resulting brain freeze cannot produce an answer.

"He's baack!" This Freddie Krueger theme very accurately describes that most formidable foe, our flesh. For just when we think that the fatal blow has been struck and that finally we'll be troubled no more, there is yet another resurgence of opposition. It was in this regard that Ian Thomas stated, "There is no climactic experience by which the evil influence of the flesh may be eradicated once and for all, though the flesh in its subtlety, would like you to believe it—in the interest of its own self-preservation."[1]

An awareness of how dominant the flesh is often comes months, or even years, after conversion. For a decidedly long while Christians will minimize their faults and fancy themselves free because they have "accepted Christ." Ray Stedman describes what happens next:

> Then gradually they begin to see that they are mastered by self, that their choices are all made with self in view. Ego, as an ugly monster, sits on the throne of their lives; and though they pay lip service to the cause of Christ, self rules, cracking a remorseless whip and driving them to even more selfishness.[2]

Andrew Murray observed, "We find Christians trying to please themselves in a thousand ways, and yet trying to be happy, good, and useful ...."[3] This will never work. They are feeding the monster that must be slain.

One reason this problem goes undiagnosed as long as it does is because the flesh isn't always putrid and petrifying in all of its ways. Sometimes it can be respectable, and even religious. Attempting to ferret out all of its facades, and to uncover each place where flesh has burrowed down, can be very draining work. In his book, *The Four Loves,* C. S. Lewis described this hide-and-seek-routine that the flesh so frequently exploits.

> ... Bunyan says, describing his first and illusory conversion, "I thought there was no man in

> England that pleased God better than I." Beaten out of this, we next offer our humility to God's admiration. Surely he'll like that? Or if not that, our clear-sighted and humble recognition that we still lack humility. Thus, depth beneath depth and subtlety within subtlety, there remains some lingering idea of our own, our very own attractiveness.[4]

Flesh! It can't be killed and, like those guerrilla soldiers hiding in the mountains, it isn't easily found. Yet, Tozer declared that "Christ has made full provision for our deliverance from the bondage of the flesh."[5]

So what strategy does Scripture offer to deal with this persistent and often times prevailing foe? There are several steps in God's strategy. The first is the need for brokenness.

The Need for Brokenness

Psalm 34:18 declares that God is near to those of a broken heart. This doesn't mean that God is a sentimental softy—a tear will draw him, a sigh will melt him. It just means that whenever someone finally comes to that place where they forsake all confidence in their native abilities, what they will then experience is not the lamented loss they had supposed but rather God himself!

Isaiah had an experience like this. He was by all accounts a good man, perhaps the most righteous person in the whole country. But then one day—and, oh, what a day!—*God* showed up! Physically, visibly, God came to the temple where Isaiah was worshipping. And when Isaiah saw him—seeing for the first time *his* holiness and *his* righteousness—Isaiah was undone! In the words of R. C. Sproul, "His was pure moral anguish, the kind that rips the heart out of a man and tears his soul to pieces. Guilt, guilt, guilt. Relentless guilt screams from his every pore."[6] All this attributable to the fact that the whiter white of God's righteousness provided a condemning contrast to what Isaiah had never seen before—the soils and stains of his own inner life. And that was enough to shame him, utterly!

David also had an experience like this. He had been walking with the Lord for many years, experiencing the blessings and victories that can only come from this kind of relationship. But then one day David slipped—which is a bit of an understatement, really, because David didn't just slip or stumble; his was a hard and stunning fall! And as a result of this fall, the spiritual life of David deteriorated drastically. For one solid year he stonewalled God.

Through the preaching of the prophet Nathan God finally overcame David's defenses, causing the heart of Israel's king to break! The result of this heartbreak can be seen in Psalm 51 where David desperately pleaded for the Lord to purge him, to wash him, to clean him, to give him a new heart and a new spirit. For David now knew that his flesh—no matter how earnest and honest it was, and how dedicated and consecrated it got—could never please God. Brokenness!

The brokenness David experienced, and later wrote about, far surpassed any downward turn of mood or any discouragement triggered by challenging circumstances. Judson Cornwall noted that "in referring to a broken spirit, David uses the Hebrew word *shabor* which means to shiver, to break to pieces, to reduce."[7] In clear view here is a breakdown so severe no restoration was possible apart from a supernatural intervention by God.

Interestingly, in Psalm 51, David identified what for many people is a substitute for brokenness. He said, "You do not desire sacrifice or else I would give it." In effect, what David was saying is, "Lord, my flesh would rather make this up to you. Instead of becoming broken and contrite, what I'd very much prefer is to undertake some service that is particularly dear to your heart, some feat of accomplishment that would be beneficial to your Kingdom. And, really, the more difficult the task, the more demanding the sacrifice—the better!"

In this frame of mind, you can well understand how the invitations to "give your all," to "dedicate your life" and to "sacrifice for God" will appeal to the flesh. Contrary to what many people suppose, the flesh loves these invitations and will be the first one down the aisle to respond to them. The one thing our flesh does not want is to be sidelined and ignored. And what it also doesn't want is to have the harsh judgments of the Bible applied: "... have no confidence in the flesh" (Philippians 3:3), " ... make no provision for the flesh" (Romans 13:14), "... they that are in the flesh cannot please God" (Romans 8:8).

Cannot please God? Well, that has to be a mistake! Why, the flesh is ready to roll up its sleeves and go to work right now! But also it must be admitted: that the flesh wouldn't exactly mind if everybody in the church took notice! With that characteristic candor of his, Oswald Chambers observed, "It wouldn't be so difficult for us to agree to the crucifixion if we could choose our own cross and choose for the right onlooker to be watching."[8] Isn't that just like the flesh—promoting self to the very end?

Had David only come to a place where he was disappointed in himself, his flesh would have breathed a sigh of relief, for that would have meant David still believed in himself. And, too, if David made some resolution, vowing to do better in the future, his flesh would have percolated gladness and glee, because that would have meant he was giving self yet another chance to perform. However, brokenness means more than a vow to never sink so low again, for true brokenness recognizes that such failures aren't random contradictions that unfairly libeled your good name. Instead, these failures expose what your self-life is like.

Therefore, to be broken isn't just to renounce the sin itself, but also the force that produced it—your flesh. God wants that judged! And the measure of this judgment is nothing less than the cross!

The Need for Crucifixion

A. B. Simpson wrote, "This is God's decree against the flesh in us. It cannot be cleansed. It cannot be improved. It cannot be cultivated. It cannot be educated into ideals and principles. It must be exterminated."[9] This verdict against the flesh is essential, Simpson wrote, because: "The flesh is hopelessly, eternally corrupt. It cannot please God, and it must be completely dethroned, renounced, and crucified with Christ."[10] All lesser measures will fail.

In order to understand the necessity of the cross, we need to understand the truth I Peter 1:23 sets forth when speaking of being born again of incorruptible seed. So what exactly is this seed? Actually, this seed is nothing other than divine life (Galatians 3:16), what the Bible elsewhere calls a "new creation" (II Corinthians 5:17), that which was created in righteousness and true holiness (Ephesians 4:24). Just know that when the Bible talks about Christ being our life (Colossians 3:4), and the fullness of God being released in the believer (Ephesians 3:19), these assertions are not the by-product of a fevered imagination or the unguarded words of religious hyperbole. The life in this seed *is* divine! And once planted within it will elevate us to an interior life that is even higher than what Adam enjoyed before the fall.

Tragically, though, most believers will live their entire life without ever experiencing their new nature. The reason for this being: their flesh isn't on the cross being judged. Consequently, the divine life within—which could so gloriously change everything—remains an inconspicuous seed.

So what must happen before a seed can yield its luxuriant life? Jesus said, "Unless a grain of wheat falls into the ground and dies, it remains alone: but if it dies, it produces much grain" (John 12:24). This tells us that unless there is brokenness, death, and the way of the cross, that seed, which has been in us since conversion—unnoticed, unimpressive, and exerting no influence whatsoever—cannot release its abundant life. Quite frankly, when many testify of an "abundant life" they are elasticizing the language of Zion beyond all recognition. What the New Testament is talking about is hidden in that seed, a reality they cannot experience until their flesh is on a cross. Only when the self-life has been put out of commission can the Holy Spirit who inhabits the new nature rise within and release its virtues.

Sometimes we confuse the cross of Christ with the cross of the believer. Of course, the accomplishments of Jesus' cross will be forever memorialized in the great romance of redemption. However, the cross that applies here is not his cross, but ours. We are to sentence our phantom self, the flesh, to the one place where it cannot function—the cross. Offering a rationale for this, Andrew Murray writes:

> Many of us would love to have sin taken away. Who loves to have a hasty temper? Who loves to have a proud disposition? Who loves to have a worldly heart? No one. We go to Christ to take it away, and he does not do it; and we ask, "Why will he not do it? I have prayed very earnestly." It is because you wanted him to take away the ugly fruits while the poisonous root stayed in you. You did not ask him to nail the flesh to ... [the] cross ... that you should henceforth give up self entirely to the power of his Spirit.[11]

Yet there is something so ruthless and final about a cross which, understandably, causes many people to shrink back. Certainly this was so at the time Jesus was crucified. The cross—so scandalous in the shame it proclaimed and so excruciating in the suffering it afflicted—caused the Roman orator Cicero to abhor the sheer horror of it all by saying, "Not only let the cross be absent from the person of Roman citizens, but its very name from their thoughts, eyes and ears." And mind you these words were addressed to a populace that gloried in gladiator violence!

In his book, *Born Crucified*, L. E. Maxwell observed that the cross merchandised today—surfaced casually in our conversations and featured commonly in our churches—wasn't ever regarded that way when Rome adopted it as a means of execution. "Two thousand years ago we find no halo of glory, no beautiful associations of history, no nobility, and no thought of heroic sacrifice attached to the cross."[12] Acknowledging the physical brutality of the cross, we mustn't, as an alternative, minimize its spiritual implications, either. So what are these implications?

Tozer tells the story of a young Christian who approached a teacher of the deeper life, asking, "What does it mean to be crucified?" The old man thought for a moment and said, "Well, crucifixion means three things. First, the man who is crucified is facing in only one direction." He's not scanning, here, there, and yonder looking for distractions that entice self-interest. Instead, because his self is at the point of death, his attention is riveted only upon Jesus—and on his promises, and on his ability to deliver. Can you imagine how much better it would be if everyone in the church were so singularly and soberly focused in this way?

Then the old man scratched his scraggly gray hair and said, "One thing more, son, about a man on a cross—he's not going back!" Going to the cross means saying a final good-bye to the world. It is to be cut-off from all of its temptations, all of its delights, since at this point all the summons, invitations, and appeals of the world are totally useless—which is why the man on the cross doesn't respond to any of them! How different this is from the repentance so commonly on display today! To renounce forever the flesh within and the world without involves a great deal more than a turning of small degrees, wherein others around you scarcely even suspect that something significant has taken place in you.

The old man went on to say, "Another thing about the man on the cross, son; he has no further plans of his own." Once he got nailed to that cross, all his plans came to an end, for his life is totally in the hands of Another. By contrast, many of us go beyond negotiating with God and start dictating instead. Bursting into the Throne Room of the universe, we unroll our blueprints, recommend this and that, then vanish in a cloud of excitement without ever hearing from God. If only we would submit! If only we would quietly and irrevocably place ourselves at the Lord's feet, waiting instead to hear from him![13] But self is so addicted to the whims of carnal desires and the preferential treatment sought by pampered pride, it whines in pitiful protest, "Can't there be some other way?" And the irrevocable answer is: There cannot!

In his book, *Not I But Christ,* Roy Hession thoroughly documented how Saul in the Old Testament represented the flesh. Due to multiple behaviors that were totally of the flesh, Saul was eventually rejected—a fact he vehemently resisted. No, sir! He wasn't about to yield his throne! Although Saul's replacement would produce the long awaited Messiah, Scripture says the prophet Samuel mourned for Saul. For a considerable time he shuffled along in a stupor, depressed in spirit, heaving great sighs of remorse, because, deeper down, this wasn't a decision Samuel would have made, even though *he* was the one who announced God's judgment!

And isn't that also just like us? We can give testimonies and teachings on the need for our flesh to be rejected. But then, when it actually comes to putting it away, we mourn that fact—our minds searching for some alternative, our eyes looking for some way of escape. Finally, the Lord came to Samuel one day and said, "How long will you mourn for Saul, seeing that I have rejected him from reigning over Israel?" This question wasn't really a question—God wanted all this mourning to stop! It was time, and really past time, for Samuel to accept the wisdom of the Lord's judgment (flesh isn't to rule)—and to move on to a better day!

Too often, though, in our sadness about what must happen first, we keep ourselves from the gladness that could happen next. Like the disciples of old who didn't see anything good about "Good Friday," all we see is the cross—the resurrection isn't even in view! Consequently, when it comes to sentencing the Saul of our soul to that cross, we lapse into the same irrational grief Samuel did, never seeing and agreeing that what God is purposing to depose never served us well to begin with.

The question we must ask ourselves, then, is this: Might God be saying to us what he said to Samuel, "How long will you mourn for Saul, seeing I have rejected him"? If so, Roy Hession encouraged a more positive response by reminding us, "There is really something rather comfortable in confessing ourselves as rejected kings. As John Bunyan once said, 'He that is down need fear no fall.'"[14]

G. D. Watson exuded exuberance when he wrote, "Oh, the blessedness of being absolutely conquered! Of losing our own strength, and wisdom, and goodness, and plans, and desires and being where every atom of our nature is like placid Galilee under the omnipotent feet of our Jesus."[15] Offering further testimony to what the crucified life produces, George Muller said this: "There was a day when I died—utterly died to George Muller, his opinions, preferences, will, died to the world, its approval or censure."[16] Just died! And this day must come for us, too, or the battle with our flesh will never be won.

The Need for Faith

The next step, which is in the opposite hemisphere from mourning the death sentence, is faith. We should keep in mind that when Jesus went to his cross, he had the faith that God would raise him up! Jesus also knew it wouldn't be long before the Father did so! And that the results would greatly reward this sacrifice! All this we must believe, too, for God isn't going to strand us on a cross. Resurrection, remember, takes place in the realm of the dead and in the territory of the impossible. So we must ask ourselves: Are we believing for this to occur? And if not, we should then ask ourselves: How can such an expectancy be generated?

To make this less theoretical and more practical, begin by bringing to mind your greatest weakness, that one area of life where you are most susceptible to defeat. In other areas, perhaps, you have experienced God's victory first-hand, but not in this area. In this area, the enemy seems to enter at will; and once in, he isn't a very thoughtful guest, because strewn all about is his lousy litter of ruin. So, again, how can you pursue the subduing of flesh more effectively?

First, come to the end of yourself—brokenness! You can do that by moving beyond being sorry for what you did and instead judge without compromise what produced it, your flesh. The flesh at work that day when Jesus was put on the cross must be seen for what it is, and be despised for what it is. Second, commit your flesh to the cross. Trust no longer in right desires, scriptural knowledge, and a lot of willpower, because victory isn't going to come that way. What you must do instead is to trust God to release his overcoming life within, for as Thomas Watson said, "God not only persuades, but enables."[17]

This enablement is found in the Lord's overcoming life, which is why Ruth Paxson said: "God does not speak of being dead to 'sins' but to 'sin'. He does not talk of 'victories' but of 'victory'. He does not command us to be troubled over our sin but to be dead to it."[18] Concurring with this counsel, F. J. Huegel wrote:

> We must never forget that it is not the Christian struggling toward a possible but hard won victory. No. It is the Christian standing in a victory already consummated. A victory consummated for all-time, one which when achieved, overcame all—the world, the flesh and the devil.[19]

And you can stand in this victory in one of two ways—the first of these is by reckoning. F. J. Huegel writes:

> The Christian ... who hungers and thirsts after righteousness, the righteousness of a perennial victory, full orbed, the more than conqueror type, is not seeking something that is not already his. In a sense, God could not make it more his than it is already. On the divine side it is a consummated thing. We get nowhere by looking at ourselves. We are not called upon as Christians to die to sin; but to recognize the fact that we have died to sin in the death of him who, on Calvary's cross, put an end to the old creation, that in the power of his resurrection he might bring forth the new. Our old man was crucified with Christ, and in view of this fact we reckon (Romans 6:11) ourselves dead to sin and alive to God. The reckoning does not produce the fact; it simply springs from the fact.[20]

The word "reckon" carries with it the idea of imaging what's true.[21] Many people have the wrong image on their mental screen when it comes to sin and self. Drawing from past experience, and also from current deception, they will see themselves in bondage to a certain overcoming problem. Hence, they remain in a prison with the door wide open—and that door has been open for a long time!

To get the right image on our mental screen we must come to terms with what Paul wrote in Romans 6. The reason we are dead to sin and alive to God is because the spirit of him that was on that cross and rose again is now in us. This spirit (I Corinthians 6:17) is who we are! It is our new nature! Jesus didn't just die *for* us, but in a profound sense he died *as* us. His being, now our being, already died to sin and is now resurrected.[22] This is the reality that should be visualized on our mental screen.

What is now in our spirit (but not in our soul) has the overcoming power of victory ready for release. Anthony Hoekema writes, "Christians should look upon themselves not as being partly in the flesh and partly in the spirit but as being in the Spirit and as having been delivered from the tyranny of enslavement to the flesh."[23]

At the time of a given temptation, you may feel utterly weak; and this in and of itself is no problem. But what you must now do is to draw on God's available strength, which can be done only in faith. Instead of bogging down in that "I-sin-every-day" mentality, faith will escape this low vision by declaring there is a power of righteousness available for this present problem! And therefore in Jesus' name I am laying claim to that power!

In response to this release of faith, God's power—which wasn't accessible before—will suddenly rise up and surge forth. When commenting on this subsequent release of power and the sure victory it obtains, F. B. Meyer wrote: "Yes, child of God, be sure that the place of defeat may become the place of victory, sublime and glorious so as to fill thine heart with adoring rapture, and heaven with consenting praise."[24] For this to occur, however, does require reckoning. J. Oswald Sanders further explained the dynamic of reckoning this way:

> When Abraham Lincoln affixed his signature to the historic Emancipation Proclamation, every slave in the United States of America was immediately and automatically released from slavery. From the moment the ink was dry on the document, every slave was potentially free. But that did not mean that every slave enjoyed actual liberty. Some masters deliberately concealed from

> their slaves the news of their emancipation. Before they experienced their freedom, the slaves had to first hear the good news. Then they had to believe that joyous news, even though it seemed too wonderful to be true. Next they had to reckon on that fact being true, not of slaves in general, but of themselves in particular. But they could do all this and still remain slaves. They had to assert their freedom and refuse any longer to remain in bondage to their former masters. In doing this, they could count on the whole might of the United States being behind them.[25]

This last step to which Sanders refers is actually an extension of reckoning. Reckoning doesn't just think and say and confess—it acts! It acts as if what has been said is true! Not to act, however, is to drastically deflate faith, rendering it, as James speaks of it, into a state of debilitating deadness.

Important to note is that the acting God requires of you is to be done with a complete dependency upon God. As you venture forth, you are to trust God for a further infusion of his supernatural strength. And sure enough, with each successive step, what wasn't there before will be released.

There have been those who said, "I tried reckoning and it didn't work." The real problem, though, is that they didn't work the reckoning. Reckoning means to believe God, to exercise faith, to draw from the reservoir of hope—and this isn't all mental! For the same chapter that tells us to reckon also tells us to yield ourselves. Moreover, the Greek makes it clear that this isn't a "twiddle-our-thumbs-and-wait-for-God-to-move" kind of yielding. In his book, *Holiness*, J. C. Ryle points out that Christians "... are not told to 'yield themselves' up as passive agents and sit still, but to arise and work. A holy violence, a conflict, a warfare, a fight, a soldier's life, a wrestling are spoken of as characteristic of the true Christian."[26]

What we know, speak, and believe must be enforced! So to reduce reckoning to a mental mantra, or to a precept that is supposed to deliver all by itself, is to court certain defeat. Yes, reckoning is essential, but it is not stand-alone truth.[27] Scarcely any truth is. Reckoning guides belief by reminding what the cross of Christ accomplished in the death of the old nature. The power connected to reckoning is unleashed when the new nature is released, thereby activating the sanctified will to pursue what God purposes.

The Need for Intimacy

Thus far we have mentioned three essential strategies for conquering the flesh: brokenness, crucifixion, and faith. The last strategy we'll consider doesn't come last but actually interweaves in the first three. This involves an intimacy with God; for without that, the flesh can't be conquered and the new nature can't be released.

There are just two verses in the Bible that specifically tell us how to get our new nature repeatedly released. In the Second Epistle of Peter, chapter 1, verses 3 and 4, we are told about the great, exceeding, precious promises of God which, as we stand on them—walking out on a limb in child-like faith—will enable us to become a partaker of the divine nature. G. D. Watson wrote, "We always find the Promiser concealed in his promise …."[28] It is when we activate faith that the presence of God manifests, as does our new nature.

The other critical factor for a new nature release is surfaced in Colossians 3:10, where we are told that our new man is renewed in knowledge. The word "renewed" means, among other things, to charge up; and the word "knowledge" means intimacy. G. D. Watson explained, "The term knowledge of God, in Scripture, means more than our mental views or intellectual information about God. It means an inward, spiritual conscious knowing of God in his personality and character."[29] So, as we experience a sweeter and stronger intimacy with God, our new nature, which is already perfect, will surge and soar, replacing our flesh and defeating our sin.

Who would not want this? The answer is, sadly enough, most of the people in church. When Jesus said, "Behold, I stand at the door and knock," it was, you should recall, a church door that was locked against him (Revelation 3:20). This stunning fact, much in evidence today, prompted A. W. Tozer to write:

> Suppose some angelic being who had since creation known the deep, still rapture of dwelling in the divine Presence would appear on earth and live a while among us Christians. Don't you imagine he might be astonished at what he saw? He might, for instance, wonder how we could be contented with our poor, common place level of spiritual experience. In our hands, after all, is a message from God not only inviting us into his holy fellowship but also giving us detailed instructions about how to get there. After feasting on the bliss of intimate communion with God, how could such a being understand the casual, easily satisfied spirit which characterizes most evangelicals today?[30]

Oh, my! Forfeiting fellowship with God, and doing so by desire and design, is an unthinkable negligence! For without this fellowship, the other strategies against the flesh are bound to fail.

We must know and never forget that brokenness (of the biblical kind) won't happen unless God draws near. Similarly, crucifixion won't occur unless, just like Jesus, we draw close to the Father first. Moreover, faith won't grip and guide unless God's presence is our familiar abode. The fellowship we seek will be limited in its benefit to us, though, unless it is what Paul called "the fellowship of his suffering" (Philippians 3:10). This is an immensely important qualifier. Hence, Jessie Penn-Lewis writes:

> Swing too far into endeavors to lay hold of all that the "new creation" means for spirit, soul and body, without the *necessary death-fellowship* maintained and deepened, and the believer will not only be holding "truth" which has no power in it, but he becomes open to the deceiving spirits of the air, who are only too ready to give all the counterfeits of the "new creation" aspects of truth the soul has eagerly stretched forward to apprehend.[3]

It is the fellowship that identifies with what Jesus did on the cross, the fellowship that is willing for brokenness and the taking up of a cross, the fellowship that seeks the higher life through deeper death, which has within it a new nature intimacy with Jesus. Based on this premise, Jessie Penn-Lewis then said of the believer: "If he wants all that the 'new creation' means, then there is no other way but to be prepared to be 'delivered unto death for Jesus sake'...."[32]

Just now you may be experiencing a dryness of the wilderness, attributable to the fact that you and the Lord are not very close. That fact alone would explain the resurgence of your flesh and the resultant pattern of succumbing to sin. Just know that making formulas out of biblical principles isn't going to get you out of this—*you need God*! And the good news is that God is ready to fill your life with his transforming presence. This is one reason I love that verse in the Bible which says, "After these things Jesus showed himself again to his disciples." Roy Hession said:

> I call it a revival text because it contains that little word "again"; and again is built into the word revival, for the prefix *re* is simply the Latin for again. Revival, then, is simply God doing something again. Although Charles Finney is right when he says that revival always presupposes a declension, that little word "again" indicates that Jesus is not defeated by our declension, but stoops to do again that work in our heart which has declined. And he does so by showing himself again to his disciples.[33]

Is this what you need? Then ask Jesus right now to show himself to you—*again*. And in making this request you can be encouraged with the knowledge that this is exactly what the Lord wants to do!

You have heard of Blaise Pascal, the famous seventeenth-century French scientist often classed as one of the six great thinkers of all time. This exceedingly brilliant man experienced an encounter with God one night that dramatically changed his life. Those who attended him at his death found an account of this experience in his pocket. In Pascal's own handwriting the note said this:

> From about half-past ten at night to about half-after midnight—fire! Oh, God of Abraham, God of Isaac, God of Jacob—not the God of the philosophers and the wise. The God of Jesus Christ who can only be known in the ways of the Gospel. Security—feeling—peace—joy—tears of joy. Amen.
>
> Commenting on Pascal's experience, Tozer asked:
>
> Were these the expressions of a fanatic, an extremist? No, Pascal's mind was one of the greatest. But the living God had broken through and beyond all that was human and intellectual and philosophical. The astonished Pascal could only describe in one word the visitation in his spirit: "Fire!"
>
> Understand that this was not a statement in sentences for others to read. It was the ecstatic utterance of a yielded man during two awesome hours in the presence of his God.[34]

The answer to the flesh problem is Jesus. Once we experience with fire and feeling his blessed presence, our new nature will rendezvous with his nature, joyously reuniting in a way that will lift us to a level of living where, thankfully, the flesh cannot go.

"He's baack!" What ominous words when spoken of a reappearance of Freddie Krueger flesh. "He's back!" What thrilling words when spoken of a fresh vision of our Lord! Once the Lord shows himself *again* to his disciples, the resulting magnetism will elevate them to an atmosphere where the self-life simply can't function. And this elevation—referred to by some as the resurrected life—means that flesh-dominated living is over and the romance of that rescuing and revitalizing rendezvous with God has begun.

Reflection Questions

1. Has the Lord led you into a spirit of brokenness over your sin? Please explain.

2. In contemplating the radical implications of the crucified life, are you ready to take up your cross? Please explain.

3. How does faith and reckoning help protect our sense of identity?

Chapter 11

The Release of the Spirit

The New Testament tells the story. After three years of living with Jesus, the disciples hadn't really changed that much. They had heard his matchless truths. They had seen his astonishing miracles. And yet, on the very night Jesus was to go to Gethsemane they were fighting amongst themselves! The reason they fought as they did was because the flesh force was still dominant in their lives—even after spending all those years in the physical presence of Jesus!

To freeze the picture at this point in the story is to be struck with colliding, colossal realities. For just when Jesus needed these men the most—as hell was about to unleash its entire arsenal—these snickering, bickering disciples were at their pathetic worst. All this, mind you, after such an enormous investment of love and the most glorious revelations from the most inspiring personality!

The provoking issue that night had to do with who was going to outrank whom in the Kingdom. Apparently, when word got around that the mother of two of the disciples had secretly met with Jesus, that became dry tinder on an easily combustible pile: The nerve of that woman, trying to gain an advantage for her sons like that!

Such a poor display of apostolic maturity was hardly a rare occurrence. On this night alone, the disciples would grieve Jesus by squabbling in the Upper Room, then grieve him again by sleeping in the garden when Jesus had asked them to pray, then grieve him another time by scattering in wild fright once the authorities arrived to make the arrest. From the evidence of this night alone, the case can be made that these obtuse and obstinate men were not easy clay to mold.

Did you know that Jesus had devoted a full week's time preparing the twelve for what would transpire during his last days? With remarkable detail, he had prophesied exactly what would happen: the arrest, the beatings, his death, his resurrection. He even told them when and where to meet him when he arose from the dead on the third day.

But did anybody show up? No, with this teaching, as with many others, not a whole lot registered. As John Henry Jowett said, "No one was anxiously watching on the third day, with eyes intently fixed upon a mysterious east."[1] This is why, when it came to the big showdown, one of the disciples betrayed him, another denied him, still another renounced his belief in him altogether, and all but one were nowhere to be found. Documenting this fact, Dorothy L. Sayers pointed out that of the four accounts of the cross in the Gospels, "John's is the only one that claims to be the direct report of an eye-witness."[2] It is likely that the other apostles didn't even show up.

To state the obvious, then: At this point in the story, these supposed shepherds of the church looked like sheep. That *these* would be the men who would turn the world upside down hardly seemed possible. And yet that, we now know, is exactly what later happened.

So how do we account for this amazing turn-around? There is, after all, such a black-and-white contrast between the disciples before Pentecost and the disciples after Pentecost.

The reason I identify Pentecost as the all-important line of demarcation (and not the resurrection) is simply because this is what Jesus did. In replaying the story's end in our minds, we can well imagine how sky-high the enthusiasm of the disciples must have been once the resurrected Jesus appeared. No one could have been more convinced than they! No one could have been more ready to serve! But instead of unleashing all this conviction and compassion upon a needy world, Jesus told them not to go anywhere or to say anything: Just wait—for the filling of the Holy Spirit.

One wonders, though, if such an instruction is likely to be heard today. Show the slightest willingness to work, and many pastors will set volunteers to serving, no questions asked. J. Gregory Mantle addressed this issue by asking:

> Does the church of Jesus Christ think she can accomplish God's work in the world without a definite experience of heart purity and the Pentecostal baptism? It is admitted that the early Christians were thus made usable to the Master; but there is an impression abroad that this qualification for successful service can be dispensed with in these days.[3]

If we were to answer that question based on the historical record alone, we would have to say that something happened on that tenth day of Upper Room waiting that is so crucial it must be investigated.

If asked, most church members would say that their walk with God is more like the disciples in the Gospels and not like the disciples in the book of Acts. The modern church-attendee would readily admit that something is wrong in his life! Despite all his advantages—the Bible, the church, the encouragement of others—something of major importance is missing. Providing a clue about what that "something" is, Andrew Murray wrote:

> While Jesus was with his disciples on earth, he could not get into their hearts in the right way. They loved him, but they could not take in his teaching, they could not partake of his disposition, and they could not receive his very spirit into their being.[4]

At the time, such a condition was unavoidable, inasmuch as the great day of Pentecost had not yet arrived. But today we *can* partake of his disposition. Indeed, not to do so is very much like trying to drive an engine-less car.

Those who have watched the Indianapolis 500 on TV know how the race begins. Every year the public address announcer will give the instruction, “Gentlemen, please start your engines!” Of course, it wouldn’t be much of a race unless they did! Yet, is it not true that Christians are trying to run a God-ordained race today without their engines being turned on?

Let’s get off the speedway for a moment, as we alter our metaphor just a bit. Imagine that you are sitting in your car about to take a trip. In preparation for this trip, you have brought along a map you have already studied in some detail. No matter how well you have studied the map, however, if the engine isn’t on, just turning the steering wheel will require a major effort on your part. True, if unusually determined, you could, I suppose, keep your hands on the steering wheel as you run alongside the car and push. But because such an effort would soon tire you out, you wouldn’t get anywhere near your desired destination.

Such a scenario is descriptive of many Christians today, in that they are diligent to study their Bibles (the map) and they have every intention of living the Christian life (the trip), but they haven’t been filled with the Spirit (the turning on of their engines). John Henry Jowett exclaimed, “... here is the secret of much of our impoverishment. We are living too much as men lived before the Holy Ghost was given.”[5]

What the Filling Is

It is interesting that of the 7,487 promises in God’s Word, one of these is so needful and special that it is referred to as “*the* promise.” Therefore, what the Father promised (Luke 24:49), the prophet prophesied (Matthew 3:11), Jesus proclaimed (Acts 1:5-8), the early church experienced (Acts 2:4) and Scripture commands (Ephesians 5:18), we are now wanting to understand—the beauty, the bounty, and the blessing of being filled with the Holy Spirit.

Lest there be any confusion, the first fact to nail down is this: Every Christian already has the Holy Spirit within. This assertion is based on Romans 8:9, which says that if we don’t have the Spirit, we are none of his. So every Christian—no matter what his denominational preference or his present level of maturity—has received (not partially, but fully) the

Holy Spirit. However, there is a big difference between the *receiving* of the Holy Spirit and the *releasing* of the Holy Spirit. The real question is not how much of him you have, but how much of you he has.

Whenever the Holy Spirit is released to fill your life, the experience is so overwhelming the Bible speaks of it elsewhere as a baptism—something that floods, engulfs, immerses, and overcomes. In the most profound and practical way, this baptism is indispensable to releasing our new nature. A. B. Simpson writes:

> It is scarcely necessary to say that the baptism of the Holy Ghost is our union with the living personality of the Spirit. It is not an influence. It is not a notion, nor a feeling, nor a power, nor a joy into which we are submerged; but it is a heart of love, a mind of intelligence, a living being as real as Jesus Christ of Nazareth, and as real as our own personality.[6]

Actually, the Bible speaks of two baptisms, not one. The fact of more than one baptism is identified in the book of Hebrews as an elementary principle (Hebrews 6:2). The first baptism is analogous to salvation (the crossing of the Red Sea); the second baptism is analogous to Promise Land living (the crossing of the Jordan River). The very distinct differences between these two baptisms can be seen in the juxtaposition of two New Testament verses.

In First Corinthians 12:13 we read: "For by one Spirit we were all baptized into one body ...." This is the baptism every Christian has already experienced. In examining this baptism, notice, first, who it is doing the baptism—the Holy Spirit. Now notice into what we were all baptized—the Church, the body of Christ. In John 1:33, though, we see a different baptism. Here we find John the Baptist saying, "... He who sent me to baptize with water said to me, 'Upon whom you shall see the Spirit descending and remaining on him, this is he who baptizes with the Holy Spirit'."

So, according to this verse, who is doing the baptizing? Jesus, the One upon whom the Holy Spirit descended. And what is the element of this baptism? The Holy Spirit, whose engulfing, rushing presence will change our whole life!

Through Scripture's characterizations of these two baptisms, we can see that the agent of each is different, the element of each is different, and the purpose of each is different. The first baptism has been experienced by every Christian. The second baptism is available to every Christian but its very existence is unknown to many. Of those in that condition, Andrew Murray said:

> A man may be an earnest Christian, a successful worker. He may be a Christian who has had a measure of growth and advance; but if he has not entered this fullness of blessing, then he needs to come to a second and deeper experience of God's saving power: He needs, just as God brought him out of Egypt, through the Red Sea, to come to a point where God brings him through Jordan into Canaan.[7]

Is this second baptism a gradual thing, the successful outcome of spiritual maturity? No, the Bible never represents this as a step-by-step improvement program. The language of Scripture always conveys sudden, definite, point-in-time action—the Spirit came, the Spirit descended, the Spirit fell upon. Martyn Lloyd-Jones says of this punctiliar and sensational experience, "... the baptism with the Holy Spirit is always something clear and unmistakable, something which can be recognized by the person to whom it happens and by others who look on at this person."[8]

Just as one can know precisely when he was baptized with water, he can also know precisely when he was baptized with the Holy Spirit. Leonard Ravenhill notes, "Some Christians cannot say when they were saved. But I never knew a man yet who was baptized with the Holy Ghost and Fire and was unable to say when it happened."[9] While the baptism with the Spirit isn't more important than salvation, it is often more dramatic.

Many Christians will view the Christian life as years and years of growth rewarded someday, they hope, by a graduation of the Holy Spirit's filling. But G. D. Watson has biblical support for chiding "the snail-crawling gradualism that gets us nowhere."[10] Andrew Murray said that "... some people want to glide into this life ... gradually, to steal in quietly, and God won't have it."[11] With equal decisiveness, Charles Trumbell said the same thing:

> No! The victorious life, the life of freedom from the power of sin, is not a gradual gift. There is no such thing as a gradual gift. And victory is a gift. It is not a growth. "Thanks be unto God who *giveth* us the victory through our Lord Jesus Christ." How long does it take you to grow into your Christmas presents? On Christmas morning, when you come downstairs, and find them there on the table with your name on them, how long does it take you to grow into those gifts? One minute a gift is not yours, though it is labeled with your name. The next minute, it is yours. Why? Because in that minute you have taken it. You did not grow into it; in an instant you took it.[12]

Likewise, A. B. Simpson spoke of this experience "as a gift, not as a growth. It is an obtainment, not an attainment."[13]

Unfortunately, as Jack Hayford points out, the image that comes to mind when many people think of the Spirit's filling is one of whipped-up emotional frenzy. They envision someone jumping up and down in a trance-like state, speaking incoherent babbling through slightly foaming lips with the staccato rapidity of a machine gun. Ecstasy! Uncorked emotions! Wild fire!

It is significant, though, that of the eight people specifically identified by the book of Acts to be filled with the Spirit, five of them were killed. So instead of their Spirit-filling being a neurotic release of cathartic emotions, the Spirit's filling was a force that drove them to the frontlines of Christian service. Thus, Paul Billheimer contended "... the Holy Spirit in the life of the believer will drive him to a life of suffering sacrifice just as he did in the life of Jesus."[14] That the Holy Spirit's work is much more pragmatic than ecstatic can be seen in those Spirit-filled evidences cited in Ephesians, chapter 5. This list focuses on such things as your marriage, your children, your work, and your relationship with others in the church (Ephesians 5:21—6:4).

Actually, the Greek word for "filled" has three compatible meanings. First, it means pressure. Just as the wind will fill out the sails and drive it along, and the river currents will take a stick and drive it along, so also the Holy Spirit will drive the life he fills in a prescribed, God-ordained direction.

Second, this word means to permeate. Like salt and other seasonings that permeate food, or the many colors of dye that permeate cloth, the Holy Spirit will permeate the life of a believer, altering the flavor and appearance of that life.

Third, this Greek word for filling, *pleroa*, means possession. The Bible tells of those who were filled with fear, filled with madness, filled with Satan—each filling completely controlling their behavior. So also our lifestyle can be decisively and dramatically changed once the Holy Spirit fills us. To be filled with the Spirit is to have our life taken over by God in such a way that we will actually feel him inside us. So awesome is this experience—the fervor of its fire, the sweetness of its strength—that we may feel that our heart is going to burst! Those who haven't experienced this have no idea that something so good is even possible on this side of heaven.

Jesus referred to this experience as "rivers of living water" that can flow with force and favor inside the believer. Dr. Jowett said, "The river is the minister of quickening, and everything it touches lifts its head in an access of refreshing life."[15]

In his book, *The Key to Triumphant Living,* Jack Taylor said:

> A river is involuntary; it doesn't have to try.
> A river is unselfish and available to all wherever it goes.
> A river is the picture of confidence and power and doesn't have to babble like a brook!

> A river is consistent and keeps on moving. You never have to prod it.
> A river is a picture of constant cleansing. Cast pollution in it, and it will sweep it away.
> A river is a symbol of courage. Put obstacles in front of it and it will overwhelm them.
> A river speaks of power. It runs factories and turns on lights all over the world.
>
> You don't have to plead for a river to flow. You can't "program" a river to stop its flow. You don't have to map its direction. It will make its own way.[16]

In view of all that a river is, what a sad and sorry scene it is to see Christians coming to church each Sunday wanting their little beggar cups filled, when in fact God wants to unloose a mighty river inside them! A. B. Simpson reminded us that "A river half-full will never become a water power."[17] Dr. Simpson said, "Only full hearts accomplish effectual work for God. Only the overflow of our blessings blesses others."[18]

The constant satisfaction and supply associated with God's rivers of living water appear to be more poetry than reality, especially if one has familiarity with the modern church. This prompted F. J. Huegel to ask:

> ... why is it that we do not see more of this living water which the Savior promised would flow from the hearts of those who believe on him? Where are those rivers? Why do they not flow as a mighty confluence of streams from the Throne and from the Lamb out upon the world's parched souls and the desert lands of her misery and death?[19]

The answer to that question we will consider next as we see what Scripture says about how to receive the filling of the Holy Spirit. There is confusion about this, causing some to claim for themselves what never happened.

How the Filling Occurs

Once the Lord causes us to desire this filling, we then will want to know just how it can be ours. Is there some formula, some method, some prescribed procedures to follow? Not exactly. We see in Scripture where prayer preceded the filling (Acts 1:4; 2:1f.; 4:31; 8:15), but this wasn't always true. We also see where praise preceded the filling (Acts 4:24), but this wasn't always true. We as well see where the laying on of hands preceded the filling (Acts 8:17; 9:17; 19:6), but this wasn't always true.

The truth is, there is no x+y= formula; so loosen up. Sometimes we make what should be natural and easy more difficult than it ought to be by being so uptight about doing everything just right. Just come in childlike faith, remembering that you are not having to persuade a reluctant God—he promised you this! Indeed, this ongoing experience of his released Spirit is the best part of your earthly inheritance.

Some people think, "Oh, I haven't been a Christian very long, and I don't know that much about the Bible." Well, the filling of the Spirit will help you with your walk with God, and it will make you want to know more about the Bible. The point being: Maturity level and Bible knowledge are not prerequisites for the inauguration of the Holy Spirit's flow. So what are the prerequisites (besides, of course, becoming a Christian)?

First, we must come to the end of ourselves, renouncing any worth that self-striving can achieve. A. B. Simpson observed:

> God has often let self have its way until it cures us effectually by showing us the misery and failure that it brings. This is the only good there is in our own struggling. It shows us the vanity of the struggle and prepares us to surrender to God.[20]

Typically, for the average Christian, this is a long time in coming, if it comes at all. Statistics show that for those pastors who eventually experienced the Spirit's release, on average at least fifteen years of ministry passed before it happened. Of course, for them and for others, it could have happened soon after conversion. It isn't God who wants many years of wilderness wandering.

Were you aware that the actual travel time from Mount Sinai to the Promise Land was only eleven days? However, we today, like those believers in that day, consign ourselves to a much-too-long wilderness wandering. But it is not until we are sick of making tracks in the sand, spiritually going nowhere fast, that we will finally make that all-important decision to leave the wilderness. Andrew Murray writes, "The first condition of all filling is emptiness. A reservoir is a hole, a great empty place prepared, waiting, thirsting, crying for the water to come. Any true abiding fullness of the Spirit is preceded by emptying."[21]

By emptying, we mean the end of all self-government and the dethroning of all rival gods. A. W. Tozer presented a probative inquiry of this issue every candidate should consider.

> Are you sure you want your personality to be taken over by One who will require obedience to the written Word? Who will not tolerate any of the self-sins in your life: self-love, self-indulgence? Who will not permit you to strut or boast or show off? Who will take the direction of your life away from you and will reserve the sovereign right to test you and discipline you? Who will strip away from you many loved objects which secretly harm your soul?
>
> Unless you can answer an eager "Yes" to these questions, you do not want to filled.[22]

R. A. Torrey said, "No man ever got this blessing who felt he could get along without it." For those who do want it and are willing for self-government to end, the cross awaits. Jessie Penn-Lewis writes: "There is no Pentecost in spiritual experience without a preceding Calvary. We have not known our Pentecost because we have not known the full meaning of Calvary."[23] The Spirit will not fill that which self continues to occupy. But this dispossessing of self is not entirely our work, for as John Owen observed, "The Spirit alone brings the cross into our hearts with its sin-killing power."[24]

A second prerequisite for the filling is belief. Lamenting the lack of belief in some, G. D. Watson wrote, "Many persons get down and pray for a baptism of the Holy Ghost who no more think of getting it than flying to the moon."[25] Upon asking God to fill us, we must believe that he *will* do this. Those who approach him with a cleansed heart and an expectant faith are not going to be turned away! This doesn't mean that heaven's response will always be immediate. D. L Moody, Smith Wigglesworth, Jack Hayford and many others did not access the Spirit-filling right away. However, because they wholeheartedly sought the filling, it did happen soon enough.

This is often the way. Seekers will get on their face before God, confessing all known sin, because they know God will never manifest himself in an atmosphere of protected, protracted sin. So bringing it all before him—their guilt, their failure, their neglect, their carelessness—they will lay these at his feet, receiving as promised a forgiveness for all. Then, pressing in further, they will seek the release of God's Spirit. But the release they seek may not come that session. It may come soon after—in a car while driving, two days later while walking down the road, or even in the middle of the night as they are awakened by the Lord. The important point, though, is because they do seek it, it does come. God will never frustrate functioning faith.

The belief God honors is not just that the Spirit-filling will occur, but also that the Spirit-filling will be every bit as good as God said it is. One criticism hurled by some denominational detractors is that the enemy will exploit all this fervent seeking. Maybe, they say, the spirit that will fill won't be holy but evil. To this objection, the following passage can be offered where Jesus himself spoke these words:

> If a son asks for bread from any father among you, will he give him a stone? Or if he asks for a

> fish, will he give him a serpent instead of a fish? Or if he asks for an egg, will he offer him a scorpion? If you then, being evil, know how to give good gifts to your children, how much more will your Heavenly Father give the Holy Spirit to them who ask him! (Luke 11:11-13)

So we ought to give God credit! Under his supernatural watch care, he can so superintend the process that only good will come and not mischievous or injurious evil.

A third prerequisite for the Spirit's filling is the exercising of our own will. Do understand that this filling isn't a seizure that will convulse the limp, the lame, and the passive. The faculty of a sanctified will must be involved, and for good reason. Remember, before the waters of the Red Sea were damned up, what did Moses have to do? Extend the rod of God! And before the waters of the River Jordan were barricaded, what did the priests have to do? Step into the onslaught of those flood-rising waters! And before the sun stood still, what did Joshua have to do? He had to verbalize a command for all to hear. And before Peter could walk on the water, what did he have to do? He had to get out of the boat!

Amazing miracles, each one, in which God came through in a most extraordinary way! But before each miracle could manifest, there was first a step of action, an exercising of the will, an obedient response to the command of God. So it must also be for those who seek *the* great miracle, the filling with God's Spirit. God wants our head lifted (this isn't a time for our minds to go out of gear), our hands lifted (this is a time to be yielded to all that he has), and our voices lifted (this is a time to honor the Lord with exuberant praise).

Just know that when the Spirit fills, those days of being immensely disappointed in yourself and all that lack in your spiritual condition will be over. Instead of being busy, but not fruitful; disciplined, but not joyful; committed, but not content; learning, but not living what the Bible does indeed teach, you will experience a takeover on the inside that is so complete the only possible explanation is God! All that you had wanted but never thought you would ever get will rush in with so much force and feeling—at which point, your new nature, the very life of God, will begin its flow.

Explaining this phenomenon and how it affects our soul, Miles Stanford declared:

> It is not that this new life of the Lord comes in to take the place of our personality, to take the place of our faculties created by God, but it comes in to take the place of the sinful life which is operating in our personality and employing our faculties. The vessel is the same, the same person, the same faculties, but the contents [are] different. No longer this same sinful element, but the very nature of the Lord Jesus Christ filling, interpenetrating, permeating.[26]

And that, as the poet put it, will make all the difference! So much love! So much power! At long last, the very life Scripture describes will be our experience! All this we will need, G. D. Watson wrote, because "it demands a 'fullness of the Spirit' to do the hard, unpopular, thankless work that must be done to save a drowsy church and a wicked world."[27]

E. Stanley Jones, missionary to India, described his own experience. He said he had been in prayer when the Lord asked him, "Will you give me your all?" Jones answered, "Yes, Lord, of course, I will. I will give you my all, all I know and all that I don't know." Then the Lord replied, "Take my all, take the Holy Spirit."

At first, Jones felt nothing. Next, doubts made their case, and he had to shoo these off like Abraham did when the birds came to scatter his sacrifice. But it was while pushing away these menacing doubts that it then happened. This is his account.

> Wave after wave of the Holy Spirit seemed to be going through me as a cleansing fire. I could only walk the floor with the tears of joy flowing down my cheeks. I could do nothing but praise him—and did. I knew this was no passing emotion; the Holy Spirit had come to abide with me forever.[28]

The life of divided loyalties can end for us, as can the deadly duality of talking one way but living yet another way. Just as it happened for those first disciples, the fire will finally be lit in us! And accompanying this fire will be a burst of compassion—toward God and toward others—that will transport truths we profess into a reality we now possess. Anything less than this just isn't the Christianity that God wants broadcast at home or beyond.

Is it now becoming clear to you why Jesus told his disciples to wait? To attempt to live the Christian life without the Holy Spirit is a hopeless prospect. Trying to convert others to a life we have never experienced is simply a doomed venture. And yet, this is precisely what is happening. Friendly flesh is trying to glad-hand a lost world into conversion. Sincere souls are talking about realities they have never experienced—and, quite frankly, do not understand. Such would have been the case in Jerusalem, too, had Jesus sent the apostles out with no Upper Room experience. Convinced and committed though they were, it would not have been enough. They needed then, as we need today, the mighty rush of the Holy Spirit engulfing, baptizing, permeating, and empowering.

While the filling of the Holy Spirit is sudden and not gradual, it is also continuous and not final. Therefore, an ongoing experience of the Spirit's filling is essential. A. B. Simpson declared, "There is such a thing as receiving the Holy Spirit at a definite moment, and there is such a thing as being filled in the present tense as a continuous experience in which we are to be workers together with God ...."[29]

Some people will say, "I got the filling in 1985!" But somewhere along the way they sprung a leak! This occurred, not because the filling is modest and momentary in its impact but because the filling was forfeited by known and deliberate sin—not inevitably, not irresistibly, as though overcome by a far greater force, but only because sin in some form was engaged irrationally, unnecessarily, and foolishly.

It is imperative for believers to understand that the mighty river flow of God's presence can be damned up if self comes off the cross or if our mind gets off the Word. Should either of these lapses occur, the filling will cease and the believer will be right back where he was before the filling ever occurred.

This need not happen, though, because, by definition, the Spirit's flow is mighty in its momentum, thus making further fillings easily accessible. It is to be remembered that those filled with the Spirit in Acts, chapter 2, were filled again in Acts, chapter 4. A. B. Simpson said of this experience, "It is, therefore, not so much a perpetual fullness as a perpetual filling."[30]

Should a forfeiting of the filling occur, it can be reversed. Indeed, it *must* be reversed! Because what the believer desperately needs, and what the Lord intensely desires, is the only kind of life that will satisfy the soul and extend the Kingdom. This life, dripping with the fragrance of God's anointing, and supernaturally charged by the turbo-power thrusts of heaven, is what Jesus died for. Only that, nothing else qualifies.

The filling of the Spirit is critical to any believer's experience of the new nature. Accordingly, G. D. Watson offered a summary statement on this truth when he wrote:

> Just as all the character and the life of the Godhead was formed and expressed in the life and person of our blessed Jesus, so, in a similar way, it is God's design that the fullness of the Christ-life shall be reformed and expressed in us by the indwelling and infilling of the Holy Spirit.[31]

The faculties of the soul—mind, will, and emotions—can never produce such a life, even among those who are converted. Only the Holy Spirit can impart and unfold Divine life in us. And this is exactly what he will do, if we, like those first disciples, will avail ourselves to him with earnest expectation for this supernatural propulsion of Divine life.

Reflection Questions

1. Is your current walk with the Lord more like that of the apostles in the gospels, or like that of the apostles in the book of Acts?

2. How do you react to the descriptions offered in this chapter of the Holy Spirit's filling?

3. If you have been filled with the Holy Spirit before, share your experience.

4. If you have not been filled with the Holy Spirit before, do you want this experience now?

Chapter 12

Getting God's Grace

Once one has been filled with the Holy Spirit, it is easy to conclude that the rest of life will be lived on what Ruth Paxson calls "a higher plane." Having escaped both the natural and the carnal, and soaring now in the stratosphere of the spiritual, there is this feeling that nothing will hinder one's flight; and, too, that nothing will ground one again in the mud of old ways. However, the filling of the Holy Spirit is one thing, while the maintaining of this filling is quite another. A. J. Gordon's rhetorical question resonates with this point: "And who has not found that it is easier to rise to lofty heights than it is to maintain one's self there?"[1]

Just how this maintaining is achieved may sadden some people, because if a choice were given between a generous annuity for life and a far more generous supply that can only come through a dependency on God, many people would prefer the annuity. Addiction to independent living is not easily cured, even after someone becomes a Christian. Confronting this agenda is the surprising fact that "... the spiritual man has no resources in himself" but "is in daily need of replenishing."[2]

In his book, *The Holy Spirit* (volume two), A. B. Simpson added commentary to this perspective when he wrote, "We are not supplied in a moment for a lifetime. We have no store of grace for tomorrow. The manna must fall each day afresh; the life must be inhaled breath by breath ...."[3] The reason this thought perplexes us is because we had it in our minds that once a Christian becomes Spirit-filled, that Christian is now vested with resources not at all available to the world. So how is it possible that the Spirit-filled Christian has no resources in himself? That this was his condition before he became a Christian, or before he became Spirit-filled, is easily understood; but why would it be true at this stage?[4]

In reply, it must first be emphasized there is an appreciable advance in the Spirit-filled life. With this new life emerging, old nemesis sidelined, and capacities for responding to the Lord ever available, life *can* be lived on a "higher plane." However, it is the nature of our born-again spirit to respond and receive from God, to constantly depend on God, rather than to function independently of him.[5] This was even true of Jesus while he was on earth. His total dependency on the Father and on the Holy Spirit is chronicled throughout the gospels.

So, yes, we are a new creation, but remember: Just as God's original creation is daily dependent on the Lord, so is his new creation. Stephen Charnock observed, "The more we grow up in the new birth, the more deeply sensible shall we be of our impotence."[6] Andrew Murray illustrated this point well with the following analogy:

> Think of a tree one-hundred years old. When it was planted, God did not give it a stock of life by which to carry on its existence ... every year *God* clothes the tree with its foliage and its fruit; every year *he* clothes the lilies afresh with their beauty. Every day and every hour it is God who maintains the life of all nature. And God created us that we might be the empty vessels in which he could work out his beauty, his will, his love, and the likeness of his blessed Son. That is what God is for, to work in us by his mighty operation without one moment's ceasing.[7]

Of course, the means by which this ongoing supply is provided is "faith laying hold of grace." In the same way our new life began—"... for by grace you have been saved through faith ...." (Ephesians 2:8)—is precisely the way God wants it continued: "As you therefore have received Christ Jesus the

Lord, so walk in him" (Colossians 2:6). This is the great simplicity of the gospel. And John Hunter offered a profound summary of this point when he wrote:

> ... my daily Christian life is a moment by moment experience of receiving Christ. Whatever problem, fear, anxiety, temptation, or frustration comes into my life, it isn't my job to meet it. My job is to expose the whole situation to Christ Jesus the Lord, and then to walk believing that what he has promised he will also perform.[8]

When we think of grace, we often think of some situation or substance—a new job, a newer house, or perhaps a brand-new car. However, the higher purposes of grace are related to our inner life. Stephen Charnock wrote, "Every inch, every spark, every joint of the new man is from grace."[9] By grace, God gave us a new nature, and—this is what is so important to learn—it is only by grace that he will enable that new nature to manifest.

Addressing this point in what was really the only book he ever wrote, *The Spiritual Man*, Watchman Nee observed:

> Man's spirit can be compared to an electric bulb. When in contact with the Holy Spirit, it shines; but should it be disconnected, it plunges into darkness. "The spirit of man is the lamp of the Lord" (Proverbs 20:27). God's aim is to fill the human spirit with light; yet the believer's spirit is sometimes darkened. Why is this? It is because it has lost contact with the Holy Spirit.[10]

True, the person without a spirit, without a new nature, would be in a far worse predicament, for then we would be talking about a brick and not a bulb. At least a bulb can shine; a brick can't.

The presence of the re-created spirit in the believer is a tremendous asset, without which the circuitry of power and light intended for this new dispensation would be impossible. Nevertheless, the point of contact is faith laying hold of grace for every situation, relationship, and discipline of the Christian life. The new nature itself, resident within us already, is released the same way grace is released. By faith we claim it in each transaction of life, instead of attempting to do the best we can with our earnest hearts and resolute wills.

F. B. Meyer explained the difference between these two approaches by first giving a warning.

> Your nature would fall within five minutes. Your resolution would carry you no further than the rush of an express train will carry a chip or straw which it catches up for a moment as it eddies over it, but soon drops it down. But if you can understand what it means to have the nature of Jesus pouring into you moment by moment, as the heat pours into the radiator when the valve is turned on, then you will never get cold and fall again. His nature through faith in his nature makes people strong.[11]

This entire operation stands in contrast with more common approaches believers activate: a dependence on common sense, human ingenuity, hard work, a network of friends, and other already possessed resources. As Ian Thomas put it, any area of life where you are not dependent on God is an area of life where you need to be repentant toward God.[12]

A Definition of Grace

Since grace is so important for living the Christian life, we need to have a working definition of what grace is. The confusion that continues to exist about grace has kept its supply out of reach for many people. Most preachers define grace as God's unmerited favor. Whenever a preacher says the word "grace," this definition immediately follows, either as apposition or exposition. However, this definition is misleading on two counts. This definition misleads, first, because grace, the favor of God, *was* merited. Before God could lavish and ravish his goodness upon us, Jesus, taking our place, had to meet the high standards of God. He who became the first-born among the born-again, he who brought humanity into the Godhead, merited grace.

Second, this grace *is* merited for the believer now, because of this one all-important fact: Once God says it belongs to us, then, on the basis of his unequaled authority, it *does* belong to us. It is by virtue of the righteousness of God, deposited both in our account and in our spirit, that we now merit God's grace! Remember, a by-product of this righteousness is a right standing with God, a certifying and credentialing that affirms we deserve to receive from God. Therefore, we should never approach God with hat in hand, shoulders stooped, eyes cast downward, feet shuffling in a supposedly contrite and humble "Aw, shucks!" routine.

The Bible says we are to *boldly* approach his throne of grace, confident that we are going to obtain (Hebrews 4:16). But we won't ever approach God the right way, if we keep thinking grace is unmerited. Remember, unmerited grace is grace we have no right to claim. And grace we have no right to claim is the grace we won't with boldness obtain. Rights and boldness are critical issues! And therefore we'll miss God's grace too often, if we aren't clear on these issues.

Besides, what father would repeatedly tell his child, "You don't really deserve what I'm giving you"? Is this the impression that a parent wants to give? I tell you, give *that* impression often enough—emphasizing how good the parent is and how unworthy the child is—and pretty soon the child will avoid this scene altogether! And you can well understand why! All these depressing, deprecating reminders only demean the child's requests.

Moreover, if the premise of unmerited grace is believed, the child will soon limit these requests to basic unmet needs *only*. Pursuing more valued aspirations would have to be omitted, since it would appear presumptuous, if not tactless and tasteless, to ask for much more than what was ever deserved.

In this way the concept of unmerited grace is not as harmless as many people think. It has afflicted extensive damage on the spiritual life of many believers.

Once we believe that we don't deserve what we are requesting, we soon back off, so our boldness diminishes and almost vanishes. Under this paradigm of thought, most of our current desires are ineligible for God's grace supply, unless we resort to pathetic begging. But if we do that, imagine how that impacts our relationship with God—such is not a good experience! So, ever aware that faith can't function under terms like these, A. B. Simpson wrote, "The distrust and dread of the guilty soul must be removed and a spirit of confidence awakened."[13]

"Must" is the operative word here—*must*! Because any semblance of confidence will be crushed if we keep reminding the child of God of his or her unworthiness. This is not the testimony of grace. Edward Hastings reminds us, "The New Testament word *charis* is derived from a Sanscrit root meaning to 'shine forth' and so to be joyful, beautiful, radiant."[14] This is the testimony of grace. The joy exists because we are now deemed worthy.

To better understand how grace is indeed merited for the believer we must see how grace is intricately connected to all the promises of God. These promises were given to us in the form of a blood covenant. Keep in mind that a blood covenant with God represented the highest jurisprudence in the universe, and as such provides a tremendous boost to faith. Since God offered these promises in the form of a legal contract, the benefits these promises convey are altogether assured. Hence, any talk of us having no merit runs exactly counter to what the covenant was intended to convey!

What God wants uppermost in our minds is not the faith-discouraging thought that tells us we don't merit these promises but instead the faith-encouraging thought that views these promises as ours, without question!

Perhaps this analogy will help clarify the issue. If a rich uncle deposited fifty thousand dollars into my bank account, would some teller at the bank have the right to tell me that I don't deserve this money? Whatever might have been true before my uncle gave me this money is now superseded by the fact that this money legally belongs to me. Indeed, there is no law in the land that would say otherwise. Accordingly, at which time I seek to make a withdrawal, I will do so with complete confidence, just as my uncle fully intended that I should. Bank employees who feel free to offer their opinions about my supposed lack of merit should be reprimanded—and if they don't cease, they should be fired! For sure, my sweet old uncle isn't going to be calling me every week to make that point!

Are you beginning to see why this talk of grace being God's unmerited favor is as inaccurate as it is unhelpful? No believer should be told that God's grace is unmerited. The context Scripture provides forbids this description. In the fifth chapter of the book of Romans, God connects two concepts—"the gift of righteousness" and an "abundance of grace" (verse 17)—in a very interesting way. Here we learn that the relationship between the two is causal and reciprocal. Meaning that if this righteousness is ours (which indeed it is; it is an accomplished fact), then as well this grace in all of its dimensions is also ours. It is our righteousness that gives us a right standing before God, as well as the confidence to expect to receive from God.

Still, we must *take* what God indeed offers. Carefully notice the wording in this verse. It says, "... they which *receive* abundance of grace and of the gift of righteousness shall reign in life ...." F. B. Meyer pointed out: "The emphasis is not on grace, not on abundance, but on *receiving* it. The whole grace of God may be around your life today, but if you have not learned to take it in, it won't help you."[15] It is only as we make this "taking" the holy habit of our life that the blessed outcome identified by this verse can become real to us. In his book, *Faith Beyond Reason*, A. W. Tozer wrote:

> We have been taught that passive acceptance is the equivalent of faith when it is not. In the Greek, this word *receive* is active, not passive. You can go to any of the modern translations and you will find that they get across the idea of "take" and "took."[16]

In his book, *With Christ in the School of Prayer*, Andrew Murray also wrote about "the faith that takes."[17] What the Lord extends to us in open hands must be taken!

A further encouragement for taking the grace God offers us is located in our heritage of royalty. To reign in life means that our life on earth will be like that of a king. While Jesus is "the King of Kings," these other kings referred to in this designation are not the potentates of this world but are really you and me, those who have been made to sit in heavenly places with Christ Jesus (Ephesians 2:6). Revelation 1:6 says that we are kings! And while that sounds good, the question we're going to have to answer is: In what sense are we kings?

Romans 5:17 answers this question directly when it says we are to "reign in life." So, unlike the European and Asian kings who are trotted out to a few ceremonies each year but have no real power themselves, we are not to be kings in this ornamental sense. God has instead elevated us to a position of actual rule. In heaven someday? No, the Bible says we're to reign in life—and life happens down here on earth! So God's forecast for believers calls for more "reign."

Not wanting this concept to float away on a cloud of imagined euphoria, we have to get honest with ourselves by asking: *Are* we reigning in life, or might it be more true to say that in one or more areas of our life things aren't going very well? The admission that there are some big-time problems in our life—painful problems, perplexing problems—doesn't mean this concept of reigning in life is only a "feel good" idea that should be relegated to an obscure footnote, or scribbled outside the margins as one might do with some eye-catching phrase.

Grace is functional! And if properly exercised, God's grace will overcome every problem just cited! But if we don't know what grace is, and if we don't know how grace is obtained, it is we who will be overcome—and not by grace!

Romans tells us that it is those who "receive abundance of grace" who reign in life. The most critical factor for a successful reign, then, is learning how to receive—not occasional grace or minimal grace, but abundant grace. For once abundant grace is finally received, that hindering circumstance will be overcome, that difficult relationship will be transformed, that unreachable goal will be surpassed, that weakness of character will be made strong. All this attributable to the fact that grace, the enabling power of God, is sufficient to meet every need we have! Indeed, whatever the need, whatever the challenge, God has a grace supply that will more than satisfy. James S. Stewart said that "for every possible predicament of man there is a corresponding grace supply of God ...."[18] This might involve salvation grace, sanctification grace, relationship grace, ministry grace, physical grace, or even financial grace. F. B. Meyer declared:

> The same grace that made a Luther, a Knox, a Latimer, a Ridley Havergal or a Spurgeon, is for you today; and if you are living a low-down life, beaten and thwarted and dashed down and constantly compelled to admit shortcomings and failure, understand it is not because there is any favoritism on God's part ....[19]

Favoritism isn't ever the issue, but learning how to receive grace is! Jerry Bridges states, "Your worst days are never so bad that you are beyond the *reach* of grace. And your best days are never so good that you are beyond the *need* of grace."[20] Whether these current days are good or bad, therefore, it is exceedingly important to learn how to lay hold of grace.

Does it make sense to you, then, why the Bible talks about grace and peace—those two, in that order, and never the other way around? In virtually every New Testament epistle we'll find the greeting, "Grace and peace unto you" or, "Grace and peace be multiplied unto you." And while we may be tempted to pass these words off as just a nice way to say "Hi," it must be stressed that these words have content. To capsulate this content it can be said: If we know that we know that our need is going to be met, that knowing will keep the unholy trinity of fear, depression, and destructive anger from muscling into our lives.

Contemplate the quantum leaps our joy would take if our peace could double and then double again! How would you like these grace/peace dynamics multiplying their presence in your life? To the extent they do, abounding grace will become a reality that will enables you to reign in life as a king. Remember, your identity affects your destiny! Therefore, you must first stake your claim on what God says about you—that you are righteous, that you are a king—and hold fast to this claim whenever opposition threatens.

Dr. Wayne Dehoney illustrated this point in a sermon:

> There is a story—almost legendary, but with some fact to it I believe—as to what happened to the son of Louis XVI and Marie Antoinette. In the French Revolution, the king and queen of France were put to the guillotine. When they brought the boy destined to be Louis XVII, if the monarchy had been preserved, the people cried, "To the guillotine!" Someone said, No, you'll just send his little soul to heaven. Send him over to Old Meg, the wickedest woman in Paris. Let her damn his soul to hell.
>
> The legend goes on to say Old Meg did try to make him wicked and evil. When she proposed extreme violence, vulgar and dehumanizing, he stomped his foot, clenched his fist, and with fire in his eyes, said, No, I won't; because I was born to be king![21]

Such a character-stiffening response will surge through any believer who "knows that he knows" that his real identity is that of a king.

The Degrees of Grace

Being a king is not an idea with which most believers readily identify. This is partly true because of a major disappointment inflicted, or a severe wounding experienced, that resulted in mere survival becoming the goal and certainly not anything so exalted as reigning in life as a king. Perhaps their vision would be higher, and the outcomes of their lives radically better, if they were more aware of the extent of God's grace.

In his book, *When God Steps In*, A. B. Simpson said, "The greatest need of our age and of every age, the greatest need of every human heart, is to know the resources and sufficiency of God."[22] True enough, there are times when our own resources are nowhere near enough and when the difficulties we face are overwhelming. But F. B. Meyer reminded us, "The greatness of our difficulties is permitted to elicit the greatness of his grace. We may even be glad to enter the storm that we may make fresh discoveries of the all-sufficiency of Jesus, who is never so near as in these days of special trial."[23]

II Corinthians 9:8 conveys the extent of this sufficiency (as well as the enormity of these resources) by saying that "... God is able to make all grace abound toward you, that you, always having all sufficiency in all things may have an abundance for every good work."[24] When looking at all the stacked superlatives in this verse—all, always, all, all, every—it becomes clearer how far-reaching this grace really is. Given all these resources promised, we can see more clearly why God won't merely sympathize with us during our time of need; for God is able—*now*! He has the resources, the will, the knowledge, to overcome every problem we've got!

The extent of grace stipulated by this verse further supports Samuel Rutherford's encouragement to make extravagant claims on God's grace—indeed, to be "greedy of grace." G. D. Watson said, "In the empire of grace there is always room for us to choose between the excellent, and the more excellent, and the most excellent."[25] Those greedy for grace go for the most excellent if they remember Thomas Goodwin's words, "You have the bottom of God's heart, the center and circumference of his degrees of grace ...."[26] God will give you as much grace as your faith will claim.

Have you ever placed an order for merchandise through a shopping catalogue? If so, perhaps you've had the experience of going to the store on your order's supposed arrival date only to learn that some of what you ordered is either out of stock or is on back order. Just know that God will never do this to you! He is able, this verse declares, to make his grace *abound*. Did you get that? Abound, not trickle—which certainly brings into question this "barely getting by" lifestyle with which you and I have become so familiar.

Nevertheless, for many Christians week after week goes by without any evidence of "abounding grace" being on the scene. One day follows another with this observation about God passing through our brains: "Well, I guess he's not going to do anything today, either."

Many believers will live their entire lives with many unmet needs, only to discover the moment they leave this world that their grace supply is still in heaven! Untouched! Unused! All of it having their name on it! All that could have been theirs, all that should have been theirs, never got to them! Why? Because they didn't know the extent of God's grace, and also because they didn't know how to lay hold of this grace. Is it any wonder, then, that this idea of being a king who reigns in life sounded like a fairytale to them?

Notice how God personalizes this promise, saying that all grace can abound toward *you*, so that *you* having all sufficiency can abound unto every good work. In the place of these pronouns, we are entitled to insert our own name with a confidence that the blessings spoken of here are intended for us. How easy it is to suppose that God's blessings are intended for someone else, that they were designed for only a rare few super, duper saints upon whom the Lord had long ago cast his eye—perhaps someone from another nation, or another generation, but apparently not for us! Scripture corrects this kind of thinking by describing the intended beneficiary of abounding grace to be any believer who will believe enough to make a faith claim upon it.

What also comforts us is the fact we can *remain* in this blessed lifestyle where we are "*always* having all sufficiency." This has to mean that even before our prayer is answered God will minister to our emotions. Can you see why this has to be true? If grace referred only to outcome, to the times when the problem was solved, then during the "in between" times, the waiting times, we might be damaged in our emotions. However, the word *always* in this verse precludes this scenario, because grace provides a sufficiency that prevents us from being dragged into the depths of despondency. The problems the psychiatrist deals with need not be our problems, *if* we tap into the sufficiency of God's ever available grace.

This verse also means that there is no situation for which God's grace won't work. When analyzed more fully, this is also the real reason eternal life is eternal. It is because grace enables a quality of life that far exceeds the self-efforts of man. Biblical scholars affirm the truth that "eternal life" has more to do with quality than quantity, although it certainly affirms both. The fact that life will go on forever is true not because of the Greek idea of "the immortality of the soul" (which predicates an eternity based on the soul's supposedly indestructible qualities), but because of the words in this verse—"grace ... always."

A further stipulation of this promise includes "all sufficiency *for all things*." So this answers the twin problems of inadequate resources and an inferiority complex. If these words from Paul's pen are true, it isn't a matter of "you win a few; you lose a few," as we are prone to think. Scripture says we can "triumph in all things" (II Corinthians 2:14).

Too often, though, we relegate words like these to the attic of intellectualism where ultra-pious precepts are frequently banished. It is there where the most precious truths from God's Word languish in stuffy darkness, while unbelieving believers plod through a life that has nothing supernatural about it.

Maybe you inherited a disposition that isn't always appealing. If so, are you going to continue saying, "that's just the way I am," even though the doctrine of the new nature says very much the opposite? The Bible says there's a better option available to you, so why not trust God, with faith laying hold of grace, to release from your spirit that which isn't present in your soul?

The very qualities you wish you had, and thus far have never experienced, are in your spirit. Actually, these character qualities couldn't be more available or more advanced than they are right now. But it takes faith to lay hold of this form of grace, character grace, to see it manifest.[27] Just know that your days of feeling inferior are going to be over, once you begin to experience the extraordinary qualities of your new nature.

The promise of being able to "abound in every good work" also inspires confidence. Remember, it's one thing to be busy, but it's another thing to be "fruitful in every good work" (Colossians 1:10). Instead of expending a lot of energy and wasting a lot of time, we believers can truly make our life count! Robert Moffat reminds us, "We'll have all eternity to celebrate our victories, but only one short hour before sunset to win them." So let us use our time wisely and use it well. Most of us want to fulfill the assignment God has for our life, right? No one wants to hang his head low at the judgment watching wood, hay, and stubble being consumed by fire. Well, through the enabling of God's grace, we *can* do something significant for the Kingdom!

Grace is a small word that speaks of amazing results. So amazing are these results that not even kings—however rich, however envied by the masses—will experience the kind of life grace provides.

The Difficulties of Grace

With so much grace at our disposal, we have to ask ourselves, why isn't life any better than it is? Since the grace being offered is so extensive, so enabling, so enduring, what seems to be the problem here? Actually, there are several problems.

One is ignorance. Hosea 4:6 speaks the Lord's lament: "My people are destroyed by a lack of knowledge." If God's people don't even know what is available to them, they will become needlessly vulnerable to lack. Did you know that out of more than 1100 pages in the Old Testament, the word "grace" is mentioned only 11 times? Grace is mentioned 124 times in the New Testament. And yet there are believers today who are every bit as unaware of grace as were those who lived during the Old Testament.

This lack of awareness will stop everything, because a believer can't operate on what he or she doesn't know. One has to know the extent of God's grace, as well as the foundational methods for obtaining it; otherwise grace will be reduced to a lovely sentiment without much practical value.

A second grace-difficulty identified in the Bible has to do with our preference for works. Even though grace seems to be a lovely idea, deep down, we really don't want grace; we want approval. What we much prefer is to think that uniquely within ourselves is some endearing quality, some notable achievement, that will bring a sparkle to the eye of God and thus merit his enduring admiration.

Sensitive to this issue, Romans 11:6 identifies a fork in the road that compels a choice for every believer. The verse states: "... if by grace then it is no longer of works; otherwise grace is no longer grace. But if it is of works, it is no longer grace; otherwise work is no longer work." So, according to this scripture, grace and works are mutually exclusive operations, having different methods, different motives, different sources, and different results. It is impossible, therefore, to be on both of these roads at the same time![28]

Despite this clear demarcation between these distinctively different operations, many Christians are asking God to bless their efforts on the works path—and he can't! Because if he did, it would only keep them on the wrong road longer! The Lord wants believers off the road that Hebrews 9:14 calls "dead works"—never to return again! When Paul used the phrase, "falling from grace" (Galatians 5:4), he wasn't talking about losing our salvation. He was talking about *this* problem: falling away from functioning grace because of a lack of dependency on God, or because of attempts to do God's work in our own power. Loss of salvation isn't the issue here, for as Martyn Lloyd-Jones pointed out, there is a difference between falling off the mountain and falling on the mountain: One can fall on the mountain and still be near its summit.[29]

A third grace-difficulty encountered by some is referred to in Galatians 2:21 as frustrating the grace of God. The word "frustrating" means to disannul, to set aside, to make void. And as it is used here in Galatians it appears to be a deliberate decision, not an unconscious one. What truly frustrates the grace of God is a "checklist" Christianity with all of its rule-setting, ritual-adding, post-Pharisee observances that has its own ideas about how to please God. Substitute any of that for the finished work of Christ, and for a daily dependency on him to meet our needs, and we will frustrate the grace of God.

A spin-off problem caused by those who frustrate the grace of God involves insulting the grace of God. Let me explain how this occurs. The one thing legalism can be counted on to produce is rebellion. Set the standard high, as legalism is prone to do, and there will be more than a few people who will end up despising that standard. The reason they do is easily enough discovered: It's because standards like these expose the flesh. We see this dynamic at work in the crucifixion of Jesus. Jesus had set the standard even higher than the Pharisees did by saying, "Be perfect even as your Father in heaven is perfect" (Matthew 5:48). This infuriated men of religion; because if Jesus was right, this had to mean their own goodness could never be good enough. So, once the standard of righteousness seemed unreachable, the people of Jesus' day rebelled against the standard—and murdered the one who articulated it.

In his book, *Christ in Isaiah*, F. B. Meyer reminded today's Christian, "You are still in the world that crucified your Lord, and it would do the same again if he were to return to it."[30] When Hebrews 10:29 talks about people who insult the Spirit of grace, we have to ask ourselves, who are these people? To answer the question, these are the people who, caring nothing about the blood of Jesus (since they won't even admit their need to be saved), flash their fangs of spite and disdain and continue to march at double-time pace on the road of supposed good works. So infectious is this disdain for grace (infectious like a disease) it should not surprise any of us when symptoms of its presence are found at the entrance of our own hearts.

A fourth grace-difficulty, so widespread in the church, involves failing the grace of God. This occurs when something hurtful happens to us, but, being unmindful of the remedy grace offers us, we become bitter instead. Hebrews 12:15 talks about a root of bitterness. Roots are often underground, if not completely out of sight. Nevertheless, these roots may be pumping poison through the whole system, causing considerable damage within. The problem with a "bitterness binge" is that it often spreads beyond the one originally afflicted, and therefore "many will be defiled." In sympathy with the one offended, someone else will take up that person's offense so that, soon enough, bitterness will belch its fury inside that person, too![31]

If a bitter person were asked why he is bitter, chances are he'd point to a certain person, or to a certain incident, and say that's the reason why. But according to this verse, that's not the reason why. "The real reason you are bitter," God says, "is because you didn't get my grace. It was available to you. It could have protected you from all this hurt. But you failed to get it."

The Delivery of Grace

This quite naturally raises the question, "So how *do* we get God's grace?" If grace is the sum and essence of God's supply, the table of contents for God's promises, the inventory for our amazing resources, it is exceedingly important that we learn how to obtain this grace.

In setting forth the needed specifics that answer this question, it is important to note that the most important prerequisite for grace-obtaining is humility. Thomas Watson noted that, "Chrysostom calls humility the mother of all the graces."[32] This assertion lines up with James 4:6, which says, "God resists the proud, but gives grace to the humble."

So who are the people who are proud? You may not think of yourself as being a proud person, since you don't hype your accomplishments and showcase your trophies. You may even become disgusted at such ostentatious displays whenever and wherever you see them. However, the Bible has something else in mind when it puts the spotlight on pride. According to I Peter, chapter 5, the one thing a proud person won't do is to cast his cares upon the Lord! He'll tough it out and, if need be, he'll suffer and go without. In fact, he may even let the devil devour him, which is what the next verse talks about (I Peter 5:8). But what he won't do is to quit his fierce independence and give his problems to God.

Our image of the humble person is also different from what the Bible teaches. The humble person doesn't deny the existence of good qualities in his life; he simply recognizes where those good qualities came from. Having been blessed by God so many times in the past, the truly humble person is that one who is ever willing to cast his care on the Lord once again, with full expectation that still more blessings will come.

The humility required goes beyond "humble talk" by holding forth the cross God would have us bear. Since the release of God's grace is part of the resurrection life, the free flow of this life, and a fresh granting of grace, necessitate diminishing pride by dying to self. Regarding the relationship of pride defeated and grace released, Roy Hession offered this insight:

> We are sometimes told by our teachers that we should not live the up-and-down life, and the saints cringe when they hear it because they know that is just the sort of life that is so often theirs. Be careful, you teachers, lest you put the saints under the law and fail to show them the way of grace and gladness. It is, however, quite true that we ought not to be living the up-and-down life, but we should be living the down-and-up life! Down to the cross in repentance and up again through the power of his blood, in praise to God; down to give in on some new point in which we are convicted and then up again to praise him for restoration and peace; down to surrender our rights on some matter and up again to have his life living anew in us.[33]

With each put-down of pride, sanctioned by Scripture and agreed to by the believer, greater grace will then manifest.

The second thing we must do if we want to get God's grace is to be bold. At first this may sound like a curious juxtaposition—first humble, and now bold? However, the boldness being commended here is not the blustery bravado of the flesh. Since biblical boldness rests on the integrity of God to perform that which he promised, Hebrews 4:16 says, "Let us therefore come boldly to the throne of grace that we may obtain mercy and find grace to help in time of need." God never wants us to approach him whining and griping, or merely wishing and hoping. He wants us to approach him with the conviction it is he who elevated us to such an exalted place, and therefore—based on his finished work and his available promises—we can be confident while making a claim on his grace. The fact that we are the righteousness of God, permitted to use his all-powerful name when we pray and to stand on his covenant promises when we petition, arouses a holy boldness to rise from within us.

Third, if we want to obtain grace, we have to have faith. Romans 4:16 says "... it is of faith that it might be according to grace." Romans 5:2 states, "... we have access by faith into this grace ...." In his book, *The Fourfold Gospel*, A. B. Simpson asserted:

> Grace without works and faith without sight must always go together as twin principles of the glorious Gospel. The one thing God asks from all who are to receive his grace is that they shall trust his simple word where they have nothing else but his word to trust."[34]

This means that if we don't get our faith bridge over to God's grace supply, we're not going to get God's grace. Tragically, most believers don't know how to make a faith transaction with God. And the primary reason they don't is because this truth isn't being taught by pastors.

To trace the problem still further: The real reason faith isn't being taught by pastors is because the inconsistency of evangelical thought disallows it. When it comes to suffering, for example, there are those who will set aside the many promises of God regarding healing, sudden calamity, or poverty, by taking refuge in their thoughts about the sovereignty of God. In doing this, they have just reduced the promises of God to mere options, something God may or may not act on, depending on whether or not he plays the sovereignty card. Consequently, where we thought was a place to stand on (the promises of God) has now become a slippery slope and treacherous terrain.

This rather recent development in certain Christian circles does something the Bible never does: It puts the sovereignty of God in competition with the promises of God, although Scripture itself does exactly the opposite. II Corinthians 1:20 declares, "For all the promises of God are Yes and in him Amen …." This means that the sovereignty of God is the guarantee of all those promises and not its reason for cancellation or suspension.

Since faith is the only bridge to grace, the enemy is going to attack that bridge. And attack it he has! I have great sympathy for those who don't know how faith works. To leave people in their confusion, as many churches do, means their faith bridge will be down, and their grace supply will be lost.

Humility, boldness, faith—three prerequisites for obtaining a grace supply that will enable us to reign in life like a king! Even the new nature God has given us, as glorious as it is, will not, and cannot, manifest by itself. This new nature, along with all the other blessings of abundant life, only manifests in one way—with faith laying hold of grace. Imperative to know, therefore, is this exceedingly important fact: If you think the Christian life is like a current of electricity which cycles through with uninterrupted force, you're going to convict yourself by a false standard and set yourself up for considerable disappointment. The Christian life isn't like that. Grace doesn't flow at its own impetus with its own momentum; grace is accessed by faith, one moment at a time.

In his book, *The Christ Life*, A. B. Simpson explained what occurs:

> … you have grace for this moment, and the next moment, and by the time life is spent, you shall have had a whole ocean of his grace. It may be a very little trickling stream at first; but let it flow through every moment and it shall become a boundless ocean before its course is done.[35]

The beauty of this arrangement is that in order for grace to show up in our lives we must remain close to Jesus.

Indeed, any faith formula that minimizes this fact is a serious miscalculation. Thomas Goodwin wrote, "The end of grace itself is the knowledge of God and communion with him."[36] Elaborating on this very critical point, Evan H. Hopkins, Anglican Bishop from Great Britain, wrote:

> Everything needed for continual growth, for perpetual freshness, and for abundant fruitfulness are found in him. All power, all purity, and all fullness—absolutely everything needed to make all grace abound toward us, in us, and through us—are stored up in him who truly dwells within us.[37]

While staying close to the Lord is essential for a free flow of grace into our lives, you should know that this required proximity is not one of a dreaded "stalker" or one of an annoying "hanger on." The prowler pursues with criminal intent, the nuisance pursues with pitiful intent, but nothing as crass as that characterizes the dynamics set forth here. Of immense encouragement to us is this most marvelous fact: It is the cherished desire of the *Lord* for us to get closer and closer to him; it is *he* who craves this constant closeness!

Put in this context, Erich Sauer is right, "Grace does not degrade, it exalts; it does not debase, but ennobles; it does not dishonor, but crowns."[38] That God gives grace in the context of a legal granting "does not destroy our human dignity," Sauer asserts. "If it were so, it would mean that every present in everyday life would be an injury to our honor."[39] And that is certainly not so!

The independent living we crave, the inexhaustible annuity we want, is not nearly as good as an ongoing intimacy with the wisest, strongest, most loving person in the whole universe. Think of it—his nature energizing our nature through intimacy and faith. The very faith which lays hold of grace to solve every problem is now leading us to glory—the preordained glory of our intended destiny, which is, the Bible tells us, the destiny of a king!

Reflection Questions

1. Do you see the pitfalls of interpreting grace as unmerited favor? How has this pitfall affected you?

2. How were you personally helped by this chapter's discussion about the degrees of grace?

3. Which of the difficulties of grace has been most troublesome to you?

4. What change, if any, will you need to give greater focus so grace will show up in a more timely way in your life?

Chapter 13

The Renewed Mind

A miracle too marvelous to describe took place during our conversion. This wasn't a gradual thing; for in an instant our whole nature changed, thus enabling us to become what we never were before and what by moral diligence we could never achieve. All this, however, happened in our spirit; it didn't happen in our mind. G. D. Watson declared, "The sanctified soul must learn, sooner or later, that there is a great distinction between being purified from all sin and being illuminated from all ignorance."[1]

Supporting this perspective, A. W. Tozer pointed out, "... the Spirit of God never promised to fill a man's head. The promise is that God will fill the heart, or man's innermost being."[2] Let's face it: Even a Christian can concoct some pretty squirrelly thoughts. So to reduce our susceptibility to wrong thinking we must learn how the new nature relates to the command and control center for our day-to-day life, the mind.

The Bible places a high premium on correct thinking. The Old Testament went to great lengths to differentiate the wise man from the fool, and in doing so provided extensive information about right and wrong thinking. Martyn Lloyd-Jones said, "The Bible is full of logic, and we must never think of faith as purely mystical." It is not. In his book, *The Christian View of God and the World*, James Orr wrote, "... a religion divorced from earnest and lofty thought has always, down the whole history of the Church, tended to become weak, jejune, and unwholesome ...."[3] By not according the mind its rightful place, the entire trajectory of faith will be put on the wrong course, and in so doing will undermine a faculty in our humanity that is critical to the image of God placed inside us.[4]

With regard to all the faculties of the soul—mind, will, emotions, and the imagination—none were replaced the day we became a Christian. Dr. Martyn Lloyd-Jones says, "They are the same as they were before; the difference is they are no longer being used on the side of sin but now on the side of God."[5] This switching of sides isn't automatic, however. Referring to these faculties of the soul, all of which have their locus in the body, the Bible tells us, and Martyn Lloyd-Jones reminds us, "... we must present the members, every one of them, all of them, to God ...."[6] This requires a deliberate act of dedication that must be reaffirmed each day. There is much work to be done in each of these faculties, work that can never be done apart from Scripture-guided discipline and those repeated fillings by the Holy Spirit.

When last I checked, the two largest computers in the world are the Roadrunner system at DOE's Los Alamos National Laboratory built by IBM and the Jaguar system installed at the DOE's Oak Ridge National Laboratory. As sophisticated as these computers are, however, they lack the capacity of the human brain. Our brain can process more than ten trillion units of information—a task it has been busily undertaking since we were babies.

But of course not everything that accessed our brains during those early years was accurate. This is largely attributable to certain disadvantages we had. For one thing, being young, our ability to access a wide range of information and to interpret accurately what we accessed wasn't fully developed. Also a problem for us during this time was the faulty data generated by our inner circle. Since our parents and peers were far from perfect, some of the things they said, and we believed, just wasn't true. Certain cultural contaminants also got into our minds—this due to a preponderance of thinking widely accepted by the world, and due also to our lack of biblical training to filter errant thinking.

Whether the data input was correct or erroneous wasn't the only problem, because of concern, too, was how that data was processed. What weight did it have? What grid did it form? This combination of the presence of the data with the processing of the data is what the Bible calls "the spirit of your mind" (Ephesians 4:23)—and it is that which God wants changed.

As any alert counselor knows, the mere presentation of preferable cognitions won't always get the job done. Although it is certainly a necessary part of the job, there is something else—more intractable to deal with and more difficult to define—that needs to be transformed. Let me furnish some examples.

The Problem

A husband comes home from work, picks up the newspaper, and begins to read, whereupon his wife says, "Why do you always do that? You seem to care more for the newspaper than you do for me. I wish that after a long day's absence you would want to come home to me."

After hearing these words, the husband, a man of reason who loves the Lord, then gets up and puts his arm around his wife, assuring her that she's right and that in the future he will do better. And for a while he does. But before long, he's back to his old ways, back in his old chair, with the newspaper and TV coming first. Why?

Across town, some new apartment buildings have been built, each subsidized by the government. A ceremony is held with a festive spirit in the air, celebrating the nicest homes these low-income families have ever had. Time passes—one year, two years—and word gets out: Don't ever get caught at night in that neighborhood! Sure enough, as you drive by one day, you can't believe your eyes—windows broken, doors off their hinges. What once was so attractive has become a dilapidated mess. But, again, why?

There was a time in your life when you daily delighted in God's Word. How his Word touched you, taught you, and often transformed your whole day! But one day you forgot, and the next day you got a little too busy, and in time what was once so easy and good became difficult and neglected. Again, why? How do we account for this enigmatic experience of knowing what's right, and wanting what's right, but for some reason or another not doing what's right? The Bible attributes this problem not to the presence or absence of raw data and brute facts, but to the spirit of our minds.

To further elaborate, the Bible describes four states of mind, each having unique characteristics. First, there is what might be called the ignorant mind. The possessor of this mind might well be endowed with a high IQ and more than one college degree. But because he or she doesn't know the Lord, Isaiah 55:8 applies, "God's ways are not our ways and his thoughts are not our thoughts." There is a great uncrossable divide between what this very intelligent person thinks and what in fact God says.

Ten times the Apostle Paul writes in his letters to the Corinthians: "Know you not?"... "know you not?" ... "know you not?" That was their problem, apparently. They were a bunch of not knowing, not understanding, not-having-a-clue Christians! And this wasn't without consequence! For Hosea 4:6 says, "My people are destroyed because of a lack of knowledge." That is, they keep walking into a buzz saw, experiencing problems they never needed to experience, all because they do not know the Word. The ignorant mindset is dangerously close to those who have only the natural capacities of their brain to rely on. A. B. Simpson said that "many of the most gifted minds of earth are dark and blind with respect to the knowledge of God. To them, he is but a name, a possible force, a remote and unreal fact."[7]

Second, there is what the book of James calls double-mindedness. This word, found only in James, was probably coined by James. It doesn't speak of the fraudulent man, but the irresolute man, alternately focusing on his thoughts and God's thoughts—first the Scripture and then reason, first the Spirit and then Satan.[8] Of such a person, the Bible says, "... let not that man suppose that he will receive anything of the Lord" (James 1:7). Now that's serious! The withdrawal of the Lord's blessings isn't in any way attributable to a lessening of his love. The real reason the blessings will stop is because double-mindedness sabotages faith, thereby relegating God to the sidelines. In this way, double-mindedness brings confusion and chaos.[9] For soon the questions are asked: Where is God? Why isn't he helping me? Why are my circumstances getting worse?

A third mindset is what might be called weak-mindedness. This describes Christians who do possess the right information; yet, this knowledge does very little for them, except perhaps to make them feel guilty. So why doesn't that husband do better with his wife, and why don't those people do better with their houses, and why aren't you doing better with God's Word? The phenomenon of people regularly coming to church, hearing all these well-prepared, life-related sermons but seeing so little difference in their own lives is referred to in the Bible as "letter and death" (II Corinthians 3:6). For these people, it's all words—words they understand, words that may even bring conviction, but words that aren't doing them any good.

One wonders how the Word of God could have so little effect. After all, God spoke only a handful of sentences and the whole world was created! Indeed, according to Jesus, the Word has the ability to feed our spirit and empower our life (John 6:63). So, since there is nothing wrong with the seed (the Word), the problem has to be with the soil (our heart). It is this problem that chronically plagues the weak-minded.

The fourth mindset belongs to the strong-minded. This describes people for whom truth has become not just information, but revelation. Not just an explanation, but an explosion. Not just facts, but a very formidable force! Instead of having a back-burner awareness of the Word—dim, hazy, and vague—the Word releases a charged-up power that penetrates and propels.

G. D. Watson said of this mindset, "It readily detects truth from error, not by a slow process of reasoning, but by a heavenly instinct, a Holy Ghost intuition which hits the mark more accurately than theological argument."[10] Those in this state of mind know how to live by the Word (Matthew 4:4) and how to let the Word richly dwell in them (John 15:7; Colossians 3:16). For this to occur, A. B. Simpson said:

> We must recognize that our natural mind is wrong and must be laid wholly down, and we

receive the mind of Christ instead, to think in us God's thoughts after God. So that our first experience is not the correcting of our thoughts, but the entire surrender of our mental being to the Lord Jesus Christ, to be crucified with him.[11]

Parenthetically, it should be noted that the parallels between Ephesians 5 and Colossians 3 are striking. Both chapters describe the superabundant life, relating this level of living to the most important dimensions of life in the same sequence: worship, marriage, parenting, and employment. Of note, the Ephesians passage begins with the command to be filled with the Spirit, while the Colossians passage, also written by Paul, begins with the command for God's Word to dwell in us richly. We need both, obviously—an ongoing infilling of the Holy Spirit and an ongoing indwelling of God's Word (see Appendix B).

Adding commentary to this point, A. B. Simpson explained:

> There is a way of coming to God occasionally for direction in great crisis, and then doing the best you can on ordinary occasions. But it is possible to have our whole life so possessed by the Holy Spirit that our very thoughts and intuitions will come to us in quietness and simplicity, with the consciousness that they have been touched by his thought and illumined by his light, that we are walking continually with our Father, and receiving constantly the testimony that we please God.[12]

A. W. Tozer said of such a way of thinking, "... there is scarcely anything on earth more beautiful than a Spirit-filled mind, certainly nothing more wonderful than an alert and eager mind made incandescent by the presence of the indwelling Christ."[13] The closer we are to our living Lord, the greater the opportunity for him to instill his thoughts into our minds. We must learn to expect this, as we avail ourselves to the anointing that teaches us. And because initial instruction for living this way is provided in the Old Testament, we would do well to reacquaint ourselves with this instruction.

The Procedure

Joshua was a man with whom most of us could easily identify. Unlike the legendary Moses and the charismatic Caleb, Joshua seemed less likely to inspire people. So one can only imagine the pressure Joshua was under! He was being charged to lead a nomadic nation of more than two-million people—people who weren't at all reticent about sharing their opinions! Had I been in Joshua's shoes at the time these people pledged that they would follow their new leader just as they had followed Moses, I would have quit! Leading a murmuring multitude like them was no enviable task!

Perhaps you find yourself in circumstances right now that are intimidating to you. What you don't need is an esoteric philosophy or some floating-out-of-the-real-world poetry. But what you do need is something that is going to work! In response to this need—for Joshua in his day, and for you today—the Lord put forward this remarkable strategy for strong-minded belief.

First, God told Joshua to meditate on his Word day and night. This assignment never necessitated a night-and-day Scripture study. The word "meditate" carries with it the idea of a cow chewing its cud. Just as a cow will repeatedly digest its food, so are we to repeatedly digest the implications of God's Word for our life. Casting a vision for such Spirit-assisted, Scripture-supported thinking, A. W. Tozer offered these expansive thoughts.

> I think that pure thinking will do more to educate a man than any other activity he can engage in. To afford sympathetic entertainment to abstract ideas, to let one idea beget another, and that another, till the mind teems with them, to compare one idea with another, to weigh, to consider, evaluate, approve, reject, correct, refine;

> to join thought with thought like an architect till a noble edifice has been created within the mind; to travel back in imagination to the beginning of the creation and then to leap swiftly forward to the end of time; to bound upward through illimitable space and downward into the nucleus of an atom; and all this without so much as moving our chair or opening our eyes—this is to soar above all the lower creation and to come near the angels of God.[14]

In undertaking this kind of thinking, this kind of meditation, it is essential to get past facts and into truth, because Jesus never said that the facts will set us free. We can have notebooks of facts stacked all the way to the ceiling—and still nothing much will change! Edward Hastings observed that "facts may lie in the mind as infertile as marbles in a boy's pocket."[15] And that's why that husband went back to his newspaper, and why we go back to things we know are not right. An assemblage of facts, even biblical facts, simply isn't enough. Truth involves processing and personalizing biblical facts for "right-now" living.

Discarding wrong ideas from our memory bank and reprogramming our thinking from Scripture is a good thing. But we can do all that and still be bogged down in the muck and mire of slow growth. So what more must be done? Meditate! Take that new fact and bathe it in prayer. Ask God to make it real to you and to connect this new fact to the area of your life that needs it the most. Then ask the Lord to show you how to implement the needed stages for biblical change and to empower each step with strength far beyond your own.

If we did these things, do we think God would honor it? Might he show us what we never would have discovered on our own? Indeed, he would! All during the day, and even late at night, his Spirit would bring to mind certain revelations that our intellectual prowess never would have generated (see Appendix C).

Perhaps there is an area in your life which you know you should change, and you want to change, but the years are going by and so far there isn't much progress. Well, there's a reason for this! Romans 12:2 says, "... do not be conformed to this world ...." That is, don't adopt their values, vision, methods, and goals—which to a large extent, perhaps, you have been doing. So this verse continues by saying, "... but be transformed by the renewing of your mind."

The word "transformed" means to change. The kind of change referenced here is a metamorphosis, such as that which occurs whenever a caterpillar becomes a butterfly. What a fantastic word picture this is! Whenever we see a caterpillar inching along, there is nothing in what we see that would ever predict a soaring work of art like a butterfly! Without prior knowledge, no one would ever guess that one would turn into the other! And similarly, once there is a renewing of the mind, changes just as marvelous will transact.

The Greek word for "renewing" in this passage has two meanings. One meaning is to update, to make current, to get rid of contaminating, erroneous thoughts. The other meaning is to charge up, to release power, to transform with a revolutionary impact. Now, since the only truth that sets free is the truth that breaks out of the realm of opinions and begins to operate with God's power, we would do well to focus on how this can happen. Remember, just finding the right theological bins to deposit scriptural knowledge falls far short of having our minds renewed.[16] Yet, many Christian institutions do little more than that in the way they teach. Protesting this approach, A. W. Tozer wrote:

> It is not what a church believes that matters so much as what that church believes enough to emphasize. It is not what a preacher will admit theologically when you pin him down and make him talk; it is what he believes with sufficient urgency to make it a living, constant part of his message.
>
> The problem with much that passes for orthodoxy in this day is not what they believe or even what they do not believe. It is what they believe enough

> to emphasize. I do not suppose that there is any gospel church but what would say, "We believe that, and we hold that as a part of our creed too." All well and good, but do they believe it enough to lay the emphasis there, to strike it and detonate it and set it off until it explodes into Christian faith and Christian living? That is what matters.[17]

Beliefs lying dormant in the brain, or in some file to document its existence, accomplish nothing. There are churches that say they believe in the filling of the Spirit, and in God's available power to live a holy life, and in the absolute necessity for letting the new nature control. And yet people sit in those churches for one year, two years, and longer and never hear a message on any of those beliefs. So what kind of a belief is that?

The belief that matters, the belief that gets the job done, isn't just catalogued; it's confessed with one's lips and confirmed with one's life. Remember: Renewing one's mind means more than data-shuffling; its real purpose, Scripture says, is, "... that you may prove what is that good and acceptable and perfect will of God." The word "prove" means to live it, to experience it! And that would be all right, wouldn't it?—to actually *experience* for yourself what this Word is talking about!

The Greek word for "acceptable" means well-pleasing. After delineating the meaning of certain words in this verse, would you agree that a pleasant, pleasing, perfect life is better than the one you are presently living? What makes this life possible, remember, is getting the mind renewed.[18] And the first step for getting this done is to meditate God's Word.

A very important aspect of meditating the Word is to image it. In Deuteronomy 6:8 God told his people to keep the Word in front of their eyes. In saying this, God never meant for these people to do what in fact some of them did—hang a bird-cage like contraption from their head gear and stick some scripture verses in it.

The "eyes" in this verse stand for the imagination. Because the pictures we have on our mental screen are much more powerful than intellectual assent, God knows that Scripture-sculpted pictures need to flash in our brains with neon brightness.

Let me give an example. In Deuteronomy 1:8, God said he would give what came to be known as "the Promise Land" to Israel. Since this word came from God, it had to be true. Still and all, at this stage it was just a word—a word that was eventually overcome, disastrously, by a picture.

In Numbers 14:12, we find twelve men crossing the River Jordan to spy out the Promise Land. Upon their return, ten of them said, "There's no way that land is going to be ours—there are giants in the land!" Well, God knew all about those giants, and not one of these giants, or even all of them combined, posed any problem to him! What these ten men said next, though, predicted the nation's eventual disobedience. To the man, each said we were in our own sight as grasshoppers, even as we were in their sight. Do you see a problem here? By adopting a perspective that agreed with the enemy's perspective, a picture flashed onto their mental screen that completely cancelled what God had said.

It is for this reason that God said in Ephesians 1:18 that the *eyes* of our understanding must be enlightened. Our ears and brain are never enough, because one picture from the enemy can dislodge what we heard the preacher say and what logic insists is true. For this reason, we need Scripture-sculpted pictures displayed on our mental screen. You may question your ability to produce such pictures, thinking this is only possible for certain "artsy" types. But in commenting on the Colossians directive to set our minds on things above, Bill Gillham offered helpful advice.

> "Setting your mind" *must* be attainable or God wouldn't command you to do it. In fact, you do it every day. Let me illustrate. Imagine you are walking down a gravel road in Arkansas. Put a cool creek bubbling beside the road. Hear the water gurgling? Let's make it an early morning in the month of May. Put a red bird in a tree, and have him singing. Imagine a light ground mist on the meadow across the road. Now, put a couple of

> cows in the pasture. See how easily you can choose to let your mind get caught up in this scene?
>
> Now let's change the imagery. I want you to set your mind on eating a hamburger at your favorite burger restaurant. It needs just a tad more seasoning. Put some on it. Now take another bite. Aw, that's better. Take a swig of your favorite beverage. Let's make it a really hot summer day and you're dying for a drink. Feel it going down? Um, so refreshing.
>
> Change the scene again. Set your mind on driving your car down the freeway. Let's make it night and you're out in the country. A truck is stalled on the shoulder ahead. See the flares? Smell the diesel fumes as you whiz by? You constantly set your mind, don't you? It's a daily practice.[19]

Perhaps your problem involves some pictures in constant reruns which you don't know how to stop! Granted, the mind doesn't have the delete button that a computer has, but this isn't an insurmountable problem. Dr. Gillham asks, "... by what process did you forget your algebra? Did you try to "overcome" it by attacking it, or did you simply "set your mind" on something else and the forgetting took care of itself?"[20]

The way to cast down imaginations is to replace them! Instead of seeing those giants having a romping, stomping good time at their expense, the spies could have imagined another scene: in one corner, the giants; and in the other corner, God! Now, let me appeal to your sense of realism with this question: Would any odds-maker have given those giants any chance at all? Nope. Not a chance!

Back to our question: How do we get our minds rightly programmed and greatly empowered? The first step is to meditate God's Word, which includes visualizing the particulars of your circumstances in a scripturally consistent way. The second step involved speaking the word. The

Hebrew word for "meditate" includes the idea of muttering. Not the muttering of a mantra as New Age proponents recommend, and certainly not peppering people with scripture verses, as some pompous, pious people are prone to do. This command to speak the Word also doesn't mean chapter-and-versing people so that Bible verses almost appear on our teeth.

Speaking the word is simply God's way of increasing the Word's impact upon our soul. God has made us in such a way that whenever our ears hear our voice speak, this transmission will impact every nerve system in our body.

It is significant that before David took on the giant Goliath, he spoke the outcome five times! To his brothers, to the king, to Goliath, to himself—over and over again David said in advance exactly what he was going to do. And you should know this wasn't just a way of "psyching himself up" like braggadocio wrestlers are prone to do. Something more principled was at work, a principle even Jesus embraced when he instructed us to speak to the mountain.

The mountain stands for those seemingly impossible problems so entrenched they're not budging! But Jesus said if we will speak to that mountain in belief, we will have whatever we will say. Remember, this wasn't some weird televangelist who said this—these words came from Jesus!

Hebrews 4:12 declares, "For the Word of God is living and powerful and sharper than any two edged sword, piercing even to the division of soul and spirit and of the joints and marrow, and as a discerner of the thoughts and intents of the heart." The literal rendering of the term "two edged sword" is two mouthed sword. Interestingly, the book of Revelation portrays Jesus with a sword coming out of his mouth. This strange and peculiar picture further emphasizes the importance of the Word being in our mouth.

Actually, one side of the sword represents the Word coming from God's mouth; the other side represents the Word coming out of our own mouth. An example of this is given in Hebrews 13:5 where we read, "For he himself has said ...."And then there's a quotation from Scripture, which the next verse follow up with these words, "So we may boldly say ...." The point being if we'll just boldly say what God has already said (see II Corinthians 4:13) the following benefits will be ours.

First, we're told that this two-mouthed sword will pierce our inner life to the extent of dividing the soul from the spirit. The submerging of the spirit into the soul, remember, was one of the most disastrous results of the fall. The fall left the kin of Adam trying to relate to God through their soulish capacities—their mind, will, and emotions—which very much limited the relationship. It is only when the spirit is pried loose from the soul's grasp that the spirit can then govern the soul.

In weighing the validity of any thought, we must first determine its origin. Did this thought come from our spirit, where the instilled wisdom of God resides? Or did it come from our soul, where natural thinking often has free reign? Hebrews 4:12 says the Word is able to divide soul and spirit, which it must do if we are to think right. Due to the fact temptation can infiltrate our thought world and thus produce false guilt, A. B. Simpson offered this insight.

> ... temptation has power to penetrate our inmost being with thoughts and feelings that seem to be our own, but are really the instigations of the evil one. *We wrestle with principalities and powers.* That is to say, they twine themselves around us as wrestlers do about the limbs of their opponents, until they seem to be a part of ourselves.[21]

The Accuser will weaken us in this battle of the mind, if we fail to distinguish between the proximity of these thoughts and the origin of these thoughts. That these thoughts blitzed in and rapidly cycled through doesn't mean that we are now guilty and thus in the grasp of Satan.

When Hebrews 4:12 mentions the thoughts and intents of the heart, it thus indicates the depths that must be negotiated for spirit-control to occur. Psychiatrists say that the greatest part of our being exists in the unconscious realm. Although this is untrue,[22] there are, no doubt, many ideations rambling around in the basement of our soul! The big problem, though, is access: How can we make contact with these very powerful forces? Much has been tried—talk, pictures, dreams, hypnosis, medication—without much success! Here, though, we are told that the Word of God can shoot right through layers and layers of rationalizations and pretense and ever so surgically expose the problem before then ministering to it (see Appendix A).

This ministry is further suggested by the reference to joints and marrow. More than once in the Psalms we find David expressing the impact of sin or sorrow on his bones. In Psalm 6 he says: "... my bones are troubled. My soul also is greatly troubled ..." (2b; 3a). This is a statement of sorrow. In Psalm 31:10 he says, "... My strength fails because of my iniquity and my bones waste away." This is a statement related to sin. Certainly, from what science is disclosing about the impact of grief or guilt on our body, we may conclude that these many references to the bones in Scripture may not be altogether metaphorical.

On the positive side, we see a ministry to the body in these Davidic words, "And my soul shall be joyful in the Lord: It shall rejoice in his salvation. All my bones shall say, "Lord, who is like you ..." (Psalm 35:9-10a). Of those who fear the Lord and depart from evil, Proverbs 3:8 says that it will be marrow (or strength) to their bones. If, as commonly supported, most illnesses today are psychosomatic (that is, caused by destructive forces of the soul), then this benefit of the spoken Word to our body is much needed, indeed.

The third step God gave Joshua was expressed in the word "Do"—"... Do *all* that I have written" (Joshua 1:8). In other words, there's to be no selective obedience. We shouldn't find ourselves equipoised between God and Satan, constantly surveying options and negotiating for a better deal. Instead—having heard the Word, meditated the Word, visualized the Word, and spoken the Word—there should almost be an unstoppable momentum building inside, a cerebral combustion just raring to go!

Do you recall how James put it—be doers of the Word and not hearers of the Word only, thereby deceiving yourselves? What can happen, according to James, is this: If there's an increasing gap between what we know and what we grow, we'll pretty soon forget who we are, just like that man who, after shaving in the morning, couldn't remember what he looks like.

This is really dangerous, because the disconnect between what the Word says and how we actually live can reduce all this talk about the new nature to just that—talk! To "do" the Word is essential, if the Word is going to release its transforming benefits. The Word itself will not be understood, even conceptually, unless a demonstrated obedience precedes the search. For this reason Athanasius, the fourth-century bishop of Alexandria, wrote: "He that would comprehend the mind of those who speak of God needs begin washing and cleansing his soul."

He said this because the pure milk of the Word (I Peter 2:1-2) is given with understanding to those who will cultivate purity in their own lives. However, that disposition of soul content with only the Word heard, need not think that anything worthy of God is likely to emerge from that practice.

Now, let's return to our friend who was more tuned in to his newspaper than he was to his wife. He really got a word from the Lord, didn't he? He might not have received it while reading his Bible, but when his wife said what she did, he knew God was involved with that. So how different do you suppose it would have been for this man had he taken the steps we have just identified?

What if he had asked God to make this insight about not being attentive to his wife more real to him? What if he had asked God to reveal all the contributing factors to this neglect, and to reveal also what he must now do to strategically overcome these? And what if he then pictured a successful outcome for this strategy and kept speaking in released faith the certainty of its accomplishment? Do you think this would have worked? Do you think this man would have finally gotten past wishful thinking and good intentions into a lasting, God-glorifying change?

The mind God has given the new creature in Christ has an orientation and capacity that are immensely important for daily living. Take the issue of relational conflict. Due to the new nature inside us, these conflicts can be processed in a way far superior than that processed by natural thinking.

The new nature, attractive when accessed and harmonious when activated, makes a huge difference.

Euodia and Syntyche, two women in the Philippi church, fell into a dispute. Paul's counsel to these women, "be of the same mind in the Lord," is not religious verbiage that should be easily dismissed. James S. Stewart got to the heart of what Paul was saying by pointing out that the words "in the Lord must be given full weight."

> It is as though he said to those two Christians who had unhappily become estranged, "Remember your common union with Christ. Remember that it is not in two different spheres that your spirits are living; the two spheres coincide, there is but one, and it is Christ. Realize that and act on it and your present differences will vanish. *In the Lord* you will agree."[23]

There is a way of thinking, embedded in the new nature, that should become operative in our relationships. In fact, any advice that bypasses the new mind believers have in the Lord is diminished in its counsel and lacking in power. Yet, much advice dispensed by pastors and counselors alike is functionally isolated from the new nature and is therefore diminished in its ability to help.

At issue is not only the substance of the new mind (its unique perspective) but also the spirit of the new mind (its supernatural functioning). G. D. Watson helped us understand this point when he wrote:

> It is a blessed proof of union with God to have the mind move promptly with the Holy Spirit, to instinctively not only take sides with God but to act with God's disposition and charity. To have all the mental faculties act under the power of a kind, gentle spirit, to put the best construction on things, to make generous allowances for others which we dare not make for ourselves, to thoughtfully take the unselfish side, to intentionally look at things through God ....[24]

It is this spirit that will bring down walls in a way that correct insight might never do. And who can deny that there are walls that need to come down—and that right quickly? Scripture tells us that the walls of Jericho—ninety feet high, thirty feet wide—tumbled down *suddenly*.

Applying this story to our life, we can anticipate the same result in some of our relationships. David Needham said, "Yes, the fortresses are real and mighty. But you will find yourself singing as you march around them when God is the biggest thing on your mind."[25] Your problems, your failings, just like those Jericho walls, *are* going to come down!

To say this wall-crumbling dynamic may occur suddenly is not to say it will occur immediately. Remember, the walls didn't fall after the first trip around them. After many days and many trips, the walls still stood, without a hint of any weakening.

Remember also that the followers of Joshua didn't run around the wall each day, they walked. G. D. Watson observed that "one of the lessons we learn as we more and more become intimately acquainted with God is the celestial art of walking slow."[26] Not in the mind-numbing way of routine, but with expectant hearts that victory is coming soon enough, even if God has to intervene directly and dramatically.

Turning our attention to God, and tuning our mind to the channel where his voice is heard, is critical to new nature manifestations. Stephen Charnock, the seventeenth-century Puritan preacher, spoke of how the "... new birth is necessary in every part of the soul. There is not a faculty but is corrupted, and therefore not a faculty but must be restored."[27] This restoration, enabled by new nature capacities, is possible not only for the mind, but, as we shall see next, also for the emotions and the will.

Reflection Questions

1. Of the four mindsets described in this chapter, which one best describes you?

2. List the procedures discussed in this chapter for securing strong-minded belief that you are practicing, then list the ones you are not practicing.

3. Which procedure do you want to focus on first in your quest for strong-minded belief?

Chapter 14

The Protected Heart

Most of us can identify with the words of the old spiritual, "Sometimes I'm Up; Sometimes I'm Down." Whether we are a happy-go-lucky sanguine or a cold, calculating choleric, we know what it is to experience intrusive, intimidating emotions. We may wake up in the morning with some buoyancy in our step and a lilt in our voice, eager and glad to greet the day. And for a while we may glide through the day, enjoying warm friendships, successful work, and the high esteem of others, when suddenly—it happens! With little or no warning, we will nosedive from euphoric "highs" to lethargic "lows"—not because we are bipolar, but because of an emotional hijacking.

The source of this attack may be situational, soulish, or satanic. Perhaps an unexpected problem, serious and distressful, surfaced at work. Or perhaps something out of our childhood (which is known to be a blackmailer) made demands we couldn't easily deal with. Or perhaps, due to no fault of our own, we walked unintentionally into a war zone, becoming a target of the spiritual underworld. However it happened—it happened! Consequently, the question we found ourselves asking then, and aren't able to answer now, was this: Is there any way to stop these emotional "down" times?

Many people think these downward turn of emotions are inevitable. Erasmus of Rotterdam, said to be the last man in history who knew everything knowable, offered this discouraging assessment of emotion's influence:

> Jupiter has bestowed far more passion than reason—you could calculate the ratio as 24 to one. He set up two raging tyrants in opposition to Reason's solitary power: anger and lust. How far Reason can prevail against the combined force of these two the common life of man makes quite clear. Reason does the only thing she can and shouts herself hoarse, repeating formulas of virtues, while the other two bid her go hang herself, and are increasingly noisy and offensive, until at last their Ruler is exhausted, gives up, and surrenders.[1]

While these words from the pen of Luther's intellectual foe satirically exaggerate, they do underscore the substantial power emotions have. On the negative side, there can be disconsolate grief, raging anger, or even something as toxic as "the Green Monster" itself, jealousy. On the positive side, there can be a throw-all-care-to-the-winds festivity, the embrace of ecstatic romance, or a flow of tears released not by sorrow but by joy. Whether these emotions are positive or negative, they do, in their ascendancy, tend to rule.[2]

Although emotions are a rich and positive part of our new nature, there are emotions existing outside the new nature that challenge our peace. One of these emotions is fear. The dictionary lists ninety-six different phobias. There is acrophobia, the fear of heights; claustrophobia, the fear of closed places; pathophobia, the fear of disease; ergophobia, the fear of work; eruthophobia, the fear of blushing; and even phobophobia, which is the fear of all things. Fear is the main way the enemy accesses our heart, tempting us to respond with pity, panic, or worse.

Upon closer examination, it becomes clear that fear is really a distorted form of worship. Worship means to respect, to revere, to believe, to bow down. And isn't this what fear will do? It will get us to respect and revere what was never from God; and having believed it, it will get us to bow down to it. Actually, fear blasphemes God, implying that his Word can't be trusted and that his resources are inadequate.

Whether the emotion is fear or some other destructive emotion, it is clear that no permanent remedy can be found for these combatants through excursion or diversion. Instead, the problem must be faced head-on! But how can we do this in a way that will rescue us from the destructive, reverse what caused it, and release from our spirit the very peace we long to preside? Fortunately, Scripture does have a prescription for peace. And this is found in the fourth chapter of the book of Philippians.

Perpetual Praise

Whenever troublesome emotions attempt to muscle in, whether they are of paralyzing proportions or not, it is easy to focus first on their assailing assaults. Such an approach, however, makes us vulnerable to defeat; and this is exactly why Scripture counsels in the opposite direction, saying: "Rejoice, in the Lord always. Again I say, rejoice!" (Philippians 4:4).[3] Instead of moaning, "Why me? Why this? Why now?" God wants us to rivet our attention on him. This, you will recall, is the same advice given in the book of James: "... count it all joy when you fall into various trials" (James 1:2). The fact life has its ups and downs doesn't mean that our emotions have to follow the same pattern. They do not. Acknowledging the highs and lows of life, F. B. Meyer writes:

> Such is life. It is filled with sharply varied experiences. Now the Angel; then the coming of Esau. Now forty days on the brow of Sinai; then the golden calf. Now the Mount of Transfiguration; then the bitter cross. Now Patmos, with its visions; then the old gray rock and the common places of captivity and loneliness.[4]

As both the good and the bad cycle through our lives—at one moment circumstances that are bright; at another moment circumstances that will blight—it would be so easy to allow our emotions to follow suit: to soar or crash, to glide or hide, with each approach and outcome (see Appendix E).

But we can get off this emotional roller coaster if we will cultivate the holy habit of perpetual praise. At the very moment sadness presents, praise should be summoned to chase it away.

The Lord specifically stipulates this sequence in Scripture—rejoicing in God *before* reacting to the circumstances—because our response to what attacks us must involve, first, a confidence in the Lord and not a fear for ourselves. The word "joy," from which the word "rejoice" is derived, finds its source in the thought that no matter what the situation, God is willing and able! Didn't God say, "Call upon me in the day of trouble and I will deliver you"? And didn't he say that he "... is our refuge and strength, a very present help in trouble" (Psalm 46:1)? Well, then, how reliable of a refuge is he? And how great is his strength? Do you think that maybe, just maybe, the All-wise, Almighty God might have the resources to solve your problem? Then start rejoicing!

The second reason God wants us to rejoice is because praising will rout the devil from the scene. A. B. Simpson wrote, "Do not ever let the devil know that he has hurt you ... Always rejoice, always be cheerful. Under no circumstances get discouraged or be depressed."[5] Instead, let Satan be the one who gets discouraged!

Did you know that the heart that rejoices in God, even in the midst of adverse circumstances, discourages Satan? According to Scripture, there is a historical, and even prehistoric, reason for this. Lucifer had been the worship leader for heaven. But when he decided he wanted to receive what he had been giving (worship and praise), he was cast out of heaven in a nanosecond!

Centuries later, when Lucifer confronted Jesus in the wilderness, the cast away cherub brought this subject up again! In fact, he offered Jesus all the kingdoms of this world (which at that point were his to give), if only Jesus would fall down and worship him.

So why was Lucifer so determined in this pursuit? Here's why. Because, better than any one of us, Lucifer knew then, and knows now, that the worship of heaven is more valuable than everything this world has to offer! Think of it:

Lucifer had already lost heaven over this issue—and now he was willing to risk losing earth! Such persistence does lead more observant ones to ask: Are there not components in Lucifer's thinking superior to ours? For he saw the value of praise, and we don't; and he was willing to give up the world for what praise had to offer, and we aren't.

Well! Having been denied what he sought most, the devil now doesn't want to be anywhere around when true worship is being offered—for such a scene brings him too much pain! Of course, evil vacating the premises helps our cause, too, does it not? And this is one of the reasons God wants us to praise him.

The third reason God wants us to praise is because praise will shrink the target the devil is aiming at—self. Whenever our hearts are lifted in praise, and our minds are set in fervent worship, our preoccupation with self is displaced by an adoring awareness of the awesomeness of our God. This fits in with the biblical injunction to put on the garment of praise instead of the spirit of heaviness (Isaiah 61:3). Praise can blast that descending darkness back to the pit from where it came. Moreover, the praise that accomplishes this feat will at the same time isolate an easily influenced self. And that's good. For if deprived of the pampering it wants, self will be far more safe and sound, due to its diminished demand for attention.

A fourth reason God wants us to praise is because praise provides a tremendous boost to faith. In his book, *Victory in Christ*, Charles G. Trumbull says, "The secret of victory is not praying, but praising; not asking, but thanking."[6] The whiny prayer that has us telling God what the devil told us does no good at all! It is far better to return God's Word in thankful rejoicing, ever grateful that Word is not going to return void!

By repeating the command to rejoice in the Lord, and by then adding the word "always," we are made to know that this is such an important step we had better not be novices in our practice of it. Perpetual praise—indeed, a lifestyle of praise—will increase our effectiveness in faith, even as it enhances our joy. In the same way exercising faith builds our faith, practicing praise develops our capacity for joy. By acquiring a praise vocabulary, and a praise instinct, we didn't have before, we steady our emotional life.

Constant Control

The second step in Scripture's prescription for peace is also one which, had we offered our counsel, would have been omitted. Philippians 4:5 says, "Let your gentleness be known to all men. The Lord is at hand." In commenting on this verse, A. B. Simpson noted:

> The Greek word translated "gentleness" is difficult to turn into English, but the various meanings that have been given to it are all suggestive and helpful, and each has certain degrees of truth in it. The first of these is the Authorized Version, "moderation." This is the temperate spirit, the disciplined heart, the self-control which comes to a well-ordered mind ....[7]

This same word is also translated "gentleness," a word which Simpson describes as "the spirit of Christian refinement, free from harshness, rudeness, coarseness, unkindness, the spirit that is harmless as the dove and gentle as the soft breath of evening."[8] It may well be, however, as Simpson points out, that "the Syriac Version has probably given us the most striking translation of this word. It is the word 'sweetness.'"[9] This is a word that calls to mind the anointing, a sweet smelling perfume that makes lasting impressions on the soul.

Lord Chesterfield, said to be the greatest gentleman in Europe, spent a few days with Archbishop Fenelon, who was as sweet as he was saintly. Deciding not to extend this visit as long as he might have, Chesterfield remarked, "If I had stayed much longer I should have been charmed into accepting his religion."[10] Equally aware of this drawing power of an anointed sweetness, Charles Spurgeon told his students, "You are the salt of the earth, and, boys, the sugar, too." In this sense, an addiction to God's sweetness is really a good thing. Whenever it diffuses strife, disengages self, calms tension, and conveys the presence of God on the scene, this anointed sweetness brings glory to God. And isn't this a trait you want more prominently exhibited in your life?

We can now see that in citing this second step God was giving us the assignment to be a worthy witness to others. Moreover, in accepting this assignment, we are to exhibit moderation, gentleness, and sweetness—a complete controlling of our emotions that only God can enable. Thomas Goodwin underscored the gospel distinctive in this assignment, since we (in his words), "... not only moderate, keep in, and smother ... contrary passions, which was the highest lesson that philosophy and the Stoics, the best of philosophers, had taught ...."[11] but we do so in the context of a joy that ministers to others.

God wants others to see a positive testimony about his faithful watch care. But if we unravel, become unglued, unhinged, and emotionally "lose it," what does that say to others about God? That he can't be trusted? That he won't help us?

Often, it's not in our actions but in our reactions that we lose control. But if we had earlier accepted this assignment from the Lord, whereby he had made us aware people are watching us, maybe our response would have been better. Some people, it seems, simply indulge their emotions, and by doing so give impulse to a lack of discipline. Living sloppy, unbuttoned lives, they care only about themselves as they perpetually cut themselves slack to say whatever they want to say.

Memories of these indulged emotions can become a real stumbling block to non-Christians! For if the abundant life is so wonderful, they wonder, why couldn't this Christian do any better than that?

Had God only given the assignment to be moderate and gentle in this verse, this advice may not have been well received. Because we all know that whenever nerves are strained and emotions are challenged (as they certainly are during the day of trouble), this business of being gentle is a lot easier said than done. Notice carefully, though, the last words in this verse, "... the Lord is at hand." With these words in mind, imagine what may be going on in you at the precise moment a major fear strikes. You are perplexed, undone, and perhaps totally engulfed by a wave of panic.

Now, if with all that going on, you were to look at Jesus—what would you see in his face? Love! And what else would you see? An extraordinary calm! And why is it that he is this calm? Because he knows what to do! The exact buttons to push, the precise insights to give, the particular path that leads to victory, are well within the domain of his understanding!

So what if the Lord didn't know these things? What if he responded to your request for help by throwing his hands in the air as he nervously paced about, saying, "I don't know about *this*! Now, go over that again: How did you get yourself into this predicament? Who did what, when?"

Of course, no such confusion will ever be found in the Lord—but only and always a contagious confidence! So how would that make you feel? Kind of relieved that someone has this all figured out—and even better, that that someone is in *your* corner, so willing to help!

The promise of God's presence is frequently made in the Bible. But never is this promise made more forcibly than in Hebrews 13:5 where God said, "I will never leave you or forsake you." This is really a tame translation, because in the original language there are five negatives. What God actually said is, "I will never, never leave you; I will never, never, never forsake you." God's five negatives—a fivefold assurance of his continuing presence! The Lord *is* at hand!

We will access the presence of the Lord more effectively, however, if we follow the advice F. B. Meyer gave when he wrote. "Many people put their circumstances always in the innermost circle, next to their heart, and they put God outside, and look at him through their wants and circumstances." But it is precisely this arrangement that causes circumstances to loom large and God to seem so far away. The better arrangement, according to Meyer, is this:

> Put God between you and everything. Weary, storm-tossed heart, put Jesus between you and the crest of the wave. The envelope is useful to protect the letter it contains from being soiled or

> damaged. So, when man lives inside God he is protected, because enveloped. God is his environment, his wall of fire, his river and stream.[12]

And this environment seals from danger! Under this arrangement, you will notice, it is God nearer the heart and the circumstances that are farther away.

Fixed Faith

So you've given yourself to a season of praise, you've accepted the assignment to be a worthy witness—what next? The next step, given in verse six, is this: "Be anxious for nothing, but in everything by prayer and supplication, with thanksgiving, let your requests be made known to God." The absoluteness of the words "nothing" and "everything" practically leap from the page! These words are comprehensive and categorical. By the rigors of definition, then, they permit no exceptions, no matter how difficult the situation is.

Many people think that fear and worry are only weaknesses, but certainly not sins. However, if God tells us not to be anxious (in the Gospel of John we are expressly told not to have a troubled heart), but we get anxious anyway, that has to be a violation of his command and, hence, a behavior that constitutes sin. A. B. Simpson wrote, "Anxiety is as much forbidden as stealing. Worry is as wicked as worldliness."[13] This view certainly helps explain John Wesley's remark, "I would as soon swear as fret." Actually, each of these sins, in their unique and respective ways, slanders God.

You should notice also a positive side to this command, because if God tells us not to worry about a thing, then—because God never gives unworkable commands—this must mean that we really don't have to worry. Hudson Taylor finally learned how to live above worry, proving as he did so that the doubts others have about such a life are false, both in premise and conclusion. In a letter to his sister he said, "It is a wonderful thing to be really one with a risen and exalted

Savior ....” Elaborating on this newly discovered life, Taylor wrote:

> The sweetest part, if one may speak about one part being sweeter than another, is the rest which full identification with Christ brings. I am no longer anxious about anything, as I realize this: for he is able to carry out his will, and his will is mine.[14]

Can you imagine how good it would be to be totally insulated from worry?

When contemplating this commandment, be very clear on its scope: God didn’t say, “Don’t worry about the mild-to-moderate problems, but of course when the major ones come, worry can’t be helped.” He said to be anxious for *nothing*. The Spirit of God then counterbalanced this message by telling us to pray about *everything*—not just the major problems, while we handle the mild-to-moderate ones with our own resources. “Everything” includes finding that parking place, losing that weight, and discovering the extra time needed to get a certain task done. The point is, to turn every concern into a prayer request, because God wants every problem removed from our shoulders.

We know that in classic mythology the great Atlas could carry the world on his shoulders, but in daily life this is something we are expressly told not to do. Instead, we are to cast our cares upon the Lord (I Peter 5:7). Sometimes, though, in attempting to obey this verse, we manage to give our problems to God ... sort of ... kind of ... a little bit—not unlike the way a little boy will bring a toy needing fixing to his father. But because he never takes his little hands off, he prevents the father from fixing it!

The word “cast” suggests an alternative approach to the one that we, like this little boy, have been known to take. This word “cast” means to let go, to relinquish control, to cease our independent efforts. And whenever we do this, we will actually feel the burden leaving. A sense of relief, a spirit of calm will come upon us, at times lifting our soul with sensations of lightness and an aura of ease. In his biography of the prophet Jeremiah, F. B. Meyer said: "... when difficulties like Atlantic breakers threaten to engulf us—we must roll our anxieties from ourselves upon the blessed Lord, our burden-bearer, and leave them with him. The care ceases to be care when it is committed to him."[15]

In praying to the Lord this way, we are also told to make our request "with thanksgiving." This doesn't mean we're to pray our "need" list and then to even it all out we are also to pray our "thanks" list. Praying with thanksgiving really means we will release our faith, thanking God *in advance* for the results. We won't plead the desperateness of our situation and the devastating impact it's having on our life. Instead, we'll stand against all that by praying God's promise.

In this very significant respect, there's all the difference in the world between praying and praying in faith. To pray in faith means we will take seriously what God said to us in his Word, and refuse to lean on our own understanding.

To the depressed disciples walking the road to Emmaus, Jesus said, "O foolish ones, and slow of heart to believe in all that the prophets have spoken!" Do not these words surprise you? What a seemingly cruel comment to make to those who obviously loved him! Picture the scene in your mind's eye. These disciples are trudging along, so crushed in spirit and overwhelmed by grief that each step follows another with little thought given as they plod without purpose, making no attempt to break the grip of depression. At the time, that part of the brain responsible for muscle memory worked; whereas that part of the brain responsible for processing emotions didn't work.

There was a reason for their disconsolate grief! When Jesus died on that cross, the very foundations of their lives were jolted so violently residual tremors unnerved the deepest part of their soul! Given this criminal's death on the town's garbage heap, all that they had thought about this man, and the kingdom he talked about, must have been false.

So as they walked along, thinking their leader was in that tomb, sealed away and gone forever, they came upon this supposed stranger, who, unknown to them, was really the risen Lord himself. Soon after, responding to his query about the cause of their sorrow, they proceeded to tell their sad story.

Now one might think the Lord would have said in reply, "My, you really loved him, didn't you? How deep your affection—and loyal your soul!" *But that's not what he said*! Instead, Jesus lit into them with words of stinging rebuke, saying, "The way you're going about this is so foolish! All this depression is a total waste! Had you just believed the Scripture, you would have known why what happened had to occur, and why it wasn't going to end in death!"

To apply this same principle to ourselves, we would have to admit that there have been times in our lives when we also misread a situation. And for the same reason, too! Because we never allowed the Word of God to interpret what was really going on. Instead, being totally absorbed in our pain, we allowed ourselves to be mugged by the problem, before then allowing ourselves to be dragged at its chariot wheels—until finally, and not too mercifully, it dropped us off in a hideous heap! Such a needless experience this is! And it is one that could have been avoided, if only the Word had been permitted to govern our thoughts!

Sometimes, the adverse emotions we experience are owing to attacks on our character. During such times, we are made to feel unworthy, maybe even contemptible, like some despicable failure who deserves to be ostracized. Of course, the reason the "Accuser of the brethren" does this to us isn't because he's mean. He *is* mean! But his strategy has designs more far-reaching than that. Satan knows that if he can mess up our self-image, our ability to release faith will also be gone, since no faith launch is possible under the threatening clouds of condemnation. This is an established principle: Sin-consciousness will *always* distance us from God, and thus make faith impossible (I John 3:21, 22).

While people tortured in this way may think that they're just being honest when they acknowledge their sins, they are really being foolish. For instead of wallowing in their painful past and affixing each accusation to the way they see themselves now, they should put on "the breastplate of righteousness," which is designed to protect the heart from attacks like these. It is in this regard that Jessie Penn-

Lewis' admonition—"do not whip yourself with vain regret"—is exactly right.

How does the breastplate protect the believer? Well, Christians have both the *imputed* righteousness of Jesus (whereby they receive full credit for the perfect life he lived) and the *imparted* righteousness of Jesus (whereby all the perfected virtues of Jesus were put into their new nature). So, whenever the Accuser fires out condemning charges against us, these two types of righteousness should be used in our defense. Imputed righteousness deals with the sins of the past by reminding Satan that every one of these sins has already been paid for. Therefore, it makes no sense to bring this case up again, since every detail has been permanently expunged from the record.

What's more, for any sin repeated since then, we can avail ourself to the sprinkled blood and be made clean again. Remember, there is power in the blood—wonder working power! Jesus has already made us the very righteousness of God (II Corinthians 5:21), and therefore that, and that alone, is who we are! Since the new nature put inside us at the time we became a Christian is actually his nature, the enemy isn't going to be too successful in attacking that!

Moreover, perpetual sinning will stop, once we get a revelation of who we are by virtue of the Lord's imparted righteousness. To see ourselves as the righteousness of God will enable a character-stiffening response whenever temptation comes knocking on our door. And to obtain a fresh release of that righteousness, by an exercise of simple faith, will engender a more consistent obedience than we ever experienced before. And how encouraging that will be!

Prevailing Peace

The result of these first three steps is what Philippians 4:7 calls "the peace of God which surpasses all understanding." Dorothy Sayers is correct: Peace is something we will likely miss if we're always aiming at it. However, if we first focus on the Lord in praise, and then focus on his Word in faith, peace will emerge as the blessed by-product.

Once peace does come, that won't be the end of the story, however, because Satan is going to want to take our peace away![16] The main way he'll attempt to do this is by throwing his "fiery darts"—certain messages and images designed to disturb peace. Sometimes, Satan will send a rush of emotions our way. Whenever he does this, it's important to understand that under the torrent of these muddied and troubled waters is a message that must first be located and then processed. Like the psalmist, we must have the presence of mind to discover what's going on—"Why are you disquieted in me, oh, my soul?" (Psalm 42:5). Instead of being blitzed and blindsided by an onslaught of feelings, we are to think (and not just feel), as we ask ourselves, what is the message the enemy is trying to get through?

The query, in this context, should not be one of panic or perplexity, for the psalmist ruled that out when he addressed his soul in confidence, saying, "Await God for I shall yet praise him—the victory of my confidence—and my God." J. A. MacMillan, the nineteenth-century missionary and writer, explained what was really being said in this particular passage:

> God is here revealed not merely as the Deliverer of the soul of the psalmist. In the existing circumstances of spiritual oppression and physical depression, that would itself have been a splendid achievement of faith. Jehovah is represented in a larger way, as the Giver of victory to the countenance of the psalmist, so that his enemies fled before his face. The Lord had endued his servant with his own authority from on high so that, as he went forward in the name of God, opposing circumstances should give way and spiritual enemies would flee apace.[17]

This is the confidence that the psalmist fully anticipates to be honored by God. It is not unlike the confidence others have known. In his book, *The Authority of the Believer*, MacMillan wrote:

> It was said of George Mueller of Bristol, in his later years, that he bore himself like a prince of God. So confident had his faith become through the years of asking and receiving, so intimate was his communion with God from uncounted hours spent in audience with him, that his countenance and his whole bearing manifested the dignity of a member of the royal household of heaven.[18]

It is with confidence, then, that the psalmist initiates his inquiry. So as we in turn follow his lead, we should know at the outset that Satan isn't likely to flash his messages in the sky, for the obvious reason he doesn't want these messages subjected to scrutiny. Instead, he'll try to smuggle his messages in through an emotional rush, or embed them in the particulars of a situation, or sneak them in through a dream, or through supposedly random thoughts. Whatever the mode of these messages, the desired outcome (from his perspective) will follow this sequence: Bad news comes, emotions get hooked, the mind goes out of gear, the Bible is set aside, and an unsanctified will is turned loose to react.

None of this will happen, though, if we will also use another part of the armor called the shield of faith. Using the shield of faith involves discerning the subtle and deceptive message Satan is sending. Instead of making no attempt to identify it, to interpret it, to check out its veracity, we should activate our spiritually informed mind in response to this attack. This is one of the reasons we read our Bibles and receive teachings from others—so we can be better prepared when temptations come against us!

So, again, instead of uncritically accepting Satan's messages, we should first determine what exactly he is saying, and then proceed to block it and defense it with what the Bible says on this subject. Something as simple as this will quench all the fiery darts of the devil. *But* we have to get our shield up, and to keep our helmet on!

Speaking in much the same way, Philippians 4:8 presents certain categories of thought—thoughts that are related to love, justice, purity, and good reports, etc.—by which we must filter all messages attempting to gain entrance into our minds. We must effectively employ this grid, because to a large degree the battle is going to be won or lost in our thought world.

What is also critical to the prevailing of our peace is a functioning biblical fellowship. In Philippians 4:9 the Apostle Paul says, "The things you learned and received and heard and saw in me, these do, and the God of peace will be with you." Here, Paul was presenting himself as a mature, flesh-and-blood example. "You follow me," he was saying, "as I follow the Lord."

How important it is to be under the wing of people who not only know the scriptural principles but also admirably put them to work in their own lives. God's designed program of biblical fellowship, set forth in those 58 "one another" statements, is exceedingly important for our protection. In the company of other believers, we are to share our inner lives within the context of God's Word and in the energy of the Holy Spirit. The German theologian, Dietrich Bonhoffer, said this:

> Sin demands to have a man by himself. It withdraws him from the community. The more isolated a person is, the more destructive will be the power of sin over him, and the more deeply involved he becomes involved in it, the more disastrous is his isolation.[19]

According to the Bible, this "Lone Ranger" Christianity, so popular today, is unbiblical. Why, even the Lone Ranger had Tonto!

Isn't it good, that in such a simple, practical way the Lord has given us his prescription for peace? Emotions are certainly powerful. Potentially, at any given moment, they can instantly overwhelm us; or, moving with subtlety and stealth, they can seep into the deepest part of our being and steadily inflict life-robbing damage—for decades!

It is commonly supposed that emotions come and go and that there's nothing much we can do about it. But this isn't true. The Bible provides an effective strategy for protecting our emotions. By implementing these principles identified in Philippians, chapter 4, our hearts will be protected from all the disturbances of peace. Thus, the new nature within us, which includes peace, can be released, enabling us to enjoy life the way God fully intended.

Reflection Questions

1. What is the most frequent threat to your peace? And what is the greatest threat to your peace?

2. Of the five processes for securing peace discussed in this chapter, which one have you exercised the most, and which one have you exercised the least?

3. Implement the peace strategy discussed in this chapter for one troublesome area of your life and report the results to your group.

Chapter 15

The Surrendered Will

The relationship between the spirit and the soul may well find an analogy in the relationship between a car's engine and its battery. The engine, like our spirit, is the source of power; the battery, like our soul, transmits that power. However, just as no car can go with only a battery; so also no believer can grow with only a soul. But, of course, the devil knows all that. And he also knows that the spirit, the new nature in man, is incapable of being harmed; so he focuses his attacks instead on the soul.[1]

Thus far, in our attempt to defend the soul from these attacks, we have examined Scripture's counterstrategies for our mind and for our emotions. What must now claim our attention is Scripture's counterstrategy for the will.

There are three occupants in every man's soul. First, there is reason. Reason gathers information, processes ideas, provides linkage to other ideas, elects to include and assimilate, or exclude and dispatch, assigns proportion and priority, specifies role and goal, and when appropriate draws conclusions, determines methods, and formulates strategies.

Second, there is emotion. Emotion reacts to positive or negative situations with a release or withdrawal of feelings. In terms of their internal impact, these emotions can either motivate or shut down. And in terms of their external impact, they can either magnetize or repel.

Third, there is the ultimate decision-maker, the will. The will determines the course of action one takes. It is for this reason that George MacDonald said, "The highest in man is neither his intellect, nor his imagination, nor his reason; all are inferior to his will, and indeed, in a grand way, dependent upon it."[2] With agreement, A. B. Simpson made this assertion:

> The will in man is the point of contact through which God acts upon us, and, like the helm and engine of the vessel, it is the directing and impelling power in life. Without a strong purpose, faith is impossible. They greatly err who look for its sphere in the emotions. Its seat is in the will.[3]

According to Andrew Murray, "The will is the royal faculty of the soul; it rules over the whole man."[4] What it comes down to is this: We can know and know and know. And we can feel and feel and feel. But if our will is on the loose, we are in real danger! The will given to us is both marvelous and awesome: marvelous, in that if harnessed it can accomplish great and wonderful things; awesome, in that if on the loose it can be like giving us enough rope with which to hang ourselves.

When assessing the power of the will, we would do well to remember just how the world got into this colossal mess. It all began when the one who eventually brought evil to this planet said "I will" five times (Isaiah 14:13, 14). This steeled determination of an unsanctified will brought catastrophic ruin to the world. For this reason, then, God wants our will surrendered—totally, unconditionally, surrendered! To become a Christian is to acknowledge at the outset that Jesus alone is the ultimate decision-maker of our lives.

The Parameters of the Will

Properly understood, our will, even when brought into alignment with God's assignment, is still critical to the way we live. Horatius Bonar said that the cross makes us decided men. It brings both our hearts and our wills to the side of God.[5] At the cross of Jesus the hard heart breaks and the resistant will yields, thus changing forever not only the direction of our will (toward godly desires, not carnal desires) but also the location of our will (under God's management, and not self's management). Once we become a Christian, our will should never again be equipoised between good and evil, or between self and God, as it awaits activation—perhaps with the participation of God, or perhaps without it—on a case-by-case basis.

If we accept what Jesus did for us on Calvary's cross, we are no longer our own; we have been bought by Jesus (I Corinthians 6:19-20). The Bible just couldn't be clearer on this point, as it insists on lordship (Romans 10:9), servanthood (I Peter 2:15, 16), and the crucifixion of self (Luke 9:22, 23). II Corinthians 5:15 puts it this way, "And he died for all, that those who live should live no longer for themselves, but for him who died for them and rose again." Despite these clear and simple words, many within the church *are* living for themselves—and then, of all things, they're asking God to help them!

I Peter 4:2 addresses this issue with forceful clarity. Speaking of the believer, it says, "... that he no longer should live the rest of his time in the flesh for the lust of men, but for the will of God." Whenever we see the words "lust" and "flesh" in the same verse, we are prone to conjure up images of seedy porno shops or some other twisted and forbidden pleasure. But that is hardly the focus of this verse. What this verse is addressing are desires that operate in the natural world, the very desires the believer was born with and even now is struggling against. These desires don't have to be a scandal to society before they qualify as an offense to God, or as a source of harm to us. At issue, is the degree they dictate the choices we make. There can be no rival to God.

Since the enemy to our soul, the flesh, is extremely formidable, there must be a clear decision on our part, not unlike the one Colonel Travis required at the Alamo. Drawing a line in the sand, Travis told his outnumbered troops that they could either flee or fight. Those willing to fight, he said, should step over the line. All others, the Colonel said, were free to make a run for it. Knowing the enemy is real, the battle is intense, and that victory can never come unless our will is exercised in whole-hearted commitment, Peter also called on believers to take a stand. As Ruth Paxson put it in her book, *Life on the Highest Plane*:

> The only cure for self-will is a deliberate, determined choice to do God's will in all things, at all times, at all costs. It is to have one's heart fixed upon the doing of God's will as the rule for daily life and to permit no exceptions to this rule.[6]

The selective obedience that wants to negotiate with God, or to defer the decision to obey him until a full assessment of the situation has been made, will invariably result in a tyrant self that can never be trusted. Therefore, the far-sighted apostle called for a more resolute decision. A. B. Simpson explained why Peter did so by pointing out what will happen to us if our obedience isn't full and immediate:

> One moment's hesitation to obey, one act of willful disobedience, will plunge us into darkness, cause withdrawal of his [God's] conscience presence from the heart, and leave the soul disarmed and exposed to temptation and sin. Those who have become wholly sanctified have given up the right of self-will and disobedience forever.[7]

Even in the Old Testament, God told Joshua to do *all* that is written in the book and not to turn from it to the right or to the left. The standard set forth that day required complete compliance and no compromise. Freedom of choice? Not in God's army! The will, even then, had to be surrendered! Summing up this point, Jessie Penn-Lewis wrote, "Our will is all that we really have to give to our blessed Lord."[8]

Unfortunately, today's church isn't so keen on doing what Peter did, preferring instead to muffle the call to lordship so as not to incite undue alarm in the heart of an evangelistic prospect. This is a huge mistake, really—and one that we have no right to make. Our job as messengers of God is to convey the Lord's message and not to edit it. Augustine stressed this point well when he said, "If you believe what you like in the Gospel, and reject what you don't like, it is not the Gospel you believe, but yourself."

Marketers of church growth are sensitive about making the gospel relevant to culture, but have displayed an appalling insensitivity to Scripture. It is with justification that Os Guinness complained, "In the past the church used to cry '*Sola Scriptura*,' nowadays all we cry is '*Sola Cultura*'." This business of adapting the gospel to the modern lifestyle, emphasizing the positive while highlighting how the Lord wants to make the lost person happy, will in the end backfire.

Remember: What the church wins them *with* is what the church will win them *to*! If converts respond to only half a message, then that's what they'll bring into the church—a petulant, at times preposterous desire for God to do their bidding! In this regard, Kierkegaard had it right: "One must either resolutely deny, combat, and persecute Christianity; or one must really live it. What lies in between is the cult of genius and deceit."

Churches that minimize the call to lordship while stimulating the atmosphere with emotion, present Christ with a lot of fervor and only a little truth. It is predictable that this kind of evangelism yields poor results. As Tozer put it, "There are some who get converted on enthusiasm and backslide on principle."[9] This must stop. Instead of minimizing lordship, or postponing it to another day which for some reason never comes, we must at the very beginning set it forth clearly. Let the sifting be done at noon day where no confusion need exist. That silly sovereign, self, must be slain! He who would wage a civil war inside us must come to terms! For how can we declare victory, if nothing happened at our spiritual Appomattox?

Even when the will is surrendered, the depth of that decision isn't entirely known to the person who offered this surrender. Although truly sincere in the original offer, the heart may later move subtly in a different direction. This is why Jessie Penn-Lewis writes: "Surrender is not talk. There is a fashion of talking about the will of God when we are all the time striving to make our will the will of God. He will put you to the test."[10]

The Lord will not do this to prove you false. His more constructive agenda is to show you what circumstances your surrendered will must yet overcome to divest itself of shallow sentiment and unworthy attachments. Anything that would compromise your surrendered will must be revealed and eliminated during the course of this testing. But the good news is, Jessie Penn-Lewis writes, "When he sees us truly surrendered there is no delay in God taking possession."[11]

Rightly understood, this call to lordship is really good news, inasmuch as self is a monster that only God can subdue! The fact our life *can* be brought under lordship means that sin need not control us one more day. But if we resist lordship, and the subduing of evil this arrangement provides, we highly endanger our usefulness to God, thereby putting at risk a forfeiture of major blessing.

In the Christian classic, *The Power-Filled Christian*, we are told what the Holy Spirit wants to give us.

> His name is at our disposal. His power is at our disposal. God's "riches in glory in Christ Jesus" are at our disposal, if only we are willing to present—to yield to him all we have, all we are: our talents, our powers, our plans, our life. But whatever we give him has no value unless we first give him our wills in loving and loyal allegiance.[12]

This point, while sufficiently made in Scripture, won't find as many proof-texts as other issues do, not because it isn't important, but simply because the existing conditions of that day already made it clear. Remember, it wasn't because Christianity attracted "down and outers" that the church began in some form of communal living. What produced instant homelessness was the fact that to come to the Lord in that day, as the three thousand did at Pentecost, meant to lose your job, your family, your standing in the synagogue, and even the acknowledgment of your existence.

If you want to see Jewish pressure at work, check out what happened to the blind man's parents in John, chapter 9. To become a Christian in Israel was to be hounded mercilessly by religious leaders. Even after the cross, they were incessantly steamed in their indignation. So there wasn't this need to keep pounding the lordship message, when already the cultural context strongly reinforced it.

If our example is Jesus, then the sustained surrender of his will should surely inspire the same from us. In John 5:30, we find Jesus saying, “I do not seek my own will, but the will of the Father who sent me.” This, in fact, was the guiding principle of his life. He who taught us to pray, “Your will be done on earth as it is in heaven” (Matthew 6:10) prayed that way even when life got harder than anyone had ever experienced it.

You know the story. While in Gethsemane, every weapon in hell was used against Jesus. This was the final countdown, the time when the “go” or “no go” decision would have to be made. Had angels watched this scene from the portals of heaven, they would have been shocked to hear Jesus asking for the cup to be removed. *Remove the cup*? Why, if this were to occur, how would mankind get saved? *Remove the cup*? But had it not been determined from the very beginning that Jesus would die to save souls? So how could a request like this ever come up?

The reason it came up was because the full fury of hell was being unleashed upon Jesus. Far worse than the nails, the thorns, the whip, and that spear, was the impending separation of Jesus from the Father, and the Holy Spirit taking flight—this excruciating misery about which we know so little! Nevertheless, in spite of the “awful, awful,” Jesus brought himself to say, “Not my will, but yours be done.” Thus, the surrender, which had never been interrupted, was now complete! George MacDonald wrote, “The highest condition of the human will is when, not seeing God and not seeming to grasp him at all, it still holds him fast.”[13] This is exactly what Jesus did that night in Gethsemane.

We think of the surrendered will almost exclusively in Gethsemane terms—and that is a big mistake! The image often flashes into our minds of agony and tears, owing to the forfeiture of something held dear. What we are contemplating borders a serious distortion of God’s will, because his will is always good. In John 4:34, Jesus said that his food was to do the will of the Father. And does not food sustain us? And satisfy us? Food helps us grow! Food helps us go! And this is exactly what the will of God accomplishes! Once accepted and activated, God’s will proves immensely satisfying to the soul—and not at all the life-depleting prospect we had assumed it would be! Of course, if Satan can get us to think otherwise, the alternative then presented will have considerable appeal.

The real issue, it should be stressed, is the character of the one to whom we surrender our will. Is he a good God? Will he always have our welfare at heart? Or will yielding to him turn out to be a bad deal? Some have thought that lordship necessitates taking away from the believer that which he likes and then forcing him to do what he doesn't like. As John MacArthur facetiously put it: If the believer enjoys athletics, God will break both of his legs and make him play the flute.

But if we could see the kind of life made possible with Jesus in control, instead of dragging our feet and moaning "Aw, gee, do we have to?" we'd be running to the front of the line to ask if the Lord would do the same for us! Even from a selfish point of view, it soon becomes evident that the best thing we could do for ourselves is to allow our lives to come under new management. For *every* word Jesus speaks, including the commandments, convey good news, once we understand the resources he offers and the outcomes he intends.

The Problem of the Will

Why, then, are we so hesitant to yield our will to the Lord? There are several major factors. One of these is confusion. In Matthew, chapter 8, verse 2, we find a leper telling Jesus, "Lord, if you are willing, you can make me clean." Confusion is embedded in these words, because for some reason this man seems to think that God may want him sick. But why would he think that? There's not one verse in Scripture that says God *wants* his people sick. To the contrary, Scripture calls sickness a curse (Deuteronomy 28), something no parent would ever put on a child. In fact, Jesus was in the process of redeeming people from such curses (Galatians 3:13). So why would the leper think that God would do that to one of his children? He could heal, but maybe he won't? What kind of a God is that?

This leper actually questioned the character of Jesus! And you will notice that as long as the leper had his doubts, he had his leprosy! It was only when these doubts were dispatched that the desired healing could then take place. And the same factor is true today: If we are uncertain about God's will, then that uncertainty will keep us from exercising our will, and from launching our faith to receive from God. So first we must know the will of God, or our own will simply won't function (see Appendix C).

A second problem that will prevent our will from establishing a proper allegiance to God is an overdependence on feelings. We in America give an undeserved reverence for feelings, quite often making our decisions on that basis alone. How did that number-one song from the 80s put it, "It can't be wrong if it feels so right"? Really? Is this a valid criterion for decision-making? No, it isn't. Feelings can be deceptive, and therefore like other false witnesses they must be thrown out of the court! Instead of letting feelings judge, they themselves ought to be judged. Indeed, of all the occupants of the soul, this is the one most in tune with the pleadings of self.

To become mature in the Lord, it is sometimes necessary to function without the support of feelings. Elaborating on this point, George MacDonald observed:

> God doesn't always make us feel right, desire good, love purity, and aspire after him and his will. The truth is this: He wants to make us in his own image, choosing the good, refusing the evil. How could he accomplish this if he were always moving us from within, as he does at divine intervals, toward the beauty of holiness?[14]

To take the next step toward holiness only if feelings inspire us to do it means we will go precisely nowhere during those times when such feelings are withdrawn (See Appendix E).

Feelings—especially those that are positive and uplifting, can cause us to draw false conclusions about ourselves; because, while experiencing some of these feelings, we may think ourselves closer to God than we really are. The fact something more vertical and transcendent triggers profound thoughts and inspiring feelings can mislead us into thinking that we are spiritual, after all. A. W. Tozer directly challenged this assumption by saying:

> It is a delusion to think that because we suddenly feel expansive and poetic in the presence of the storm or stars or space that we are spiritual. I need only remind you that the drunkards or tyrants or criminals can have those "sublime" feelings, too. Let us not imagine that they constitute worship.[15]

It is not uncommon, though, for some Christians to judge their spiritual status almost entirely by the presence or absence of feelings. If feelings are in decline at the moment, the tendency is to lose motivation and slack off in their pursuit of God. Responding to this pronounced and prevailing tendency in our churches, J. C. Ryle wrote:

> Truly holiness ... does not consist merely of inward sensations and impressions. It is much more than tears, and sighs, and bodily excitement, and a quickened pulse, and a passionate feeling of attachment to our favorite preachers and our own religious party.[16]

Were holiness this susceptible to the suspension of feelings, its stamina would soon fail when under assault. And the outcome of that would be anything but holy.

Although a supernatural radiance shined forth from the first believers, this radiance wasn't subject to the ebb and flow of feelings; its source went much deeper. When these believers worshipped their God, they found a reality that generated this supernatural glow. But being smitten with strong feelings didn't produce this glow, and it didn't sustain it. "How many mistake emotional life for life in the Holy Ghost," exclaimed England's twentieth-century author, Jessie Penn-Lewis.[17]And how many activate the excitement of the flesh in their aspiration for the joy of the Spirit. But why? In the words of Charles Spurgeon, “Feelings are more fickle than the winds, more unsubstantial than bubbles ....”[18]

The temper of the times in modern America—where it isn’t one nation under God but one nation under therapy—has feelings being regarded in an overly exalted way. We go to great lengths these days to discover feelings. Like an archeologist searching for treasure, we dig and dig, until all that has been suppressed and repressed has been duly uncovered and thoroughly examined. Then, with bended knee, we do whatever the great god, Feelings, demands.

And what a compelling case feelings can make! Like a seductress, it begs for what it wants. Like a circus barker, it promotes what it seeks. Like a thief, it conspires a way to get it. Like a sociopath, it blocks the hurt of those wounded in the process. And we would follow the lead of this?

Sadly, we do follow feelings—and do so with an undeserved loyalty. Our motive? To avoid the immense pain feelings can inflict. Like a punished child, it will throw a tantrum. Like an offended woman, it will sulk and pout. Like a scorned lover, it will seek revenge. And like a cruel gangster, it will get that revenge in a swift and terrible way. Of course, none of this is biblical or godly, and therefore feelings shouldn’t be highly regarded. In his book, *Full Assurance*, Dr. H. A. Ironside writes:

> It is a remarkable fact that the word “feel” is only found once in the New Testament, and that is in Paul’s sermon to the Athenians, where he rebukes them ... it has nothing to do with the gospel, but rather with the heathen groping in the dark, “... if happily they might feel after God.” You are not in their ignorant condition. You have heard the gospel. You know of the one living and true God. You are not told to feel anything, but to believe his record.[19]

Jay Adams said it well: We are to be commandment-motivated, not feeling-motivated. The Word of God must take precedence over the subterranean flow of potentially precarious feelings. What God says is the determinative factor, not what we feel. In this same vein of thought, A. W. Tozer comments:

> "Religion," say the theologians, "lies in the will" ... "If any man will," said Jesus; he did not say, "If any man feel." Feeling is a play of emotions over the will, a kind of musical accompaniment to the business of living, and while it is indeed most enjoyable to have the band play as we march to Zion; it is by no means indispensable. We can work and walk without music and if we have true faith we can walk with God without feeling.[20]

Yes, when properly motivated and theologically trained, feelings can be a rich part of our experience. So in *that* context its full participation is very much welcomed, and even expected. But if there is going to be a healthy connection between spirit and soul, feelings dare not lead the way!

Other generations have made another mistake by exaggerating the importance of the mind. This was certainly true during the Renaissance, when one's native abilities to reason and comprehend were unduly exalted. During the "Age of Reason," there were intellectuals on the scene who contended that revelation wasn't necessary: While those with limited brain power needed it, others could arrive at the same conclusions without any help from God. The arrogance of this view became immediately obvious to anyone who read what these rationalists wrote. Sophisticated? Yes! Clever? Yes! Wise? No! For as Paul put it in the book of Romans, "claiming to be wise, they became fools" (Romans 1:22).

Even today, one can ask some university professor to summon his best views about a particular problem he is encountering, and it will become obvious, certainly to one taught in the Scripture, that there is a Grand Canyon gap between what man thinks and what God thinks.

At other times in history, it was the will that was too strongly emphasized. During the Renaissance, humanism took on an intoxicating euphoria when it elevated man's will with dreamy eye delusions. Leon Battista Alberti echoed with amplification the strong sentiment of the times when he said, "A man can do all things if he will."[21] This notion that a person can do whatever he sets his mind to do crossed the Atlantic during the early years of American history and was largely accepted coast to coast—by early settlers in the first colonies and later by those rugged frontiersmen in the old American West. Today, overachievers in business, sports, and other high-profile endeavors will talk about giving a hundred and ten percent. And in doing so, they unabashedly enthrone willpower as the key to their success.

Our culture simply loves those pick-yourself-up-by-the-bootstraps success stories, especially the one that prove former failures wrong. Louisa May Alcott was told that she couldn't write and therefore she should stick to sewing. She persisted in her writing anyway, however, and eventually wrote the classic, *Little Women,* which sold millions of books. F. W. Woolsworth wasn't allowed to wait on customers, because they said he didn't have enough sense to meet the public. He, too, persisted in his dream, and one day started a business that franchised stores all over the nation. Richard Byrd was forced to retire from the military with the designation "unfit for service." Not giving up, though, he later made his legendary trips to the North and South poles. Thomas Edison was said to be too stupid to learn, as was Albert Einstein when he was a boy. However, everyone now knows what those two accomplished.

Yes, our flesh has ready ears for stories like these and admiring eyes for those who overcome all odds through diligence and desire. It should be noted, however, that in religion the Pharisees thought this way, too, and they became the target of Jesus' strongest criticism! The Pharisees invested an undeserved and unexamined confidence in what the will could achieve. However, as Henry Drummond, the nineteenth-century Scottish writer, said, "In willpower, in mere spasms of earnestness, there is no salvation."[22]

A third problem that plagues many a soul is simply passivity, the abdication of any initiative and purpose until the will has been captured by guaranteed knowledge, or by irrepressible feelings, or by a supernatural intervention of

God. This almost magical view imagines that God will undertake and accomplish his will without the activation of our will. In some unexpected beatific moment the transformation will suddenly occur. But Jessie Penn-Lewis took this view to task when she wrote:

> God will not change even the tone of your voice for you as if you were a machine. He will put his laws into your mind and write them upon your heart, but you are the person to act upon them—and it is possible to have them in your mind and heart and not act upon them. It is for *you* to choose the way you will think, speak and act, and as you choose, the Holy Spirit will enable you to carry out God's laws.[23]

The overly passive person is certainly not passive about one thing, though, because within him is a determined avoidance of commitment! Persistently, he seeks not to get involved. Studiously, he avoids all entanglements. Aggressively, he stiff-arms any pledge, any promise. And this is exactly why, whenever some commitment-seeking belief comes knocking at the door, the only response is one of silence—and later, perhaps, a sneaking away from the premises. And should this commitment-seeking belief then pursue him, discover him, and present its truth claims at some new place of hiding, the passive soul will file away the entire presentation in planned neglect by saying politely, "I'll think about it." Bible commentator William Barclay questioned the honesty of this response:

> Often when we say, "I'll think about it," all that we really mean is that I don't want to decide ... The phrase is just an evasion, an excuse for inaction ... We ought to be very careful that when we say, "I'll think about it," we don't in fact mean precisely the opposite.[24]

What an artful dodger the soul can be! The years pass as the soul goes be-bopping along, wary of commitments, suspicious of fervent come-ons, unimpressed with the supposedly irrefragable truths of the gospel (even though it had never checked one of them out). Throughout this escapism romp, the high standard the soul holds forth is this: The only way it will surrender is if some totally convincing, no-room-for-doubt belief leaps from its hiding place and flashes its impressive credentials. Reflecting on the likelihood of this prospect, C. S. Lewis wrote:

> We have been warned that all but conclusive evidence against Christianity, evidence that would deceive (if it were possible) the very elect, will appear with Anti-Christ. And after that there will be wholly conclusive evidence on the other side.
>
> But not, I fancy, till then on either side.[25]

In search of this undeniable proof, the cry goes forth from Scripture, "If only one were raised from the dead"—surely *that* would be the kind of proof that would compel belief! But then came that day outside the tomb of Lazarus. The religious enemies looked on as Jesus sent his summons to the lower regions of the dead. In response, the mummified Lazarus arose and walked straight toward them! He that had been dead and buried for four days was now undeniably alive! And did that secure belief from those who had been withholding it? No, it did not! For less than two weeks later, the very ones who watched Jesus perform this miracle were shouting with tantrum insistence for his death. But why? Hadn't they believed what they had seen at the tomb of Lazarus? Indeed, they did; there could be no disputing the fact. But so perverse is the human heart that not even undeniable proof will do what we think it will do.

What is really needed, as Jesus had earlier said, is a witness of another sort—the testimony of Moses and the prophets (that is, the truth of Scripture born by the Holy Spirit into the human heart). This is why there wasn't an Easter parade on the morning of the resurrection. Jesus could have marched down Main Street, the Grand Marshall of Jerusalem's greatest celebration. He could have suspended everyone forty feet above the earth, where they would all remain until they were ready to become a follower of his. Jesus did no such thing, of course, because displays like that fail to provide what our hearts really need.

Lloyd J. Ogilvie once wrote, "God never burglarizes the human will. He may long to come in and help, but he will never cross the picket line of our unwillingness."[26] Therefore, to be passive and evasive with our will is to court first-rate disaster! Despite this fact, there is a strand of eastern mysticism that has successfully infiltrated the church today. This mysticism promotes a complete disengagement from all earthly influences until passivity settles in, which in turn waits for divine aggression to motivate. When such aggression occurs, the believer will become a passive automaton, a subject who obeys the mesmerist only, but does not use mind or will. Jessie Penn-Lewis decisively rejected this kind of mysticism, saying, "No soul can be fully used of God unless he becomes *intelligently* and volitionally obedient to the will of God."[27]

There is another type of passivity in evidence in the church. But this passivity has nothing to do with mysticism; it is rooted instead in rebellion. More than a few people in the faith haven't completely divested their soul of its capacities for passive resistance. Hence, the very scripture that accomplished the miraculous in others does next to nothing for them. They can sit there in the midst of Holy Spirit excitement and look on in utter skepticism, if not disgust. This happens because their will won't get off dead center and take on the assignments of faith.

Even when it comes to spiritual warfare, we see the same problem recurring—an uninvolved will. J. C. Ryle brought clarity to this issue by reminding us of the relationship between faith and the exercising of one's will.

> The very same Apostle who says in one place, "The life that I live in the flesh I live by the faith of the Son of God," says in another place, "I fight ... I run ... I keep under my body"; and in other places, "Let us cleanse ourselves ... Let us labor ... Let us lay aside every weight."[28]

It is true that the Spirit of God will move upon us, but only in response to faith! And having so moved, he'll then require more faith! But for all this to occur, our will has to be involved. Amplifying this point in his influential classic, *A Serious Call to a Devout and Holy Life*, William Law wrote:

> ... the reason why you see no real mortification, or self-denial, or eminent charity, or profound humility, no heavenly affection, no true contempt of the world, no Christian meekness, no sincere zeal, no eminent piety in the common lives of Christians, is this, because they do not so much as intend to be exact and exemplary in these virtues.[29]

What a concise exposure of the truth! According to this nineteenth-century British cleric, the real reason we're not experiencing what God is offering is because *we never intended to*. We may have said otherwise in the language of wishes and wants, but there was never any serious purposing—and hence, predictably, there were no observable results. This perspective certainly lines up with Tozer's observation, "Every man is as close to God as he wants to be; he is as holy and as full of the Spirit as he wills to be."[30]

Still another problem of the will, familiar to anyone who has attempted to exercise it, is the challenge to sustain our will as strongly as when we first commissioned it. The passion for some Christians lasts about three days! Their eyes, their voice, are full of excitement—at least in the beginning when Jesus seems so near and the promise seems so sure. But then feelings fade, flesh intrudes, God tests, and the world resists. And it is under this duress that the once emboldened will slowly retreats. But why?

George D. Watson explains, "There are two great departments of the will—choice and execution; or the elective and persevering acts. Both of these forms of the will are involved in holiness."[31] The initial decision to employ the will is obviously essential, for apart from this decision that which the will seeks to secure would remain forever out of reach. Yet, Watson explains that "all choices of the will are fruitful only according to the amount of perseverance accompanying them, which is the will's executive side."[32] It is the cessation of the will (during those circumstances that challenge and confuse) which constitutes the objective of Satan and the cause of our defeat.[33]

In cataloguing all these problems of the will, we must again point out the equal and opposite problem: having too great a reliance on the will, for even a godly person can succumb to this problem. There are times when self-will intrudes, sticks out its chest, struts in undeserved confidence, and decides to do God's work in its own way. We learn from Scripture that the greatest of Israel's leaders succumbed to this mistake. God had told Moses to speak to the rock at Kadesh—only that, and then the water would flow to quench these people's thirst. But Moses decided to do something more spectacular: not to speak to the rock only, but to strike the rock—and not once, but twice! Commenting on what occurred that day, Roy Hession said:

> ... like Moses, we cannot believe that so little on our part as just speaking to the rock can produce as big a result as is needed. We must do something, and do something strong. Failing in faith, we act in the flesh—a further intrusion of self.[34]

Nothing appeals to religious flesh more than an appeal to strongly exercise one's will. It was certainly no lack of willpower that accounted for Paul's failures, first in Damascus and later in Jerusalem. He who was one of the greatest intellects in history had a will so resolute, so determined, scarcely anyone could rival its zeal. And yet, this will, well-intentioned though it was and scripture-informed though it was, failed.

As we seek to define the will accurately, we must see beyond the apparent. In the realm of the flesh the will seems to be applauded, but in the realm of the spirit the will seems to be demoted. This perception needs clarification. Miles Stanford helped us better understand the redefined role of the will when he wrote:

> The effortless life is not the will-less life. We use our will to believe, to receive, but not to exert effort in trying to accomplish what only God can do. Our hope for victory over sin is not "Christ plus my efforts," but "Christ plus my receiving."[35]

It is only when we depend on God as our only source—not just for the extra twenty percent that will put us over the top, but for the full one-hundred percent—that our will is properly related at last to our spirit. In this proper alignment we will then experience the truth of Andrew Murray's words, "The Lord Jesus, who is exalted high in heaven, penetrates my whole nature by his Spirit, until all my willing, thinking, and feeling are moved by him."[36] Murray further clarified this assertion by making a very important distinction between willing and doing. Read these words slowly.

> The new will is a permanent gift, an attribute of the new nature. The power to do is not a permanent gift, but must be each moment received from the Holy Spirit. It is the man who is conscious of his own impotence as a believer who will learn that by the Holy Spirit he will live a holy life.[37]

In her Christian classic, *The Christian's Secret of a Happy Life*, Hannah Whitall Smith added to this insight when she wrote: "When God is working 'within us to will,' we must set our faces like a flint to carry out his will, and must respond with an emphatic 'I will' to every 'Thou shalt' of his."[38] He will enable—that is true—but we must receive and respond to this enabling with a determination steeled by his Spirit. Not to do so will eventually stop the work of God, for as F. J. Huegel observed, "God *cannot* when man *will* not."[39]

"The secret of saintliness," Tozer said, "is not the destruction of the will but the submergence of it in God's will."[40] Likewise, Charles Finney wrote, "Let your will be lost in his will; not lost in the sense of being annihilated, but in the better sense of being submitted—merged in his will."[41] He that is the Alpha and Omega of your faith will utilize his will to strengthen your will, if you yield to his participation he undertakes in this way.

Samuel Rutherford, the seventeenth-century Puritan from Scotland, expressed a sentiment other Christians have had when he wrote, "I pray God, that I may never find my will again. Oh, if Christ would subject my will to his, and trample it under his feet, and liberate me from that lawless lord."[42] The elimination of our will would make life easier, but nowhere in Scripture do we find any hope for this prayer to be answered. The exercising of our will is necessary, which is why A. B. Simpson wrote, "Will is the mightiest thing God has given to mankind. No person can receive much from God without making a firm and decided choice."[43]

Yes, there is truth in the call for a surrendered will, but error can enter still if we don't see the surrendered will as something God will sustain. Andrew Murray said, "When God has begun the work of absolute surrender in you, and when God has accepted your surrender, then God holds himself bound to care for it and to keep it."[44] In the words of A. B. Simpson: "When the life is surrendered to God, it will be as strong as omnipotence and as sweet as heaven."[45]

Even this surrender is hardly a work for which we are solely responsible, for the indwelling Christ is more powerful than indwelling sin, and more steady in resolve than the vacillations of human will. A. J. Gordon saw the supreme importance of this factor when he pondered this question: "To have Christ dwelling in us, his will encircling ours with its holy constraints, and his heart within us the fountain of all blessed desires, do we count this a rich prerogative of the gospel?"[46] And the answer is, we do, indeed! His will, shaping and supplying our will, is at the heart of the Christian life.

In summing up these chapters on the soul we can say that each occupant of the soul—mind, emotion, and will—can achieve optimal results, if duly submissive to the Spirit. For this to occur, however, these resident capacities of the soul mustn't be relied upon, in part or in whole, or else the native abilities of each, inferior and inadequate, will surely exhibit. With the release of new nature capacities, though, all that changes.

Reflection Questions

1. Do you allow your will to be on the loose, to negotiate what you perceive to be a better deal for yourself? If so, what is the most recent example of this?

2. This chapter discusses several hindrances to the will's proper release—confusion, a reliance upon feelings, passivity, an attempt to avoid commitments, and an overreliance on willpower. Which of these hindrances troubles you the most?

3. The quotes by Andrew Murray and A. J. Gordon on the last page of this chapter are certainly worth pondering. How do you react to what these men said? Do you have personal examples to illustrate their point?

Chapter 16

New Nature Benefits

Have you ever read the biography of some admired person, only to finish the last chapter with a sense of disappointment? Hero books designed for an eleven-year old won't have this problem, but biographies portraying a person "warts and all" (to quote Churchill) will cause us to see, even when we don't want to see, some serious moral failings. Not just idiosyncrasies and quirky peccadilloes, but offenses that are much more objectionable.

The biographies of Jesus are quite different, however. For the closer we look at his life, the more we see the incomparable Christ. Simply put: No other life in no other day exhibits the beauty of soul and winsomeness of personality we find in Jesus! The wisdom of his words, the power unleashed in his documented deeds, are unmatched in the history of man. Therefore, applause and admiration fall far short in the honor due him. Only the reverential awe that gives him life-long loyalty is sufficient as an initial response.

What if all the best writers, individually or collectively, were to try to invent a character as inspiring as Jesus, could they do it? With their abilities to capture the best of human genius, to develop plot lines that fascinate and background details that enrich, could they create a character so deft in understanding, mighty in deed, and magnificent in personality, that people throughout the ages would be continually enraptured by what they see? No, as talented as all these writers are, they could never rival what these fishermen wrote! The difference in outcome, of course, is attributable to the subject and not to the writers. What the

New Testament reports about Jesus is far superior to what the genius of man could ever imagine!

It is true that the Old Testament has its share of inspiring people—Moses, David, and Elijah, to name a few. Each of these men, though, was obviously flawed: Moses with his anger, David with his lust, Elijah with his bitterness. But there is another life in Scripture considerably higher than all of these! Read the book of Acts, the second letter to the Corinthians, and elsewhere in the New Testament, and you'll see a life so remarkably like that of our Lord's. This is the life of the Apostle Paul. Indeed, so extraordinary was this life that Henry Drummond said of Paul: "Judged by his influence on human history, no single life is entitled to more admiration for what it has done, or is indeed more worthy of imitation for what it was."

That there should be a life in the New Testament much superior to anyone's in the Old Testament credentials the importance of the new nature. We could extol the new nature for all its supposed virtues, but at best our commentary would only be theoretical were there not extensive evidence that theory actually converted to practice. Given what we know about Paul, our commentary on this subject has been elevated to another level, one that is both historical and biographical. And amazing, too, is the fact that the very life that was in Jesus, and then in Paul, is now in us![1]

A. W. Tozer said, "The truly regenerated man is a new creature; he belongs to another order of being; he has another kind of life, another origin, another destiny."[2] Based on this truth, what we want to consider next are the benefits of the new nature. There are many. Testifying to this fact, A. J. Gordon declared, "Nothing is more striking than the breadth of application which this principle of union with Christ has in the Gospel."[3]

The Solving of Sin

The strangest murder case in the files of the famous French detective force, the Surete, had its beginnings one morning in the year 1888. It began with the discovery of a body on the beach. As soon as the discovery was made, a telegram was sent to Robert LeDru, considered the most brilliant detective on the force. LeDru would often work a case twenty-two hours a day, driving himself to near exhaustion as he did it.

Upon arrival at the scene, LeDru roped off the beach area, and then proceeded to comb it for clues, inch by inch. After an extensive investigation, he finally found the clue that broke the case open—footprints of the stocking-footed murderer. The next morning LeDru presented a plaster of paris cast of the footprint to police headquarters. The cast, he said, indicated that the large toe on the murderer's left foot was missing. Then, taking off his own left shoe, LeDru startled headquarters by announcing, "Messieurs, I am the murderer!"

Apparently, those nightmares where he dreamed he was committing murder were more than nightmares. LeDru had set out looking for a murderer, but the trail led to himself.

Likewise, we also have known what it is to do wrong, but, being in a spiritual stupor, didn't have any conviction about it. Then, as we studied the evidence of God's Word, the painful conclusion began to dawn on us—*we* are the ones who are guilty! This is one of the functions of God's Word, to radically unmask us and thereby expose our guilt.

Many years ago The London Times ran a series of articles addressing the issue, what is wrong with the world? Inviting readers to respond to this question, many erudite explanations were subsequently submitted. Interestingly, the most thoughtful response was also the briefest. "Dear Sirs," the entry began—and then with telegraphic brevity came the two-word answer—"I am." That was the totality of the response, after which the author signed his name, G. K. Chesterton, who happened to be one of the most brilliant Christian writers of his day.

Doesn't this reply get to the heart of the issue? The self that sins, the self that pursues what it wants even if morality is compromised and other people get hurt—that self, more than anything else, is the problem of our world!

Many people, even people in the church, are living with a self they don't want exposed, and with a guilt they don't want discovered. It is said that Arthur Conan Doyle, the author of Sherlock Holmes, was a bit of a prankster. One day his inner imp got the better of him when he decided to send telegrams to twelve prominent people. The telegrams briefly stated how all was now known and that they should immediately flee. Upon receipt of these telegrams, all twelve men fled the country—an outcome Mr. Doyle never expected!

Whether our sin is known or unknown to others, who can deny that our sin is a pervasive pollutant whose harm can hardly be overstated? From our first day on earth, evil showed up to inflict its damage. E. M. Bounds said of Satan, "He is at the cradle of every baby."[4] Viciously, maliciously he stalks every infant, setting traps that may take years to spring. Commenting on the impact of sin, the famous Southern Baptist pastor, Dr. R. G. Lee, said:

> Sin has ruined men, ruined women, ruined angels. Sin has occasioned every tear of sorrow, every sigh of grief, every pang of remorse. Sin has withered everything that is fair, blasted everything that is good, made bitter everything that is sweet.[5]

G. D. Watson observed, "Surely it is a blessing to loathe sin, and a still greater blessing to loathe that particular sin that has done us the most damage."[6] This is true if such loathing doesn't turn inward to condemn but instead strategizes a somber, serious response. The gravity of our situation certainly warrants this response, for the words of the Puritan theologian, John Owen, have put us all on notice: "Kill sin or it be killing you." As we contemplate our response to this warning, we have to ask ourselves, is there a way, any way, for the forces of sin to be stopped?

The Bible declares in Romans 6:14 that "sin shall have no dominion over you." Similarly, Galatians 5:16 contends, "... walk in the Spirit and you shall not fulfill the lust of the flesh." This sounds good, but how do we square such claims with the loose talk heard from the modern pulpit, "We sin every day"? While such talk may appear to be in agreement with John's assertion, "If we say we have no sin, we deceive ourselves, and the truth is not in us" (I John 1:8), it really isn't. John was simply pointing out that nobody, Christian or non-Christian, has lived this life without a sin problem. Even the best of Christians—and even after they had been saved, sanctified, and Spirit-filled—have sinned. That is simply a fact, but it is not a necessity; nor must it be anything close to daily reality.

Ruth Paxson correctly argued, "God nowhere says that we are not able to sin, but he clearly says that we are able not to sin."[7] At no time when a believer sins is this sin inevitable, owing to the fact that the forces of temptation have overmatched the resources of grace. The extent of God's provision for defeating sin seems not to be clear to J. I. Packer, however. In his book, *Keep in Step with the Spirit*, Packer speaks approvingly of Benjamin Warfield's description of believers as "miserable-sinner Christianity," and Robert Murray McCheyne's petition, "Lord, make me as holy as a saved sinner can be."[8] Talk like this is not realism, as Packer supposes, but a theological deficit discrediting the believer's true identity and current resources.[9]

According to Thomas Watson, "Tertullian thought he was born for no other end but to repent."[10] However, the Spirit-filled believer, as is evidenced in the life of Paul, can live a sustained period of time without succumbing to sin. Theoretically, he could do it forever, but what is entirely possible isn't always actual. Nevertheless, the successes others have achieved, and the teachings of Scripture itself, are enough to refute this "I-sin-every-day" talk.

Because the Lord has made the provision he did to overcome sin, E. M. Bounds offered, with some indignation surfacing, the following assessment:

> There is no denying that the unrenewed man cannot obey God. But to declare that—after one is renewed by the Holy Spirit, has received a new nature, and become a child of the King—he *cannot* obey God is to assume a ridiculous attitude. It is to show a lamentable ignorance of the work and implications of the Atonement.[11]

To get to the victory side of this struggle, it is important to recognize the right way and the wrong way to encounter sin. The Galatian Christians are an example of the wrong way, as they sought to operate on the formula: The Scripture plus a dedicated will can secure the victory. Horrified at this updated Pharisee-like belief, Paul contended that these Galatians were really reverting to the way of the law and thus back to the defeats incurred whenever the might and mind of the individual were relied on to produce a worthy life. In his book, *In Search of Spiritual Excellence*, Andrew Murray said:

> A believer can encounter and strive against sin in two ways. One is to endeavor to ward it off with all his might, seeking his strength in the Word and in prayer. In this form of conflict, we use the power of the will. The other is to turn at the very moment of temptation to the Lord Jesus in the silent exercise of faith and say to him: "Lord, I have no strength. You are my keeper."
>
> This is the method of faith.[12]

Moreover, this is the method the Apostle Paul discovered and disclosed. His struggle against sin had been an arduous, agonizing process! For Paul, it was just as the Latin poet Ovid said of himself, "I see the better course and approve it; but the worst is the one I follow." One might think that once the mind is enlightened, the heart is delighted, and the will is consecrated to do God's will that evil would recede into the background and that good could be accessed through widely opened gates. But, no, evil runs ahead and hides where we would least suspect to find it.

In a sermon entitled "The Dangers of Virtue," Edward Cleal said:

> We expect evil to be present when we would do wrong, when we deliberately set out along the black path of sin, but it lurks along the upward way. It crouches in the holiest places. It drags its

> slimy tail through the very sanctuaries of our lives.[13]

Many temptations are not to do wrong, exactly, but to take shortcuts to righteousness. This is what Jesus encountered in the wilderness temptations. The counsel given seemed sympathetic and well-intended. But its subtlety, which many never would have detected, came right out of the pit.

The man personified in Romans 7 also aspired to do good, but admitted, finally, that despite his enlightened mind, he was eventually deceived; and that despite his delighted heart, he was cast into utter anguish; and that despite his consecrated will, he was repeatedly defeated.[14] The good news, though, is that this man escaped this Romans 7 dilemma. Indeed, in Romans 8:2 he declared this to be the case when he made the triumphant declaration, "... the Spirit of life in Christ Jesus has made me free ...."

By definition, the Spirit of life in Christ Jesus is the new nature. And according to Paul only the new nature is sufficient. Adding commentary to this point, A. B. Simpson wrote:

> No higher school of ethics was ever known than the teaching of Moses and the Jewish law. But Paul had found the utter worthlessness of the righteousness of the law and the powerlessness of the highest ideals to lift man above his fallen nature. And so he came to his fellow men to tell them that our fallen race must have, not an evolution, but a revolution. Humanity is too far gone for self-improvement or any principle of recuperation. There must be a new creation.[15]

Once man gives up his soulish attempts to be good and allows instead for his new nature to flow, that elusive but desired victory finally becomes his.[16] Judson Cornwall reasoned, "If holiness is the essential nature of God—and the angels proclaim that it is—then living in holiness is living in the nature of God ...."[17] This is one of the best benefits of the new nature.

The Inspiring of Image

Another benefit of the new nature deals with self-image. Josh McDowell says that, "Persons with a poor sense of self-worth ... struggle with the tension of trying to be acceptable while believing they are not."[18] Jessie Penn-Lewis said this effort isn't helped when the Accuser "pours on you morning, noon, and night ...."[19] All these condemning conclusions, whatever their basis in fact, only serve to drive another nail into the coffin of self-respect. Actually, such performance-based respect is bound to end in accusation. With heightened drama, this point was surely taught at Sinai when it belched its fury, thundering the message of guilt to anyone, anywhere, who thinks one's own goodness might be good enough.

But aren't you glad this isn't the end of the story? Self-worth is essential, and properly deriving that worth is indispensable to eternal life. For this reason, then, Jesus came to earth to establish a new identity for us by giving us a new nature.[20] A. W. Tozer reflected on the new nature's relationship to our image by first asking, "Now how could it be that this eternal God who had no beginning, no creation, no origin, this mighty God—how could it be that he could assume to himself the nature he had created?" Tozer's answer is logical, and easily discoverable: "... because human nature was made in the image of God, it is therefore appropriate and consistent that the divine nature could assume the human nature ...."[21]

From the very beginning God had determined that we would have his image, and that determination resulted in a divine intervention to restore the image that Satan shattered in Eden. Concerning this restored image that lifted the child of God above every condemnation, Tozer wrote:

> Nothing in heaven is higher than this. All the earth scraped together and all its riches would not be as high as this. All the celestial heavens and the astronomic heavens rolled together would not be as high as this. Not all those strange and mysterious beauties we read about in heaven and

see by the eye of faith—not all these things together would be as much as this: Christ in you, the hope of glory.[22]

It would be good if the story ended with the restoration of the image of God in man, but there's a thug and thief on the scene today. And, as was true in the beginning, with renewed efforts he moves with concealed cunning to steal our restored identity. Identity theft, we know, is a major problem in modern society, resulting in much loss and great frustration. But all the havoc and chaos of identity theft is even more evident in the spiritual domain. Thus, there's a need to expose mistaken thinking, and to disclose the truth of our real identity.

The story is told of a tiger cub that somehow got lost and fell in with sheep. Quite naturally—because he lived with the sheep, grew up with the sheep, and had as his only environment these sheep—he began to think of himself as a sheep. But one day a sure enough tiger approached, giving off a roar. Alarmed by what he heard, the tiger who thought he was a sheep responded with a feeble "baah." Again, the larger tiger roared, this time louder than before! Once more, though, the tiger with a confused identity bleated his pitiful, strange-sounding "baahs." When this ferocious tiger roared a third time, something within that younger tiger began to resonate. Thus, he soon returned the roar, and with each successive roar, he awakened to his true identity. Impressively, the story ends with this once confused tiger walking over territory he formerly feared to enter.[23]

Thomas Howard asked the question, is there not a sense in which Christ the Tiger roars to us from his Word, awakening in us an identity that is higher than the one we had? Our true identity, the Bible makes clear, is not to be found in our past; it is to be found instead in our new nature.

In II Corinthians 5:16, the Apostle Paul said, "Therefore, from now on, we regard no one according to the flesh." Where people live, what they wear, what they look like, are inadequate criteria, because who they really are is not what we *see*, but what God *says*. And God says that they are a brand-new creation—the precise point Paul makes in the next verse! All the perfections of the divine life, and all that satisfies God's law, forever defines the essence of a true believer.

Who we are can never be improved and can never be diminished. Since the new nature is the Lord's life within us, it is perfect and will always be so. Therefore, once this teaching about the new nature becomes a revelation to us, our struggle with inferiority will be over. And what will also be over is our difficulty in believing that God loves us. Theologian Charles Hodge accurately described the problem that plagues many people.

> The great difficulty with many Christians is that they cannot persuade themselves that Christ (or God) loves them; and the reason they cannot feel confident of the love of God, is, that they know that they do not deserve his love, on the contrary, that they are in the highest degree unlovely. How can an infinitely pure God love those who are defiled with sin, who are proud, selfish, discontented, ungrateful, disobedient? This, indeed, is hard to believe.[24]

The premise of this problem is erroneous, however, because, due to the new nature, a believer doesn't have to identify with the behaviors Charles Hodge cited. Whatever sins are allowed to attach to a believer's life represent a contradiction to the believer's true identity and not an expression of it. *What God loves is what he gave: the new nature, the life of Jesus within.* Therefore, there's no difficulty in believing that God loves the person who has this new nature, and who in fact *is* this new nature. What's not to love?

The implications the new nature has for relationships are enormous, because what we believe for ourselves we can also believe for others. Ephesians 2:15, which talks about God making one new man, refers to the centuries-old animosity that existed between the Jews and the Gentiles. The scathing invectives that passed between these two groups would shatter anyone's sensitivities. Such blistering, biting rebukes! Such a grab-them-by-the-throat contempt! And somehow God was going to reconcile people who acted like this?

He did so, this verse confirms, by creating "in himself one new man from the two, thus making peace." God gave the Jew a new nature and the Gentile a new nature; and therefore what was impossible before, soon became a reality. These former enemies, each blessed with a new nature, could now enjoy with each other a remarkably rewarding relationship. And just think: If God could do that for people like these, who at the time would have been at the top of anyone's impossibility list, imagine what the new nature could do for believers today.

One implication of this fact is that whenever we see a Christian bogged down in the muck of sin, we don't have to identify the muck—covered in it though he may be—with the believer. Instead, we can be encouraged to conclude that what we see is a contradiction and not a reflection of who this believer really is. Consequently, we should do what the Bible says love does and believe in him (I Corinthians 13:7), and then look for opportunities to articulate God's view of this person. This is one of the most powerful things we can do, attributable to the fact that identity precedes destiny! What we see is the way we'll be! Therefore, to get the image right, and articulate to another in extended faith what this image is, can release that person into a new way of life.

It must be stressed, repeatedly, that the vision being articulated isn't just mental; it's actual—it is a reality that can be experienced! Oswald Chambers, whose devotional book, *My Utmost for His Highest*, has blessed millions of people, once suffered four years of a broken intimacy with God. During this time, the Bible was a dull, uninteresting book to him. But then one day God broke through, enabling Oswald Chambers to experience who he really was. "I was filled with the love of God," Chambers said. "It is no wonder that I should talk about an altered disposition. God altered mine; I was there when he did it."

For this to be our experience as well, we must become teachable before the Lord and allow him to show us what is true about the new nature he has given us. But if we still think of ourselves as sinners, we'll never ask God to make actual what we really don't think exists. Moreover, if God did release our new nature within, that release would soon be shut-off by the contaminated thinking we have about ourselves. So off we would go for another season of stale worship and sterile service.

Experiencing what Oswald Chambers called "the altered disposition" produces an enormous impact on our self-image. It is regrettable that so many people, for so long a time, have languished under a spirit of self-doubting—or worse still, self-loathing! People who have known this kind of agony, find the eternal elevation of one's self-esteem all the more special. It is one of the best benefits of the new nature.

The Determining of Destiny

Another benefit of the new nature has to do with finding one's purpose in life. Many people, even Christian people, seem to be sleepwalking through life with scarcely a clue about why God has put them here on this earth. In response to this dilemma, First Corinthians 15:34 says, "Awake to righteousness." In reading these words, even for the first time, one need not become overly imaginative to sense the passion in that word "awake." One can even imagine a shaking that is almost violent, given how much is at stake. This shaking occurs because of three facts true of those asleep, especially spiritual asleep. One, they have no idea who they are. Two, they have no idea what's going on around them. Three, they have no capacity to set goals, to reach goals, or to do anything useful. But once there is a shaking and an awakening, and once the new nature rises and releases within them, that changes!

David Needham illustrated this truth in his splendid book, *Birthright*. He wrote:

> There is a most remarkable bird called the arctic tern. Once a year it travels on the longest migratory journey of any bird known on earth; all the way from one pole to the other. The bird soars across trackless oceans, thousands of miles to its

particular resting place. That alone would make it a very unusual bird, indeed. But there is something even more remarkable about it.

After the tiny terns are hatched and old enough to feed and care for themselves, the parent birds leave for the South Pole. Weeks pass by and the young birds grow and exercise their wings, enjoying all the games that sea gulls seem to play in the sky. But finally the time comes when the young terns take one last look at the only place they have ever known, and begin a journey to a place they have never been!

Somehow, deep within them, they know they cannot stay, they must go; they *want* to go. But which way? Did Mama and Papa tern leave a set of directions propped up in the nest? "Follow the star Arturus until you see the Southern Cross, then, going south by southeast …." No! The trip is very deep in their natures.[25]

Isn't that good? Bound within our new nature is a purpose that will define our life! This is especially true when contemplating the moral and spiritual dimensions of life. The impact of our new nature will decidedly direct us away from choices we would have otherwise made. The life goals we choose, the way we spend our time, the way we spend our money, the way we choose our friends—the trajectory of our life will change, certainly and dramatically, once we receive our new nature.

This change isn't spiritual and moral only (although these are the changes most important), for there is also a vocational change involved. Figuring out vocation and vocational direction cannot be done just by examining spiritual gifts, native abilities, personality temperament, and identifiable passions, since God has been known to give vocational assignments to people who didn't want these assignments. Ask Jonah. Ask Moses. Ask Jeremiah. Ask Paul. It is imperative, therefore, that we be led by the Spirit and not trust our own thinking too much. For even godly men have made painful errors in precisely this way.

When God leads in a direction we don't want, our own thinking may mount a strong argument for a direction of our choosing. Yet, to our consternation, there is a knowing inside us that refuses to budge but instead obligates us to follow a direction different than our desire. And so we do, perplexed—only to have a similar experience at another juncture in our life's journey. Once again, we fail to understand, since the direction urged upon us doesn't seem to make sense. Of concern, too, is the fact that we can't explain how this sudden and strong knowing gained our attention. We only know that it did, and that it was of God. So we followed once more, only to discover, perhaps decades later, exactly what God was purposing.

When looking back across the years, design and purpose finally became clear. What didn't make sense before, in time makes perfect sense. Benefiting from this retrospective vantage point, it became more than apparent to us that all along the Lord had been in control and knew exactly what he was doing. Dr. F. B. Meyer acknowledged the tumultuous feelings we may have: the rain of tears, the shrinking of soul, the perplexity of mind while we navigate the circumstances God has chosen for us in life. But then, Dr. Meyer said, "... as days pass, some incident, some turn in the road, some concurrence of unforeseen circumstances will suddenly flash the conviction of mind that God's way was right, the wisest, and the best."[26]

So significant to us as well is the manner and method these turns and redirections transacted. Whether by vision or voice or some less sensational medium, we were led by his Spirit through our spirit, the new nature.[27]

Late one night a professor sat at his desk working on the next day's lectures. Shuffling through a collection of mail put there by the housekeeper, this professor quickly did his sorting of desired and undesired mail. After discarding the undesired mail into the trash, a green magazine, not even addressed to him, caught his attention. In retrieving this magazine from the wastebasket, the professor flipped its pages momentarily before seeing an article by Alfred

Baenger titled, "The Needs of the Congo Mission." Without knowing exactly why, this professor began to read it; and as he turned from page to page, what he read strangely captured his interest. The article told of the great need in the northern province of Gabon, located in what was then called the central Congo. The professor then closed the magazine and, without further inquiry, wrote in his diary that his life's direction was now set.

Who was he? Some highly impressionistic flake? A goofy gadfly who indiscriminately found meaning where there was none? No, this man had a doctor's degree in theology, philosophy, music, and medicine. In fact, he was the world's foremost interpreter of Bach! It was none other than Albert Schweitzer who went to French Equatorial Africa, sight unseen, because there was something inside him that urged him to go. This illustrates one of the benefits exclusive to the new nature.

Taking in the whole picture, A. B. Simpson wrote:

> Outside of Christ you are trembling on crumbling ground; beneath you are a yawning grave and an eternal fire, and above you is a cloud all lurid with judgment and despair. In him alone do you meet God and enter into his plan of love. That plan you can never understand until you get inside.[28]

But once you are inside, the plan he has put inside you becomes discoverable.

The Augmenting of Abilities

The solving of sin, the inspiring of image, the determining of destiny—but now the important question is, how? How is a Christian to move into this divinely determined destiny? Most of us know what it is like to worship, pray, and serve the Lord ineffectively—in fact, to live our lives ineffectively! This constantly occurs whenever we try to respond to God with our innate abilities. If this truth hasn't registered with you yet, I hope it will: Capacities of the soul are incapable of spiritual growth. Yet, when many of us come to church, only our soul participates. And when we engage other spiritual disciplines or duties, only our soul is activated for that, too. Addressing this dilemma, Andrew Murray writes:

> This is ... the reason for the weakness in the lives of many believers who read and know a great deal of Scripture. They do not know that it is the Spirit who quickens. The human understanding, however intelligent, however earnest, profits nothing.[29]

We can read a passage so loaded with life and power; nevertheless, the words of that passage will drift in the shallows of the mental unless they engage our spirit, in which the Holy Spirit indwells. Similarly, true prayer involves the Holy Spirit birthing in our human spirit those utterances that he will then bear to the Throne Room of the universe. It is a Spirit-to-spirit transaction. And for this precise reason Andrew Murray contended, "There can be no true worship except through the indwelling and unceasing operation of the Holy Spirit."[30]

Judson Cornwall correctly observed that "worship is fundamentally God's Spirit within us contacting the Spirit in God." Cornwall further explained, "God knows what changes are necessary on man's side ... to make worshippers out of us, so by living within man's spirit, God is able ... to overcome the barriers of worship which may be sin-generated, culturally induced, or religiously ingrained ...."[31]

When the Lord undertakes this work, he, to us, will be more than a fuzzy image evoked from the pages of Scripture, or a fading memory jostled from some long-ago encounter. Instead, the presence of God will break upon us, exciting a wonder so full, so overwhelming, it defies description. This will set truth on fire, prompting alternate responses of holy fear and exhilarating joy.

Without this infusion of the Spirit's presence, all will be hay and stubble, even if our efforts appear impressive in the eyes of the world. Whether we're talking about worship, prayer, or finding our purpose in life, the Third Person of the

Trinity is essential to the success of our endeavors. He must not only lead us (a task he will only undertake through the spirit within us where he abides), but he must also enable us. By an alignment of our heart with the providence of God, the Holy Spirit will set us on a course unique to our destiny, and will do so in a way that harnesses the passions of the heart.

Jessie Penn-Lewis explained: "Love converts what would otherwise be work into the spontaneous activity of the life within him. In doing what he loves to do he labors just as much as the birds do when they fly and sing."[32] Let there be another alignment, though, one not in accord with the divine life within, and the outcome will be different.

"Do you know you are a failure here, that you are making a great mistake in your ministry, that what you are doing does not count for much?" These were words that D. L. Moody spoke to a supposedly successful pastor, Wilbur Chapman. And, as you might well expect, these were words that wounded deeply.

Could it be that if the Lord were to give a present assessment of your service to him, he would say the same thing? Maybe you're not a preacher or a globe-trotting evangelist. Nevertheless, as you periodically examine your service to the Lord, do you at times wonder if you're doing this right?

Deeper down, Wilbur Chapman knew something was missing in his ministry. Convicted at last by a truth he had routinely deflected, Wilbur Chapman became desperate for the Holy Spirit's filling. On the sixteenth day of October in the year 1892, Wilbur Chapman experienced what had been missing in his life. The result, history reports, was an impact so revolutionary that years later Wilbur Chapman said, "If there has been any helpfulness in my ministry, if there has been any ability to win souls, I know when the change came."

There was a point in time, a specific date and a sudden occurrence, when all that God had put into this pastor's new nature was finally set free to minister. And having thus been loosed, it was the gates of hell that came under siege! Wouldn't you want dynamics like that released in your life? Wouldn't you want God to use you fully, without your flesh impeding his will?

To drive this lesson home, Andrew Murray asked:

> Do you want to have a heart overflowing with love to every believer, even to those outside your circle? Do you want a heart of love which can set others on fire? Do you want the very love of heaven to flow out from you? Do you want the self-sacrificing love of Jesus to take possession of you, so that you can bear and forebear, so that with the long suffering and tenderness and gentleness and the very meekness of Christ, the Lamb of God, you are willing to be the helper and servant of everyone, however unlovable or unlovely? Then you need to be filled with the Spirit.[33]

It is only when the Spirit fills that the new nature's attributes, anointed already, can be released to soften formerly hardened hearts and to illumine formerly darkened minds. G. D. Watson summed up the excellence and equilibrium of the new nature, once released by the Spirit's filling, when he wrote:

> A soul filled with God is serious but not sad, cheerful but not volatile; firm but not stubborn; gentle but not effeminate; discreet but not timid; bold but not rash; sweet but not sentimental; elevated but not proud; lowly but not cringing; holy but not harsh.[34]

There's little wonder God can achieve so much through a personality like this! As important as the new nature is, though, it is imperative to put on record that our trust must never be placed in the new nature, as if it has resident powers that can function independently of God. It does not. Jessie Penn-Lewis expounded this point, which should be obvious to all.

> In union with Christ we become "partakers of the divine nature" (II Peter 1:4), and have the very life

> of Jesus imparted to us. God revealed his Son—the very nature of his Son—in Paul, but Paul always proclaimed and relied upon the Man Christ Jesus in heaven, not upon his nature or his Spirit in himself.[35]

Our reliance must be on the provider of the new nature, but never on the new nature itself.

Still, we can rejoice over the benefits the new nature offers, and in gratitude we must do so, for as one of the Puritans put it, "I wrong the work of grace in my heart if I deny my new nature ...."[36] The new nature must always be affirmed, understood, and activated if it is going to solve sin, inspire image, determine destiny, and augment our abilities to serve and worship God.

Such blessed benefits, wouldn't you say? From such a great God! And for such a great purpose!

Reflection Questions

1. Of the four benefits the new nature provides, which one do you experience best?

2. Of the four benefits the new nature provides, which one do you need the most right now?

Chapter 17

Clarifying Contrasts

It was Erasmus, the influential Renaissance thinker, who said that all definitions are dangerous. This may be particularly true in theology, for once definitions are given a near creedal status, there is a tendency to equate those definitions with the Word of God itself. But, whether done through coercion or blind loyalty, this is a huge mistake, resulting in a mindless succumbing to rote, catechetical thinking. You know the routine: Just ask the question and—presto!—back comes the revered memorized response. And if parroted long enough, a rigidity of thought, if not a frigidity of atmosphere, will eventually solidify.

What must be remembered is that theological definitions resemble scaffolding. They are useful, but they mustn't be confused with the edifice they surround. With the passage of time, therefore, we should periodically check to see if our definitions have a proper proximity to what God has revealed. Where there are some theological loose ends flopping around, we must be honest enough to deal with these. And if relevant facts were erroneously excluded earlier, we must revisit the issue now with an agenda to assimilate.

Of course, a theology that doesn't define would be even more dangerous, since the Bible is hardly a compilation of vague, mysterious, untranslatable thoughts. To the contrary, our God—whose intent is to reveal and not conceal—is an excellent communicator! Therefore, taking confidence in this fact, we should seek an intelligent understanding of what the Bible says.

For some people, this concluding chapter may be unnecessary. However, for those less acquainted with this subject, a consideration of clarifying contrasts may be helpful. Sometimes we can read a book and be favorably impressed, only to later read another book on the same subject and be equally impressed, even though the two books have substantial disagreements. Our ability to interpret is going to be handicapped, obviously, if we don't have the necessary grid to process what we are reading. Therefore, to provide some pegs on which to hang this material, we will identify some "this, but not this" contrasts. The first contrast is easy.

Grace, Not Works

The one thing that people of other religions and the people of no religion have in common is this belief that if there is any justice at all, our final destiny will be determined by works. That is: If a person is good, he'll be rewarded; but if a person is bad, he'll be punished. Christianity is the only religion which says that the road of good works is the wrong road to be on.

According to Scripture, our goodness can never be good enough—and therefore grace is our *only* hope! Due, however, to the widespread appeal of "good works" thinking, and the penchant for this thinking to weasel back into New Testament theology, finding the proper relationship between law and grace is still an addressable issue.

The subject of law and grace is a major theme not only for the Book of Galatians but for twenty-seven other New Testament chapters as well. While Christians today may not get caught up in the intricacies of this debate, some "law/good works thinking" may creep into their minds if the appeals of "try harder" and "do better" are made. If Christians perceive that God's job is to hold up the standard and the Christian's job is to comply with that standard, then "law/good works thinking" has already contaminated their beliefs.

There is hardly any Christian anywhere who believes the flesh profits nothing. In practice, most Christians think that self can do a lot—not everything, which is why sometimes God must be called on to intervene. But, for the most part, their method of operation is this: Upon hearing *God's* will, they will then try to exercise *their* will, attempting to become dedicated, consecrated, conscientious, and committed. And should the struggle turn out to be harder, and their own resources weaker than they first thought, they will then ask God to bless these efforts with a divine intervention sufficient to put them over the top.

Grace says something quite different. Grace says that our contribution to the Kingdom of God is zero. Not fifty percent, or eighty percent, or some other worthy percentage. Our inability is such that we need God to undertake *every* time—and having undertaken, to then sustain and eventually consummate! This does not eliminate our will, but it does refuse to trust it. If we're going to rightly choose between gumption and gospel, we're going to have to acknowledge that we are weak—pathetically weak! And this will still be so even at the most advanced stage of Christian maturity.

Many years ago, a young lady named Charlotte Elliott went to see a minister, Caesar Milan. The purpose of her visit was to find out how to become a Christian. When this minister explained the gospel to her, she responded in surprise, "Do you mean that God will save me just as I am?" "My dear, Charlotte," he answered, "that is the only way he will save you—just as you are."

Stunned by this offer, she went home and wrote one of the most beloved hymns of the Christian faith, "Just As I Am." This, indeed, is how God wants us to come to him—and not just for salvation, but for everything, every time! Colossians 2:6 says that in the same way we received Jesus, we are now to live. So how did we receive him? We did so with a released faith that laid hold of God's grace. Well, as was true at the outset of our walk with God, this is how we are to live now. Acknowledging that we are weak, we are to release our faith in God with a determined dependence that recognizes that he is the source of all grace.

In fact, in that 1834 composition Charlotte Elliott included the line: "Yea, all I need in Thee to find, Oh Lamb of God, I come! I come!" And she came—not to be pitied, not to be comforted—but with an expectation to receive that which was currently lacking in her life.

Without question, there is a place for our will, as well as a place for good works. The Reformer Philip Melancthon wisely said that although salvation is by grace alone, once salvation is received, grace won't be alone—there will be good works! Yet, it must be remembered that the only works that can be regarded good are those that are generated by God's grace and not by human gusto. And what also must be remembered is that there is no quota, no certain threshold, which if not met excludes one from salvation. Holiness teachers raise a false standard if they ever suggest something like this.

Actual, Not Just Positional

A second contrast is a little more difficult to pin down. In the New Testament, there are numerous statements that declare how a believer is perceived by God. In Philippians 1:1 believers are called "saints." This word "saint," an appellation used 56 times in the New Testament, acknowledges the righteousness that Jesus achieved which, in the record books of heaven, was credited to our account. Technically, everybody is either a saint or an "ain't"—that is, either a Christian or a non-Christian.

Positional truth describes all those virtues Jesus merited on our behalf. Practical truth describes what we are presently experiencing, which may be far beneath the positional level. Although positionally I am a saint, in practice I may have told three lies today, and it's not even noon yet.

Too often in our interpretation of Scripture, we put all the honorific descriptions of a believer in the positional truth category, thinking that if it doesn't describe present behavior, that's where it must go. For example, when Ephesians 4:24 says that our new man is created in righteousness and true holiness, we've made the mistake of thinking this is referring to positional righteousness—the kind of righteousness depicted by the phrase: when God looks at us he sees Jesus. This aspect of righteousness is not anything we experience; instead, it is a declaration of God officially recorded in heaven the moment we became a Christian. Theologians call this imputed righteousness. In this forensic sense, a judicial accounting is rendered.

Ephesians 4:24, however, doesn't belong in this category, because this verse is describing a righteousness that actually exists in the believer. Stephen Charnock declared, "Righteousness and holiness is the very constitution of the new creature."[1] Not in heaven someday, now! Not an imputing, but an imparting—it is a reality that can be experienced and not just explained. J. N. Darby said, "The very essence of practical Christianity is our partaking of the divine nature, and having God's moral attributes conferred on us, or implanted with his nature in us."[2]

If positional righteousness is our only answer, then consistent obedience in this life is a lost cause. For under that schematic, the forces of sin have been downgraded only slightly. Whereas before, these forces overmatched us *always*; now, they overmatch us *often*. And there's not much of a gospel in that!

By overloading the positional truth category, and by disregarding the actual truth category, Christians have set themselves up for a doublespeak deception that leads to moral ineptitude. This is why so much of new nature teaching has been watered down. We've been putting what belongs in the actual truth category in the positional truth category.

Immediate, Not Gradual

One of the biggest misconceptions of the Christian life can be described as the stair-case approach to maturity. Principle by principle, obedience by obedience, we begin the long, arduous ascent, bit by bit getting better and better, until qualities resembling Jesus finally begin to appear. Some enthusiasts for this approach will use Jeremiah's symbolism of the potter's wheel, wherein we are the recalcitrant clay in this metaphor, a big glob of goo which, because of the skilled and indomitable patience of God, finally takes shape. C. S. Lewis spoke in a similar vein when he imagined our lives under construction. With so much sawing and banging going on, we begin to wonder, he said, what's God up to? Shouldn't all this construction work be over by now? According to Lewis, the reason we're disturbed is we thought the Lord was building a cottage, when in fact his designs called for a palace.[3]

What all these metaphors have in common is the view that the Christian life begins with an unrealized potential—the seed that grows, the baby that crawls—that kind of potential. And while there is some truth to these observations, the doctrine of the new nature conveys a truth that is in a very different direction. In his book, *Forever Triumphant*, F. J. Huegel wrote:

> Give up the fight if in your own strength you have been struggling to obtain a victory which you seem never quite able to achieve, in spite of prayers and tears and effort and consecration and what not. You do not have to climb this stony, thorn-infested, unscalable mountain. You can begin at the top.[4]

And the reason you can begin there is because at the very moment you became a Christian, God put a new nature in you that is already perfect. In was in this context that Alfred Edersheim contrasted the ethics of the gospel from every other system of ethics:

> Every moral system is a road by which, through self-denial, discipline and effort, men seek to reach the goal. Christ begins with the goal, and places his disciples at once in a position to which all other teachers point as the end. They work up to the goal ... What the others labor for, Christ gives.[5]

Depicting this truth in a somewhat facetious way, the story is told of two farmers, a father and a son, who had never been to the big city before. As they drove to the city in their old truck, they saw, for the very first time, all those skyscrapers! Well! Their mouths dropped, their eyes bulged; they could do little more than stare at each other in stunned silence.

Upon entering a huge, modern hospital, the two men noticed a homely, heavy-set woman walk toward two big doors which, to their amazement, opened and closed all by themselves. Utterly fascinated, they moved closer to inspect this phenomenon. In doing so, they saw numbers above the door start to light up: two-three-four-five. What were they for? Where was this woman going? They had no answer. But as they continued to watch, suddenly the numbers began to reverse: twenty-four, twenty-three, twenty-two, twenty-one. Momentarily, the doors soon swung open, and out came this very attractive woman!

Father and son looked at her and then at each other, neither of them knowing what to make of it all. Then the father's eyes lit up when he said, "Son, let's go get your mother; I want to run her through that thing!"

What seems humorous, if not fanciful, is that a very radical transformation could so instantly occur. And yet, on a far more profound level, that is precisely what the Bible teaches. Colossians 2:10 says, "... you are complete in him ...." This isn't a crawl-walk-and-run sort of a thing. Everything God ever wanted you to be, he already put inside you at the time you were born again. The issue, then, isn't one of a progressive *rebuilding* of the image of God inside you (God has already done that), but a progressive *releasing* of this glorious, no-way-to-improve-upon-it image.

One Nature, Not Two

The image we have of ourselves is a powerful determinant for our future. The choices we make, the dreams we pursue, are going to be confined to the framing of that image.

The statement—"If you see you as you, you'll be you!"—may seem to be a tautology, but it really isn't. Tautologies rename their antecedents, but in this case the renaming is based on confusion. We are not a compilation of all that has flowed into our lives, either by heredity or experience.

Though our past may say otherwise, we are who God says we are—a brand-new creation.

But due to the fact contrary forces within militate against Christians, successfully, it's easy for Christians to believe that they have two natures. A popular illustration often used to depict our two nature conflict is that of two dogs. According to this illustration, we have a good dog and a bad dog; and whichever one we feed the most is going to be the most active. But if we see ourselves in this way—the possessor of two natures, one good and one bad—then we will live that way!

The biggest problem of the two nature theory is that it lethally lowers the ceiling of our vision of what the Christian life can be. What should properly be defined as an alien sin-force, has now been elevated to the level of our nature. And to make matters worse, this "nature" is regarded as permanent by those who espouse the two-nature theory! But if we believe this theory, this "half and half" identity stuff is going to cause us a lot of problems. The two tributaries, one pure and the other polluted, will ceaselessly intermingle.

The Scripture, however, never says that we have two natures. To the contrary, it very specifically says that our old man was crucified (Romans 6:6), that we "*were* by nature the children of wrath" (Ephesians 2:3) but that now we are a new creation; the old has passed away (II Corinthians 5:17). As previously noted, when Paul contended against those contrary sin forces, he twice said, and accurately so, "it is not I" (Romans 7:17, 20). This we must also say, because just as a wrong labeling of medicine can be injurious to our health, so also a wrong labeling of our identity can be detrimental to our spiritual life.

Let's be clear on this: This discussion of one nature versus two natures isn't just the fussiness of airhead academia—much more is at stake here! Indeed, carelessness on this issue brings casualties!

The hyphenated, bifurcated view of man that sees us as part new nature and part something else produces disastrous results (see Appendix A). A belief in two natures is a belief that severely reduces God's real remedy for sin. If convinced we have two natures, we will have all the explanation we need for ongoing sin in our life and therefore may tend to yield to the inevitable.

Victorious, Not Defeated

It is commonly supposed that the sin struggle of Romans 7 is an unavoidable, inescapable model. Paul is admired for his noble efforts, and gets our sympathies for his feelings of guilt. But to ourselves we think: That's just the way it is in this world; the sinning will never stop. And as further proof of the ongoing sin, we recall some other words the great Apostle wrote: "O wretched man that I am" ... "Not that I have already attained" ... "I am the chief of sinners." All such verses cause us to think if that were true of Paul, the greatest missionary theologian of all time, then the rest of us are sunk.

Could it be, though, that Paul's words have been misunderstood? For example, when Paul said, "not that I have already attained," he wasn't saying that he was bogged down in the swamp of sin and hadn't laid hold of anything that would pull him out. It should be remembered that this same Paul spoke of the Christian life as a "glory to glory" journey (II Corinthians 3:18). One has to wonder, though, how it could possibly be that, if he were constantly defeated by sin.

I submit that the "not attaining" in Philippians 3:12 refers not to a freedom from sin but to these increasing and elevating glories. To support this point of view, Paul also said in Philippians 3:12 that he was not "already perfected." In our minds, these words have been reduced to mean, "Nobody's perfect; we're all in the same boat, adrift on a sea of sin." But Paul was really saying something much more positive! He was in essence saying there was more of God's good he had yet to receive—a greater intimacy, a greater release of his spirit to dominate his soul, a greater capacity to serve God. Properly understood, then, Philippians 3:12 has more a mountain-top atmosphere to it, and not the valley-bound spin less observant ones have given it.

When Paul said that he was the chief of sinners (I Timothy 1:15), the very worst of the worst, this wasn't referring to his present status with God. This couldn't be the case, because just two verses prior to this statement Paul referred to his pre-Christian days saying, "I was formerly a blasphemer, a persecutor, and an insolent man." It was the fact that Paul had been the arch-enemy of the Church during her infant and vulnerable days that potentially merited his hall of shame status. This wasn't the end of the story, obviously, since Paul then speaks of what changed the whole picture—God's mercy and grace. In one supernatural encounter of the road to Damascus, Paul underwent a radical change.

Indeed, this change so transformed his life the term "chief of sinners" no longer applied to the Spirit-filled apostle. Just a little reasoning will make the point clear. For how could the man who told us that sin would not have dominion over us (Romans 6:14), and that by walking in the Spirit we would not fulfill the lust of the flesh (Galatians 5:16), be bogged down in sin more deeply than anyone else? That would make no sense! And further: It would completely disagree with the biblical account of this missionary's life! And as for those words, "O, wretched man that I am," Paul wasn't saying how evil he was; he was just saying how unhappy he *was*. These are words that characterize emotions and not the true identity of a believer (see Appendix F).

Again, it must be emphasized that Paul got out of a Romans 7 defeat and into a Romans 8 victory.[6] The defeat Paul reported in Romans 7 is not what the Christian is doomed to live. God has given believers power over sin and authority over Satan, although many Christians aren't aware of what God has given. By lacking this knowledge, Satan gained an advantage. In his book, *Destined to Overcome*, Paul Billheimer writes:

> Satan has succeeded in keeping God's people in the dark about what happened to him at the cross. By brainwashing and deception, he has succeeded in convincing the church that he is almost, if not quite, as powerful as God, when actually he has no power at all. He has no legal standing, no right, no authority. He knows that

when the church fully realizes the utterness of his defeat and how to use the authority which has been delegated to her, he is done for.[7]

The accomplishments of the cross are only partially known by most believers, and that part isn't the half of it! Paul knew what these accomplishments were, every one of them, and he knew what they meant. Hence, the biblical record of his ongoing victory!

Constant, Not Sporadic

Another contrast to contemplate differentiates between a religion of fits and starts and a relationship that is ongoing and reliable. When Scripture likens the indwelling Spirit to a river of living water, it intentionally leaves the impression this is a sustained, satisfying experience. The model is not one of an oasis thirst-quencher, where there's so much dryness until finally some welcome relief arrives. For instead of occasional spurts, God's river is like the one sung about in the musical "Showboat"—a river that "just keeps rolling along."

Repeatedly Scripture promises a quality of life that is enduring: an abiding in Jesus, being kept in perfect peace, the joy no one can take away, the promise of never thirsting again. Hudson Taylor remarked, "The cause of thirst may be irremediable. One coming, one drinking may refresh and comfort: but we are to be ever coming, ever drinking. No fear of emptying the fountain or exhausting the river!"[8] Charles Finney, who knew well the constancy of God's supply, said, "Though all else should fail, still his joy would be overflowing, perennial. No circumstances whatever could have the power to quench the flame of love, no wind to parch the soil or dry the current of holy joy in the soul."[9]

There are times when the Lord seems to withdraw some of these things. The real purpose for brief withdrawals, though, is the enlargement of our hearts and the increasing of our fellowship capacity. His is but a lover's retreat that invites us to pursue him. It was in this regard that the great English writer, F. B. Myer, once wrote:

> … we must learn to know and believe the constancy of God's love. We may not feel it. We may deem it shut up and gone forever. We may imagine that we have forfeited all claims to it. We may think of it as Arctic travelers, dying in the icy darkness, dream of the summers of early childhood. But, nevertheless, it has not altered. Staunch as the affection of a friend, true as the love of a mother, the love of God abides unchangeable as himself. Mists, born of the swamps and marshes of your own sin, obscure the light of that; but [this love] is shining yet as brilliantly as ever and will shine on until it has dispelled all shrouding veils and bathes you again in its warm and blessed glow.[10]

The experience of many Christians is one of declensions and detours. Just when they get on track, they get off again. Just when they experience a spiritual high, their spiritual temperature plummets soon afterward. And, yes, not too long after the revival is over, they're in need of someone to prop their sagging faith. But surely this isn't the Spirit-to-spirit intimacy (our nature enmeshing intimately with his) that the Bible talks about. Instead of all those lectures on the unimportance of feelings, what is really needed is a recognition that something *is* wrong. Watchman Nee observed that whenever our spirit is properly related to God's spirit (like a light bulb in a socket), there is going to be a consistent glow, and not a flickering, fading spark.

Confident, Not Confused

Another paradigm to ponder involves faith—and since faith is the victory, we have to get this right! If faith is the one bridge to the resources of God, then the enemy is going to do what all military generals would do—attack it! The enemy's rationale is obvious: If the supply routes can be cut off, then the opposition's ability to mount an offensive will be greatly weakened. Today, to a large extent, we would have to admit that the enemy has succeeded at this, since only a small minority of Christians know how to make a faith transaction with God.

The reason they don't know is because it's not being taught in many churches. And one of the reasons it's not being taught is because the evangelical world holds views that make this teaching impossible. For example, as long as we think that the sovereignty of God can cancel out the promises of God; that our knowledge of God's will is uncertain; that any claim to know it is presumptuous; that faith claims amount to "putting God in a box," that we should keep asking God for what we've already asked him, we are undermining truths foundational to a successful faith transaction.

Moreover, as long as we put all suffering in the same category, thinking, perhaps, that for character-building reasons God wants us to be sick, or wants us to be poor; and, too, as long as we contend that this "we live in a fallen world" rationale is the proper explanation for what often happens to us, then these and other thoughts like these are going to sabotage faith.[11]

Let me throw the gauntlet down. Evangelicals cannot put forward a consistent how-to view on faith, because too much of what they believe knocks the props out from what faith requires. Of course, exhorting people to have faith, without offering a systematic reflection on how to do it, will lead them exactly where they are—confused and ineffective.

Any thoughtful analysis of what's happening in today's church must compel the conclusion that the faith bridge *is* down, and some of the most revered teachings in the church are responsible for this. Yet the problem of reconciling a God who is all-wise, all-powerful, and all-loving with the presence of sin and suffering in this world need not be as vexing as we have made it out to be. Theologians refer to this as the problem of theodicy—be it of the Aristotelian variety, or of the Augustinian variety, or some other spin-off theory. However, as all theologians readily admit none of these approaches solve the problem. The reason our present formulations leave us scratching our heads and shrugging our shoulders is because some of the things we've assumed to be axiomatic aren't even true?

Significant contributions have been made by the Deeper Life movement, the Pentecostal movement, and the Charismatic movement which now make the problem of theodicy more solvable. One of these contributions relates to implications engendered by the new nature. Another contribution comes from the delegated authority God has given to believers, for which faith transactions, properly undertaken, are essential. Yet, many Christians know very little about the new nature or how to release faith.

It goes without saying that whenever an army lacks proper intelligence, and whenever its soldiers receive conflicting reports, that army and those soldiers are going to be vulnerable to the menacing attacks of the enemy. But for the Church of the living God, a predicament like this is altogether needless! Because the promises of God *are* true! And the revelation he gave *is* clear! And his faithfulness to perform *is* unimpeachable!

Active, Not Passive

There are those who malign faith by supposing it is too passive, and others who overly exalt the will by demanding it to be too active. To conclude that the antidote to a grinding-it-out-in-the-flesh-righteousness is a sit-back-and-watch-what-God-will-do passivity is a major mistake. Clearly, we are to work out what God works in; and if we don't do this, the spiritual growth enterprise will come to a grinding halt.

Bishop Handley Moule declared, "The Scripture doctrine of sanctification teaches no effortless passivity."[12] Those who would criticize the teaching "Let go and let God" as being a call to passivity do so on a false and fictitious basis. Of course we are to let go of our problem as we cast it upon the Lord (I Peter 1:7)! And of course we are to let God do his work without the ill-advised intrusions of our fleshly efforts! But this hardly sanctions idleness and slothfulness. Bishop Moule is right, "No will is so fully constituted for work as the regenerate and surrendered will."[13]

Likewise, Charles Finney declared, "A passive holiness is impossible and absurd. Let no one say that when we exhort people to trust wholly in Christ we teach that anyone should be or can be passive in receiving and co-operating with the divine influence within."[14]

Remember: God lives *in* me, not *instead* of me. His life in my new nature is so powerful, however, I can live in a way that far surpasses previously set goals. The fact that I can, however, doesn't necessarily mean that I will. I could, for example, be driving a car that has a two-hundred mile per hour capacity and a two-hundred thousand mile engine endurance; but if I'm only going to the store once a week, what would be the point? My resources aren't being utilized.

The little quip, "The law says do, the gospel says done," speaks a wonderful truth, especially when the "done" includes our new nature. But these little sayings have their limitations; and if not explained properly, they may spawn distortions. The fact that God made my new nature perfect, doesn't mean that automatically, without any exercise of my faith or will, perfection is going to behaviorally manifest. It won't. Yes, the steering is a lot easier when the engine is on, but one still has to steer ... and study the map ... and maintain the car.

The directive of Scripture to put on the new man indicates an active role we are to undertake. In his book, *The Psychology of Redemption*, Oswald Chambers wrote:

> The putting on of the new man means we must not allow our natural life to dictate to the Son of God, but see to it that we give him ample chance to dominate every bit of us. He has delivered us from sin, now we must see that he dominates our natural life also until the life of Jesus manifests ....[15]

The term "putting on" implies purposing. It is the language of will, intent, determination. The author of *Knowing God's Secrets*, John Hunter, put it this way. "God wants me to avail myself of his full salvation—not only the 'act of Christ' when he died for me on the cross of Calvary, but also the 'activity of Christ' as he lives in my heart through his Holy Spirit."[16] This availing requires continual purposing on our part.

A vivid contrast to this way of life is illustrated by Ephraim in the Old Testament, who, on the day of battle, turned their backs and left. It wasn't because these people were weak or ill-prepared that they did this, because they had enjoyed impressive victories before, as their name implies (Ephraim means "twice faithful"). Despite these past victories, though, and despite present and ample resources, Ephraim simply made the decision to take the easy way out. And therefore they became exhibit A for dodging one's duty.

Centuries later, when reflecting on this inexplicable incident, the psalmist said of them, "They were turned aside like a deceitful bow" (Psalm 78:57). A more literal rendering of this text would be a "slack bow." In his book, *Limiting God*, John Hunter pointed out: "All the pieces were there—the wooden upright which gave the tension, the string that thrust forward the arrow—but the whole thing was slack. The string hung limp and useless as the bow was utterly ineffective."[17] What produced this slackness? A lack of will, a lack of faith, the lack of a proper intimacy with God. John Hunter reminds us, "... backsliding" comes from "slack abiding." If we don't stay close to Jesus, we will fail the Lord by taking an undeserved rest at the very time we are needed.

Some people may wonder, "But doesn't the Bible talk about rest?" Yes, but not the kind of rest that is passive and unresponsive. There are people who gather in "holy huddles" but never break out to play the game. Norman Grubb described a more biblical view of "rest" when he offered this illustration of people thrown to sea because of a shipwreck:

> In the struggling position they are in the water fighting with the waves and are in need of help themselves. In the clinging position they are holding on to the boat; they are quite safe themselves, but cannot help anyone else, because both of their hands are occupied. In the resting position they are sitting in the boat with both their hands free to help others.[18]

Instead of the underutilized car, the slack bow, the perpetual huddle, and the "automatic pilot" view of

Christianity, God wants us busily engaged from a place of rest. Whereas before, we were struggling too much with ourselves to be able to help others, now, with our own needs met, we are to be actively engaged in those people-helping tasks that God has given us to do. Too often we wrestle when we should rest.

It is hoped that these eight contrasts will clarify what new nature living is, and is not, like. And it is further hoped that you will increasingly show forth the new nature's fruit. John 15 speaks of "fruit," "more fruit" and "much fruit." This perhaps has some parallel with other New Testament labels: thirtyfold, sixtyfold, a hundredfold; or babes, young men, and fathers. The stage one level of growth, fruit, may be minimal. Some Christians may have produced a shriveled grape that only the all-seeing eye of God can find!

The stage two level of growth, which the Bible calls "more fruit," *will* be noticed by others—and very favorably so! However, in this more moderate and incomplete stage, the attention given may go no further than, "He's a really nice guy!" or "She's a very wonderful person."

By contrast, at the stage three level of growth, what Jesus called "much fruit," the assurance is given that what so marvelously manifested will neither be overlooked nor confused; instead, the Father will be glorified!

This should be our goal: not just token changes the world can scarcely see, not just halfway changes that the world may misinterpret, but changes that are so supernatural in their source, and abundant in their extent, that everyone will instinctively know this is of God!

We are told that when the twelve spies came back from the Promise Land, it took two of them to carry just one cluster of grapes (Numbers 13:23). Have you ever heard of such a thing—two men, one cluster of grapes? What kind of grapes were these? They couldn't have been ordinary grapes or Israel's leaders would have left them behind, and the Bible would have never mentioned them. So these had to be extraordinary grapes, a testimony of God's great provisions.

This is exactly what our world needs to see in us—fruit so extraordinary in quality and quantity that all will know its true source, the Lord Jesus, the originator of our new nature.

Reflection Questions

1. Of the eight contrasts provided in this chapter, which one helped you the most?

2. How has this study of the new nature changed your life?

Introduction to the Appendices

The following appendices will appeal to some readers and not others. These appendices further credential this teaching on the new nature, and for that purpose a more advanced theological reasoning is used. Although advanced in thought, this material is not academic; and it does use an accessible writing style.

Theologically, the first and last appendices are the most significant, whereas the other appendices are more practical. The practical appendices offer further reflections on chapters 13-15, the chapters that relate the new nature to our thinking, feeling, and doing. Getting a more complete picture of the new nature's relationship to these faculties of the soul is helpful.

Too often, those in the Pentecostal and Charismatic communities tend to end the story with the filling of the Spirit, as if that experience settles everything. It does not. What we must also understand is how the Spirit-filling, and how new nature, relate to these functions of the soul. The dynamics involving these functions fundamentally changed after Jesus came into our life. Their capacities changed. Their processes changed. And their outcomes could dramatically change if the truths in these appendices were understood and utilized.

Other parts of the church have likewise addressed our thoughts, feelings, and will with little regard for the new nature, or for the Spirit's filling. Consequently, the Word-to-soul dynamics that failed in the Old Testament are needlessly continued today. Earnest and sincere Christians will spend hours hearing and reading the Word, yet wonder why the results are so disappointing. The reason is not that difficult to discover.

Any spiritual growth that bypasses the new nature, or simply assumes the new nature will automatically function once we are Christians, is bound to fail. And has failed. Miserably. Do understand: God will not set aside what he has so marvelously created in the new nature to help us grow in some other way. When the Bible calls for changed behavior, it repeatedly mentions the new man. This instruction is given to believers, you will notice. So just because you are a believer doesn't mean you are functioning in the flow of the new nature. There are principles to learn, steps to take, which if not learned and implemented will leave you without the abilities you need to grow as you could in the life of God.

In more recent days, many in the church have come to see that the believer has one nature, not two. After asserting this truth, however, the conversation largely stopped. Why? One reason for this is attributable to one-nature adherents seeing no difference between soul and spirit. This inevitably throws up a barrier. Because unless distinctions between soul and spirit can be proven, the new nature cannot be defined. This is exactly why preachers and publishers have offered so little information about the new nature. This first appendix, I submit, is critical to averting this impasse, because it answers the objections dichotomists make.

The last appendix deals with the agony of that man in Romans chapter 7. Many in the church believe this is what Christians must go through. Consequently, the level of living the new nature is supposed to enable is seriously challenged by their view of Romans 7. Precisely for this reason, then, a better understanding of Romans 7 is essential, if the doctrine of the new nature is to maintain its credibility.

Appendix A
Soul and Spirit

Theologians will form their view of man not on the basis of human observation—whether external in nature (like the behaviorist approach) or internal in nature (like the psychoanalytic approach)—but on the more reliable basis of divine revelation. Although psychology has its contributions to make, there can be no source of knowledge superior to that given by the One who first formed man before breathing into him the breath of life. Think of it. When man first saw the morning dew, God was there! The glistening of this dew cast its diamond-like luster, but even more captivating than those sun rays beaming through the trees above was the glory radiating from the Creator! For there shone from the face of God that day expressions of pleasure and favor! Man! Bearer of the divine image! Partner with God in earthly government! And one-day friend with God in heavenly joy!

That which God designed man to be, and all the means and methods necessary to fulfill this design, are simply not knowable on the basis of human observation. To get this information, one must consult a higher source. It is true that the sociologist, anthropologist, and historian provide useful information. But none of these disciplines can offer summary judgments about man, because their perspectives are limited by time, by selective sampling, by an inability to account for divergent moral outcomes, and by an inability to know the human heart (John 2:24).

Likewise, the poet, playwright, and song writer have their reflections to offer—sometimes insightful, at other times even inspiring. But like the observation of man, so, too, the inspiration of man can never trump the revelation of God. Shakespeare wrote with much inspiration, certainly, when he had Hamlet saying:

> What a piece of work is man! How noble in reason! How infinite in faculty! In form, in moving, how express and admirable! In action,

how like an angel! In apprehension, how like a god!

Still, what is needed most is a revelation from outside the rim of human genius, since only an assessment from man's Maker—determinative in value and definitive in insight—can tell us what we need to know.

When it comes to the nature of man, there are no words loftier in theme and more revealing in content than the words Jesus spoke to Nicodemus that night, declaring that he (and really we) "must be born again." To be born again means that the essence of man, whose source had been Adam, is radically changed so that a new life, whose source is Jesus, reconstitutes man's inner being.

The believer's union with Jesus is obviously crucial to understanding the new nature. So logic requires asking the question: How are we to understand this union? In a sermon entitled, "True Christian Union," R. A. Torrey answered: It is "... one of the grandest, one of the most glorious, one of the divinest, one of the most beneficent things on earth. It is the life of God the Father and the Son reproduced in the Church."[1]

Like most theologians, Charles Hodge strongly affirmed the union between Christ and the believer when he said that "they have a common life analogous to that which exists between the vine and its branches, and between the head and members of the body. The believer is truly a partaker of the life of Christ."[2] However, unlike most theologians, Hodge was equally forthright in admitting that a lack of clarity exists about this union. According to Hodge, "... representations of Scripture concerning the union between Christ and his people are neither to be explained nor explained away."[3] According to him, attempts to further define our union with Christ are speculative and unwarranted.[4]

This perceived inability to define our union with Christ, and hence the new nature the believer has, is not without consequence. Succumbing to a view like Hodge put forth has caused new nature teaching today to be more abstract than useful and, hence, to float away into what C. S. Lewis called "idealistic gas." That this should happen to a doctrine so essential to spiritual growth is nothing short of tragic. That it has happened, though, becomes obvious by how seldom the pulpit talks about the new nature and how infrequently books on this subject are published. Most church members do not have a functional understanding of the new nature. This deficit accounts for an enormous harm to their souls, one exceedingly difficult to overstate and quite impossible to ignore.

Further complicating this inability to define the new nature is the dominant suasion of the dichotomous view of man among theologians.[5] Gordon Clark states that for almost 1500 years "trichotomous thinking was largely entombed in silence; and although it enjoys some popularity today this popularity does not extend to theologians."[6] In his book, *The Bible Doctrine of Man*, Professor John Laidlaw explained:

> The trichotomy of body, soul, and spirit held an important place in the theology of some of the Greek Christian Fathers; but, in consequence of its seeming bias towards a Platonic doctrine of the soul and of evil, still more because of its use by Apollinaris to underprop grave heresy as to the Person of Christ, it fell into disfavor, and may be said to have been discarded from the time of Augustine till its revival within a quite modern period.[7]

The belief that there is no difference between soul and spirit has the effect of shutting down discussions about what the new nature is and how the new nature operates. For if soul and spirit are indistinguishable from each other, as almost every theological scholar contends, then where in the immaterial part of our makeup is the new nature? If all our attitudes—the good and bad, the counterfeit and the authentic—co-mingle in our interior life, how can we ever speak persuasively about the new nature? Would not the new nature in this context be confined to the theoretical, a distant idealism that is neither provable nor practical?

In attempting to resolve this problem (is there a difference between soul and spirit?), of necessity we begin with what we know. And we know the soul is far from perfect. Indeed, all the core functions of the soul—the way we think, the way we feel, the way we decide—are chronically problematic for us even after we become a Christian. So how can the new nature be part and parcel with that? If the soul is indistinguishable from the spirit, and if the soul is contaminated by Adamic infection and is thus hampered with daily dysfunction, an extension of this logic leads to the conclusion that the spirit is also contaminated and dysfunctional. According to this theory, then, the question—in what way is our soul and spirit connected to divine life?—appears to have no answer.

The inability to be more specific about the location of the new nature triggers a blurring and blinding that renders the new nature a theological abstraction—at best, an ideal that is affirmed but not explained; at worst, a tantalizing fantasy that bears little resemblance to daily life. This supposed inability, however, is more apparent than real.

It was with profound understanding that A. B. Simpson wrote, "Christianity is the religion of the spirit."[8] Extending this thought, Samuel Chadwick wrote, "The Christian life is above all else a matter of spirit. It is not a philosophy to be debated; not an ordinance to be observed; not an ethic to be achieved."[9] Underscoring the implications of this issue, Watchman Nee wrote, "To fail to distinguish between spirit and soul is fatal to spiritual maturity."[10] That may be a bit of an overstatement, but the problem this statement portends is very real. In his book, *What is Man?* T. Austin Sparks contended strongly for the need to distinguish soul from spirit.

> We cannot but feel that a very great deal of loss would have been prevented, and gain would have been secured, if that distinguishing had been applied to the matter of soul and spirit. This is no matter of merely technical interest to Bible students, but one which involves and touches the spiritual life of God's people at almost every

point, and governs the whole question of life and death in spiritual things. There are few things more vital to fullness of life and effectiveness of service than this.[11]

Yet, much of the church, for most of the time, has failed to make the distinction between soul and spirit. And in this regard theologians have not helped us very much; because once they interjected the theory of spirit/soul sameness, a dense cloud descended—one so dark and thick in its composition that peering through it was virtually impossible. Notions about the new nature in *this* context became vague, theoretical, and impractical, rendering believers vulnerable to an outcome Scripture warned against: "having a form of godliness but denying the power thereof" (II Timothy 3:5). This, unfortunately, is a much documented reality plaguing today's church.

There is a need to respond to dichotomists' objections to soul/spirit distinctions. Making contrary assertions, and setting forth alternative views, aren't good enough if dichotomists' objections aren't directly refuted on the terms these objections were offered. Indeed, not to do so, allows credibility to the dichotomist view to continue and further relegates new nature teaching to the status of vision and theory.

The major reason most theologians see no difference between the soul and the spirit is because they believe every function the Bible attributes to the spirit is also attributed to the soul. Moreover, every function the Bible attributes to the heart (which is said to be a part of the soul) is also attributed to the spirit. Therefore, given the sameness of these attributions, supposed differences between the soul and spirit seem to dissipate upon examination. Without further examination, of course, the debate ends; and the only conclusion that seems possible (the wrong one) prevails.

Although an examination of soul and spirit can be lengthy and tedious, it is possible to deal more briefly with this subject if we identify pivotal premises that differentiate dichotomists (those who believe soul and spirit are not distinguishable) from trichotomists (those who think soul and spirit are distinguishable). The dichotomists believe there are two parts to man—the material part, the body; and the immaterial part, the soul and spirit. The trichotomists believe there are three parts to man—spirit, soul, and body. For trichotomists, the new nature is located in the realm of our spirit. For dichotomists, this location is less certain. Some claim its location is in the soul. Others claim its location is in the soul and body—the whole man.[12]

Downgrading the Spirit

One pivotal premise foundational to the dichotomist view is succinctly stated by Wayne Grudem in his admirable work, *Systematic Theology*. Professor Grudem declares:

> The human spirit is not something that is dead in an unbeliever but comes to life when someone trusts in Christ, because the Bible talks about unbelievers having a spirit that is obviously alive but is in rebellion against God—whether Sihon, King of Heshbon (Deuteronomy 2:30: "the Lord hardened his spirit"), or Nebuchadnezzar (Daniel 5:20: "his spirit was hardened so that he dealt proudly"), or the unfaithful people of Israel (Psalm 78:8: their "spirit was not faithful to God").[13]

What Grudem says here is typical of dichotomists: They tend to minimize the radical change God made in our spirit. Logically, dichotomists have to do this, since they think the soul and spirit are virtually identical. For this reason, then, any discussion elevating the spirit beyond that of the soul is going to be challenged by dichotomists. Grudem concludes, "It is not just that one part of us (called the spirit) has been made alive; we as whole persons are a 'new creation' in Christ (2 Corinthians 5:17)."[14]

Really? The soul is alive to the same extent the spirit is? And our bodies are also alive in some way different from the bodies of the Old Testament faithful? This doesn't make sense, for we all know what our bodies are like; and we also know what our souls are like. Therefore, hope sinks and encouragement deflates, if the new nature is presented in terms like these. By making body and soul referents for the new nature—the domains for its residence, the proofs of its existence, the displays of its genius, and the exhibits of what it can produce—the doctrine of the new nature becomes more hollow than the wispy sentiments of a Romantic poet. And by saying that the spirit we have now is capable of sin today, just as it was during the Old Testament, and just as the soul is capable of sin, smashes hope with the sledgehammer of doubt.

Dr. Grudem further elaborates his theory about our spirit by saying outright: "When Paul encourages the Corinthians to 'cleanse themselves from every defilement of body and spirit' (II Corinthians 7:1), he clearly implies that there can be defilement and (or sin) in our spirits."[15] Spurgeon argued otherwise, though, saying, "... there is no sin in the newborn nature, it cannot sin because it is born of God ...."[16]

The downgrading of the spirit, a major premise in the dichotomist argument, can be tracked in its direction as we plot three points on a graph. Point one: the soul and spirit are the same. Point two: The spirit in a believer today isn't entirely new; it's an extension of what existed during the Old Testament. Point three: The spirit in us today is capable of sinning, just as it has always been capable of sinning throughout human history. But if all this is true, if the spirit part of our being is as limited and vulnerable as any other part of our being, the new nature is almost unintelligible in this kind of paradigm.

To answer Grudem's latter point, there is a need to recall that most commentators think that II Corinthians 7:1, for reasons of substance and style, belongs to the previous chapter. The main thrust of the previous chapter deals with the need for separation from unrighteousness (verse 17) and from the perilous condition of being unequally yoked (verse 14). It is instructive that the Greek word for "cleanse" in II Corinthians 7:1, in its root, includes a connotation from agriculture that means to clear away, as one might clear away weeds from plants or from vegetation of value. Again, separation is the prevailing theme of this passage, and so the idea of separation extends to II Corinthians 7:1.

Even if cleansing is the preferred rendering, this still involves dirt being separated from what it is attached to. Something defiling may have close proximity to my spirit, but that doesn't mean that my spirit produced this defilement, participated in this defilement, or was in essence diminished by this defilement. The implication Dr. Grudem finds in this verse is a construct he imposes on it. The concept of the new spirit sinning is not borne out by the text itself. When A. B. Simpson instructs us to "detach our spirit from every evil thing that touches it,"[16] he is in line with Scripture. This detaching, this steering away, is necessary because evil approached, and not because our spirit welcomed the approach.

The Greek word for "defilement" in this same verse, *molusmos*, is used nowhere else in the New Testament. Three times this word is used in the Greek Old Testament, the Septuagint, and each time the reference denotes religious defilement. False religion, error, and heresy appear to be the concerns targeted. Since this passage in II Corinthians isn't focused on the makeup of the believer's inner life, it is likely that Paul's mention of body and spirit in this verse simply suggests totality, completeness, and nothing more. The broadly stated directive from Paul in this passage—don't let false religion affect you in any way—must be seen as just that. To say more than this is to offer conclusions which are the product of dubious deductions.

Moreover, all the references Dr. Grudem finds in the Old Testament where the spirit is said to sin have no reference to New Testament believers, since God said he would give us a new spirit, and not just improve the old spirit. That God did so is emphatically declared by the Apostle Paul when he spoke of the distinct and dramatic differences between the constitution and essence of the Old Testament person, faithful or unfaithful, and the New Testament believer. In I Corinthians 15:45, Paul teaches "And so it is written the first man Adam is made a living soul; the last Adam was made a quickening spirit." John Laidlaw renders these words, "For the first head of the race was made a living *psyche*; the Second Adam is a life-giving *Pneuma* (1 Corinthians 15:44—47)."[17] Here, a contrast is made between soul and spirit that contradicts the claim of those who contend that these components of our inner lives are the same. They are different!

According to the apostle, Adam and his offspring, from Eden to Zion, were limited by the incompetence of the soul. But all the offspring of Jesus, those truly born again, have something inside them far better, a spirit which is none other than the spirit of Jesus. Jesus himself said, "That which is born of the spirit is spirit" (John 3:6). The miracle of the new birth—indeed, the necessity of the new birth—is this need for a spirit, literally *of* God and not just *from* God, a spirit which is so perfect in essence and divine in character that the ability to control the soul was at last made possible.

In his classic book, *The Bible Doctrine of Man*, the nineteenth-century Scottish professor John Laidlaw further explained this point by observing the distinctions between psychical man, having to do with the soul, and pneumatic man, having to do with the spirit.

> The psychical or "soulish" man is man as nature now constitutes him, and as sin has infected him ... The pneumatic or spiritual man, again, is man as grace has re-constituted him, and as God's Spirit dwells in him and bestows gifts upon him (I Corinthians 2:15).[18]

When Paul says in I Corinthians 6:17, "He that is joined to the Lord is one spirit," he indicated a commonality of essence between a New Testament believer and God. Willing to take a stand where the Bible does, A. T. Pierson rightly declared:

> In this language we have represented the highest conceivable unity. The stones of the building may be removed; the branch may be cut off from the vine, and the limb severed from the body; the sheep may wander from the shepherd, the child from the father; the bride may be divorced from

> the bridegroom; but you cannot divide spirit asunder.[19]

The spirit that unites the believer with the Lord is indissoluble. Distinct in its composition, it is also incapable of mixture, dilution, subtraction, addition, or alteration of any sort. Hence, Jessie Penn-Lewis wrote, "It is important to distinguish things that differ. When Scripture speaks of the soul it does not mean the spirit."[20]

When Paul speaks of the struggle between flesh and spirit in Galatians 5:17, and proceeds to delineate the works of one and the fruit of the other, the term "spirit" in each instance refers to the new nature and not, as such, to the Third Person of the Trinity. This is a view that was held by Martin Luther [21] and C. H. Lenski [22] among others, since the focus in this Galatians, chapter 5, passage is on two parallel capacities: our flesh, operating in the soul, and our spirit, which is inhabited by the Holy Spirit. Calvin thought the spirit in Galatians 5 refers to both the Holy Spirit and the recreated human spirit.[23]

Dividing Soul and Spirit

A second premise that is indeed pivotal and critical to the dichotomous/trichotomous debate relates to claims and counterclaims about boundaries of essence distinguishing soul and spirit. Hebrews 4:12 speaks of the Scripture's ability to divide soul and spirit, encouraging trichotomists to believe that each represents a different part of man. Again, Wayne Grudem weighs in on this point to argue:

> The author is not saying that the Word of God can divide "soul *from* spirit," but he is using a number of terms (soul, spirit, joint, marrow, thoughts, and intentions of the heart) that speak of the deep inward parts of our being that are not hid from the penetrating power from the Word of God.[24]

Actually, this verse says more than what Grudem claims it says. By selecting one point made in this verse, and only that, dichotomists seek to avoid the unavoidable: namely, that the differences between all these terms *already exist*. For example, thoughts are at one level, intentions are at another. A thought may go unheeded and remain just that, a thought; or it may grip the will with motivation and become an intention, and still later a deed.

Similarly, there are differences in makeup and function between marrow and joints. The two are not contiguous. If we were looking at a diagram of the human body, one arrow would point to a joint and another arrow would point to the interior of, say, the femur bone where marrow exists. Since one doesn't fuse into the other, a medical student would have no problem at all in distinguishing a joint from marrow. Likewise, the spirit and soul are different from each other—*already*! Grudem obfuscates, not wanting to concede this point, and in the process dares to argue that division doesn't mean division after all. But it does!

Why would the Word divide thought from intention? Perhaps to focus on a thought that hasn't been acted upon but needs to be acted upon; or perhaps to focus on a certain wayward intention so that the thought that inspired it can now be identified, isolated, scrutinized, and redirected. Even the thought itself must be analyzed by the penetrating Word. Jessie Penn-Lewis writes:

> The division of soul and spirit is intensely necessary. You find difficulty in guidance simply because God is not able to make his guidance clear to you, because of your inability to discern the difference between the things of your mind and the things of your spirit.[25]

It takes the Word of God to make these distinctions by separating God's thoughts, revealed in the Word, from our thoughts residing in that compartment of the soul called intellect.

And why else would the Word divide soul and spirit, one asks? To show, perhaps, how the inferior strength of the soul is being relied upon to supply what only the power of the spirit can supply. Or perhaps to show how some other inadequacy of the soul—for example, ecstatic emotions—is being substituted for the filling of the Spirit. Or perhaps to show that a counterfeit thought embraced by the soul doesn't measure up to its authentic representation revealed to the spirit. Or perhaps also to ward off false accusations from Satan who seeks to diminish the believer's true identity by insisting that some mood, thought, or temptation that appears in the soulish realm is indictable evidence, when it is not.

Norman Grubb suggested yet another reason for dividing soul from spirit when he wrote:

> We may feel exalted at one moment or abased at another; dry at one time, fresh at another; fervent or apathetic, bold or fearful; compassionate or indifferent. If, therefore, we confuse soul with spirit, we quickly fall into false condemnation.[26]

Something is wrong with us, we may erroneously conclude before then making exclamations of panic: Where is God? I've lost my victory! I need an inner revival! By identifying all that cycles through our soul as expressions of our true self, we set ourselves up to draw erroneous conclusions.[27] A proper division between soul and spirit is useful, therefore, to avoid the inner tumult these erroneous conclusions excite. Norman Grubb argued, "We have to learn how to discern between soul and spirit (Hebrews 4:12). We have to refuse in our spirit, our real selves, to be dominated by the reactions of the emotions or the reasons—our soul."[28]

Unless this division between soul and spirit is understood and utilized, Satan gains continual and considerable advantages over the believer. All this makes sense. Attempting to say that Hebrews 4:12 recognizes no differences between soul and spirit makes no sense. Even a cursory glance at this verse discloses that the rationale of some dichotomists—the division of soul and spirit used in this verse is hyperbole for separating the inseparable and dividing the indivisible—simply doesn't fit.

In his book, *Beyond Redemption*, Dr. Jay Adams argued that the translations of Hebrews 4:12 which declare that this two-edged sword divides *between* soul and spirit is in error. The Greek word used in this passage, he insisted, shouldn't be translated "between," since this is an imported idea that distorts the text's meaning. According to Adams, the sword cuts deeply into each part, not between each part.[30] But the dichotomist argument articulated by Dr. Adams is refutable.

The Greek word for "dividing asunder" used in this verse, *merismos*, is more accurately translated in the active sense, according to W. E. Vine, as division or separation.[31] Moreover, the instrument used to accomplish this dividing is said to be sharper than a two-edged sword. *Tomoteros*, the Greek word for sharper, supports this active sense of dividing, as it suggests in its etymology decisive consequences, something achieved by one blow as opposed to repeated hacking. Even the attribute accorded to the Word of God of being a "discerner" carries with it the idea of division, wherein truth is separated from deception, and carnality is separated from holiness. Given this repeated stress of active dividing accomplished by the Word of God, one need not concede the point to dichotomists that the outcome of division caused by the Word is foreign to this text. It is not.

The dichotomist argument that only cutting and piercing is indicated by this verse is then linked, somewhat clumsily, to another argument that also attempts to minimize these distinctions by saying that Scripture depicts man in his entirety (which it does numerous times). And therefore, according to this argument, distinctions between the immaterial parts (soul and spirit) of man cannot be made.

This argument is hardly persuasive. To refute it, let me give a parallel example. Just because I refer to my hand in its entirety almost every time I make reference to my hand, doesn't mean there are no functional distinctions between palm and fingers, between joints and skin, between fingernails and knuckles. By naming parts of the hand even once, I acknowledge differences. To conclude that only my whole hand should be thought of, because that's the way I usually refer to it, hardly precludes acknowledging at some point that there are different parts and functions of my hand. To say otherwise is an *a priori* assumption that only sets up circuitous reasoning whereby presuppositions become conclusions.

Missing from the dichotomists' interpretation of this verse is an appreciation of its context. Hebrews 4:11 talks about entering into rest, as opposed to futile striving. For this reason, then, there is a need to divide the soul from the spirit. Indeed, the futility of the soul is exactly why God gave man a new spirit. A fundamental difference between the Old Testament and the New Testament is this: The Old Testament involved these Word-to-soul transactions that consistently failed; whereas the New Testament involves Word-to-spirit transactions that consistently succeed. That there is a definite need for God's Word to divide our soul from our spirit is a point that F. J. Huegel makes quite well:

> Now the purpose of God in the great work of redemption is to bring man once more to a God-consciousness through the spirit; to quicken and to release the spirit of man, disentangling it from that which is soulish and fleshly, and bring it once more into the ascendancy so that man might be dominated by the spirit.[31]

Not to see this point, and to be governed by it, severely hinders what God purposes to do in our lives. John Laidlaw's view of this verse is conciliatory and helpful. He says of Hebrews 4:12 that it means "either that the word of God divides and discriminates between what is psychical and what is spiritual; or, that it penetrates both regions of human nature."[32] In either case, the distinction between soul and spirit is valid, since more than one region does exist.

Determining Context for Soul and Spirit

A third pivotal premise that invites polar responses from the dichotomist's camp and the trichotomist's camp centers on the assertion of overlapping and duplicate functions attributed by Scripture to both soul and spirit.

Dichotomists affirm this assertion; trichotomists ignore it. I submit that the apparent sameness of soul and spirit, claimed by dichotomists, dissolves if a proper protocol is used for determining the appropriate theological bin that verses addressing this subject correctly belong.

When reading a verse about the heart or some function of the soul involving volition, cognition, or emotion, the first criterion in this protocol is obvious: Which Testament, the Old Testament or the New Testament, is applicable when it comes to understanding context?

There are verses in the Old Testament which describe a heart that seeks God (Psalm 119:145), trusts God (Psalm 28:7), meditates upon the truths of God (Psalm 19:14), applies the wisdom of God (Psalm 90:12) and even welcomes God's testing (Psalm 139:23). So is this heart to be identified with our new nature? No, it is not, because the Bible says of this Old Testament heart that it is desperately wicked (Jeremiah 17:9) and therefore would have to be replaced by a new heart (Ezekiel 36:26) that would have a capacity the old heart didn't have: the ability to obey God's laws (Jeremiah 31:3).[33]

David's plea for God to create a new heart within him (Psalm 51:10) may have been more profound than he ever realized. It is clear that the heart David wanted replaced—indeed, that God wanted replaced—is not at all the same heart as the new heart God provided to New Testament believers (Hebrews 8:8-13). Therefore, as we seek to understand the new nature and locate the domain inside us where this new nature exists, we can place all the verses in the Old Testament that describe the heart available then into a different theological bin than the one where verses descriptive of the new nature belong.

A second protocol applicable for determining context implements a criterion that distinguishes aspiration from achievement. In Romans, chapter 7, Paul speaks of several functions of the soul that were operative in him, ostensibly, during an earlier stage of his pursued victory over sin.[34] It is clear that the decision-making faculty, his volition, was at work during this pursuit, given Paul's acknowledgment of this in verse 18, where he said, "... for to will is present with me ....” Knowing what we do about the Apostle Paul, we can be sure that his will, once the will of a zealot, was steeled in determination, since mere wishing, hoping, and halfhearted efforts never characterized the extent of Paul’s devotion.

As well, the very formidable intellect of Paul was at work. Paul stipulated this to be the case when he said in verse 25 “... with the mind I myself serve the law of God ....” Others may be moved only by goose bumps and tears, or by the sensational and the awe-inspiring only, but Paul did more than chase visions, voices, and dreams. The probative powers of his mind were called upon to weigh and sift, to deduct and construct coherent understandings about meaning and design.

A consecrated will, an analytical mind, but notice also that Paul’s emotions were involved in this pursuit, inasmuch as he speaks of “delighting” in verse 22. Paul was a passionate man, and this passion was much in evidence throughout his life.[35] While others could be cold and calculating, vacant in emotions and robotically functionary in their routines, Paul had a big heart. And his heart was certainly on display in his determination to win over sin.

Yet, despite all this, his will collapsed (verse 19), his mind deceived (verse 11), and his heart eventually broke. This heart-cry in the end—“O wretched man that I am ...” (verse 24)—was just that, remember, deep emotion expressing utter anguish. It was not, as some say, an evaluation of his “inner man” (verse 22).

All these functions of the soul—will, mind, and emotion—noble though they were in their *aspiration*, failed when it came to *achievement*. And this will always be the case, even for a believer, if these soulish qualities are not empowered by the spirit. The futility Paul experienced, we will experience, too, until a proper alignment of soul and spirit finally occurs, as it eventually did for Paul, thus exciting his announcement of victory in Romans 8:2, “... the Spirit of life in Christ Jesus has made me free ....” Notice, his soul didn’t make him free. His spirit did—that is, his new nature where the Holy Spirit dwells.

There are many verses in Old Testament and New which describe efforts and energies spent by will, mind, and emotions. Instead of indiscriminately lumping all these verses together and seeing supposed commonality, we need to determine whether the verse being examined is one conveying an aspiration of the soul functioning on its own, or an achievement of the soul empowered by the spirit.

A third criterion to use in this suggested protocol is one that distinguishes between source and agency. Often, this distinction isn't located in the words of a particular verse but can be determined by contextual clues. Let me give an example by using a passage that connects both testaments of Scripture. A scribe approached Jesus one day to ask him, what is the first or greatest commandment? Quoting from the Old Testament, Jesus said, "... you shall love the Lord your God with all your heart, with all your soul, with all your mind, and with all your strength" (Mark 12:30). Taken in isolation, one might think that heart, mind, soul, and will are capable of loving like this. In this verse, the agents and instruments of love are cited but not the source of it.

It is elsewhere we learn that the love of God is shed abroad in our hearts by the Holy Spirit (Romans 5:5), that the Spirit was sent forth by God into our hearts (Galatians 4:6), that our minds can be instructed by the Spirit (I John 2:27) so that we can know the mind of the Spirit (Romans 8:27), and that we can be strengthened with might by God's Spirit (Ephesians 3:16). When Scripture's full testimony is considered, we are made to know that the Spirit who indwells our human spirit is the source. The heart, the soul, the mind, and one's strength are all instruments—capacities for expression but not sufficient generators of these expressions.

It is important, therefore, that when we read scriptures about mind, will, heart, and soul that we keep in mind the context of these verses. For as in the great commandment Jesus recited, outcome and means may be identified (the instrument used, the expression conveyed) and source may not. There's nothing unusual about this kind of communication, really. For example, I may say that I went to work this morning, without saying anything about my car. The source for my travel, the real power I actually relied on for the trip, was provided by the car. Nevertheless, I need not stipulate always what can be well understood. Assuming that there should be this much detail is to assume too much.

In this same manner of speech, Peter tells us to serve one another (I Peter 4:10). However, Paul said something different, at least on surface, "... I serve with my spirit ...." (Romans 1:9). So was Peter saying something less accurate, less spiritual, than what Paul was saying? No, in fact just four verses prior to the verse we referred to in I Peter, the Apostle Peter writes of how we should live according to God in the spirit. Hence, Peter knew what Paul knew. Nevertheless, to select and seize certain words written by Peter and then include them, and organize them, in a topical study may lead to conclusions in this proof text arrangement that are very wide of the truth.

A fourth protocol needed for establishing clarity about soul and spirit involves recognition that same attributions do not mean sameness of identity. For example, Scripture describes the soul departing at death (Genesis 35:18; I Kings 17:21) and the spirit departing at death (Psalm 31:5; Luke 23:46; Acts 7:59). So does this mean that the soul and spirit are the same? Not really. What it does mean, minimally, is that both the soul and the spirit depart at death. Those dearly departed are sometimes referred to as spirits (Hebrews 12:23; I Peter 3:19), and sometimes they are referred to as souls (Revelation 6:9; 20:4). However, such designations hardly secure the conclusion that soul and spirit are the same.

The intent of these verses, remember, is simply to refer to individuals; and so functional speech such as this shouldn't be pressed to say more than what it was intended to say. Just as I have an individual soul, I have an individual spirit, and therefore referring to me one way or the other is accurate.

One could also refer to me by describing my physical body, which, according to science, is sufficiently capable in its characteristics to distinguish me from every other person on earth. But just because I can be accurately identified physically doesn't mean that my true identity can *only* be explained by my physical attributes. Let me give an example from Scripture. When Scripture says Stephen saw Jesus in heaven standing (Acts 7:55), in some sense it was the physical attributes of Jesus that came into view and thus clearly distinguished Jesus from all the angels in heaven. Yet, no one would use this verse to claim that the body of Jesus is the same as his spirit, since Jesus is also referred to as a spirit.

While there are accounts in Scripture that refer to Jesus in terms of one aspect of his person, his physical presence; there are also accounts that refer to another aspect of his person, his effervescent glory. But even though Jesus' identity is established in both ways doesn't mean each criterion for establishing his identity is interchangeable, one equating with the other.

We are making much too much of this supposed sameness between soul and spirit, ignoring as we do so the common usage of daily language that sometimes substitutes the part for the whole. Referring to a new car, for example, I might say, "I can hardly wait to get behind the wheel." Or maybe, if I'm one of those thrill-seeker types, I might talk about taking that new car on some country road and "putting the pedal to the metal." By referring to a car in this way, no one would ever conclude that the steering wheel and the gas pedal are the same, even though the car in each instance was referred to in such a singular and summary way. Nor would it ever be assumed that because one part of the car was identified and not another that there aren't any other parts to the car.

Putting the right protocols in place, such as those suggested in this appendix, will help to make clear what never should have been a mystery in the first place. Once we follow a protocol that distinguishes between attributions and identity, between agency and source, between aspiration and achievement, and between what was possible during the Old Testament and what is possible in the New Testament, the dichotomist argument begins to crumble, so that appearance gives way to reality and theory yields to truth.

In I Thessalonians 5:23 Paul clearly divides man into three distinct parts when he describes our makeup as a believer in terms of spirit, soul, and body. The very fact that there is a different name for each part affirms the obvious:

that each part *is* different! Also, the fact that each part is preceded by the definite article, and each part is also connected by the conjunction "and," reinforces the declared and obvious differences between each part. Fausett contends that this verse describes man as originally designed in Genesis and later restored in the New Testament. It does not refer to every human being.[36]

In her book, *Soul and Spirit*, Jessie Penn-Lewis says that the soul is the domain for self.[37] Citing Tertullian, the third-century Montanist, she wrote:

> The soul stands between the spirit and the body, for "direct communication between spirit and flesh is impossible; their intercourse can be carried on only by means of a medium"—the soul being that medium.[38]

What the soul should never be relied on to do is to function as the primary medium between God and man. In his book, *Things of the Spirit*, T. Austin Sparks addresses this issue when he writes: "The trouble lies not in the fact that man has a soul, but that when the soul is made the basis of attempted ingress into Divine things it is exceeding its province, and will create trouble."[39]

In reflecting on the soul as Scripture defines it, it has often been observed that in the Old Testament the Hebrew concept of man *being* a soul predominates; whereas, in the New Testament the Greek concept of man *having* a soul predominates. However, we need to keep in mind whose book this is, for the Greek/Hebrew debate on this topic didn't spillover into the Bible, as many seminary professors suppose. In his book, *The Bible Doctrine of Man*, Professor John Laidlaw observed that Paul's usage of the word "spirit" (*pneuma*) had never been debased by ethnic thought.

> It was never used in the Greek psychology. Even Plato's highest human principle is not *pneuma*, but *nous*, and its derivatives. While therefore the ethical distinction between "soulish" and "spiritual" may have had some dim parallel in

Graeco-Jewish philosophy, the terms themselves were biblical.[40]

In the Old Testament, man's identity was totally soulish, but in the New Testament that changed! The born-again believer should now draw his identity from his re-created spirit, although he still has a soul through which his new nature can be expressed. Thomas Goodwin, the seventeenth-century Puritan, said of the believer, "... it is not the soul that is inner man properly, but the inner man is that which is opposite to corruption ...."[41] The corruption that exists in the soul does not exist in the spirit.[42] Moreover, the holy dispositions of the spirit are not products of the soul.

When creating the new nature, "there is," Goodwin reminds us, "a passing away, a taking away of old things, and there is not a whit of the old that remaineth in the new."[43] The re-created spirit in man, Goodwin says, "is more than the soul and the faculties of it."[44]

I Corinthians 15:45 delineates further the difference between soul and spirit when it declares, "Thus it is written, 'The first man, Adam, became a living being [soul]; the last Adam [Christ] became a life-giving spirit.'" George Ladd said, "Spirit is often used of God; soul is never so used."[45] A. B. Simpson declared:

> The predominant characteristic of natural man is expressed by this word, "soul," just as the predominant characteristic of the new man in the New Testament is expressed by the word, "spirit." The soul represents the intellectual and emotional elements that constitute man. The spirit represents the higher and the divine life which links us directly to God, and enables us to know and to come into relationship with divine things.[46]

Both Adams originated a nature. The first nature, created by Adam, was badly flawed and under judgment. But the second nature, created by Jesus, is absolutely perfect and has already been glorified. A. B. Simpson concluded, "So the spirit born of God is separated in its own divine nature from its own self and the sinful heart."[47] What God wants, then, is for our spirit, the new nature, to radically impact our soul.[48] It is true that the soul, contaminated as it is with fleshly programming, won't be rendered extinct by such an impact, but it can be transformed.[49]

In this regard, it can accurately be said that there are two kinds of people—soulish people and spiritual people. This perspective is most clearly conveyed in I Corinthians 2, where the apostle speaks of one "who is spiritual" (verse 15) and another who is a "soulish person" (verse 14). Technically, the spiritual speaks of the believer and the soulish speak of the unbeliever. However, even a Christian can act soulishly (I Corinthians 3:1) whenever he allows natural capacities (some form of intellectualism, emotionalism, passivism, or activism) instead of the new nature to prevail. At which point the spiritual in us is by-passed, set aside, or ignored, fleshly/soulish forces will rush in to replace it.

Christianity is a religion of the spirit, G. D. Watson exclaimed, "The human spirit is the vehicle through which the Holy Ghost pours his deep, divine yearnings ...."[50] Accordingly, there are more compelling reasons to call us Pneumatics than Charismatics, since the first deals with being and the second deals with doing. The term Pneumatics describes who we are; the term Charismatics describes how we function in certain aspects of ministry.

The Genesis of Soul and Spirit

As a postscript to this discussion of soul and spirit, a theological footnote needs to be offered regarding the genesis of soul and spirit. The theory of Traducianism, which I believe to be correct (as do Grudem and Adams), contends that the soul has qualities that are derivative from prior generations. We have all observed this fact to some degree, in that it is almost immediately apparent to us that babies are not "blank slates" when they are born, waiting the imprinting of environment and education to shape their personalities. Babies exhibit both personal traits and physical traits from day one, traits that have identifiable antecedents in a family's genealogy. Some of these traits may come from the mother, others may come from the father, while other traits, physical or personal, may come from an uncle, a grandparent, or another person in the extended family.

The main alternative to Traducianism is a creationist view that contends that each individual soul is created by God sometime after conception. But if that is true, when does this occur? The Bible doesn't say. Then how do we know it does occur? The Bible doesn't say. Well, then! These are two good reasons for refuting this theory!

Two more reasons for refuting the notion that God creates each individual soul after conception are: 1) If souls aren't in existence at the time of conception, then abortion becomes more viable; and 2) If God creates the soul for each person today, then what he creates is obviously predisposed to moral corruption, an idea that is not at all consistent with the nature of God. The *only* time God created a soul, the Bible says, was in the very beginning, and that soul was said to be good.

The Bible doesn't say a word about God creating souls today, but it says a lot about the nature we inherited from Adam and the problem of sins from one generation being passed on to subsequent generations (Exodus 20:5; Numbers 14:18; Ezekiel 18:1-2,19). In discussing the generational sins issue, the Bible makes clear that little Johnny won't be called to account for what his grandfather did. More the problem, according to Scripture, is the fact that some of the moral flaws of grandfather are now exhibiting in little Johnny much worse than they ever did in grandfather.

For example, Abraham was known to tell a lie or two, but his grandson Jacob—the schemer, the cheat—earned the reputation of being a chronic liar. We also see this deterioration of behavior in the first family when the first child born to Adam and Eve—each sinners, to be sure—committed the horrendous act of murdering his brother.

It is most significant that Scripture tells us how God created first man and made him a living soul but says nothing about God creating another soul at the time Cain was born. Cain, the world's first murderer, actually inherited his sinful nature from his father, and then exhibited the extremes of this nature in a way his parents never did. Here, again, we see an obvious difference between soul and spirit. The new spirit promised in the Old Testament and made available to us at Pentecost isn't what we are born with. Instead, it becomes ours long after conception and birth. This distinction presents yet another reason for affirming that soul and spirit are not the same.

Appendix B
Enlightenment Through Our Spirit

The Bible says we are spirit, soul, and body (I Thessalonians 5:23)—three parts that constitute the whole, each part having different characteristics from the other. When a person is born again, it is the spirit within that person that is instantly and totally changed (John 3:5, 6), but nothing as complete as that takes place in the body or in the soul. Our body still has its limitations, still has its problems, as does our soul with all of its aspirations, both good and evil. However, it is God's plan to progressively transform the disciplines of the body and the performance of soul *through* our spirit.

In her book, *War on the Saints*, Jesse-Penn Lewis observed that Satan attempts to controvert this order.

> The Devil's scheme is therefore to make the believer to cease walking after the spirit, and to draw him out into the realm of soul and body. Then the spirit, which is the organ of the Holy Spirit in conflict against a spiritual foe, drops into inactivity and is ignored ....[1]

The spirit within us is the domain of the new nature, and therefore God isn't going to bypass what he so marvelously created to produce spiritual growth in some other way. This is why we are expressly told to put on the new man whenever improved behavior is needed. *Word to soul transactions failed in the Old Testament and they will fail today.* Our spirit, the new nature, is the only conduit by which, and through which, God achieves his perfecting work.

Trusting resident capacities of the soul to accomplish this perfecting is a doomed venture. Yet, a high percentage of church members come to church each week with their soul capacities active and their spirit capacities dormant. Addressing the futility of this pattern, Oswald Chambers said of the Occupier of our new nature, the Holy Spirit:

> He will never witness to our wits, or to our intelligence, or to our physical perfections, or to our insights and genius, or to anything at all that is natural to us: He will only witness to that which has been reproduced in us by his redemption.[2]

By such witness, the Holy Spirit does his perfecting work through that which he inhabits, the spirit of a born-again believer.

Yet, there are many Christians, earnest Christians, who find themselves trapped today similar to the way that one in Romans 7 had been trapped. Tragically, they do not know how this man got free and stayed free.[3] Paul attributed this victory to what God made available to and through the new nature (Romans 8:2). This new nature—possessed from the first day of conversion, but for many believers not accessed until sometime later—is critical to our spiritual growth.

The role the new nature has for our spiritual growth is not incidental or optional, since our spirit has capacities that our soul doesn't have. One of these capacities is a heightened sensitivity to the truths of God. Apart from a revelation from God—available through the Word, ministered by the Spirit—man knows nothing with certainty.

Skepticism will quickly acknowledge this fact; dogmatism will not. In the warfare between skepticism and dogmatism, where one perspective claims to know too little and the other claims to know too much, Pascal cast deserved aspersion. Note the juxtapositions he uses whereby the overly exalted and over debased views of man are contrasted.

> What a chimera then is man! What a novelty! What a monster, what a chaos, what a contradiction, what a prodigy! Judge of all things, imbecile worm of the earth; depository of truth, sink of uncertainty and error; the pride and refuse of the universe!
>
> Who will unravel this tangle? Nature confounds the skeptics and reason confounds the dogmatists.[4]

Actually, God unraveled this tangle! And he did it by giving us revelation (which extends far above reason) and illumination (which extends far beyond intellect). G. D. Watson observed, "The power of the mind can never illuminate your heart; unless God shines in your spirit it remains in total darkness."[5] Dr. Martyn Lloyd-Jones observed that "man's trouble by nature is not that he merely lacks intelligence. What he lacks is spiritual understanding. Man's trouble is not in his mind alone but in his lack of the capacity and ability to understand, and to believe and to follow, spiritual truth."[6]

Soon after Paul's conversion, he went to the deserts of Arabia for three years to be taught in that solitary place by the Holy Spirit. When comparing what Paul gained under the tutelage of the Spirit with what the disciples gained after a comparable period of time with Jesus, F. J. Huegel concluded, "Paul was always ahead of them—as a missionary, as a theologian, as a preacher, as an organizer, as a saint."[7] And although there are many variables that help to account for this difference, what must not be overlooked is the enormous benefit Paul gained by allowing his spirit to be taught by God's Spirit.

When the Bible says that the truths of God are "spiritually discerned" (I Corinthians 2:14) and "he that is spiritual" discerns all things (I Corinthians 2:15), and that there is an anointing within you which teaches all things (I John 2:20), our attention is directed to the realm where this anointing abides, our born-again spirit. The anointing—a symbol of the Holy Spirit and a function of the Holy Spirit—reveals what our intellect—diligent and dedicated though our exercise of it may be—cannot on its own know. It can be argued that this enlightening could be a Word-to-soul transaction executed by the Third Person of the Trinity, but saying this would marginalize the new creation and run counter to its necessity and functional importance.

The anointing within inhabits our spirit, the re-created spirit we were given when we were "born again." However, the amazing capacities of our spirit will certainly get sidelined if our soul (how we think, feel, and decide) dominates our spirit. Should this occur (as is actually the case for most Christians today), our spiritual sensitivities will greatly diminish. But while activated in a peak operational mode, the spirit within us will enable the Word to transcend "letter and death" and become "spirit and life" (II Corinthians 3:6). Quite the opposite will occur if our spirit within isn't permitted to function in ascertaining and processing God's Word. For then there will be light without sight, a phenomenon amply documented in Scripture.

The Reality of Darkness

One day Jesus stood near the temple and declared, "I am the light of the world." This was a statement much more shocking than what our routine quoting of it may indicate, because when Jesus spoke these words he stood by a lamp stand that gave off a light so bright it could almost light the entire city. Historians report that this light (hung in the Court of the Women) was turned on only three times a year (the Feast of Tabernacles being one of the occasions), and that when lit, it astonished all the people.

More astonishing still was the radical claim Jesus made that night. The authoritative assertion he made was that he could light not just a city but the entire world! What's more, his light, he said, could extend not just to certain people at their sanctimonious best but to the entire population at their acrimonious worst. It is no wonder, then, that when attempting to describe the power of this light, Charles Williams said of Jesus: "A light that shone from behind the sun, the sun was not so fierce to pierce where that light could."[8]

The astounding claim made by the Lord that night does present some problems, though. For if his was a light that could span the entire globe, why didn't more people recognize his real identity, especially those to whom he presented himself and lived amongst? Never mind those people who lived hundreds of miles away and thus never saw him; the more puzzling question is: Why were most of the people who had seen Jesus still in the dark about his identity when he left this world? Perplexing as well: Why were some in his own family skeptical about his identity?

The answer to this question relates more to the processes of illumination than to the product of revelation. The difference between these two being: Revelation is given by Jesus and his Word; illumination deals with our capacity to understand the revelation that has been given. To communicate this problem in a more familiar way, we could say that the TV we purchased may be the most expensive on the market, but if we don't have an antenna, a dish, or cable services, we could sit before that TV for hours and never see a program.

Proverbs 4:18 describes the "path of the just" (meaning the person who is rightly walking with God) "... as the shining light that shines more and more until that perfect day" (KJV). This speaks of an increasingly clear and vivid picture. Keep in the mind that the light itself, the Word of God, is not the light of a meteor—very bright, but quickly gone. Nor is it the light of a candle—steady, but slowly diminishing in its glow. And nor is it the light of the sun, which according to the second law of thermodynamics is gradually losing its energy. No, in contrast to all these other lights, this is a light that will glow with a fixed and fabled brightness.

Unfortunately, the "more and more" promised in this verse isn't exactly the experience of many Christians today. Instead, the wattage of their spiritual sensitivity has gone from 500 to 50. And for some Christians, it's a lot worse than that! Like those lightening bugs the children chase on a summer night, there's a brief flicker of light followed by a darkness so dark a person can't even see his own hand. Such darkness, especially in the spiritual realm, should be feared.

Darkness may well have its charm while offering cool breezes, opportunities for romance, and repeated invitations for rest. But the seductiveness of these appeals would vanish instantly if the dangers of the night were more clearly in view. Darkness in this sense means not knowing that you don't know, making decisions without adequate criteria and yet being deluded into thinking that you made good decisions. For such a dilemma, a Savior is needed.

The Bible says that Jesus came to this world to give light to those who sit in darkness and in the shadow of death

(Luke 1:79). The ominous picture conveyed here depicts a person who dare not move, lest he plummet over a cliff or risk catastrophic injury in some other way. Paralyzed by fear, unable to solve his problem (much less to understand it), he is without any options; so he has given up. A deep and dense darkness surrounds. Death is nearby. All this man can do is sit, frozen in fear, utterly helpless.

The phrase "abide in darkness," as it appears elsewhere in Scripture, isn't referring to back alley thugs who frequent what even society would call "the dark side of life." The sinister, malevolent person who roams the sewers under the city, that person who is always lurking in the shadows, he who is motivated only by mischief and malice, does not profile the darkness-dweller Scripture describes. By all appearances, the person Jesus described as abiding in darkness may be sincere, affable, polite, and overtly kind. With regards to the wisdom of God, however, this person is wandering through life in a condition of cognitive contamination. Life may seem pleasant at times, but it is what he doesn't know that will destroy him! So, pressing beyond mere curiosity, we must ask: Why is this person in such a condition?

The Resistance to Light

John Milton had it right when he said, "There are none so blind as those who will not see." I don't know why, but there are more than a few people who want nothing to do with God. Mention his name and they'll tune out; convey what his Word has to say and they'll walk out. It is in this regard that Isaiah inquired, "Lord, who has believed our report? And to whom has the arm of the Lord been revealed?" The implied answer is, not many. Despite all the teachings and testimonies given, and all the miracles and manifestations bestowed, the world's response has been rather small. But, again, why has this outcome been so common?

David Watson offered one explanation by recalling this true-life story that took place in his native country, England. In a locale where public debates were common and where fiery rhetoric was often unleashed, the following scene played out between a scorner and a believer.

> A man once stood on a soapbox at Hyde Park Corner, pouring scorn on Christianity. "People tell me that God exists; but I can't see him. People tell me that there is life after death; but I can't see it. People tell me that there is a judgment to come; but I can't see it. People tell me that there is a heaven and hell; but I can't see them ...." He won cheap applause and climbed down from his "pulpit." Another struggled on to the soap-box. "People tell me there is green grass all around; but I can't see it. People tell me there is a blue sky above; but I can't see it. People tell me there are green trees all around; but I can't see them. You see, I'm blind!"[9]

Spiritual blindness certainly accounts for many who can't see. Scoffers and scorners actually say more about themselves than they do about the revelation they reject. It is true that Hosea talks about the destruction that comes from a lack of knowledge, but the same verse points out that the knowledge offered by God was rejected (Hosea 4:6).

This rejection, ranging from apathy in its milder form to disgust in its more egregious form, prompted Oswald Chambers to observe: "Jesus was crucified at 'a place called Golgotha, that is to say, Place of a Skull.' That is where he has always been put to shame, in the thinking part of man ...."[10]

The deliberately darkened mind, no matter what its shade, refuses the light Jesus offers. G. D. Watson wrote, "God calls earth to bear witness that the rejection of spiritual light by his people has ever been followed by gross darkness of soul and spiritual death."[11] Remember, the Dark Ages descended on the Church, too, and for almost a thousand years the lights went out.

Residual blindness is the condition we are all born with, and have all lived with, until that time when God enabled a measure of light and sight to reach our unsaved soul. Once this light was emitted, the opportunity to accept God's Son as our Savior soon presented. To accept the gift of salvation, if we chose to do this, meant that even more truth and more light would be given to us. But to run from the light, if we chose to do that, meant that such hurried flight constituted the basis of our judgment (John 3:19) and guaranteed the cessation of further light.

A. W. Tozer warned, "The searcher for truth must be willing to obey truth without reservation or it will elude him. Let him refuse to follow the truth and it dooms him to darkness."[12]

Again, to the extent a believer runs toward the light, sees his need, receives Jesus into his heart, and lives under his lordship, the ability to see the eternal is increased. Commenting on the relationship of spiritual sight with consistent obedience, Andrew Murray writes:

> There is a general will of God for all his children which we can, in some measure, learn out of the Bible. But there is a special individual application of these commands—God's will concerning us personally—which only the Holy Spirit can teach. And he will not teach it except to those who have taken the vow of obedience.[13]

Light comes where it is treasured and will not be wasted. If we want to discover God's unique purpose for our lives, we must first submit our lives to him for direction. In encouraging precisely this step, Paul prayed for wisdom, revelation, knowledge, understanding, and enlightenment (Ephesians 1:17, 18). These noetic functions have distinct differences, but are all necessary for God's people to see with clarity not only their calling but also the resources God has provided to pursue this calling.

For many Christians today this call is only faintly heard; and the resources needed to fulfill this calling are scarcely known. Thus, their light is hid under a bushel. That bushel may be ignorance, a sense of inferiority, incriminating sin, indiscriminate choices. The reasons, no doubt, are many and the consequences severe, but how different the lives of God's people would be if this light were permitted to shine!

In John 5:35 Jesus said of John the Baptist, "He was a burning and shining light." This explains why everyone in Judea left town and went into the wilderness to hear this preacher. Contrary to all the church growth predictors (the location wasn't convenient, the group wasn't homogeneous, and the message wasn't positive), John was used in a most extraordinary way. What we see in John, someone flesh-and-blood just like us, is an example of what a burning light can be. And in seeing this we must remember that people, then and today, are drawn to a fire!

The warmth and glow of God's incendiary influence functions like a magnet. Commenting on the life transformed by God's light, A. W. Tozer observed of the early church:

> One distinguishing mark of those first Christians was a supernatural radiance that shined out from within them. The sun had come up in their hearts and its warmth and light made unnecessary any secondary sources of assurance. They had the inner witness. It is obvious that the average evangelical Christian today is without this radiance. Instead of the inner witness we now substitute logical conclusions drawn from a text.[14]

Thus, we plod through life without an effervescence emanating from within. Our libraries grow, our notebooks stack up, the "a-has" of mental discovery are repeated, but it is obvious to others, and even to ourselves, that something very important is missing. The look of eye, the tone of voice, and all the intangibles emanating from us lack the radiance of a life lit up by God.

The Reliance on Light

Just as light is essential to life, the light God gives to our spirit is critical for new nature functioning. At issue, though, is the kind of light needed. Is the light of philosophy sufficient? Or the light of psychology? Or the light of science?

Of course, the frenzy of fanaticism produces its own ghastly glow. The Bible calls this "wildfire," a quality and experience we are deliberately discouraged from pursuing. So, if not the light of fanaticism or one of these other sources of light, what kind of a light should we seek?

Surely, we need a light bright enough to generate certainty and confidence, a light that exceeds opinion and speculation. Because what if our beliefs are speculations, no truer or wiser than anyone else's speculations? And what if the ideas we founded our life upon prove untrue, and what we thought was rock solid becomes shifting sand? The light that guides to peace (Luke 1:79) has to be reliable in what it shows us, or else we shouldn't trust it.

Such disparity between opinion and truth need not be the dilemma of the child of God, because the Apostle John writes, "But you have an anointing from the Holy One and you know all things" (I John 2:20). By all things, John doesn't mean nuclear physics or some foreign dialect spoken on a remote South Sea island. He simply means everything necessary for decision-making, everything necessary for an essential understanding of God's Word, everything vital to grip and guide, and to thrill and fulfill.

Later in this chapter, John makes an astounding claim about the anointing when he said: "But the anointing which you have received from him, abides in you and you do not need that anyone should teach you; but as the same anointing teaches you concerning all things ..." (I John 2:27). According to John, this anointing within is all-sufficient. It doesn't matter how high the IQ is, or how mature the Christian is, or how extensive his bible training is. This anointing is enough to make the Word clear and life-giving.

In I Corinthians 2:16, the Apostle Paul makes another astounding statement: "But we have the mind of Christ." Now if you are a thinking person, you have to wonder how anyone could possibly say that. Had Paul qualified this statement by limiting it to some topic the Bible clearly addresses, we could better understand. And had he referred to the mind of Christ, as he did in Philippians, chapter 2, to a disposition of humility, we, likewise, could better understand. But the absence of these qualifiers leaves us stunned, shocked. Can any sane man make this claim? And if this claim is true, how can it be true for us?

Our only hope for gaining this much-needed wisdom is clearly addressed in I Corinthians 2:10, where Paul says, "But God has revealed them to us through his Spirit ...." The Holy Spirit, associated elsewhere with the very anointing we've been talking about, is charged with the responsibility of bringing truth-bearing images to our spirit. In Paul's words, "no one knows the things of God except the Spirit of God" (verse 11b). The knowledge that informs, the principles that direct, the wisdom that guides, comes to us through a Spirit-to-spirit infusion.

Someone else can hear what we hear and understand what we understand; yet, the result is remarkably different. In one life, where there may be willing, delighting, and a commitment to obey (Romans 7:18, 19, 22,), defeat takes place and hope gives way to anguish (Romans 7:24). While in the other life, truth so resonates in a man's spirit that there is a radiant energy that comes forth, the magnetism of what Scripture calls a "life to life" anointing (II Corinthians 2:16). Drawn by this anointing, people get closer and closer to the Lord.

In pursuing this anointing, there is a mistake we can make, one we must be careful to avoid. While we are right to avoid an overreliance on intellect, we must not fall into the trap of disparaging this function of the soul and becoming poor stewards of it. The excitement engendered by a vision from God, the voice of God, a message communicated by prophecy, or wisdom-granting deposited in our spirit, should never become more precious to us than Scripture. We dishonor God if we allow a preoccupation with these other ways of gaining knowledge to surpass, or even rival, our devotion to Scripture.

It is true that Scripture study and a proper use of intellect do require a dependence on God that utilizes the capacities and sensitivities of our spirit. For having only the Bible and our brain, one revered and the other respected, will never be enough. Therefore, another gift has been given to us, not to compete but to complete; and this gift is the new nature within which alone has been made alive to the truth and truths of God. The new nature has an anointing receptive to truth. On this point A. B. Simpson wrote:

> Some persons are so zealous for the Word of God that they deny any direct guidance from the Spirit apart from the Word. If we truly believe the Word itself we will be forced to accept its distinct statements that the personal presence of God is given to the humble and obedient disciple for the needed direction in every step of life.[15]

William Law frames the issue more broadly by saying that because all the functions of the soul operate in an ongoing manner, of necessity the Holy Spirit's work in us must also be ongoing and perpetual in order to gain needed dominance over the soul. In the book, *Wholly for God*, Law writes: "... if we can have no holiness or goodness but as the life of thought, will, and affection works in us ... then a perpetual, always existing operation of the Spirit of God within us is absolutely necessary."[16] This operation includes, at times, a direct conveyance of guidance by the Holy Spirit, the exalted guest residing in our new nature.

Unless the Holy Spirit illumines biblical truth in our spirit, that truth, when heard, will have a minimal impact on our lives. The self that dwells in the soul, confident in its own abilities to gain truth and discern error, can be utterly dense when truth seeks to make itself known. This caused Whittier to write:

> A Tender light than moon or sun,
> Than song of earth a sweeter hymn
> May shine and sound forever on,
> And thou be deaf and dim.
>
> Forever round the Mercy-seat
> The guiding lights of love shall burn:
> But what if, habit-bound, thy feet
> Shall lack the will to turn?
>
> What if thy eye refuse to see,

Thine ear of Heaven's free welcome fail,
And thou a willing captive be,
Thyself thy own dark jail?

What then? From the very beginning of our walk with the Lord, the anointing was needed to make truth accessible to us. And this is still true today. Without the anointing, the lights go off, and the jail of our choosing will be dark, indeed. However, our very lives will be lit with that supernatural radiance Tozer identified, and John the Baptist exhibited, if a Holy Spirit anointing becomes operational when ascertaining and processing the revealed truth of God.

In his book, *Joy Unspeakable*, Dr. Martyn Lloyd-Jones, for thirty years pastor to Westminster Chapel in London, tells how the Holy Spirit "gives a kind of luminosity, a clarity of understanding and apprehension."[17] Answering the argument that a Pentecostal-like baptism with the Spirit is for the less educated and more emotional, Lloyd-Jones identifies several first-rate scholars—revered theologians and respected philosophers among them—who experienced this baptism. One aspect of this experience of particular interest to Lloyd-Jones was the contribution this baptism made to intellect.

The Radiance of Light

It is the nature of a baptism to transact in mere moments but to have consequences that are momentous. These blessed consequences are varied in their scope, altering personality and augmenting ability. One such consequence is a radiance that is immediately noticeable to the believer and to all others who know him. Describing the legacy of this light, G. D. Watson explained:

> ... so when a believer is filled with the Holy Ghost, there is a part of that uncreated lustre that comes out; nay, it begins in conversion, when he is pardoned. It shines out—the faint beginning of the transfiguring glory; and when you are fully sanctified, the glow in your face is brighter, the

> flash of your eye is stronger; and when we are glorified it will be the complete shining of the internal glory. Every saint shall outshine the sun![18]

So strong is this radiance, even on earth, it will cast its illuminating glow on the mind. Martyn Lloyd-Jones introduces us to some remarkable men who had this experience.

John Flavel—a graduate of Oxford, a prolific writer, and seventeenth-century Presbyterian pastor—was sitting by a well when suddenly overwhelmed by the baptism with the Holy Spirit. Describing this experience afterwards, Flavel said he learned more of the life of heaven in that one encounter than he had from all the books he had ever read and from all the discourses he had ever heard. Because John Flavel was a major thinker, his books are still being sold today, more than three centuries after his death. Yet, what he experienced one day, in one hour, added more to his understanding than a huge library of books.[19]

Dr. John Owen, considered by many to be the most formidable intellect among the Puritans, described his baptism with the Spirit as a filling with gladness and exultations, but also something else—"unspeakable raptures of the mind."[20] The mind doesn't grow blank, said this professor at Oxford University. The mind is given a knowledge that couldn't come in any other way.

Thomas Aquinas, long considered the official theologian of the Roman Catholic Church, lived during the twelfth century. In his attempts to blend Aristotle with Scripture, Aquinas came to believe that there could be no direct contact between man and God. In his major work, *The Summa Theologica*, a work of many volumes, Aquinas offered instead five classical proofs of God, arguments that are studied by most theological students today. But then one day something very powerful happened to Aquinas which is described by one of his biographers.

> ... after spending the whole of his life demonstrating how man has no direct contact

> with immaterial reality, Aquinas shortly before his death had such an overwhelming direct experience with God that he wrote no more. Urged by his friend to complete his great work, *The Summa Theologica*, he answered, "I can do no more, such things have been revealed to me that all I have written seem as straw, and now I await the end of my life."[21]

That which was revealed to this extraordinary theologian persuaded him that his previous theological reflections were unworthy. No one who reads the various accounts of Aquinas' experience would ever dismiss what occurred as the humble talk of a dying man. An intellectual enlightenment had occurred—suddenly, in mere moments—forever altering the perspective of this brilliant theologian.

Earlier in this book, we read what Pascal wrote when a similar experience happened to him. In a space of two hours, this scientist and philosopher had an overwhelming experience with God that well describes what others have called a baptism with the Holy Spirit. In recording what occurred to him, Pascal attributed the source of this experience as being, "God, the living God, not of the philosophers and the wise."

The knowledge Pascal gained that day that must be distinguished from the yield of philosophy and science, two disciplines in which Pascal had gained acclaimed proficiency. Unlike Aquinas, though, who thought he should retire his pen given what he had already written, Pascal became deeply motivated to dedicate his remaining years toward communicating the truth God had so marvelously illumined. Hence, he wrote his now famous works, *The Provincial Letters* and *Pensees*.[22]

A. B. Simpson said of himself, "I had a poor sort of mind, heavy and cumbrous, that did not think or work quickly."[23] Just getting through high school proved challenging for young Simpson. He suffered a breakdown that kept him out of school. His doctor required him to stay away from books for one year. But in childlike faith Simpson went to the Lord to get his provision for this problem.

Well, the provision came, enabling Simpson to write more than a hundred books while serving as a pastor, evangelist, missionary leader, and, as it turned out, the founder of a denomination. No one can read what he wrote and without seeing on every page a God-given ability.

There are few men who surpass A. B. Simpson as an effective communicator of God's truth. Speaking with experience, A. B. Simpson later declared, "There is a distinct baptism of the Holy Spirit for the mind as well as for the spirit."[24] According to Dr. Simpson, "Minds that have been dull and obscure before have risen beneath his touch to the highest intellectual attainments and the mightiest achievements of human genius."[25] This baptism of the mind, Simpson explained, "gives soundness of judgment, clearness of expression, pungency of thought, power of utterance, attractiveness of style"[26] and other supernaturally endowed essentials that God uses to speak to a generation.

We see, from the didactic statements of Scripture and from corresponding examples of history, that the Holy Spirit does bless our minds, but he does so in a way that disallows the mind from assuming singular responsibility or credit. Always the product of blessed thinking is attributable, by source and agency, to a gift distinctive from the genius of intellect. The intellect applied in faith receives; it doesn't grasp. As it roams what Oswald Chambers calls "the universe of revelation facts,"[27] the mind attuned to the Spirit of God is illumined with insights that research and contemplation could never on their own attain. A. W. Tozer explained:

> Man is a worshipper and only in the spirit of worship does he find release for all the powers of his amazing intellect. A religious writer has warned us that it may be fatal to "trust ... the squirrel-work of the industrious brain rather than to the piercing vision of the desirous heart."[28]

The intellect applied to a study of biblical history, biblical languages, biblical theology, and comparative religions will not yield, despite the efforts of native genius and dedicated discipline, what the worshipping heart tuned into the Spirit of God will yield. As Thomas Watson put it, "Knowledge in a natural man's head is like a torch in a dead man's hand."[29] Overstuffing the brain with the minutiae of research will not yield what an anointed mind yields.

Consider what happened on the day of Pentecost. Did the preacher that day, this formerly fearful fisherman, have any idea that he would be preaching a sermon to thousands of people? From the biblical record, there is no indication that Peter prepared to speak. Yet, when we read what he said (in the second chapter of Acts), we are amazed that a fisherman could use the Scripture in such an insightful way. Commenting on the sermon Peter preached that day, Jessie Penn-Lewis wrote:

> How different this is to the idea that to be "filled with the Holy Spirit" you must not use your mind, and that when he fills a believer he uses his tongue like an automaton. It is not so with Peter, for there we find the illumination of the mind and the flood of light upon Scriptures and the intelligent utterance of what he had grasped and knew by the enlightening of the mind.[30]

Truth ministered through and to our spirit by the Holy Spirit is what we should therefore aspire to obtain. G. D. Watson wrote, "A fire-baptized intellect is a 'secret pavilion,' a 'second veil,' into a which a soul may quietly and softly enter and rest beneath the golden cherubim and listen to the voice of God, for he said to Moses, 'I will speak to thee from between the wings of the cherubim.'"[31]

There are times when the prelude to God's speaking requires an isolation that purposes an intense intimacy with God. The innate capacities of one's spirit and the special gifting granted to one's mind could never substitute for this intimacy, and would never want to do so. In his book, *Our Own God*, G. D. Watson elaborates on this point.

> St. John, banished to the Isle of Patmos, cut off from human society, surrounded by wild beasts and the melancholy roar of sea surf on the shore,

> was the occasion for the most glorious revelation of the Lord Jesus, the opening of the Heavenly world and the crowning revelations of Scripture truth ....
>
> Sometimes God's saints are islanded in a mysterious ocean of his dealings where no ships are allowed to stop, on purpose that he may draw them more deeply unto himself, and give them unfoldings so deep and still and powerful that the least intrusion of another would spoil them.[32]

What was in evidence during the Old Testament, and most assuredly on the first day of the Holy Spirit's filling, should be in evidence today as well—a ministry to the mind resulting from an intense intimacy with God. Actually, how we live our lives is much dependent on this ministry. For without it, that which is neat, plausible, logical, and wrong will run us into a lot of dead-ends, wasting time instead of redeeming it, resulting in frustration only, and not in fulfillment.

A. B. Simpson writes, "Is it not inspiring to think that this Holy Ghost who fills our heart, is no mere sentiment of spiritual ecstasy or emotional joy, but is the great Mind from which all minds come ...?"[33] What is in the Spirit's mind can increasingly be in ours. But this can only occur if he teaches, illumines, enlightens, and anoints. Summing up, J. H. Jowett concluded, "The Word of God has a great deal to say about 'discernment.' Again and again it is implied that the mental powers are sharpened, that the judgment is quickened when life is pervaded by the fine presence of the Spirit of God.[34] Indeed, it is under the Spirit's tutelage that the mind is enlightened by eternity for eternity.

So the darkness-dweller can sit there if he chooses to, despairing his dilemma and never budging from the core beliefs that put him there. But if he'll look up to the Father of lights, and follow where that light leads, the despair will be left behind, as a life he never could have imagined will welcome him with its joy.

Appendix C
Our Spirit and God's Will

In his book, *Christ Our Healer*, F. F. Bosworth makes the statement: "... faith begins where the will of God is known."[1] Without having assured and reliable knowledge, other dynamics can kick in—trust, for example, and maybe even hope to some degree. But faith will always remain grounded, unless and until the will of God is known.

Many Christians are stuck at the level of trust in their relationship with God. Stuck? This is a thought they never would have conceived, since they can't imagine why there's anything wrong with trust, or why the word "stuck" should ever be attached to it. Let me explain.

While trust is commended in Scripture, the dynamics of trust are not the same dynamics set forth by Scripture to describe faith. The Bible tells us to live by faith, and by that declaration four times given sets forth an expectation that all of life is to be a series of faith transactions through which God will reward and without which God is not pleased (Hebrews 11:6). But adherence to *this* agenda requires a significant upgrade from simple trust.

Trust is a worthy quality, to the extent respect is given and reliance is activated. A baby trusts his mother, for example, and a toddler trusts his father. However, in both instances reflection is shallow and maturity doesn't exist. The infant, the toddler, relate positively to their parents; yet this is due to their near total dependence on them, and perhaps also to positive perception about them that hover somewhere between instinct and learned experience. The point being: Although trust is foundational to a relationship, it is elementary at best. Therefore, God wants believers to progress beyond an infantile Christianity that only trusts.

The strongest reason that trust should graduate to faith is because only faith lays hold of grace (Romans 5:2) and thereby gains the victory (I John 5:4). Mere trust won't achieve this. In the beginning, while we are "babes in Christ" and thus incapable of a higher level of functioning faith, the

Lord will provide as we simply trust him. But later it won't be this way. There will come a time when the Lord will require us to use our faith more and more. And when that time comes, provisions previously granted by love and mercy won't be forthcoming unless faith is exercised.

The Necessity of Faith

Be aware that the church is filled with people who trust and hope and believe—and yet find the promises of God are out of reach! Why is this true? Because faith isn't being exercised. And why isn't it being exercised? Because church members don't know how to do it. And why don't they know how to do it? Because they aren't being taught the processes of faith. Not many in the church know how to make a faith transaction with God. Therefore many of God's promises go unfulfilled in their lives.

You will recall that God made great promises to the Children of Israel when they came out of Egypt. Yet, most of those people died in the wilderness without experiencing the fulfillment of any these promises. Even though the Promise Land, for them, was only days away, decades went by—and most of these people never got there!

The reason they didn't isn't exactly a mystery, because Scripture says, "... the word preached did not profit them, not being mixed with faith in them that heard it" (Hebrews 4:2). All kinds of promises recorded in the Word, and preached from the pulpit, will go unfulfilled in our lives, too, unless faith is activated.

We may believe these promises are true. And this, it can be parenthetically pointed out, is where hope comes in. Hope is produced by the promises of Scripture at the point belief considers these promises true. In tracking the differences between belief, hope, trust, and faith, the issue of verb tenses looms large. All that the Bible says *was* true and *will be* true are embraced by hope and undergirded by trust. But as strong as this belief is in its past and future perspectives, it will come to nothing in these present days unless faith takes up this belief and asserts that the God of yesterday and the God of tomorrow will be faithful to me today. Faith draws from the reservoir of hope and commences a specific transaction with God in the here and now.

Trust, worthy though it is, isn't enough. Hope, worthy though it is, isn't enough. Belief, worthy though it is, isn't enough. All are essential, but none is sufficient. Remember, the Bible tells us that even the devils believe (James 2:19—but of course such belief hasn't done anything for them! Hope, the Bible tells us, does anchor the soul (Hebrews 6:19); so there is some benefit to this dynamic. But there are limitations as well, inasmuch as hope won't launch a ship—and it won't complete a voyage! Similarly, there are distinct limitations to trust. Trust encourages us to grow faith, and it even helps us to sustain faith, but if faith doesn't remain on the job, then the job won't get done! And should that be the outcome, trust—badly injured and severely compromised—will languish somewhere between perplexity and extinction.[2]

The Active Function of Faith

Colossians 2:6 says that in the same way we were saved, that's exactly the way we are to live. So how were we saved? Ephesians 2:8 we were saved by faith laying hold of grace. Then that's how we should live: using our faith to lay hold of God's grace. When addressing the issue of the extent of grace and why no aspect of life should be negotiated without it, II Corinthians 9:8 speaks of "abounding grace." The word "abounding" denotes grace in all its forms operating with optimum capacity. The immediate reference in this passage is to financial grace, but there is also healing grace, relationship grace, grace for times of trouble, grace for spiritual growth. Indeed, whatever the need, whatever the concern, God has a grace supply with our name on it!

So does he just give us this supply? Almost, but not quite in the way we may be thinking. The Lord certainly offers it to us, but this grace may very well remain in the extended hands of Jesus unless faith reaches out to receive it. The Greek word for "receive" can be accurately translated "take." This is another very important distinction to make between trust, belief, hope, and faith. Unlike the trust that believes, and the hope that waits, faith *takes*. Faith makes a claim on grace, firmly taking hold before sight can affirm its reality or confirm its coming manifestation. So faith is not as passive as the word "receive" may seem to indicate. This word "take" may help believers better understand what is required of them so they won't miss out like that generation which died in the wilderness. A. B. Simpson, said, "There is a great difference between asking and claiming, between wanting and taking."[3]

Many Christians fail to understand why there are so many promises in the Bible that haven't been fulfilled in their lives. Since they believe these promises are true, they wonder why these promises aren't being fulfilled. Ephesians 3:20 further extols the generosity of God by saying that he will do exceedingly above all that we ask and think. He will? There's little evidence of that thus far! Why, God hasn't done even half of what they've asked for! In examining this very common problem we would have to say that yes, they asked; and yes, they sought. But did they proceed to the next step of knocking? Knowing and finding are essential outcomes; but according to Jesus, the process is incomplete unless one boldly marches up to that door to receive (Matthew 7:7).

Perhaps we are identifying a major reason for unanswered prayer. It is because God's grace, conveyed by God's promises, has to be *taken* in faith (Romans 5:2). In order to secure the blessings of God, the virtues of trusting, hoping, and believing will have to progress to the higher level of faith. Should this not occur, though, then the all-too-familiar scene of desperately wanting, and forever waiting, will result in much confusion and great consternation, which in turn will present huge targets to the enemy. Especially will this be so when the glories of grace are still extolled from the pulpit.

Romans 5:17, for example, speaks of an abundance of grace that will enable us to reign in life! Reign in life? Many believers feel they're being beaten up by life, or, at best, just trying to hang on and survive. This notion of reigning in life seems way beyond their experience! Again, though, the reigning is connected to the grace. And the grace is released by a faith that takes.

The Specificity of Faith

Since we are to live in the same manner we became a Christian—that is, with faith laying hold of grace—we must further inspect this conversion dynamic so there won't be any confusion about how to live. With this agenda in mind, let me ask you these questions. When you got saved, did you release only a general belief in God, agreeing that he is loving, and wise, and powerful—and simply leave it at that? Or did you get more specific? You got more specific, right? What you released was a faith for sin's forgiveness, for acceptance into God's family, for the entrance of Jesus into your life, and for your one-day entrance into heaven. There were additional benefits that came, but initially you were quite specific about these benefits.

Now, what if you never got specific? What if you never nailed anything down but let all sorts of loose ends fly in the breeze? Regarding salvation, for example, you could have said something like this, "I know that God will do what is best ... in his time ... in his way. I'm sure that whatever God decides will be good." Now I ask you: Would you have gotten saved with that kind of belief?

Attempting to sound broadminded, you might have also said, "Maybe God will let me into heaven, and maybe he won't. One never knows. After all, our understanding is so limited! We don't want to presume upon God!" Again, I ask you: Would you have gotten saved that way? Of course, you wouldn't have. Floating along on such broad-based platitudes would have gotten you precisely nowhere. What was required for salvation is a faith that *takes* based on a specific promise from God's Word. And what was required then is also required now, because Scripture tells us: "As you have received Christ Jesus, so walk in him" (Colossians 2:6).

This verse brings us back to Mr. Bosworth's observation of faith being impossible unless the will of God is known. As we reflect on the dynamics critical to receiving the Lord, it is indisputably clear that we had to know about sin's forgiveness, heaven's assurance, and Jesus' willingness to come into our lives before we could exercise our faith regarding these matters. To trust God only in a general way would have secured none of these blessings. And yet many have drifted from this very simple premise when it comes to obtaining other blessings from God.

There is a view, widely assumed to be true by many in the church, which says that God moves in mysterious ways. You've heard people say that, I'm sure. Accompanying this view are honorific pronouncements about the omniscience of God as compared with the limited knowledge of man. Once the conversation takes this direction, someone will pipe up and point out, almost on cue, that we don't even know what to pray for much of the time, which is why the Holy Spirit must make up this deficit by interceding for us. Sound familiar?

I submit that notions like these put the believer in a quandary in two respects. First, if we *don't* know—and, as we've been told often, *can't* know, due to the wide span that exists between Creator omniscience and creature understanding—how can we ever be specific in our prayers as faith requires? Would not this lack of knowledge inevitably downgrade us back to the level of trust every time we pray? And in the second place, if this factor of not knowing is as extensive as many believe it is, might not this factor bear application to *every* attempt to launch faith, and thus bring insurmountable doubt on the scene that compels the faith-killing words, "if it be thy will"?

Again, if we don't know a certain prayer petition is God's will, *that cancels faith*! Given this neutralization of faith, these words, "if it be thy will," must be examined more carefully, lest they degenerate into generalities that get dangerously close to the concept of "whatever." Proponents of the "if-it-be-thy-will" usage in prayer, point out that Jesus prayed this way at a very important time in his life. So if he did, so should we. Furthermore, they tell us, we will never come to a time in life more important than Gethsemane, so surely our prayer requests must not be offered in a manner that has less humility than what Jesus used.

This argument falls apart for several reasons, one of these being that there will never come a time in the believer's life analogous to Gethsemane, inasmuch as it will never be our role to redeem the world![4] Moreover, nowhere does

Scripture tell us to model our prayers after the blood-sweat prayer Jesus prayed. Using Jesus words, "if it be thy will" as a tack-on for every prayer is simply without scriptural warrant. A closer examination of Gethsemane further discloses that a lack of information wasn't the issue for Jesus, as we say it is for us whenever we unwisely transport these words into our prayers. Scripture tells us that just before Jesus went into the garden he said, "For this cause came I unto the world." For what cause? To die a Savior's death, the pressure of which bore down on him at Gethsemane in ways we'll never understand. Yet, important to remember is the fact that Jesus wasn't confused! He knew then, what he had known from eternity past, that his mission was to die to save sinners. There was no confusion about God's will in the garden that night.

I acknowledge there *is* a time for speaking these words, "if it be your will," but this is much more limited in its applicability than we have supposed. The only reason for saying these words is to gain knowledge from God that will be necessary for a future faith transaction with God. James tells us not to assume too much as we project a far-off future with details that came from our own minds and never came from the Lord. G. D. Watson notes, "It is not the divine plan to reveal all things to us from beginning to end at once, but to open up our way little by little in distinct steps ...."[5] The idea that the next year has been disclosed in complete detail warrants this reprimand from James to reign in some of this stuff by first inquiring "if the Lord wills" (James 4:13-15).

Again, there is danger in any grandiose grasping of the future, which G. D. Watson succinctly addressed when he wrote: "If God should reveal to us his plans for a long time ahead, it would cause us to depend on our knowledge, and to some extent it would wean us from that life of momentary trust ...."[6] The Bible talks about a light sufficient for where we are walking, this lamp unto our feet, and not about a light so bright it instantly illumines our entire life path.

A. B. Simpson offered further counsel on this subject when he wrote, "Many of you have the way all mapped out. You have heard someone's experience, and want that itinerary for your journey."[7] Projections of one's future patterned after someone else's experience is just as much a mistake as conceiving these projections from the desires and creativity of one's own mind. To guard against presumption, it is necessary to submit all plans to the Lord before launching in supposed faith.

To caution against presumption is one thing, but we mustn't interpret this caution to mean what it clearly does not mean: namely, that we can never know God's will. To think that specificity about God's will is reserved only for omniscience, and that such knowledge isn't available to believers today, even if sought to a lesser degree, is wrong. What James discourages is claiming to know too much; he does not discourage claiming to know anything. Therefore, allowing God to blue pencil our plans before extending these plans to him in a faith transaction is a wise thing to do. However, the "if" part of these words has to be resolved or no faith can commence. Addressing this point, Charles Finney wrote:

> To put an "if" in God's promise when God has put none there, is tantamount to charging God with being insincere. It is like saying, "O God, if Thou art in earnest in making these promises, grant us the blessing we pray for."[8]

R. A. Torrey also cautioned against hedging our prayer requests with "if-it-be-thy-will" postscripts.

> If you plead any plain promise in God's Word, you need not put any "ifs" in your petition. You may know that you are asking something that is according to God's will, and it is your privilege to know that God has heard you, and it is your privilege to know that you have the thing you have asked; it is your privilege to get up from prayer with the same absolute certainty that that thing is yours that you will afterward have.[9]

Jessie Penn-Lewis fully supported the perspectives of Finney and Torrey. In her book, *Face to Face*, she writes:

> Ignorance of God and his heart and his written Word lie at the bottom of much aimless prayer. How can we say, "if it be thy will," when he has plainly revealed his will as to much that we ask for? We need but to point him to his Word, and say reverently, and with the boldness of faith, "*Do as Thou hast said.*"[10]

A. B. Simpson warned, "There is much subtle unbelief often in the prayer, 'Thy will be done.'"[11] An over-usage of the prayer addendum, "if it be thy will," clearly conflicts with other examples of prayer more frequently taught by the Lord. In fact, Jesus *never* taught us to pray, "if it be thy will." Instead, he taught us to pray "thy will be done on earth as it is in heaven," which assumes at the outset adequate knowledge about heaven.

Instead of cautioning us not to get too specific with our prayer requests, as many pastors do, Jesus did the precise opposite! In Matthew 21:22, Jesus said, "And *whatsoever* you ask in prayer, believing, you shall receive." Andrew Murray noted, "The tendency of human reason is to interpose here, and with certain qualifying clauses, 'if expedient,' 'if according to God's will,' to break the force of a statement which seems dangerous. O let us beware of dealing thus with the Master's words."[12]

In Mark 11:24, Jesus said, "*What things so ever you desire*, believe that you receive them and you shall have them." In John 14:13, Jesus said, "And *whatsoever* things you shall ask in my name, that will I do ...." In John 15:7, Jesus said, "If you abide in me, and my Word abides in you, you shall ask *what you will* and it shall be done unto you." J. A. MacMillan writes:

> Note carefully the significance of the statement, "Ye shall ask what *ye* will." How many believers content themselves with a submissive uttering of the words, 'Thy will be done," in all matters which they bring before the Lord. Their spirits assume a passive attitude which assumes that anything that comes to them comes as the will of the Father.

> This is not scriptural, and it is very far from the desire of God for his children.[13]

In John 16:23, we see this same promise given again: "*Whatsoever you shall ask the Father* in my name, he shall give it to you." These verses are sufficient in number and clear enough in their wording to convince us that prayer is not a shotgun exercise whereby we get enough rounds off and hope we occasionally hit some elusive target.

There is a guarantee attached to each promise Jesus made about prayer, which hardly resembles the talk of supposed humility that says, "You just never know ... whatever the Lord wills .... We'll just have to wait and see." Listen, what the Lord wills is faith! And faith *cannot* begin until sufficient knowledge is given!

True, there are conditions cited in these verses—namely: belief, not doubt; petitions consistent with God's character and not with carnal wishes; and abiding in God's Word instead of enmeshing with the world. Nevertheless, in all of these verses you will notice affirmative answers *guaranteed*, and not this abundance of caution about the possibility of denial, delay, or even the use of the sovereignty card whenever God decides to overrule. Scripture says that *all* the promises of God are in him yea and in him amen (II Corinthians 1:20). Therefore, sovereignty is the guarantee of God's affirmative answers to prayer and not, as many moderns believe, the reason for their suspension.

The Revealing Essential to Faith

How different these verses are in their direction than what is commonly heard today from the pulpit. One reason for this difference, and it is a major reason, is the common belief among moderns that God's will is quite uncertain and that our knowledge of it is largely limited. But is this assumption true? No, it is not true. The metaphor of Jesus being the head and we the body conveys frequent messages being sent from the head to members of the body! This metaphor makes no sense, really, unless these messages come frequently, clearly, and accurately. The idea of God's will being done on earth as it is done in heaven assumes sufficient understanding about heaven. The binding and loosing on earth, each to be reciprocated in heaven, envisions heaven and earth in sync, and not a clueless church for whom the Holy Spirit has to do much of the praying.

Embedded in the assumption of those who counsel that we must be tentative in the way we pray is a minimalist view of the revealing ministry of God. But knowing quite well that faith requires knowledge, even specific knowledge if faith is to progress beyond trust, God has been faithful to reveal this needed knowledge. Thus Scripture declares, "Be not unwise, but understand what the will of the Lord is" (Ephesians 5:17). In Colossians 1:9 Scripture speaks of being filled with the knowledge of his will." And the Greek for knowledge here, *epignosis*, isn't just talking about spiritual knowledge universally applicable, but may well indicate specific knowledge needed for a decision next Wednesday.

In Ephesians chapter 1 the inspired Word of God loads up these noetic concepts when it commends to us wisdom, revelation, knowledge, understanding, and enlightenment. Would God inspire a prayer like this, if all these things couldn't be ours? In James 2:5 we are told that if we lack wisdom, God will give it to us. In I Corinthians 1:30 we are told that Jesus has been made wisdom unto us. In I John 2:17 we are told that we have an anointing within sufficient for us to know all things. And in I Corinthians 2:16 Paul asks, "For who has known the mind of the Lord that he may instruct him?" Of course, the implied answer is, no one. But then Paul concludes this verse by writing the exact opposite of what we would have thought when he declares, "But we have the mind of Christ." *What*?

This just can't be! Paul must have meant here in I Corinthians, chapter 2, what he said in Philippians 2:5 when he wrote, "Let this mind be in you which was also in Christ Jesus." And there, you will recall, Paul goes on to talk about humility, death, and trusting in the Lord, etc. However, in I Corinthians, chapter 2, no such context is given to these words about having the mind of Christ. Instead, Paul talks about a faith that doesn't stand in the wisdom of men (verse 5)—which is precisely why it does stand! Additionally, in verse 10 Paul talks about a revealing available to us through the Holy Spirit and, in verse 12 he talks about how this revealing is transmitted through our spirit.

Are you getting the idea that God intends for us to know? Of course we're not omniscient or even anything close to that. But the Holy Spirit doesn't keep us in the dark where it is impossible for faith to function. Moreover, Scripture never assumes that we're inevitably vulnerable to ignorance and that this is why the Holy Spirit is going to have to pray for us.

Translation or Interpretation?

With this background in mind, I now want us to look at a scriptural passage that many have interpreted to mean: The Holy Spirit prays for us because we don't know enough to pray for ourselves like we should. Some people think that this verse should be interpreted in a more limited way, meaning there are gaps in our knowledge which *at times* require such praying by the Spirit. This is possible, but I'm not sure that this verse is even saying that. Others think this verse addresses a more prevailing condition—our profound inability to know, which is constantly a factor in our lives—and that's why the Holy Spirit has to do all this praying.

This latter view can't possibly be correct, because there are too many verses that say otherwise. But let's see to what extent, if any, the former view is true.

First, we will quote the verses in question. Romans 8:26-27 states:

> Likewise the Spirit also helps our infirmities: for we know not how we should pray as we ought: for the spirit itself makes intercession for us with groanings which cannot be uttered. And he which searches the hearts knows what is the mind of the spirit, because he makes intercession for the saints according to the will of God.

At first glance, these verses appear to indicate believers lack the needed knowledge for praying and so the Holy Spirit must do so on our behalf. This is certainly the traditional view of this verse. However, there are textual reasons for doubting this is the case. Let's examine some of these, briefly.

Notice first that the passage begins with a word that causes us to back up, the word "likewise." This word obviously links us to prior verses, since a comparison involving some antecedent is set forth. The word "groanings" in verse 26 also connects with an earlier verse, the creation groaning mentioned in verse 22. This refers to our planet, the physical world, which waits that glorious day when a new heaven and a new earth will be on the scene.[14] Verse 23 then talks about believers groaning, signifying a desire for our physical bodies to be free from its current imperfections and glorified. Perhaps we do groan when our bodies are in pain, but we probably don't do so with profound aspirations for a glorified body. Then verse 26 mentions the groanings of the spirit. Literally? No, the Greek word for "groaning" is a figurative word that means longing with hope. "Likewise," Scripture says—in the same manner the physical cosmos doesn't release audible sounds, and our physical bodies don't release audible sounds, the spirit within us doesn't release audible sounds. Thus, the idea embraced by some Charismatics that speaking in tongues is indicated by this verse is not likely the case.

In attempting to ascertain the meaning of this passage, we must do a word study more than once. Chuck Swindoll has said that emphasizing the necessity of knowing the original languages of the Bible—Hebrew, Greek, Aramaic, Chaldean—may create a suspicion in the minds of church members that the Bible they have can't be trusted. This is a point well-taken, and explains why an overemphasis on the need to know Greek, for example, may needlessly discourage believers from reading their Bibles written in English. However, in the two verses that presently claim our attention, there are some textual difficulties that can cause translation to become interpretation. I shall comment on some of these.

First, the Greek word for "spirit" in verse 26—that is, the second time the word "spirit" is used in this verse (where we're told that the spirit makes intercession for us with groanings that can't be uttered), that word "spirit" is neuter in gender, and therefore by itself can't be referring to the Third Person of the Trinity, the Holy Spirit. When referring to the Holy Spirit, the pronoun *autos* is used, thus indicating a person. The King James Version of Scripture gets this right when it translates "the spirit itself." This has to mean, then, that the spirit referred to in this part of the verse is our spirit and not the Holy Spirit.

This affects interpretation. But, you say, it also causes problems, for how can it be that our spirit intercedes for us? Well, this question introduces another textual difficulty. The Greek word for "intercede," used only here in the entire Bible, *huperentunchano*, can mean petition or appeal or intercede, but that is not its likely meaning here. This same word can also be translated to meet, to approach, to turn to—in effect, to connect. So what connection are we talking about? The connection between the first reference to "spirit" in this verse, the Holy Spirit, and the second reference to "spirit" in this verse, our own spirit. A connection is made when our spirit turns for direction to the Holy Spirit.

Now, when this same verse talks about the Holy Spirit helping our infirmities, the Greek word for infirmities, *astheneia*, means weaknesses or an inability to produce results. Therefore, on its own, our spirit can't produce needed results. Notice, though, that this verse says that the Holy Spirit "helps" our infirmities. But how does he do this, by praying for us? That's the interpretation many give, but this interpretation doesn't really make sense, because if the Holy Spirit just takes over, we may reasonably ask, has my spirit really been helped? In one sense, it has, I understand. But this is not the sense this verse indicates, because the Greek word for help, *sunantilambanomai*, means to take hold of, to cooperate.[15] So here in this one verse we see, twice, the ideas of connecting and cooperating. What is communicated is conjoint activity between the Holy Spirit and our spirit, and not substitute activity, where one party simply takes over.

This point is further stressed by the Greek word for "ought," the word *dei*. This word is translated variously: as "should," "must," and "necessarily." Notice, though, the subject for this verb. Is it the Holy Spirit? Or is it the believer? It's the believer! *We* ought, *we* must. Well, if *we* must, then why is the Holy Spirit taking over and doing this all in our place? He's not, and other words in this verse, when properly explained, tell us he's not. This is a conjoint activity, a cooperative activity. The Holy Spirit is working with our spirit. In what way?

Verse 26 discounts audible words, or even words at all. However, verse 27 talks about the mind of the spirit. This refers to content possessed. The Greek for "know," *eido*, informs us the Holy Spirit perfectly knows what the spiritual mind is, spoken of earlier in this chapter, in verse 6, where Christians are told to be spiritually minded. Now, if we couldn't follow this command to be spiritually minded, why give it? The emphasis in this chapter is on believers functioning, and not on our inability to do so and therefore the Holy Spirit having to take over.

The Holy Spirit does have a role to play, obviously, since he knows perfectly what we know partially. Therefore, verse 27 tells us that the Holy Spirit does what for us? Translators render the Greek word in this verse, *entugchano*, "makes intercession," which is certainly one option consistent with this Greek word, but it's not the only option. This same Greek word can also be translated "confer with," or "deal with." And with either of these last two options further qualifiers can be added with the words "strongly" and "suitably."

If translated this way, verse 27 indicates that the Holy Spirit confers with our spirit suitably, strong enough for us to get the message. When considering the other words in this passage that stress conjoint activity and not singular and independent activity, I submit this is a better way to translate this word.

The rest of verse 27 says that the Holy Spirit confers with the saints "according to the will of God." Many people take this to mean that only the Holy Spirit knows what God's will is, and therefore he has to pray for us. But that isn't what this verse is saying at all. Instead, this verse is saying it is God's will for the Holy Spirit to confer with our spirit suitably enough so we will be helped to pray as we ought—indeed, as we must!

When commenting on this verse, Norman Grubb said that the phrase, "we know not what to pray for as we ought," has been misinterpreted. With regard to the Holy Spirit, Grubb said, this "does not mean that he is praying for our personal needs on our behalf, but that he is inspiring us to pray for the things and people we ought to pray for ...."[16] Thomas Goodwin's seventeenth-century commentary on this passage speaks similarly: "The Holy Ghost comes and imprints a skill upon a man's heart, and teacheth him to pray acceptably to God, which no man in the world can do."[17]

I Corinthians 2:10 says that the Holy Spirit searches all things, which is similar to what is said here in verse 27. However, I Corinthians 2:10 further tells us God reveals unto us by his Spirit. The Spirit doesn't search and then keep this information to himself! He reveals! It is God's will that he do so! Jessie Penn-Lewis writes:

> When your spirit is in unbroken communion with Christ, you will know what he wants you to do. The Holy Spirit dwells in your spirit: If you live in the deep stillness with him, you will come to detect the slightest movings of that Spirit.[18]

Quite often, this detecting, knowing, and revealing will come in quiet stillness and not with great sensation. This underscores our need to enter that stillness, since divine disclosures aren't likely while we're watching TV or while we're yucking it up friends at the ballgame. Protracted praying is the usual context for divine disclosures. Accordingly, Paul Billheimer writes:

> God's deepest secrets are reserved for those who take time to wait upon the Lord, who take time to be alone with him. He has many secrets, many spiritual visions, many hidden revelations and insights which will be shared only in long hours of waiting upon God in the secret place of prayer. If we begrudge the time spent alone with God, if we

> will not wait upon him, we must be content to remain spiritually naïve, inexperienced and immature.[19]

Undeniable is the fact that God has reconstituted the spirit of a believer in such a way that Omniscience rectifies ignorance and sets out a course the believer knows to follow. G. D. Watson exclaimed, "It is the highest glory of our nature that we can be knit to the living God by union with Jesus, and so partake of his character as to be possessed of his thoughts and plans in such a way that we make them our own."[20]

Again, if we don't know, faith can't function. Therefore, there are a multitude of verses in Scripture that tell us how God has provided the knowledge we need. It is true that we don't know everything, but God makes sure that we *can* know what we need to know at the time we need to know it, so we can then use our faith. Had God done this in any other way, we would be consigned to the lower levels of trust, hope, and belief—benefiting in some ways, but not in the way that most pleases the Lord.

Appendix D
Getting God's Guidance

In his commentary on the Psalms, James Hastings stressed the need for daily guidance, given the fact that "life is so strangely perplexing, appearances are so misleading, errors and mistakes are so easy, and their consequences are so serious ...."[1] Yet, seeking answers with the aid of natural light only is a dilemma experienced by many people today. German humorist Karl Vallentin staged this dilemma well, so that when the curtain rises, the audience sees a man walking with his head down, apparently searching for something he lost. And because it is nighttime, as the stage setting makes clear, the search is difficult.

A policeman approaches the scene to see what is going on. Seeing the worried look on this man's face, the policeman asks, "What are you looking for?" "I lost the key to my house," the man answers. Nodding his head with understanding, the policeman walks to where the man is standing and joins the search. One man walks clockwise, the other man walks counterclockwise, in a small circle of light provided by a nearby streetlamp.

Unsuccessful in these efforts, the policeman stopped and asked, "Are you sure you lost it here?" "Oh, no," the man answered, pointing to a dark place a good distance away, "I lost it over there." There was a long pause ... and then the most quizzical look ... before the somewhat perturbed policeman said, "Then why on earth are you looking *here*?" "Because," the man answered with a shrug and a snort, "there's no light over *there*!"[2]

Patches of darkness will indeed cover much of life's landscape if alternatives to the Word are all that we have. Fully aware of this dilemma, Satan has kept those philosophers in full employment who could produce yet another epistemological problem that calls into question our ability to know. Seeing the effect of this in his day, G. K. Chesterton remarked, "A man was supposed to be doubtful about himself, but undoubting about the truth; this has been exactly reversed. We are on the road to produce a race of men too mentally modest to believe in the multiplication table."[3] The shadows of darkness, it seems, are lengthening in these modern times.

There is no justifiable reason for all this uncertainty, since the Bible is a sufficient revelation, a reliable source of knowledge, a depository of supernatural revelation that tells us all we need to know about life and eternity. And as for those questions that can't be answered by a Bible verse, there is a leading the Holy Spirit provides. However, even this guidance must be evaluated by the obvious scriptures that do apply. Regarding such guidance, G. D. Watson noted:

> There are two extreme views with reference to the particular leadings of the Lord. One view is that there is nothing of the supernatural in our daily guidance, but that we have only the light of reason and the force of circumstances, which is the view of skeptics and materialists. The other extreme view is that we may expect infallible guidance in every detail of life, and should claim it, but they always run off into great foolishness and the wildest errors ....[4]

Hannah Whitall Smith took to task those Christians who overly relied on an inner voice for guidance. One woman, she reports, stayed in bed each day waiting for the voice of God to tell her when to get up. And when she finally did get up, she then waited for the Lord to tell her what clothes to wear. Sometimes she wore only one shoe, or only one stocking. The combinations selected from day-to-day seldom suited society's standards but well suited the standards for comedy. It all depended on the direction of the inner voice, this woman said.

Then there was an invalid who returned the kindness of her visiting friend by keeping the friend's money that had accidentally been left on the dressing table. Upon discovering that her money was missing, the friend returned to the house to check the whereabouts of her money. But the invalid pretended not to know. During that interval between friend departed and friend returned an inner voice had told the invalid that the scripture "all things are yours" applied to this situation; so the invalid took the money and hid it.

Another woman, also uncritical in her acceptance of the inner voice, felt distinctly led to get seekers of the Holy Spirit's baptism in bed with her and, in her words, "lie back to back without any nightgown between."[5] Of course, Scripture never sanctions a guidance that supports immaturity or immorality. Jessie Penn-Lewis observed: "If the believer ceases to use mind, reason, will, and all his other faculties as a person and depends upon voices and impulses for guidance, he will be led or guided by evil spirits feigning to be God."[6] Providing additional insight into this issue, Jessie Penn-Lewis wrote:

> Many define guidance or "leading," as purely and only supernatural, such as by a voice saying "Do this" or "Do that," or by a compulsory movement or impulse apart from the action or volition of the believer himself, thinking of the expression used concerning the Lord, "the Spirit drove him into the wilderness" (Mark 1:12). But this was abnormal in the life of Christ ....[7]

Supernatural leading, for Jesus and the apostles, occurred occasionally, but even for them it wasn't normative. G. D. Watson openly confronted the expectation of some, that direct guidance should come to believers today more often than it did to people in the Bible, when he said, "There are hundreds of comparatively good people at this moment lazily waiting for some special revelation to do something which Scripture and common sense would lead them to go at immediately."[8]

Getting God's guidance is obviously essential, because if the Lord's will is not known, and in many churches it is not, utter confusion will lead to a wrong conclusion. You've heard it said that "God moves in mysterious ways." This is a saying that has a measure of truth in it. However, this mystery business poses a big problem, especially if God is going to be our covenant partner—for how can we partner with someone who is always a mystery? Faith becomes impossible if God's will is lost in some inscrutable, unfathomable domain reserved for the Deity.

Aware of this problem, the Bible presents God as a revealing God; and according to Alexander Maclaren, "The darker the night, the brighter the guidance."[9] G. D. Watson pointed out how "the whole Trinity unite and agree in the guidance of the believer." Watson explained:

> In examining the Scripture on this matter we find the peculiar sphere of the Father's leading is providence, the peculiar sphere of Christ's guidance is the written Word, and the peculiar sphere of the Spirit's guidance is direct conviction and illumination upon the heart and spiritual senses.[10]

But if this is true, how are we to interpret that verse where God says, "... my thoughts are not your thoughts, nor are your ways my ways ...."? We do so by recalling that this verse describes what would naturally be so, if the Lord withheld his revelation. We read in I Corinthians 2:9, for example, "Eye has not seen, nor ear heard, nor have entered into the heart of man the things which God has prepared for those who love him." It all sounds like a big mystery, right? However, the very next verse says, "But God has revealed them to us through his Spirit ...." And this is always his way! If there is something we have to know to release our faith, the Lord will reveal that to us. Indeed, once we are in receipt of his revelation, and then act on that revelation, the world will say of us what it says about God, that *we* move in mysterious ways!

Why God Restrains Advice

We are not saying that God is constantly downloading private information to us. There are at least four reasons why he won't do this. First, to do so would result in a "pushy parenting" that would hinder our growth. The psalmist said, "Do not be like the horse or like the mule which have no understanding ..." (Psalm 32:9). In this context, God has no intention of saying, "To the right, to the left; do this, do that."[11] When we were young, our parents had to furnish a lot of instruction; but as we grew older, they quite rightly relinquished this approach. With each new year they increased our freedom along with our responsibility. This makes sense. The ever instructing, exhorting, admonishing, and even rebuking God envisions a model of parenting that wouldn't be good for us at all! This is why God says in John 15:7, "Ask what *you* will and it will be done unto you." You see, God wants us to grow to the place where we can take the initiative in our relationship with him. This growing into peership (with a small "p," of course) is to God a desirable goal, and not a sign of presumption or willful arrogance.

A second reason God won't tell us everything is because he doesn't want private audiences with him to bypass the Word already given or the wisdom already deposited in our spirit. In James 1:5 we are told, "If any of you lack wisdom, let him ask of God who gives to all liberally and without reproach ...." Taking encouragement from this verse, Christians will pray with fervency—but, as it turns out, all under a silent heaven with no hint of a forthcoming answer! This outcome produces great consternation: What went wrong? Why didn't I get an answer? Actually, nothing went wrong, except perhaps a failure to notice the first word in this verse, "if." It may be that this person doesn't lack wisdom. I Corinthians 1:30 says that Jesus has been made wisdom to us. Inside our spirit, there is a reservoir of wisdom, owing not to the investigations of the human mind or to the hard lessons learned from actual life, but owing to a gracious deposit that was made when Jesus came into our lives. Therefore, we may already know all that we need to know to make a particular decision.

A third reason God may not provide additional information is due to a degree of latitude he allows, within which we are permitted to make God-pleasing decisions. When it comes to *moral* decision-making, Scripture speaks with clarity and comprehension. In the area of *non-moral* decision-making, though, (which car to buy, which house to rent, which school to attend), God may say very little.

Actually, there may be several options available to us, all of which are acceptable to God. In his book, *The Set of the Sail*, A. W. Tozer further elucidated this point.

> Now, a happy truth too often overlooked in our search for the will of God is that in the majority of decisions touching our earthly lives God expresses no choice, but leaves everything to our own preference. Some Christians walk under a cloud of uncertainty, worrying about which profession they should enter, which car they should drive, which school they should attend, where they should live and a dozen or score of other such matters, when the Lord has set them free to follow their own personal bent, guided only by their love for him and for their fellow men.
>
> On the surface it appears more spiritual to seek God's leading than just to go ahead and do the obvious thing. But it is not. If God gave you a watch would you honor him more by asking for the time of day or by consulting the watch? If God gave a sailor a compass would the sailor please God more by kneeling in a frenzy of prayer to persuade God to show him which way to go or by steering according to the compass?[12]

The idea that in every decision only one option is God's will is biblically inaccurate. In Matthew 9:29 Jesus said, "According to your faith let it be to you." If your faith is somewhat small, then God will bless the option selected commensurate with that. But if your faith is impressively large, then God will bless the option elected commensurate with that. Again, there is latitude here; and this is why God isn't always telling us what to do.

A fourth reason God restrains his leading is because he wants our sense of direction to come in a less authoritarian way. Psalm 37:4 says, "Delight yourself also in the Lord and he shall give you the desires of your heart." Since delight is the premise of this promise, Stephen Charnock asked, "What delight do you find in God and his ways? This indeed is an evident sign of the new nature ...."[13] —but is it evident in you? In the Hebrew, the word "delight" means to be moldable, to be pliable. The softness of heart this verse commends is one that says, "Because I belong to you, Lord, spend my life any way you please."

The reason Jesus could say in John 15:7 "Ask what *you* will" is because of what he said just before: "If you abide in me and my words abide in you." Whenever there's an unhindered intimacy with Jesus and a number of life-giving experiences with his Word, God can readily trust the desires that come from this kind of heart. But even so, it is still good to bring our best thoughts to the Lord, allowing him to blue-pencil any amendments he might want to make (James 4:13-15). Remember, getting the goal is one thing; getting the plan is another. Some people get the goal, but in their resulting excitement they leave God in the dust and never get the plan.

If, in a given situation, the mature believer petitions heaven for directions that don't come, what should he do? Assuming that his relationship with the Lord is good and no check in his spirit encourages him to wait, he should proceed! His confidence that God will bless the decision he makes stems from the fact that he approached God the right way. Having been totally yielded and totally willing to do anything God said, means that God will now support the decision made. If God doesn't intend for the believer to proceed, God will infuse an awareness within that persuades the believer to continue waiting.

False Criteria for Decisions

Other people, not drawing their confidence from their faithfulness to a process that was rightly engaged, will attempt to draw confidence from dubious criteria. For example, appealing to Colossians 3:15, there are people who will make their decision based on the presence or absence of "peace." "I just have peace about this decision," they will say. Or they might say, "I don't think I can do that because I don't have peace about it." But was the peace of Jesus challenged in the Garden of Gethsemane? And were you at peace just before your wedding? Remember, these challenges to peace don't always mean that a decision is wrong or that the course you are following is a mistake. To the contrary, it may mean that the decision is so right that the devil is attacking it!

The problem with using Colossians 3:15 as a proof-text for guidance is that this verse isn't talking about nonmoral decision-making. What this verse is talking about is the harmony God wants to see among church members. Relational peace, and not a peace that guides decision-making, is the subject of this verse. Therefore, we shouldn't explain our decision-making on the basis of peace, but rather on the basis of a sense of leading from the Lord or some clear criteria found in his Word.

Another false criterion for decision-making is "open doors" and "closed doors." When Paul began his missionary journey, he went to a place where no one seemed to want him to go. There was great danger en route, robbers lying in wait to steal and harm, all of which caused one team member to quit and the other team member to become so upset with Paul this man eventually quit. On surface, this certainly looked like a closed door, especially when the danger included possible murder. Nevertheless, Paul went bulldozing through—and God blessed it!

Later in Paul's missionary journey, he very specifically tells us that the door to Troas was open to him (II Corinthians 2:12)—which, without censure from God, Paul didn't go through! Therefore, the ease or difficulty of circumstances is not always the predictor of God's will. Closed doors, in the power of God, can be forced open, and open doors can be rightly bypassed, if God is purposing a different direction for our lives.

The notion of getting "confirmations" is another high-risk venture when it comes to determining the will of God! When Gideon did the "fleece" routine (in Judges, chapter 6), that clearly upset God! Seeking some sort of tangible sign, as Gideon did, elevates the credibility of this supposed "confirmation" above the Word of God—which, in this instance, Gideon had heard already! Moreover, because God says we are to live by faith and not by sight (II Corinthians

5:7), this pursuit of confirmations will lead us to the very realm where faith isn't, the realm of sense and sight.

When the twelve spies went into the Promise Land, did this visual confirmation help them? Not really. The confirmation they sought and got discouraged most of them. A. B. Simpson explained how this can happen to us, too: "The spirit of human reasoning is the natural enemy of faith; and the command of God will often lead us into the face of improbabilities and seeming impossibilities."[14] Therefore, confirmations are more likely to hurt us, and not help us.

Most of these so-called "confirmations" people identify are highly questionable. Despite the breathy piety that reports them, the confirmation itself is capable of multiple interpretations—at least one of which is considerably more plausible than what is being recommended.

On several occasions New Testament leaders operated on humbler and more honest criteria as they spoke of "reason" (Acts 6:2) and what "seemed" (Luke 1:3; Acts 15:25, 28). There wasn't this penchant to explain every decision made by attributing ozone layer atmospherics to the decision-making process. God clearly spoke when Paul's first missionary journey was launched, but this wasn't the way it happened for the second missionary journey. In his commentary on the second missionary journey, A. B. Simpson observed, "We note the absence of the special call of God to go forth as in their first missionary journey. It was voluntary, and came directly from the prompting of Paul himself. 'Let us go back,' he said to Barnabas, 'and visit the brothers' (Acts 15:36). And so we learn that when God has once called us to his work we are to be about our Father's business and not wait for some special revelation ...."[15]

Still and all, if we are in need of a sure word from God, God will give that to us—either through an audible voice, a quiet instilling of thought, a dream, or some other form of communication. He'll tell us what we need to know when we need to know it.

Does this mean that our understanding will always be in accord with the ways of God? No, even the Apostle Paul spoke of being perplexed (II Corinthians 4:8). And for us as well there will be those times when God will act, or not act, in ways we don't understand. Addressing this point, F. B. Meyer counseled:

> Do not be surprised, then, if there should be matters in the Bible, in your own life, and in the providential government of the world, which baffle your thought. Remember you are only a little child in an infant class, and it is not likely that you can comprehend the whole system of your instructor. God would cease to be God to us, if we by searching could find him out.[16]

Just know that reason without revelation will never discover God, and even a searching into revelation will come short of an exhaustive understanding of God. What the revelation of God's Word discloses is a sufficient revelation. It is true that the Lord will never act contrary to his Word, but he may very well act contrary to what we would have predicted. Should this occur, as well it might, this simply means the knowledge withheld from us is not knowledge we needed to have. And therefore, like Paul, we can carry on without despair (II Corinthians 4:8).

In appreciating the revelation God has given, and the knowledge he does give, it is important to avoid the error of supposing this knowledge is complete. It is not. But to think that it is will produce a spectacle that either contrives wrong answers (and sometimes downright silly answers) or convulses in anguish about a deficit in knowledge that is assumed to be resolvable. Accordingly, when all efforts to achieve resolution fail, false guilt becomes the result, a result that was perpetrated by error in the first place and then exploited by the enemy after that. By learning how God does and does not disclose his will for our lives, we can stay out of the darkness where Satan abides, and out of the confusion that Satan authors.

Still, it must be affirmed that God does guide. G. D. Watson said, "The Holy Spirit illuminates the Word of God, enlightens our judgment, gives clear perceptions of divine providences, convinces and impels the heart, using all of them in his guidance of the child of God."[17] James S. Stewart declared, "... it is literally a new world you enter on—a world of glorious meaning and zest and happiness—when you come awake to a God who guides." And yet Stewart had to lament, "I am convinced that half the strain, half the feverishness in the world today is that we won't believe that ...."[18] Therefore, we trudge through life as if we're alone, as if there are no certain answers and no reliable guidance upon which to depend. To consign ourselves to such darkness is without scriptural warrant. Because God does guide, and his light is sufficient for where we are walking.

Yet, there will come those times when we feel more alone in our decision-making than we want to be. This should not surprise us, really, for the wise parent will not always hold the child's hand. The parent may even step out of the room, giving the impression of absence. But what the child doesn't know is that the parent is peering through a door, slightly ajar, ready to reenter the room as soon as the need arises. Until a more direct intervention is needed, however, the parent will limit his or her role to watching. And if prior training was effective, these intervals of seeming absence will grow longer, precisely because the child's ability to do what's right is becoming stronger.

Appendix E
Examining Emotions

The role emotions should have in the believer's life has often been subjected to hidden assumptions and their predictable conclusions. For example, those in a high church tradition where ceremony is prominent tend to downplay the role emotions should have, as do those in a more scholarly tradition where theology is scrutinized. But those in a more revivalist tradition, or in a more Charismatic tradition, seem to elevate the role emotions should have.

For other people, the deciding factor for promoting or demoting emotions relates more to personal temperament than it does to church tradition. If a person tends to be more sanguine and outgoing, then emotions will be warmly welcomed. But if a person is more reserved by nature, emotions may be more buttoned down and restrained. Sometimes, too, an appeal is made to gender, wherein women are said to be more emotional than men; or to geography, wherein those of African or South American descent are said to be more emotional than those of British or Scandinavian descent.

These generalizations are overly broad and not particularly useful. C. S. Lewis differentiated between "thick" religion and "thin" religion, saying that those more cerebral in their approach (thick religion) should venture toward a more emotional venue of expression (thin religion); and vice versa—the more emotional should become more cerebral.

Although there is some wisdom in this suggestion, it doesn't say enough. At issue, really, is this: What does Scripture say? Is the participation of emotions in our faith to be decided by church tradition, personal temperament, national origin, gender, or some formula designed to achieve balance? Or does Scripture set forth more definitive principles addressing the extent emotions should participate in our life?

In pursuing this question further, it would be helpful to know to what extent, if any, emotions are to be found in God.

Does God Have Emotions?

It may be something of a surprise to learn that some theologians say God doesn't have emotions. The Westminster Confession of Faith asserts that God has neither "parts nor passions." The word "parts" in this document refers to the body; the word "passions" refers to emotions. In other words, since God doesn't have a body, he therefore doesn't experience emotions. The argument, according to this historic confession, is that those scriptures attributing emotions to God are anthropomorphic—that is, an adaptation of language used to accommodate the experience and understanding of man. So we shouldn't suppose that God has emotions.

We shouldn't? But isn't this kind of thinking a philosophical intrusion upon theology? It is regrettable that some Reformers (not Luther) allowed the resurging Platonism of their day to creep into their theology. The argument that emotions are singularly linked to a physical body is circular in its construction. Who says that emotions can only transact through a physical body? Scripture never makes this point. Moreover, who says that the impassibility of God and the supposed fluctuations of emotions are incompatible? Scripture never makes this point, either. It is philosophers wrestling with what they don't know who talk this way, but theologians should know better.

Whenever an argument is largely deductive, has the structure of linked hypothesis, has one or more premises that are philosophical in nature, the conclusion of that argument is almost always in error. And such is the case with this notion that scriptural declarations of God feeling are anthropopathic. This is a construct imposed on Scripture. The genre of the text gives no indication at all that the language employed in these passages is figurative. Thus, Wayne Grudem, a classical theist, is correct to call this tenet from the creeds (The Westminster Confession, The Thirty-Nine Articles) into question. Those who have ventured away from Scripture to formulate an interpretation of emotions seemed not to have realized the number of theories about emotion that exist in philosophy, psychology, and psychiatry, none of which should ever be decisive when it comes to postulating what God feels.

Fully aware of this theological belief espoused by the Reformers, Charles Spurgeon, a Reformer himself, said, "I believe in a God who can feel. As to Baal, and the gods of the heathen, they may be passionless and without emotion, or without anything that is akin to feeling. Not so do I find Jehovah to be described." Horatius Bonar, a contemporary of Spurgeon, wrote:

> We are apt to associate God only with what is cold and abstract and ideal; ourselves with what is emotional and personal. Herein we greatly err. We must reverse the picture if we would know the truth concerning him with whom is no coldness, no abstraction, no impersonality.[1]

Also rejecting the view of an emotionless God, A. W. Tozer wrote, "It is a strange and beautiful eccentricity of the free God that he has allowed his heart to be emotionally identified with men."[2]

Reflecting more narrowly on this subject, the Puritan writer, Stephen Charnock, said, "God is a Spirit infinitely happy ...."[3] All day, every day, he is supremely happy! But what if this weren't true? For purposes of analysis, John Piper allowed himself to contemplate that possibility.

> Can you imagine what it would be like if the God who ruled the world were not happy? What if God were given to grumbling and pouting and depression ...? What if God were frustrated and despondent and gloomy and dismal and discontented and dejected?[4]

That God's emotions are always elevated above every negative emotion is a profound truth, as is the fact that never once has any outside circumstance, or any inside emotion, diminished his joy in the slightest.

God certainly has emotions, as do we who were created in his image. And while it is of course true that these emotions shouldn't rule us, it is patently untrue to say they shouldn't be allowed to participate in our lives. Contrary to the rationalists of his day who rejected the emotional displays seen at revivals, Jonathan Edwards argued for the necessity of emotion in our faith. In a document published in 1746, Jonathan Edwards' *Treatise Concerning the Religious Affections* offered this summary statement:

> I am bold to assert that there never was any considerable change wrought in the mind or conversation of any person, by anything of a religious nature which he read, heard, or saw, who had not his affections moved ... Nor was there ever a saint awakened out of a cold, lifeless flame, or recovered from a declining state in religion, and brought back from a lamentable departure from God, without having his heart affected. In a word, there never was anything considerable brought to pass in the heart or life of any man, by the things of religion, that had not his heart deeply affected by those things.[5]

Strong surges of feelings—what some call enthusiasm—is not alien to our faith. G. D. Watson exclaimed, "What a vast ocean of heart life and pathos and feelings pervade the whole Bible! It is not a stoical, human, philosophical book; it throbs with deep feeling from beginning to end."[6] In fact, the very word "enthusiasm" comes from two words, one means "in" and the other means "God." True enthusiasm, therefore, comes from being in God. "Without enthusiasm," Joseph Parker cried, "what is the church? It is Vesuvius without fire, it is Niagara without water, it is the firmament without the sun."[7]

Yet, not wanting to elevate emotions too much, Stephen Charnock also made a valid point when he said, "We shall gain nothing by our applaudings and praises of Christ, without a renewed nature."[8] The worship of superficial emotions means nothing. Tears may sparkle from the eye, the face may be flushed with passion, and yet soon after the service the ways of the flesh are reengaged.

Emotions: Authentic or Eccentric?

Whenever emotions become the goal in worship (or for that matter in life), idolatry has reemerged and a drug mentality has taken over. To measure a worship service by the degree the emotions were stirred is a false assessment, by which the Spirit of God is reduced to a stimulant, and "getting high" becomes the result of an inferior intoxicant rather than godly inspiration. There are worship leaders who will seek to "rev" the crowd up, and will never deviate from this agenda, not from their first syllable to their last sigh. In worship services like these only the sensational is sought. Everything else is deliberately omitted.

To see the bizarre and dramatic emphasized to this extent goes a long way toward discrediting exuberance in worship, public or private. And yet when one reads the Psalms, exuberance in worship is actually commanded. Therefore, any criterion which attempts to set aside emotional worship, or to reduce it to only one of a cafeteria of options offered by Scripture, is simply wrong. Exuberance in worship is not only right, it is expected.

Still, however, without in any way attempting to modify this point, it must be acknowledged that Scripture's thoughts on this subject are more nuanced than what at first might seem to be the case.

Mature faith engages the emotions, and need not ever repress all of them! Love, joy, peace, and many other parts of the Holy Spirit's fruit would become most unappealing, if not altogether unintelligible, if emotions were stripped away from their definitions. The resulting difference in that case would be as obvious as that which exists between artificial, plastic fruit bought in a department store versus natural, juicy fruit bought in a grocery store. Besides, what is worship without emotion? And why would God even want such worship if he weren't also emotional? Commenting on what occurred in the book of Acts, A. W. Tozer noted:

> The joy of the first Christians was not the joy of logic working on facts. They did not reason, "Christ is risen from the dead; therefore we ought

> to be glad." Their gladness was as great a miracle as the resurrection itself ... The moral happiness of the Creator had taken residence in the breasts of redeemed creatures and they could not but be glad.[9]

This joy and gladness infused their worship in a way contagious among those who also believed and compelling in its witness to those who didn't yet believe. It is in this context that Charles Kingsley spoke of "the sacred duty of being happy."[10] We certainly see such happiness in Jesus. Harry Emerson Fosdick tells us that Jesus "let the ripple of a happy breeze play over the surface of his mighty deep." And Thomas Carlyle noted: "True humor ... issues not in laughter, but in still smiles which lie far deeper." According to Louis Sabatier, the nineteenth-century French theologian, in Jesus alone "optimism is without frivolity, and seriousness without despair."[11]

How nearly the opposite is Scripture's depiction of Satan! G. D. Watson observed: "... Scripture never reveals Satan as a being of levity in himself. The starless gloom of eternal night is fastened upon his awful malignant nature, and his very laugh would indicate a fiendish misery."[12] A very different destiny was forecast by Jesus for those blessed ones who weep now. According to the Sermon on the Mount, the Master said, "They shall laugh." Once the great battle with Satan is over and none of his work is left on the scene, the impulse of laughter will need no restraint. In his book, *The Hierarchy of Heaven and Earth*, D. E. Harding said that "... heaven is lighthearted and merry ... the skies are one broad smile, and the galaxies are even now shaking their fiery manes with laughter ...."[13]

The notion that feelings are a valid and valued part of worship is defensible. What cannot be defended is an inversion of this order, whereby our culture worships feelings. To enthrone feelings—so that, like one who responds to a tyrannical king, we constantly bow to its preferences and offer nonstop pampering for its continued favor—is a mistake of the first order. Samuel Chadwick wrote, "A religion of mere emotion and sensationalism is the most terrible of all curses that come upon any people." Comparing this display of emotions with fireworks, Chadwick writes, "Fireworks are brilliant but they end with the hour. No ideas are kindled, no ministry impelled, no sacrifice inspired."[14] In one sense, a religion rooted in feelings is a religion frustrated in its desires and unstable in its ways. But if feelings are properly demoted in one's priorities, a better outcome more likely occurs. According to F. B. Meyer, "Seek feeling, and you will miss it; be content to live without it, and you will have all you require."

The Fervent Feelings of Faith

Jonathan Edwards, one of the greatest intellects America ever produced, was used by the Lord to bring one of the greatest revivals America ever experienced. The overflow of this revival deeply touched his wife Sarah. Describing her experience, Edwards said that her soul was "perfectly overwhelmed, and swallowed up with light and love and sweet solace, and a rest and joy of soul altogether unspeakable."[15] Edwards also said that she "felt a great delight in singing praises to God and Jesus Christ, and longing that this present life may be, as it were, one continued song of praise to God." Further describing this blessed state of his wife, Edwards said, "... there was a longing to sit and sing this life away, and an overcoming pleasure in the thoughts of spending an eternity in that exercise."[16]

Such a deep communion with God, wherein there is an adoring fascination by the beauty of his character and the excellence of his work, cannot help but touch our affections to the point of releasing exuberant and overwhelming joy. It is this quality of heart, this depth of experience, that comes to those who allow the Spirit's filling to continue its flow. So overwhelming was this flow in Francis Xavier's life, he said, "I prayed to God to restrain the overflowing fullness of joy which constantly fills my soul."[17] There were times when heart and mind could scarcely assimilate these tumultuous feelings. D. L. Moody also asked the Lord to restrain his joy, for fear he couldn't bear it anymore.

Describing mountaintop joy with an emphasis on how sublime this satisfaction of soul can be is accurate if we don't leave the impression that such exalted feelings are automatic, happily greeting us at the first waking moment of the day. As described already, joy is accessible by operating in Scripture-stipulated ways, but it is not automatic. There are reasons for the Lord not allowing joy to replace the needed environment for faith to grow. *Accessible* joy belongs to this environment; *automatic* joy may not. This is especially so if joy functions more as a prop than as a by-product.

It is with this rationale in mind that Tozer—in his book, *That Incredible Christian*—made the following observation:

> The smile of God will be for the time withdrawn, or at least hidden from your eyes. Then you will learn what faith is; you will find out the hard way, but the only way open to you, that true faith lies in the will, that the joy unspeakable of which the apostle speaks is not itself faith but a slow ripening fruit of faith ....[18]

Describing further these periods of withdrawn feelings, G. D. Watson wrote:

> There come periods to the most perfectly consecrated soul when it must push its way through a sameness of things and over dreary and monotonous plains where the thoughts and emotions and prayers and duties are like a tiresome treadmill, day after day, week after week, and month after month, in which there are no new visions, no fresh gushes of prayer, no bright thoughts of heavenly beauty, and everything in religion seems to be dull and tiresome.[19]

If at such times you know that welcomed sin, slackened obedience, and weakened faith didn't cause this, you won't misread what's happening to you and seek a false solution.

Instead, you will know that God is giving an opportunity for your will to strengthen. So go ahead and let your will undergo this strengthening exercise, unburdened by a perplexed mind or by an accusing conscience.

The joy that is faith's reward will strengthen faith, certainly, if faith strengthens it. But if faith can only function while smitten with strong surges of automatic joy, then faith weakens and may not be restored until the cross summons, the will yields, the night passes, and the morning comes with God's deeper joy. G. D. Watson repeated the point: "After the exuberance of the Spirit's baptism has subsided, there may come a strange emptiness; the blessing may seem to have vanished."[20] This occurs, Watson said, because God "has simply withdrawn his radiance to teach the soul a lesson which could not be learned in the glare of noon, and that is to rest solely on Christ ... It must learn to repose in the eternal Blesser. Then God can send the blessings as hallowed pulses beating through the soul when it pleaseth him."[21]

There are other times when the trial of faith is intense, yet—quite unexplainably—joy soars with supernatural grace. Such was the case when Paul and Silas were beaten at Philippi. A. B. Simpson said, "... their bones were aching, and they were sore from the stripes of the inner prison. They could not keep it back. They sang for joy." Speaking about this joy in the midst of persecution, A. B. Simpson wrote: "It came to the martyrs when they were roasting at slow fires, and they turned to their persecutors and said, 'We do not feel the flames, the joy is so great; it fills our being and quenches our pain.'"[22]

Even as early as the third-century, these reports of God protecting the faithful with joy were well-known. Despite the fact the torture lasted for hours, the joy lasted longer.

> Tertullian and other of the early Christian fathers affirm that the minds of the martyrs, when subjected to the most terrible tortures which their tormentors could inflict, were so completely occupied with the manifested love and glory of Christ, that they did not seem to be affected at all by bodily suffering.[23]

The takeaway principle that applies to our lives is this: As the guardian of our soul, the Lord knows when strong dosages of joy are helpful and when they are not.

Whenever joy does come, we must receive—but not grab, grip, or snatch, for that may indicate a joy addiction that isn't healthy. Counteracting what may easily become a problem, Tozer counseled: "We must not cling even to our peace and joy and spiritual comfort. Sometimes the flower must fade so that the fruit may be more abundant and that we may learn to walk by faith and not by sight."[24] The joy of the Lord is an encouragement of faith, certainly a reward of faith, but it must never be a substitute for faith, or even the focus of faith.[25] The focus of faith should be the Lord, and not the joy of the Lord.

Of course, when God releases this joy, as he delights to do, it is so good! Extoling this fact, Andrew Murray said that "joy in God is the strongest proof there is that I have in God what satisfies and satiates me."[26] True joy is a powerful witness to those outside the church, an immense encouragement to those in the church, and of enormous pleasure to God, who is not only the sole source of this joy but is also the recipient of that effusive praise joy bestows.

Very much related to joy, but distinct from it, is a fervent spirit. To address the subject of emotions with breadth requires devoting some attention to the passion a fervent spirit generates. In his introduction to the book, *The Awakening in Wales*, the Presbyterian pastor, J. Cynndyland Jones, commented on the great emotion that exhibited during this revival by first asking the rhetorical question:

> Is enthusiasm permissible in every other department of life but forbidden in church life? A thousand times, *No*. How speaks the Apostle? "Fervent in spirit, serving the Lord." Fervent, literally, *boiling*. "Boiling in Spirit." Let none be ashamed of "boiling" in the service of the Savior.[27]

The fervent spirit commended by Paul (Romans 12:11) and the fervent prayer commended by James (James 5:16) relate to the passionate plea commended by Jesus: to be hot or cold, but not lukewarm (Revelation 3:15). To our surprise, the moderation preferred by the modern church—polite, cordial, and full of smiles—is declared the worst of all options by the Lord of glory. According to him, even the freeze of stone-cold faith is better than that insipid taste of lukewarm Christianity with its friendly ways and chit-chat conversations. G. D. Watson warned that "lukewarmness of spirit is so decent and well-behaved that it chloroforms its victim and kills him without a scream of terror."[28] But what the Lord wants is steamy hot faith—the boiling prayer, the burning heart, the fiery worship. Thomas Watson said, "Zeal is the flame of the affections, it turns a saint into a seraphim."[29] And that is perhaps why peace and joy are not the highest state of our soul; the spirit set ablaze by the presence of God is even higher![30]

The white heat of a fervent spirit is made that way by proximity to the Lord of glory. The closer one gets to his glory, the more the light of that glory releases its glow—illuminating, yes; warming, certainly; but more than that: igniting an unquenchable passion, incendiary in its convictions and explosive in its impact. Oswald Chambers knew this experience well, and thus wrote, "I have no difficulty in seeing how the saints will meet the Lord in the air, for when the Lord blesses so much here, and your physical frame seems incandescent with God's fire—why, it is just a wonder you don't rise ...."[31]

Dr. George W. Peters said, "God, the Church, and the world are looking for men with burning hearts ...." T. A. Hegre wrote: "It is fire we need: fire to stir our cold and flat emotions, fire to drive us to do something for those who are going into Christless graves. Untold millions today are dying untold because we as Christians have no fire. We need fire—the fire of the Holy Ghost."

Such fire did indeed burn brightly in the life of William Taylor, the nineteenth-century missionary to India, Africa, Australia, and South America. It was said of this man who preached on every inhabited continent of the world—"What a flame of revival he had become! The living God was with him, and Pentecostal fire fell upon the people wherever he went."[32]

Were that it were so today! But whenever God's people are confronted by higher truth, deeper holiness, fervent feelings, or sacrificial service, there is a tendency to recoil at what they see and to reduce its legitimacy by finding fault. Authenticity isn't the issue, though, for J. H. Jowett said it well, "The holy fire of God will reveal its presence in the soul of man in an ardent enthusiasm which cannot be quenched."[33] Those wanting to quench this enthusiasm prefer a heaven where polite applause is routine and where starchy souls maintain their decorum. This must not be.

The intense worship that makes carnal souls uncomfortable—that prompts looks of disgust, and makes rigid the body that refuses to dance—is exactly the worship God wants. So get use to it! In obedience to God, begin to give him the worship he wants now, the worship your new nature is ready to release. And if getting ready requires an honest assessment of those blockages within that have nothing to do with all those rebuttals you've been putting forth, then cease masking these issues hindering your relationship with the Lord, and deal with them.

A new normal needs to be discovered, wherein our truth-touched emotions are granted the freedom to bless the Lord with all their might—and for all he is due! Those emotions informed by the Word and generated by the Spirit carry worthy freight: gratitude for God's goodness, praise for God's works, delight from his daily fellowship, gladness for promises yet to be filled, and worship motivated by every glance at the beauty of God's holiness.

Feelings of this sort should rightly be released from our new nature where abiding peace and abounding joy already exist. Tozer went so far as to say, "The Christian owes it to the world to be supernaturally joyful."[34] The lukewarmness that makes God sick (but makes everybody else comfortable) is in need of the Holy Spirit's fire, the full flame of which can only be gained when God is supremely valued during extended prayer, consistent obedience, and devoted service.

Appendix F
The Romans 7 Debate

The seventh chapter of Romans, if not interpreted correctly, can unleash devastating consequences upon the church, and has done so. There can be little doubt that most Christians today are living defeated lives, much like the life of that one described in Romans, chapter 7. The church has been told that this is what Paul experienced after he became a Christian. So, left with this impression, it was entirely predictable that any expectation of consistent victory for us would drastically deflate. Because if none other than the greatest missionary theologian of all time was thrown into so much turmoil, so much defeat, what hope do the rest of us have?

The seventh chapter of Romans has perplexed theologians for centuries now and, still worse, has left many beleaguered believers in substantial unbelief about significant gospel truth. Some theological debates are of little consequence. This debate about Romans 7 isn't one of them. Those debates confined to the musty halls of academia may proliferate into theological libraries, and may even make their way into scholarly conferences where professors present their papers. But unfortunately the Romans 7 debate escaped those confines to infect the church. Had perplexity been the only result of this debate, the church might have fared better than it did. But something worse than perplexity resulted. As it turned out, some very wrong conclusions cemented into everyday thinking, and thus became conducive to the low level of living widespread in the church today.

There are misunderstandings about Romans 7 that need to be, and can be, corrected. To do so, however, we must first point out that it isn't at all certain that the words penned by Paul in Romans, chapter 7, are autobiographical. Paul's use of the personal pronouns "I," "me," "my," and "myself" in this chapter do not require the conclusion that this chapter is personal testimony. Werner Georg Kümmel cites passages in Romans (Romans 3:7-8; 7:7a, 9) and in I Corinthians (I Corinthians 6:12, 15; 13:1-3) where Paul uses personal pronouns as an understood rhetorical device and not as indicators of biographical experience. According to Kümmel, these pronouns aren't personal (referring to Paul) or typical (referring to humanity in general) but are dialogical (a manner of speaking about a subject under discussion).[1] Theologian Johannes Weiss considered these pronouns a literary convention.[2] This personifying and usage of the "dramatic present" are well-known forms of address even today, each serving to project empathy, to invite inclusion, and thereby to gain interest. Nevertheless, we may assume that the observations Paul made in this chapter weren't altogether theoretical, either.

More the issue in this chapter is the spiritual status that is under review in Romans 7. Is this chapter descriptive of a nonbeliever, or does this chapter describe the struggle every believer will have? It is difficult to exaggerate the importance of this question, since the answer given will inform the believer to what extent victory is possible in his or her spiritual journey.

If it is true that this chapter describes the struggle of a Christian, then Paul's statement in verse 14 about being carnal and sold under sin, in verse 18 about nothing good dwelling in him, in verse 19 about not being able to do what is right, and in verse 24 about being wretched and in desperate need of deliverance, hardly forecast a future of consistent obedience. Minimally, these verses predict many heartbreaking defeats. And therefore for projections like these to find supposed credentialing in Scripture is most concerning. This concern prompted John Laidlaw to challenge the view that Romans 7 describes a Christian.

> Considerable injustice has been done, not only to the interpretation of an important passage of Scripture, but, what is more serious, to the entire doctrine of sanctification, by some of those who are bent on maintaining that the latter half of the seventh chapter of Romans describes the experience of a converted man. It has been too

> often read as if it described the ordinary and normal state of a child of God; as if nature and grace were so exactly balanced in believers that "they cannot do the things that they would"; as if the sum and substance of sanctification were this death in life, or this living death expressed by the perpetual cry, "wretched man that I am!" Now it has been well said, that if this were all that grace did for its votaries, St. Paul would only have proved that it was as futile and insufficient as the law. If all that regeneration could accomplish were only to awaken a sense of inward discord without being able to take it away, this would certainly destroy the influence of spiritual Christianity and disgrace its character.[3]

Equally indignant, Johannes Weiss argued, "What would be the use of the new birth or redemption at all, if it could not end that miserable stress and slavery?"[4] For a believer to be thrown into the throes of anguish, convulsed by continuing sin in one's life just as this man in Romans 7 was, hardly conveys the biblical view of how a believer should respond to sin. G. D. Watson reminded us:

> God's thoughts are not as our thoughts, and when we lie in self-abhorrence at Jesus' feet, with our religious ideals shattered to fragments, he sees his ideal being carried out in us. Fretting over ourselves is a very subtle form of self-righteousness. Self-upbraiding and calling ourselves harsh names may seem like humility, but in reality it is spiritual pride ... Any view of ourselves which disturbs our repose in Jesus is a wrong view.[5]

Yet, this is exactly what we see exhibited in Romans 7. This man is in deep despondency. He knows no way out. He can't endure this amount of failure. He blames only himself. Extending his commentary on this situation, G. D. Watson concluded by saying:

> In human sorrow over sin there is a chafing, fretting, recrimination, self-denunciation which is itself sinful ... When God takes us up into sweet, holy union with himself, we will see that it is as great sin to fret and rage at ourselves as at our fellows.[6]

Godly sorrow looks quite different from what we see in Romans 7. The despair and disgust seen in this chapter, cited with much elaboration but without censure, offers further proof that this chapter does not describe a believer. That a lost man would respond this way is understandable, but no believer should ever respond this way.

Nevertheless, most of the respected theologians in the Reformed tradition—Augustine, Luther, Calvin, and Barth among them—have argued that Romans 7 *is* describing the sin-struggle every believer will encounter. Luther said of the believer "... for one and the same man is spiritual and carnal, righteous and a sinner, good and evil."[7] Calvin viewed the believer's condition in a more improved state than that, saying that while the one Romans 7 describes is not enmeshed in sin, sin did reside in this man's soul.[8] Yet, still Calvin believed, as do many theologians today, that Romans 7 does describe the sin-struggle of a regenerate person.[9]

Interestingly, the Reformer's view does not reflect the views of the theologians during the first three centuries. Protestant theologian Frederick L. Godet said the view that Romans 7 described a believer's experience was practically unknown during the first three centuries. Most of the Anti-Nicene Fathers, as well as many other theologians through the years, have denied that Romans 7 is speaking about a Christian.[10] Andrew Murray said Romans 7 described "the impotency of the unregenerate man to do God's will.[11]

There are many other variations to Luther's view, some of which I will cite, none of which I will fully analyze for reasons that will soon become apparent. One variation is the view that the verb tenses in Romans 7 provide clues for the spiritual stage being addressed. Because Paul uses the first person, past tense in verse 7-13, it is argued that this part of the passage refers to his pre-conversion days. In verse 14 through verse 4 in Romans 8, however, the first person, present tense is used, thus indicating, according to this argument, that this part of the passage refers to Paul's post-conversion days.

But if we say that Paul wrote these words in a manner that dramatizes a point, the shift in verb tenses matters little. Moreover, upon further examination, as we shall see, it becomes clear that other factors are far more decisive for interpretation. Besides, how can a believer be freed from the power of sin in Romans 6, so he finally serves God and produces the fruit of holiness (verses 20-22), but then in Romans 7 (verses 23-25) become a captive to sin again, dispossessed of the knowledge he once had of how to be delivered from sin (verse 18), and thus ended up marinating in misery? This interpretation is too simple in its approach and unsatisfactory in its conclusion.

The two-nature view of man, another construct imposed on Romans 7, sees the genesis of Paul's struggle in the old nature which, while judicially dead, still actually exists. This particular forensic view was disposed of already in this book (in the chapter entitled, "Getting Rid of Our Old Man"), and therefore we won't reproduce that argument here.

Yet another construct offered, which is supposed to help us interpret Romans 7, is one that posits the born-again believer in proximity to the Romans 7 sin-struggle by interpreting the new nature in him in a more minimalist way. John Murray contended that the believer is a new man, a new creation, but he is a new man not yet made perfect.[12] Benjamin Warfield, a predecessor to Murray as articulator of orthodox Presbyterian theology, described the new nature as a change in direction, a change in disposition.[13] But this view severely minimizes the concept of divine life, as do those views that refer to divine life as a principle, instinct, aptitude, receptor, or force. Those who characterize the new nature this way do so because their dichotomist view leaves them no other choice. They aren't able to locate the new nature in a unique aspect of man's being (man's spirit); so they *have* to resort to language like this, even if Scripture doesn't speak this way.

Divine life cannot be reduced to mere turning toward the spiritual realities of God, or to an inclination where there is increased appreciation of those realities. The term, "new creation," speaks of essence, not mere capacities or the receptor for those capacities. The very life of Jesus is placed in the believer, not just an ability to progress toward that life. Moreover, the views of Murray and Warfield are susceptible to the errors of the so-called spiritual formation movement today which envisions the new nature forming, or extending, or improving. This view also was refuted in footnote 32 from chapter 1. The unanswerable question is: How does one increase or improve divine life?

While the concept of spiritual progress is valid, the progress the believer does experience, noted already in this book, is one of release, not one of formation; one of exercise, not one of expansion. As maturity is approached, and eventually accessed, there will be an increased impact of the divine life, resident already in the spirit, upon the soul. The Bible talks about this journey, this maturation, as "walking in the Spirit." And walking denotes progress, purpose, and practice. The *Dictionary of Paul and His Letters* states, "*Practice of the Spirit* makes more explicit the *intentionality* and *discipline* anticipated by Paul's language of 'walking.'"[14] G. D. Watson said, "The word 'walk' applies to all the activities of life, whether in the mind, or in the affection, or the will, or the outward life, in business or conversation."[15] It charts its course from the spirit to the soul, from the center to the circumference, from the inner life to the outer life.

So there is a progressive dimension to the Christian life, but not in the sense of improving or increasing the essence of divine life. The progress is one of increased access, increased activation, and not one of increasing the life of Christ, borne by the Holy Spirit and put into the spirit of the born-again at the time of conversion. The Spirit of Life in Christ Jesus (Romans 8:2) doesn't come in installments. When the Bible says we were created in righteousness and true holiness (Ephesians 4:24), that righteousness wasn't partial or potential righteousness; and that holiness wasn't incremental or conditional holiness. This righteousness and holiness was complete in its essence.

Other variations of the view that Romans 7 describes the sin-struggle of a believer include the notions that two contradictory volitional tendencies appear in the new nature (but there is no scriptural foundation at all for saying that divine life ever gives impulse to sin) and that the new nature was implanted in the ego (which wrongly imports Freudian language into theology) or in the soul (a view dispensed with in Appendix A). The problem of contrary wills and the locus of the new nature is a dichotomist's dilemma. Trichotomists don't have this problem.

What we can all agree on is that Christians do have an ongoing struggle with sin. At issue, though, is how this struggle is to be defined. Does Romans 7 provide this description? Those who say it does will point out that Paul talks about delighting in the law in verse 22, something, they say, an unregenerate person cannot do. However, Psalm 1:3 describes a pre-Christian follower of God as one who delights in the law of the Lord. In fact, effusive praise of the law, the Word, God's statutes, and God's wisdom appears in many places in the Old Testament. It simply isn't true, therefore, to say that such delighting (at least in some measure) is impossible for, say, the pre-converted Jew.

Those who contend that Romans 7 describes the sin-struggle Christians face also point out that Paul talks about delighting in the law according "to the inward man" (Romans 7:22), which they assume to be a reference to the new nature. But the inner man doesn't always mean the new nature. The Greek word for "inward" in this passage is also used to describe being *in* a house (John 20:26), *in* a prison (Acts 5:23) and *in* a church (I Corinthians 5:12). The simple meaning of this word indicates inward and not outward. What is being asserted is that this man had an inner desire. While the term "inward man" can refer to the new nature (Ephesians 3:16, II Corinthians 4:16, etc.), the book of Romans also describes "inward" in contradistinction to outward formalism (Romans 2:29). So we must be careful not to import a static definition of this term into Romans 7, given the fact that this adjective is more fluidly used in Scripture, and also given the fact that the context of Romans 7 disputes the import.

The case against Romans 7 being descriptive of a believer's struggle against sin is compelling. For how can it be said of a believer that he is enslaved in sin, that nothing good indwells him, that he is a wretched person not yet delivered from sin? In Romans 6, Paul speaks of the believer as being no longer under the dominion of sin (verse 14) but being freed from sin (verse 18). This is a declaration that Paul reaffirmed in Romans 8 (verse 2). Charles Wesley's words, "He breaks the power of canceled sin and sets the prisoner free," are all the more encouraging when it becomes known that the setting free in Romans 6 is presented in the perfect tense, describing a past action with a continuing affect or force.

So if the believer's freedom in Christ is permanent and ongoing, how can this same believer be sold under sin (verse 14)? The heart-cry for deliverance expressed in Romans 7 is inexplicable if this same believer had already been set free in Romans 6. Besides, didn't Jesus say that a person couldn't serve two masters? Well, then, how can a believer be a servant to God in Romans 6 (verse 22) but then be a captive to sin in Romans 7 (verse 23)? This doesn't make sense, at least not in any way that should be deemed normative.

It is true that a Christian who acts in carnal ways can do almost anything that a non-Christian can do. That fact is not in dispute. What is in dispute is that this failure, in the manner described in Romans 7, ever happened to Paul, or that it is bound to happen to believers today. In refuting both these points, we will consider first the possibility of Romans 7 describing Paul.

The supposedly saved and miserable Christian we see in Romans 7 certainly does not describe the Paul we see elsewhere in Scripture—the Paul who tells others to imitate him (I Corinthians 11:1), the Paul who says that he gets stronger and stronger on the inside (II Corinthians 4:16), the Paul who declares that by walking in the Spirit we will not fulfill the lust of the flesh (Galatians 5:16). The fact is: The Bible provides extensive biographical details about Paul, and nowhere do we see the defeat described in Romans 7 as being characteristic of the life he lived as a believer, or even being an episode in his life. From the time Paul reappears on the scene in Acts 13 to become the great missionary of the church to the end of his life on this earth, there isn't any evidence at all that the sin-struggle Romans 7 describes manifested in this man's life.

For that matter, there isn't any evidence that Romans 7 describes Paul prior to his conversion, either. Would a Pharisee ever say that he didn't know how to do good? Typical of the zealous Jew, and particularly a Pharisee, was a strong confidence that he could pass God's inspection with flying colors. This is what Pharisees prided themselves in being able to do. Therefore, Romans 7 is not likely an account of Paul's personal life, at any time or during any stage of his spiritual development. Like most Pharisees, self-doubting did not manifest. And there's not a hint from Scripture that Paul ever exhibited such doubting.

We may ask ourselves: Was Paul the Pharisee ever wondering about who would deliver him from sin, as the man in Romans 7 did (verse 25)? Scripture paints the opposite picture when it says that Saul, "breathing out threatenings and slaughter" (Acts 9:1), charged out across the countryside—intent on finding the secret to the sin problem? No, he charged out to "deliver" other people! From captivity of sin? No, into the captivity of Jewish leaders! These other people, of course, being Christians and their forced destination being prison! Apparently, the only anguish present at that time wasn't *in* him but was *because* of him.

According to the biblical record, there was no meltdown in Paul's attitude, a time of softening, a time of reassessing himself and the rightful role the law ought to have in his life. For Paul it was full steam ahead! In fact, so fierce and resolute was this man's attack that it took none other than God Almighty to stop him! With a quiet instilling of thoughts, you ask? No, with a blinding light and a voice straight out of heaven! Had there been any ambivalence in Paul, at least some self-doubting about his spiritual standing, perhaps lesser measures would have been sufficient to turn him around. But there's no indication from Scripture that Paul was ever conflicted in this way. His confidence wasn't challenged until Damascus.

Important to note also is that Paul's conversion transacted suddenly and that thereafter his relationship with the Lord progressed quickly. As we further track what happened, we discover that soon after Damascus Paul is filled with the Spirit (Acts 9:17), becomes a powerful preacher (Acts 9:22, 29), before then going into the desert of Arabia for three years to commune directly with God, full-time, all the time (Galatians 1:17, 18). So, again, we have to ask ourselves, where in the biblical record do we see Paul lamenting there is nothing good in him and that he doesn't even know how to be good? Harvard professor Krister Stendahl contended that Paul consistently viewed himself as a free and holy man and did not exhibit the conflict of conscience that troubles so many in their struggles against sin. The sense of personal disappointment from any current or recent failures in his moral life is remarkably absent from his writings.[16]

It should also be noted that years later Paul expressed outright amazement that the Galatians reverted to old ways so soon after they received the gospel (Galatians 1:6). But if Paul had done the same thing, as those who think Romans 7 describes him say, would he have been so amazed? One would think that a softer, more empathetic approach would have been forthcoming. But this isn't what happened.

The confrontation Paul launched in the Galatians letter was serious and sobering. With strong and pulsating emotion, Paul called these people fools and wondered openly who had bewitched them (Galatians 3:1). Of considerable relevance to our discussion is the fact the issue at Galatia was exactly the same issue Paul addressed in Romans 7 (Galatians 3:2; Romans 7:6)—newness of spirit versus the letter of the law. But instead of telling these believers that what they are going through is a normal stage in Christian growth, something we all have to go through, Paul renounced their thinking in no uncertain terms! He even told them their beliefs and behaviors were outside the gospel, instead of being a part of the gospel. This intolerant response by the apostle further supports the notion that the pronouns used in Romans 7 are more likely fictive and not actual. And it also supports the notion Romans 7 is an aberration.

Further undermining the view that Romans 7 describes a Christian transitioning to maturity is the total lack of transitional language in this chapter. We see no linkage, no similarities, no blending; we only see contrasts. Moreover, the contrast between Romans 7 and Romans 8 couldn't be more vivid! In Romans 7 we see a man enmeshed with flesh (verse 14); in Romans 8 we see a man who isn't enmeshed with flesh (verse 9). In Romans 7 sin wins (verse 17); in Romans 8 righteousness wins (verse 4). In Romans 7 we see a man totally confused and utterly confounded in his struggle against sin (verse 18); in Romans 8 we see a man spiritually minded and confused no longer (verse 6). In Romans 7 we see a man who is miserable (verse 25); in Romans 8 we see a man who is very much at peace (verse 6).

So is this the *same* man? Are we to understand the Christian life is one that fluctuates and vacillates between Romans 7 and Romans 8? If this be the case, then the strong language of Romans 6:14 ("sin shall have no dominion in you") cannot be true. For if the Christian has been set free, as Romans 6 and Romans 8 both declare, but then reverts—periodically, if not more routinely—to the defeat and despair of Romans 7, in what possible sense has he been set free? And further we may ask: How can a believer keep on being filled with the Spirit, as Ephesians 5:18 instructs, yet succumb to sin repeatedly? Moreover, how can a believer never thirst, never be dissatisfied again, according to Jesus (John 4:13; 7:37-39), but then be thrown back into Romans 7 despair, as many people today claim? The incongruence of possessing a joy that is full and a joy that remains (described by Jesus in John 16) with all these repeated lapses into the defeat dynamics described by Paul in Romans 7 cannot be resolved.

Even as these questions are posed, and some of these declarations are made, theological rationalists are ready to burst into the room to offer answers that are supposed to satisfy. But these answers do not satisfy. I will give one example. Wanting to sound a word of realism about the sin problem believers will continue to encounter even after conversion, Horatius Bonar offered this comment regarding Paul's words about being carnal and sold under sin:

> This is not the language of an unregenerate or half-regenerate man. When, however, he adds, "I am carnal, sold under sin," is it really Paul, the new creature in Christ, that he is describing? It is; and they who think it impossible for a saint to speak thus, must know little of sin, and less of themselves.[17]

Such supposed realism simply doesn't line up with Scripture. For while the dangers of sin are real, the believer's warfare against sin is not nearly as formidable in conflict, and discouraging in results, as what Romans 7 describes. Actually, this conflict is far less formidable, Romans 6 tells us, because of what Jesus did for us and in us. And the results are much more certain, much more positive, Romans 8 tells us, because of what the Holy Spirit does in us and for us today.

The man in Romans 7, however, seems not to know any of this! He frankly admits he doesn't know how to do good (verse 18). But why doesn't he, when the chapters before and after Romans 7 provide specific instructions for winning over sinning? How can it be, then, that Romans 7 is descriptive of a believer? In arguing that Romans 7 *is* descriptive of a believer, John Murray states:

> There must be a constant and increasing appreciation that though sin still remains it does not have the mastery. There is a total difference between surviving sin and reigning sin, the degenerate in conflict with sin and the unregenerate complacent to sin. It is one thing for sin to live in us; it is another thing for us to live in sin.[18]

While there is much wisdom in Murray's words, these words actually refute his argument rather than support it. This is true, first, because the man in Romans 7 is not complacent in effort—he *wills* to perform the good of God's law (verse 18). And, two, he is not complacent about outcome, either—for he abhors the defeat in which he finds himself (verse 24). Third, sin *does* reign within this man and has total mastery over him (verses 14 and 24). So, parachuting wisdom into this passage, irrespective of the details presented, is not helpful. Nor is Anthony A. Hoekema's assertion that "the new self is not yet perfect."[19] If our new nature consists of the very life of Jesus, how is that not perfect? And how is it not totally sufficient to defeat every temptation to sin?[20]

As we step back to see the broader perspective that motivates this debate, what it comes down to are two different sensitivities: on the one hand, a concern that the believer's problem with sin is being minimized; and on the other hand, a concern that God's solution to the sin problem is being minimized. While there can be no question at all that believers will encounter ongoing temptations, it is a major mistake to suggest that Romans 7 is normative for believers. Such an assertion marginalizes Romans 6 and 8 almost out of the picture!

Yet, the outcome of much teaching on this topic has had that precise effect, in that the sin-struggle of Romans 7 has strongly emerged to resonate with believers. They know the scene all too well—the conflict of opposing desires, a weak will, chronic defeat, overwhelming guilt—but what they don't know nearly so well is the way to avoid this scene. Instructions for that are amply provided in Romans, chapter 6 and in Romans, chapter 8. Nevertheless, those instructions have receded into the background, almost becoming a blur, while the defeat of Romans 7 looms large in the forefront.

It almost seems that once the congregation has been told that Romans 7 describes a believer, then the teachings of chapters 6 and 8 are relegated to the status of lofty, unworkable ideals. The protrusion of Romans 7 and the receding of the chapters that precede and follow it are not without explanation. Because if we say that Romans 7 describes believers, we are telling Christians the defeat dynamics of Romans 7 are likely to show up in their lives (which need not happen at all), even to the point where they are enmeshed in flesh, sold under sin, utterly deceived, constantly defeated, and are completely miserable.

There are several weak points in the traditional understanding of Romans 7 that need to be exposed. One of these weaknesses is an inability to show how the descriptors provided in this chapter demonstrates this chapter is profiling a believer. Those who contend that the seventh chapter of Romans describes a believer must show how *all* the descriptors of Romans 7 can be reconciled with that point of view. One can't select parts of the profile, omit other parts of the profile, and draw accurate conclusions with that methodology. The *full* profile of Romans 7 must be examined and explained. But when examined, as we have already seen, irreconcilable differences between the person in Romans 7 and the person in Romans 6 and Romans 8 become obvious. The only consistency in these profiles is that these profiles consistently clash.

A second weakness in the traditional view of Romans 7 is the assertion that this chapter exhibits transition. Many commentators contend that Romans 7 describes the typical transition most Christians experience as they move from functioning in a carnal way to functioning in a spiritual way. While such a transition is indeed common (but unnecessarily so), there is no indication at all in the text itself of *any* transition occurring in Romans 7. The direction of Romans 7 is not forward but sideward. Just because the numeral 7 follows the numeral 6 doesn't mean that chapter 7 presents a new development in the believer's walk with God. It does not. There's not one word in chapter 7 that adds any instruction for spiritual growth. None! Chapter 6 provides this instruction. Chapter 8 provides this instruction. Chapter 7 does not.

More properly understood, Romans 7 holds the ground Romans 5 gained (and Romans 6 defended) by further explaining why the law way to God, described in Romans 7, had to be displaced by the gospel way, described in chapters 5 and 6. Chapter 7 shows a contrast between the law approach to God and the gospel approach to God. It does not show transition from a carnal believer to a spiritual believer. Furthermore, not only does Romans 7 not embark on some new stage, but even *within* this supposed new stage (imagined by some) there isn't any transition evident.

Instead, Romans 7 describes one condition in a singular and emotional way. In setting forth this condition, there is no lesser-to-greater language describing the condition, no entrance and exit language that describes onset and departure, and, again, no clear evidence that this condition is descriptive of a believer.

The disruption of context flow is nothing short of startling if we assume that Romans 7 shows transition. Keep in mind that the book of Romans is the most systematic theological treatise Paul ever wrote. And he would interrupt that by providing extensive biographical material? Such an assertion doesn't fit the schematic. What also doesn't fit this schematic is the idea that Paul interrupted this meticulous presentation of gospel theology by telling his readers how this theology didn't work for him. All the astounding declarations Paul presented in the previous chapters, in which he explains stunning salvation realities, hardly flow into the idea that the misery and defeat described in Romans 7 is common for Christians.

This supposed transition Romans 7 is said to exhibit is actually a major barrier to correctly interpreting this chapter. To reinforce this point of view, Martyn Lloyd-Jones offered this observation about Romans 7:

> Its primary object, its fundamental theme is to deal with the place and the function of the Law in God's dealings with the human race. Every detail must be considered in the light of that purpose, and of nothing else. To start by thinking that the object of this chapter is that Paul should give us his experience is to miss the whole point. That is not his purpose at all.

Lloyd-Jones rightly asserts that misunderstandings about the role of the law were triggered in chapter 5, where Paul states that no man can be justified by the law. Of course, this statement runs directly counter to what the Jews had thought. And more shocking still in their minds was this seeming diminution of the law, so long revered by the Jewish people. So, to bring clarity to this issue, chapter 6 focuses on the truth that the morality the law espoused is actually enhanced by the gospel and not set aside, as some in his audience might have feared. Then in chapter 7 Paul further defends his statements about the limitations of the law by explaining why it was also inadequate for sanctification, and not just justification, as chapter 5 had pointed out. Again, to understand chapter 7, one must track the logic of the arguments which precede it.

Context matters. Content matters. The point being: We can't jump into Romans 7 and start interpreting. We must first see the *intent* that motivated these words, the *approach* Paul took to affect this intent, and the logical *framework* he used to encase the arguments which pursued this intent. Staying within the parameters of Romans 7, I now want to propose a solution to the theological dilemma that emerged regarding the meaning of this chapter.

First, the primary *intent* of Romans 7 is to explain to one of Jewish understanding, since the audience was heavily Jewish,[21] why the law should not be regarded in the way they had previously regarded it. This rationale was needed because in the previous chapters Paul had explained revolutionary new developments in the economy of God's salvation that would certainly prompt the traditional Jew to wonder how the law fits in. The "gospel of God," spoken of in the very first verse of this book, had (with the advent and accomplishments of Jesus) produced fundamental changes that now altered, or should have altered, the previous view these Jews had toward God's law. The intent of Romans 7, therefore, is to explain why the law was inadequate for establishing a right relationship with God.

Second, the *approach* adopted by Paul is that of teaching a somewhat singular point in a more human and less theoretical way through the use of personal pronouns. Understand that fact and this passage will make total sense. Put the focus on Paul, though, instead of on the point he is attempting to make, and this passage will present insurmountable problems. Romans 7 isn't focusing on the personal experiences of the pre-converted Paul or the subsequent experiences of the saved-but-spiritually-floundering Paul. Instead, the pronouns in this passage represent Paul's attempt to dramatize this teaching about why the law couldn't affect a right relationship with God but could only bring about misery.[22] Andrew Murray observed:

> You will find that in this passage (Romans 7:6-25) the name of the Holy Spirit does not occur once, nor does the name of Christ occur. The man is wrestling and struggling to fulfill God's law. Instead of the Holy Spirit and of Christ, the law is mentioned nearly twenty times.[23]

Echoing this observation, Professor James S. Stewart wrote:

> The very fact that the name of Christ is not heard until the closing verse, that Jesus is nowhere in all this chapter until he comes in suddenly in the doxology which proclaims the conflict ended and the victory won, is a clear indication that it is the life still requiring to be born again that is being described.[24]

Third, the basic *framework* of this passage can be summarized in this way. In verses 1-4, Paul states, with uniquely Jewish reasoning, the fundamental fact that the relationship the converted Jew had with the law is now different from what it used to be. In verse 5, Paul begins to explain why this change had to occur, stating that one reason the law could not do what the typical Jew thought it could do (enable a right standing with God) is because the law triggered an arousal of sin. This is the point Paul elaborates in verses 7-16, as well as in the last part of verse 25. This is the basic framework of the passage.

There are, however, instances in this logical framework when Paul interrupts the flow of his commentary on the inadequacy of the law to make a contrast with the sufficiency of the gospel. He does this in verses 6, 17, and 20 by using the word "now."[25] In the Greek, the word "now" (*nuni*) is a strengthened form of the Greek word *nun*. According to W. E. Vine, this word *nun* may indicate the logical conclusion of an argument, or it may mean what is true about the present in contrast with what was true in the past.[26] The latter meaning, I suggest, is clearly applicable to verses 6 and 17. In a strong manner, Paul is making a contrast between what was true under the law with what is now true under the gospel.

He does this again in chapter 8, verse 1: "There is therefore *now* no condemnation …." The word "now" here isn't a transitional word, nor is it a word that indicates the conclusion of an argument. It couldn't possibly be that, because the verses prior to Romans 8:1 do not lead to this conclusion. Instead, this is a word that makes a contrast in time: under the time of the law versus under this new day of the gospel.[27]

A critical principle for interpreting Romans 7 is the recognition that all the verses that use the word "now" are exceptions to the profile presented in this chapter and should not represent inclusions in the profile. Every time this word is used, what follows is a description of a believer. All the other verses describe an unbeliever. Once the word "now" is interpreted as a contrast, and not as words of transition or conclusion, the enigma is solved. Further commentary on this point, however, is necessary.

In verse 6, Paul speaks of what is true under this new dispensation of the gospel ("we are delivered"), but continues in the next verse to explain what it is like under the law, which culminates in verse 24 with that agony of soul that life under the law was designed to produce ("who shall deliver me"). Notice further the word "we" and not "I". Under the law, we experienced this; under the gospel, we experience that. At this point, therefore, the dramatization of the problem with its usage of "I" language hasn't begun. It begins in verse 7. For all these reasons, verse 6 hardly supports the notion that the person described by the rest of chapter 7 is regenerate.

Verse 17, which uses the same Greek word for "now" as verse 6 does, is often interpreted as if a conclusion based on prior verses is being offered. Grammatically, this is possible, although such an interpretation is certainly not required. Theologically, however, this interpretation is not at all possible. For how can one under the law say what Paul says in verses 17 and 20, "It is no more I that do it"? The unregenerate man—one without the old man crucified (Romans 6:6), one who has never been made "alive unto God" (Romans 6:11)—could not plausibly say this. Context, therefore favors the interpretation that the "now" of verse 17 has the same force as the "now" of verse 6: a contrast between life under the law versus life under the gospel. This verse interrupts the narrative of the unregenerate man's plight to make this contrast with the old "I" of verse 16 with the new "I" gained by the gospel, which is really the new nature.

There is one other comment interjected in Romans 7 that also expresses a gospel perspective instead of a law perspective. That comment is made in the first part of verse 25 where Paul says, "I thank God through Jesus Christ our Lord." This is the talk of one who lives under the gospel, and as such echoes the thanks given to God in Romans 6:17f. Verse 25 then concludes with a summary statement of what it is like to live under the law, a statement that contrasts with the summary statement given in verse 6 of what it is like to live under the gospel.

Once the *intent* of Romans 7 is clear (Paul explains how the gospel reveals the inadequacy of the law), the *approach* of Romans 7 is clear (Paul uses personal pronouns to convey truth in a less abstract manner) and the *framework* of Romans 7 is clear (the focus is on the failure and misery produced by the law approach to God and the fact the gospel counteracts this misery), Romans 7 easily makes sense. Thus, all those contrived explanations, distorted definitions, and other errors spawned by the traditional view of Romans 7 can now be set aside.

These errors have hindered believers from living in the gospel realities the book of Romans strongly sets forth. The sufficiency of what God has done for us, and the new identity to which he has elevated us, have been encumbered with a burden they never should have had to bear. The practical effect of this has been an unintended muting and morphing of God's message about the saved life so that millions of people today have become spiritually stuck. These people have so resonated with what they thought Romans 7 said, that the glorious gospel proclaimed in Romans lost its luster. That part of the gospel which teaches how to be saved (Romans 3-5), they got. That part of the gospel which teaches how to live the saved life (Romans 6 and 8), they didn't get.

The theological contortions made necessary by assuming that Romans 7 describes the life of a believer is of serious consequence. By exaggerating the dilemma the believer faces, and by minimizing the resources the believer has, a message has reverberated throughout the church that has hurt the church. This is the baggage that the traditional view of Romans 7 carries.

Believers all over this world have a severely reduced vision of what the Christian life can be. As F. J. Huegel put it, "... there are millions of professing Christians who in their secret souls know, so far as their life and walk are concerned, that the power of Satan is not yet broken ...."[28] And they also know, with painful clarity, that they are not yet free! It is hoped that a more accurate understanding of Romans 7 will help reverse this course by allowing the truths of Romans 6 and 8 to reclaim the attention these truths rightly deserve. Norman Grubb's concise summary bears repeating, "... Paul says we believers have nothing to do with Romans 7. It is not a chapter for us, we do not live there."[29]

But for those who think we do live there and seek to persuade the church that this is so, the questions Hannah Whitall Smith asked need to be considered:

> Must this crooked heart and perverse will always remain? Must I be a believer and yet have no faith that reacheth to sanctification and holy living? Is there no mastery to be had, no getting victory over sin? Must it prevail over me as long as I live?[30]

Not convinced by the theology that tells us this is the case, the author of these words set forth this challenge:

> ... settle down on this one thing, that Jesus came to save you now, in this life, from the power and

> dominion of sin, and to make you more than conquerors through his power. If you doubt this, search your Bible, and collect together every announcement or declaration concerning the purposes and object of his death on the cross. You will be astonished to find how full they are. Everywhere and always, his work is said to be to deliver us from our sins, from our bondage, from our defilement; and not a hint is given anywhere, that this deliverance was to be only the limited and partial one with which Christians so continually try to be satisfied.[31]

The theology that states that Romans 7 applies to believers will never satisfy! Indeed, it is a serious error to tell believers that the power of sin in their lives has been reduced only slightly, from that of being conquered always to that of being conquered often. The Bible speaks otherwise, saying that we have been delivered from the power of darkness (Colossians 1:13) so that we can be strengthened with all might according to his glorious power (Colossians 1:11), giving us weapons of warfare that are mighty through God (II Corinthians 10:4). To somehow think that such a power is insufficient and that Romans 7 episodes are bound to repeat in our lives is to run counter to Scripture and, to some extent, is to gut the gospel.

Thomas Goodwin, the Puritan scholar, wrote: "To destroy the power of sin in a man's soul is as great a work as to take away the guilt of sin."[32] Therefore, such a truth should be heralded as gospel truth, as Peter did when he said that "divine power has given us everything that pertains to life and godliness" (II Peter 2:3). Everything! The believer has been fully supplied to be a "partaker of the divine nature" (II Peter 2:4). And this is why Thomas Goodwin said of the believer, that when God, "... put holiness into him, to aim at God in all things, it changeth the whole man presently; it changeth all his course, all his affections, everything in him ... it will make him sail after a different compass."[33]

To succumb to the wrong view of Romans 7 is to fail to see how great our "so great salvation" really is. Coming to terms with what the hymn writer called "sin's dreadful sway," Thomas Goodwin declared, "... if there be such a power in sin as there is, to detain a man, that will not yield, will hold a man to the utmost, there must be *an almighty power of God to subdue it*."[34] And such a power is indeed available through the Lord Jesus! According to Thomas Goodwin, "The weakest Christian and Jesus Christ are too hard for all the world and all their lusts."[35] This is the message set forth in Romans 6 and Romans 8, a message that for too long has been put in jeopardy by a wrong interpretation of Romans 7.

Subject Index

Subject Index

Subject Index

Subject Index

Subject Index

Subject Index

Subject Index

Subject Index

Subject Index

Subject Index

Subject Index

Scripture Index

Scripture Index

Scripture Index

Scripture Index

Scripture Index

Endnotes

Chapter 1 —The Greatest Treasure

1. Paul Tillich, *The New Being*, (New York, Charles Scribner's Sons, 1955), p.15.
2. John Murray, *Redemption Accomplished and Applied*, (Grand Rapids, William B. Eerdmans Publishing Company, 1970), p.170.
3. A. J. Gordon, *Rest in Christ*, (Dixon, MO., Rare Christian books, n.d.), p.3.
4. F. J. Huegel, *John Looks at the Cross*, (Dixon, MO., Rare Christian books, n.d.), p.14.
5. Robert Letham noted how sparingly pulpits and publishers have addressed this subject when he said, "From the middle of the seventeen century on, however, this great jewel in the crown of God's grace has gone into eclipse. Today not much is said about union with Christ from the pulpit, and until recently, little is written about it." (*Union with Christ*, Philipsburg, NJ., P&R Publishing, 2011), p.2.
6. R. Mauculay and J. Barrs, *Being Human: The Nature of Spiritual Experience*, Downers Grove, InterVarsity Press, 1978), p.82.
7. Robert Letham is correct to say, "... we have more than fellowship with Christ. Fellowship takes place between separate persons by means of presence, recognition, conversation, shared interests, and the like. Adam had fellowship with God before the fall. Redemption has not restored us to the condition of Adam ... It goes beyond communion. It entails union. (*Union with Christ*, pp.126-127.)
8. D. Martyn Lloyd-Jones, *God's Ultimate Purpose: An Exposition of Ephesians 1:1 to 2:3* (Grand Rapids, MI., Baker Book House), p.441.
9. Paul Billheimer, *Destined for the Throne*, (Minneapolis, Bethany House Publishers, 1975), p.35.
10. A. W. Tozer, *Whatever Happened to Worship?*, (Camp Hill, Christian Publications, 1985), p.107.
11. Andrew Murray, *The Ministry of Intercessory Prayer*, (Grand Rapids, Baker, 1981), p.117.
12. Ruth Paxson, *Rivers of Living Water*, (Chicago, Moody Press, 1989), p.65.
13. Ibid., p.65.
14. A. B. Simpson, *All in All*, (Telford, PA., Worthy Christian Library), Chapter 2, paragraph 8.
15. A. B. Simpson, *The Supernatural*, (Camp Hill, PA., Christian Publications 1984), p.38.

16. A. W. Pink, *Spiritual Union and Communion*, (Grand Rapids, Baker, 1971), p.7.
17. Abraham Kuyper, in his book—*The Work of the Holy Spirit*, (Grand Rapids, William B. Eerdman's Publishing Company, 1979), p.333—does more than ignore spiritual union with God, he severely downgrades it by stating, "The union of believers with Christ their Head is not effected by instilling a divine-human life-tincture into the soul. There is no divine-human life ... And since there is no divine-human life in Jesus, he cannot instill it into us."
18. William Law, *Wholly for God*, (Minneapolis, Minnesota, Bethany House, 1976), p.123.
19. Martyn Lloyd-Jones, *Romans, Exposition of Chapter 6, The New Man*, (Edinburgh, UK, The Banner of Truth Trust, 2008), p.30.
20. Throughout this book the author's insertion within a quotation will be indicated with brackets.
21. A. W. Tozer, *Gems from Tozer*, (Harrisburg, Christian Publications, 1969), p.21.
22. Andrew Murray, *An Exciting New Life*, (Springdale, PA., Whitaker House, 1982), p.186.
23. Francis A. Schaeffer, *He is There and He is Not Silent*, (Wheaton, Illinois, Tyndale House Publishers, 1972), p.3.
24. A. B. Simpson, *The Holy Spirit*, Volume 1, (Telfair, PA., Worthy Christian Library), Chapter 2, paragraph 23.
25. G. D. Watson, *Our Own God*, (Hampton, TN., Harvey Christian Publishers, 2008), pp. 10, 11.
26. Blaise Pascal, *Pensees: Thoughts on Religion and Other Subjects*, (New York, Washington Square Press, 1965), p.113.
27. Jessie Penn-Lewis, *The Story of Job*, (Ft. Washington, PA., CLC Publications, 1996), p.230.

Chapter 2—A Higher Order

1. Warren W. Wiersbe, *Why Us?*, (Grand Rapids, Fleming H. Revell, 1984), p.21.
2. Os Guinncss, *The Dust of Death*, (Downers Grove, Inter-Varsity Press, 1973), p.233.
3. Helmut Thielicke, *Between God and Satan*, (Grand Rapids, Wm. B. Eerdmans Publishing Company, 1973), p.19.
4. Billy Graham, *The Challenge*, (New York, Pocketbooks, 1971), p.99.
5. C. S. Lewis, *Mere Christianity*, (New York, Macmillan

Publishing Company, 1977), p.182.

6. Ibid., p.183.
7. A. W. Tozer, *Gems from Tozer*, p.20.
8. Charles H. Spurgeon, *Christ's Glorious Achievements*, (Grand Rapids, Baker Book House, 1975), p.71.
9. Watchman Nee made a similar point in a conversation with a friend. Here is his account: "When I called on Mr. Wong his pet dog was by his bedside, and after speaking with him of the things of God and of the nature of his work in us, I pointed to the dog and inquired his name. He told me he was called Fido. 'Is Fido his Christian name or his surname?' I asked (using the common Chinese terms for 'personal name' and 'family name'). 'Oh, that is just his name', he said. 'Do you mean that is just his Christian name? Can I call him Fido Wong?' I continued. 'Certainly not!' came the emphatic reply. 'But he lives in your family', I protested, 'Why don't you call him Fido Wong?' Then, indicating his two daughters, I asked 'Are your daughters not called Miss Wong?' 'Yes!' 'Well then, why cannot I call your dog Master Wong?' The Doctor laughed, and I went on: 'Do you see what I am getting at? Your daughters were born into your family and they bear your name because you have communicated your life to them. Your dog may be an intelligent dog, a well-behaved dog, and altogether a most remarkable dog; but the question is not, Is he a good or a bad dog? It is merely, Is he a dog? He does not need to be bad to be disqualified from being a member of your family; he only needs to be a dog." Watchman Nee, *The Normal Christian Life*, (Fort Washington, PA., Christian Literature Crusade, 1974), p.80. Used by permission of CLC Publications.
10. In his book, *What is Man?*, T. Austin Sparks has a chapter entitled, "Man Now Another Species than God Created." T. Austin Sparks contends this shocking title is scriptural.
11. Quoted from Stephen Charnock's sermon, "The Chief of Sinners Saved."
12. A. B. Simpson, *The Christ Life*, (Harrisburg, PA., Christian Publications, 1980), p.31. On this point, Erich Sauer argues that a "son for the Oriental is always one who is his nature, in the essence of his being, is determined and formed by him for whom he springs." Erich Sauer, *The King of all the Earth*, (Grand Rapids, William. B. Eerdmans Publishing Co., 1967), p.147.
13. Articulating this same point, Stephen Charnock wrote, "...

the new creature is framed according to the most exact pattern, even God himself ... The new creature is begotten; begotten, then, in the likeness of the begetter, which is God." Stephen Charnock, *The Works of Stephen Charnock*, Kindle Locations: 1244-1245.

14. The doctrine of *theosis* (man becoming God) was suggested in the fourth century by Athanasius, who wrote the Son of God became man "that he might deify us in himself." While Athanasius didn't mean what these words suggest, such comments are nonetheless objectionable and should not be allowed for discourse on the new nature. The doctrine of *theosis*, long revered by the Eastern Orthodox Church and too quickly dismissed by the Western Church, must rid itself of scandalous impediments so as not to hinder the perception and reception of glorious truth. Yet, Reformed scholar Robert Letham points out that Calvin expressed views that were largely compatible with Athanasius' view of *theosis*, as did the theologian Polanus whose views were representative of Reformed theology contemporaneous with Calvin. (Robert Letham, *Union with Christ*, pp.107, 117.)
15. Samuel Chadwick, *Humanity and God*, (Salem, Ohio, Schmul Publishing Company, 1982), p.19.
16. Ibid., p.40.
17. A. B. Simpson, *In Step with the Spirit*, (Camp Hill, PA, Christian Publications, 1998), p.34.
18. Erich Sauer, *The King of all the Earth*, p.185.
19. Horatius Bonar, *God's Way of Holiness*, (Chicago, Moody Press, 1970), p.10.
20. G. Campbell Morgan points out that the words "he is" do not actually appear in the text but were supplied by translators. Morgan prefers to place the words "a new creation" in apposition to Christ and not as a referent to the believer. However, this exegesis appears arbitrary, given the fact that that the subject of the verse is the believer and not Christ; and that the preceding verse focuses on how we should view a believer and not how we should view Christ. Therefore, these contextual factors favor the way most translators translate this verse.
21. On page 80 of his book, *God's Eagles*, (Salem, Ohio, Schmul Publishing Company, 1989), G. D. Watson observed, "There are two words for *all* in the Greek New Testament; one is *halos*, which means the entirety of anything, and the other is *pantos*, which means all parts,

or all of the number. The word here is *pantos* ...." Watson then illustrated the meaning of this Greek word when he wrote: "The water in the ocean contains gold, salt, iron, sugar, oxygen, hydrogen, nitrogen, and a great many different elements. You can take a thimble full of that water, and that thimble contains as many aspects of the sea as the ocean contains." We must acknowledge, therefore, the restraint the Greek word places on this concept of being filled with all the fullness of God, but at the same time we must acknowledge the limitations of language. For if a person swallowed a thimble of water, the affect on him would be somewhat inconsequential; and the actual ratio of that swallowed water, when compared with everything else inside him, would be miniscule. In this way, overdependence on a Greek word penalizes accuracy.

22. Donald Barnhouse, *How to Live a Holy Life*, (Old Tappan, New Jersey, Fleming H. Revell, 1975), p.46.
23. John Tauler, *The Inner Way*, Christian Classics Ethereal Library, Kindle Edition, 2009, Kindle Locations: 3012-3013.
24. In his book, *Making Men Whole*, (Waco, Texas, Word Books, 1973), pp.114, 115, J. B. Phillips reminds of the corporate implications of "one new man" and how those capacities of God given evidence through the gifts of the Spirit are bestowed upon the entire church and not one individual. Likewise, Herman Bavink, the Dutch theologian born in the mid-nineteenth-century, wrote, "The image of God is far too rich to be completely represented by a single human being ...." Martin Luther appeared to interpret the new man as Christ himself, of which we are only a part: T. F. Torrance, *Kingdom and Church*, (Edinburgh, Oliver and Boyd, 1956), p.46.
25. A. T. Pierson, *In Christ Jesus*, whatsaiththescripture.com, webpage 6.
26. James A. Fowler is correct to point out that our union with Christ "... is not a metaphysical merging or commingling with God wherein a person is consubstantially and essentially deified in an organic union that constitutes the person as 'no longer human'." Nor does this union mean "... that you are essentially, inherently, intrinsically Jesus Christ. That would be blasphemy. This is not an essential union of fused coalescence or absorbed equivalence." *Spirit-Union Allows for Soul-Rest*, christinyou.net, 2004, pp.5, 6.

Endnotes

27. G. D. Watson, *Pure Gold*, (Hampton, TN., Harvey Christian Publishers, 1996), p.7.
28. Walter Marshall, *Gospel Mystery of Sanctification*, Public Domain, first published 1692, Monergism Book, Kindle Location: page 24.
29. From a sermon by Charles Spurgeon entitled "The New Nature," delivered June 30, 1861.
30. Dale Yocum, *Conformed to Christ*, (Salem, Ohio, Schmul Publishing Company, 1986), p.75.
31. Even with regard to the moral qualities of God, qualities that belong to the domain of character, fullness in the sense of quantity and extent are incommunicable. Fullness is better understood in the sense of the range of these qualities (i.e. the fruit of the spirit) and their inherent perfections.
32. The metaphor of a seed can be misleading if it includes the notion of being without form beyond that of a seed. The phrase "until Christ be formed in you" (Galatians 4:19) refers to conversion, which Paul doubted had occurred yet to these people (Galatians 4:11, 20). These Galatians—about whom A. B. Simpson said, "they were as quick to be perverted as to be converted"—represented an enigma. Hence, Charles Finney noted, "Many professors have not Christ formed within them." (Charles Finney, *How to Experience the Higher Life*, Kindle Edition, 2010, Location: 2418). To interpret Paul's words in Galatians 4:19 as ongoing process sets up the problem experienced in eighteenth-century Europe and America, where conversions were regarded as probationary for an extensive period of time and half-way covenants were established to accommodate this arrangement. No, just as a fetus takes form in the womb, Christ is formed in us during conversion. The formation is complete, although growth is not. When the Bible says that God formed man from the dust of the ground and animated him with Divine breath, the picture depicted is one of completion. Charles Spurgeon agreed with this perspective, saying "In the old birth, and in the new birth also, a life is also brought forth which is complete in all its parts and only needs to be developed." (From a sermon preached June 30, 1861 entitled "The New Nature")

    Recent interest in spiritual formation (Richard Foster, Dallas Willard) lacks accuracy when mystical disciplines, contrary to Scripture, are said to *add* to spiritual formation. The terminology, the "Spirit-formed life," also lacks biblical accuracy (even if more orthodox disciplines are used), if these disciplines are thought to contribute to formation. Growth, yes; formation, no. If we succumb to the wrong paradigm here, it will set us up for needless problems later. For example, the phrase "conformed to the image of Christ" (Romans 8:29) doesn't refer to a daily, step-by-step procedure. To say that it does imports a construct onto the text which the text itself doesn't indicate. The conforming refers to essence, not behavior. When Jesus died for us, he didn't just die for what we did, he died for who we were. Who we were was worse than what we did. Similarly, when we were conformed to the image of Christ, this was done with regard to essence, suddenly, and not with regard to behavior, gradually. Who we are in the new creation is also greater than the way we act, no matter how extensive our progress turns out to be. Colossians 2:10 uses the widest inclusion language when it says that we are complete in the Lord. There is no sorting out criteria introduced for the purpose of distinguishing which believers are conformed to Christ and which ones aren't. All are conformed to him at the point they have been born again. If we interpret Galatians 4 and Romans 8 in a behavioral context, at what point does this forming/conforming occur? And by what criteria are we to judge this? Scripture never provides criteria, precisely because this isn't an issue.

33. A. B. Simpson, *The Supernatural*, (Camp Hill, PA., Christian Publications, 1994), p.36.
34. Oswald Chambers, *Shade of His Hand*, (Grand Rapids, Discovery House Publishing, 1991), p.71.
35. A. B. Simpson, *The Christ Life*, p.36.
36. A. T. Pierson, *In Christ Jesus*, webpage 3.
37. Paul E. Billheimer, *Destined For the Throne*, p.33.
38. Ibid. p.34.
39. A. W. Tozer, *The Attributes of God*, Volume One (Camp Hill, PA., Christian Publications, 1997), p.122.
40. On page 15 of his book, *Humanity and God*, Samuel Chadwick further addresses the supposed contrast between the nature of God and the nature of man by writing, "Many of our difficulties have arisen from regarding the two natures as dissimilar, if not antagonistic and irreconcilable. We have looked upon God as radically

different from ourselves, remote from all that was vital to our humanity and alien to all the instincts of our nature."

41. John Flavel seemed to have thought of the incarnational God in this way when he allowed himself to ponder, "For the sun to fall from its sphere, and be degraded into a wandering atom; for an angel to be turned out of heaven, and be converted into a silly fly ...." Flavel's search for extreme metaphors continued in this vein until he wrote, "But for the infinite glorious Creator of all things, to become a creature, is a mystery exceeding all human understanding."
42. E. J. Carnell, *The Case for Biblical Christianity*, (Grand Rapids, William B. Eerdmans Publishing Company, 1969), p.148.
43. F. B. Meyer, *Christ in Isaiah*, (Fort Washington, PA., CLS Publications, 2001), p.165.

Chapter 3—The Ultimate Makeover

1. G. D. Watson, *Soul Food*, (Hampton, TN., Harvey Christian Publishers, 2000), p.90.
2. Affirming this principle, C. S. Lewis wrote, "The value of the individual does not lie in him. He is capable of receiving value. He receives it by union with Christ." C. S. Lewis, *The Weight of Glory*, Grand Rapids, William B. Eerdmans Publishing Company, 1973P, p.41.
3. G. D. Watson, *Soul Food*, p.35.
4. G. D. Watson, *A Pot of Oil*, (Hampton, TN., Harvey Christian Publishers, n. d.), p.62.
5. Oswald Chambers, *God's Workmanship*, (Fort Washington, Christian Literature Crusade, 1936), p.55.
6. Tony Lane, *Timeless Witness*, (Peabody, MA., Hendrickson Press, 2004), p.45.
7. The amazing benefits made possible by the new birth prompted the Puritan writer Thomas Watson to exclaim, "At our first birth we come weeping into the world, but at our new birth there is cause of rejoicing ...." Thomas Watson, *The Lord's Prayer*, Kindle Edition, 2010, Kindle Locations: 213-214.
8. A. W. Tozer, *Faith Beyond Reason*, (Camp Hill, PA., WingSpread Publishers, 2009), p.99.
9. In his book, *In Darkest England*, William Booth, the founder of the Salvation Army, tells the story of many unsavory characters, considered the dredges of London society, who were gloriously saved. In drawing conclusions

about this great work of God, Booth said, "To get a man soundly saved ... you must in some way or another graft upon the man's nature a new nature, which has in it the element of the divine. To change the nature of the individual ... is the only real lasting method of doing him any good." (*The Speaker's Bible, The Epistle to the Romans*, Volume I, Aberdeen, Scotland, G. & W. Fraser, 1936), p.108.

10. Donald Barnhouse, *How to Live a Holy Life*, p.70.
11. A. W. Tozer, *Jesus, Our Man in Glory*, (Camp Hill, PA., WingSpread Publishers, 1987), p.37.
12. Thomas Watson points out, "The Hebrew word for glory signifies a weight, to show how solid and weighty the glory of the celestial kingdom is." By contrast, Watson said, "The glory of the worldly kingdom is airy and imaginary ...." Thomas Watson, *The Lord's Prayer*, Kindle Locations: 1697-1698.
13. Paul Billheimer, *Destined for the Throne*, p.37.
14. Martyn Lloyd-Jones, *Romans, Exposition of Chapter 6 The New Man*, (Edinburgh, UK, The Banner of Truth Trust, 2008), p.135.
15. A. B. Simpson, *The Christ Life*, p.84.
16. Paul Billheimer, *Destined for the Throne*, p.37.
17. *The Works of Thomas Goodwin, Volume I*, (Lafayette, IN., Sovereign Grace Publishers, Inc., 2000), p.95.
18. Miles J. Stanford, *The Complete Green Letters*, (Grand Rapids, Zondervan, 1983), p.65.
19. Lest anyone think that this is only an evangelical problem, and not a Charismatic or Pentecostal one, it must be pointed out that a person can be baptized with the Spirit and then forfeit the enormous benefits of that extraordinary experience, if the wrong goal of trying to create what God already created is subsequently undertaken. God wants what he has already given! The victory we are to experience is his victory, and not one of our own making.
20. When inspecting the consequences of the fall and the vast differences between sinful man and a holy God, the attempt to describe the enormity of these differences tempts extreme comparisons. Profoundly true as well, however, are the significances of being made in the image of God. Though inflicted with damages so extreme as to make divine abiding impossible, still there was a way open to God with man that was never open to any other part of

God's creation. In this sense, man was not a species too foreign in his makeup, in his original constitution, for divine visitation and later divine habitation. The image of God in man may have been rendered, as Calvin said, "frightfully deformed" through the fall, yet it was not annihilated. There was some part of the image left that could be renovated and renewed by the Son of God.

21. A. B. Simpson, *The Christ in the Bible Commentary*, Volume Five, (Camp Hill, PA., WingSpread Publishers, 2009), p.40.
22. A. W. Tozer, *And He Dwelt Among Us*, (Ventura, CA/. Regal, 2009), p.62.
23. Ibid., p.63.
24. Andrew Murray, *The Believer's Secret of the Masters Indwelling*, (Minneapolis, Minnesota, Bethany House Publishers, 1977), p.89.
25. Francis Schaeffer, *Genesis in Space and Time*, (Glendale, CA., Regal Press, 1972), p.113.
26. Oswald Chambers, *Making All Things New*, (Grand Rapids, Discovery House Publishers, 1991), p.195.
27. James S. Stewart, *A Man in Christ*, (Vancouver, Regent College Publishing, 2002), pp.314, 315.
28. C. S. Lewis, *Miracles*, (New York, NY: HarperCollins, 1947), pp.236-237.
29. Bradley G. Green, ed., *Shapers of Christian Orthodoxy*, (Downers Grove, Illinois, IVP Academic, 2010), p.57.
30. George D. Watson, *Love Abounding*, (Cincinnati, Ohio, God's Revivalist Press, n.d.), p.208.
31. Paul Billheimer, *Destined for the Throne*, (Minneapolis, Bethany House, 1975), p.16.
32. A. W. Tozer, *The Set of the Sail*, (Camp Hill, PA., Christian Publications, 1986), p.103.
33. James S. Stewart, *The Strong Name*, (New York, Charles Scribner's Sons, 1941), p.65.

Chapter 4—Introducing the New You

1. Anthony A. Hoekema, *Created in God's Image*, (Grand Rapids, MI/Cambridge UK, William B. Eerdmans Publishing Company, 1986), p.110.
2. Earl Jabay, *The God Players*, (Grand Rapids, Zondervan, 1969), p.14.
3. John Calvin, *Calvin's Commentaries: Romans–Galatians* (Wilmington, DE: Associated Publishers and Authors,

n.d.), p.1921.

4. G. D. Watson, *Heavenly Life*, (Salem, Ohio, Schmul Publishing Company, 1994), p.9.
5. James S. Stewart, *A Man in Christ*, p.309.
6. In his book, *A New Creature*, the Puritan Thomas Watson made a strong distinction between the virtues the flesh produces and those that are imparted into the believer's new nature: "Natural honesty, moral virtue, prudence, justice, liberality, temperance—these are not the new creature. These make a glorious show in the eye of the world—but differ as much from the new creature as a stick differs from a star."
7. Will Durant, *The Pleasures of Philosophy*, (New *York, Simon and Shuster*, 1953), p.186.
8. Andrew Murray, *The Believer's Secret of Holiness*, (Minneapolis, Bethany House Publishers, 1984), p.66.
9. A. B. Simpson, *The Christ in the Bible Commentary*, Volume 6 (Camp Hill, PA., WingSpread Publishers, 2009), p.27.
10. James S. Stewart, *River of Life*, (Nashville and New York, Abingdon, 1972), pp.86, 87.
11. C. S. Lewis noted our tendency to commend or reject rather than to conceptualize with precision. "The human mind is generally far more eager to praise and dispraise than to define and describe." C.S. Lewis, *The Four Loves*, New York, Harcourt Brace Jovanovich, Inc., 1960), p.27.
12. A. B. Simpson, *The Christ in the Bible Commentary*, Volume 6, p.225.
13. J. H. Jowett graphically illustrated the width of God's love when he wrote, "There is love whose measure is that of an umbrella. There is love whose inclusiveness is that of a great marquee. And there is love whose comprehension is that of the immeasurable sky. The aim of the New Testament is the conversion of the umbrella into a tent, and the merging of the tent into the glorious canopy of the all-enfolding heavens." J. H. Jowett, *The Epistles of St. Peter*, Kindle Edition, 2010, Kindle Locations: 1400-1403.
14. C. S. Lewis, *Miracles*, p.116.
15. Alexander Maclaren emphasized the ongoing dimension of God's seeking love when he wrote, "God's seeking love lingers round every one of us, yearning over us, besetting us behind and before, courting us with kindnesses, lavishing on us its treasures, seeking to win our poor love." Alexander Maclaren, *Exposition of Holy Scriptures*,

Psalms, Public Domain Books, Kindle Locations: 697-698.

16. F. J. Huegel, *Bone of His Bone*, (Fort Washington, PA., CLC Publications, 2009), p.65.
17. A. W. Tozer, *The Knowledge of the Holy*, (Harper and Brothers, 1961), p.121.
18. On page 28 of his book, *Entire Sanctification* (Salem, Ohio, Schmul Publishing Company, 2000), Dr. Wilbur T. Dayton, Professor of Biblical Literature and Historical Theology at Wesley Biblical Seminary, said that this love "is the kind of love for which the pagan Greeks had no noun until later Christian centuries because they knew no such love. The word *agape* was coined to translate the Old Testament word *hesed* into the Septuagint Greek and then became very much a key word in the New Testament."
19. C. S. Lewis also downgraded feelings in his definition of love when he wrote, "Love is not affectionate feeling, but a steady wish for the loved person's ultimate good as far as it can be obtained." *God in the Dock*, Grand Rapids, Michigan, William B. Eerdmans Publishing Company, 1970), p.49.
20. The relationship between love and doing good is also at the core of Jesus' words, "If you love me, you will keep my commandments." In his book, *Grace Walk*, Steve McVey points out how easy it is to misunderstand these words. In our minds we may think that consistent commandment-keeping is what we must crank out if we want to prove our love to Jesus. "However, that is not what the verse said," McVey writes. "Jesus said that if we love him we *will* keep his commandments. Do you see the difference?" Steve McVey, *Grace Walk*, (Eugene, OR., Harvest House Publishers, 1995), p.131.
21. Richard Sibbes, *The Bruised Reed*, (Carlisle, PA., The Banner of Truth Trust, 1998), p.89.
22. Andrew Murray, *The Spirit of Christ*, (Springdale, Whitaker House, n.d.) p.226.
23. Ibid. p.229.
24. Dr. and Mrs. Howard Taylor, *Hudson Taylor's Spiritual Secret*, (Chicago, Moody Press, 1990), p.234.
25. A. B. Simpson, *The Christ in the Bible Commentary*, Volume Six, (Camp Hill, PA., WingSpread Publishers, 2009), p.307.
26. J. H. Jowett, *The Passion for Souls*, (London and Edinburgh, Fleming H. Revell Company, 1905), p.96.
27. G. D. Watson, *Love and Duty*, (Salem, Ohio, Schmul

Publishing Company, Inc., 1984), p.77.

28. J. H. Jowett, *Brooks by the Traveler's Way*, New York A. C. Armstrong and Son; London, H. R. Allerson, 1902), p.38.

29. J. H. Jowett, *Silver Lining: Messages of Cheer and Hope*, Kindle Edition, 2010, Locations: 997-998.

30. J. I. Packer, *Knowing Man*, (Westchester, IL., Crossway Books, 1979), p.47.

31. The extent of sin's control over an individual was well-illustrated by Thomas Brooks' remark. "When the physicians told Theotimus that except he did abstain from drunkenness and uncleanness he would lose his eyes; his heart was so bewitched to his sins, that he answered, 'Then farewell, sweet light'...." Thomas Brooks, *Precious Remedies Against Satan's Devices*, (Carlisle, PA., Banner of Truth, 1968), p.18.

32. Oswald Chambers, *The Psychology of Redemption*, (London, Simpkin Marshall LTD, 1941), pp.92, 93.

33. Stephen Charnock accorded the pleasure principle a profound foundational status when he observed, "... for all sinful dispositions are rooted in one, namely, in 'love of pleasure more than of God' ...." *The Works of Stephen Charnock*, (Kindle Locations: 1787-1788). And John Flavel, a contemporary of Charnock, lamented, "O how many have been wheeled to hell in the chariots of earthly pleasures ...." *Keeping the Heart*, Kindle Edition, 2010; Kindle Location: p.24.

34. A. B. Simpson, *The Christ in the Bible Commentary*, Volume Two, (Camp Hill, PA., WingSpread Publishers, 2009), p.58.

35. On page 134 of his book, *Born After Midnight*, A. W. Tozer decries the Church's addiction to pleasure when he writes: "In these times religion has become jolly good fun ... Christianity, contrary to what some have thought, is another and higher form of entertainment. Christ has done all the suffering. He has shed all the tears and carried all the crosses. We have but to enjoy the benefits of his heartbreak in the form of religious pleasures modeled after the world but carried on in the name of Jesus."

36. Alexander Maclaren, *Expositions of Holy Scripture, Isaiah and Jeremiah*, Public Domain Books, Kindle Locations: 924-925.

37. Ibid., Kindle Locations: 1776-1777.

38. Reminding us of the context of Jesus' words about joy, J.

H. Jowett writes, "Hatreds had deepened into black passions of the midnight. Malicious nets were being woven around him. Calvary was only a stone's throw away, and on the morrow the grim cross would be on the hill! ... And yet the Master quietly spoke about His joy." John Henry Jowett, *Friend on the Road and Other Studies in the Gospels*, Kindle Edition, 2010, Kindle Locations: 1140-1142.

39. Henry Scougal, *The Life of God in the Soul of Man*, (Harrisonburg, VA., Sprinkle Publications, 1986), p.71.
40. R. A. Torrey, "How to be Inexpressibly Happy," Sermonindex.net
41. Andrew Murray, *The Believer's Secret of the Master's Indwelling*, p.144.
42. When comparing today's church with that of the apostles, J. H. Jowett said that "we lack the apostolic exhilarancy, their power of nimble rebound, their song, their praise, their joy." John Henry Jowett, *Friend on the Road and Other Studies in the Gospels*, Kindle Location: 1163.
43. John E. Hunter, *Knowing God's Secret*, (Grand Rapids, Zondervan, 1972), p.35.
44. Ibid., p.62.
45. Amy Carmichael, *Learning of God*, compiled by Stuart and Brenda Blanch, (Ft. Washington, PA., CLC Publications, 2000), p.13.
46. Andrew Murray, *The Believer's Secret of the Master's Indwelling*, p.144.
47. J. C. Ryle records a similar testimony, true of Goethe. "His works were read and admired by thousands. His name was known and honored, wherever German was read, all over the world. And yet the praise of man, of which he reaped such an abundant harvest, was utterly unable to make Goethe happy. He confessed, when about eighty years old, that he could not remember being in a really happy state of mind even for a few weeks together ...." *Practical Religion*, (Kindle Edition, 2010, Locations: 3707-3710).
48. Dr. and Mrs. Howard Taylor, *Hudson Taylor in Early Years: The Growth of a Soul*, (New York: Hodder and Stoughton; George H. Doran Co., 1912), p.125.

Chapter 5—Seeing the Picture

1. Charles R. Hembree, *Spiritual Stirrings*, (Grand Rapids, Baker, 1973), p.40.
2. William Barclay, *And Jesus Said*, (Philadelphia, The

Westminster Press, 1970), p.74.

3. James Stewart, *The Gates of New Life*, (Edinburgh, T. and T. Clark, 1956), pp.144-145.
4. Rollo May, *Love and Will*, (New York, Dell Publishing, 1970), p.16.
5. We find this counterfeit peace challenged in *The Speaker's Bible* with this entry: "No sentiment is more untrue, and none if acted upon more baneful, than that of the Latin poet who declared, 'The only way to be happy is to care for nothing much'." *Speaker's Bible, The First and Second Epistles of Peter, The Epistle of Jude*, ed., James Hastings, (Aberdeen, Scotland, G. & W. Fraser, 1924), p.71.
6. J. H. Jowett, *The Epistles of St. Peter*, Kindle Edition, 2010, Kindle Location: 1755.
7. Charles R. Swindoll, *The Church Awakening*, (New York, Boston, Nashville, Faith Words, 2010), p.229.
8. Supporting this emphasis, G. D. Watson offered this reflection: "Of all the millions of professed Christians, only a small percent reach that state of life where the mind of God is habitually stayed on God. And yet we never get into the very heart of religion, or into a true scriptural life, until God becomes the paramount abiding and ever increasing attraction of the mind ...." G. D. Watson, *Spiritual Feasts*, (Salem, Ohio, Schmul Publishing Company, 1991), p.70.
9. Dr. and Mrs. Hudson, *Hudson Taylor's Spiritual Secret*, p.178.
10. Emphasizing the point that what Satan offers can never produce peace, Thomas Watson wrote, "You may as well suck health out of poison, as peace out of sin." *A Body of Divinity: Contained in Sermons upon the Westminster Assembly's Catechism* (Kindle Locations: 5857-5858).
11. G. D. Watson, *White Robes*, (Hampton, TN., Harvey Christian Publishers, 2000), p.41.
12. L. E. Maxwell, *Born Crucified*, (Chicago, Moody Press, 1945), p.56.
13. W. E. Boardman, *The Higher Christian Life*, (Charleston, S. C., Bibliolife, n.d.), p.246.
14. G. D. Watson, *God's First Words*, (Hampton, TN., Harvey Christian Publishers, 1992), p.53.
15. Abraham Kuyper, *The Practice of Godliness*, (Grand Rapids, Baker, 1977), p.65.
16. James S. Stewart, *River of Life*, p.144.
17. John Henry Jowett offered an example of this principle: "Take the apostle Peter—once his strength was the

strength of impulse, a spurt and then a collapse, a spasm and then a retreat, proud beginnings bereft of patience and perseverance. But see him when the Spirit of God has got hold upon him ....” After Pentecost and the releasing of his new nature, a pattern of godly endurance prevailed. John Henry Newton, *The Whole Armor of God*, Kindle Edition, 2011, Kindle Locations: 1443-1445.

18. Thomas Watson, *The Godly Man's Picture*, (Carlisle, PA., the Banner of Truth Trust, 2009), p.127.
19. Ibid., p.123.
20. A. W. Tozer, *The Attributes of God*, Volume 1, (Camp Hill, PA., Christian Publications, 1997), p.185.
21. Puritan theologian John Owen correctly observed, “There is no word in the Scripture whereby this perfection, and being perfect, is expressed, that in its use is restrained to such an absolute perfection as should admit of no mixture of failing or defect.” Owen points out that “the words used in the New Testament are chiefly *teleios* and *artios* ...” and that “this is a perfection in a tendency to that which is complete ....” The trajectory is straight; the point of termination not yet reached. John Owen, *The Ultimate Collected Works of 22 Books*, Kindle Edition, 2011, Kindle Locations: 119057-119084).
22. Asa Mahan, *Out of Darkness into Light*, (Boston, Willard Tract Repository, originally published 1896, Holy Data Ministry digital edition, 1997), p.136.
23. Ibid., p.31.
24. With grace and eloquence, John Henry Jowett characterized the astonishment we have to God's offer of perfection: “Christ kindles hope in the perfectibility of self. He comes to me, a poor sensitive, devil-governed man, and whispers to me that I too can attain to freedom and put on the strength of the ideal man. I stand amazed before the suggestion. Quietly He reassures me and tells me that I too can be perfected. What, I; with the fires out, a poor bit of driftage upon life's sea, that I can be renewed and filled with power and made master of circumstances, and voyage happily and safely to the desired haven? Can I be perfected?” John Henry Jowett, *Silver lining: Messages of Hope and Cheer*, Kindle Edition, 2010, Kindle Locations: 1025-1028.
25. On page 90 of her book, *The Christian's Secret of a Happy Life* (Old Tappan, N. J., Fleming H. Revell Company, 1974), Hannah Whitall Smith correctly notes, “No safe

teacher of this interior life ever says that it becomes impossible to sin; they only insist that sin ceases to be a necessity, and that a possibility of continual victory is open before us."

26. In one place Stephen Charnock wrote, "Fix your aims on a state of perfection. You are to walk, not to stand still. Never rest till all that righteousness which of right belongs to that divine nature in you, be conferred upon you: breathe after a more close conjunction with the original." (*The Works of Stephen Charnock*, Kindle Locations: 2143-2144). And in another place Charnock wrote: "Not to walk as new creatures is a dishonor to God. You that do not walk answerable to your high calling do more highly dishonor him than all other persons" (*The Works of Stephen Charnock*, Kindle Locations: 2192-2193). For one not to aspire to the kind of life the new nature enables is discrediting to a degree so deep in disgrace that having to answer for it before God would not be a welcomed prospect.

Chapter 6—There Must Be a Difference

1. G. D. Watson, *Coals of Fire*, (Salem, Ohio, Schmul Publisher, n.d.), p.100.
2. Hannah Whitall Smith, *The Christian's Secret of a Happy Life*, (Old Tappan, N. J., Fleming H. Revell Company, 1974), p.140.
3. Lloyd Ogilvie, *Life Without Limits*, (Waco, Word, 1979), p.60.
4. Richard J. Foster, *Money, Sex, and Power*, (San Francisco, Harper and Row, 1985), p.104.
5. Lloyd John Ogilvie, *You've Got Charisma*, (Nashville, Abingdon, 1975), p.150.
6. George MacDonald, *The Best of George MacDonald*, (Colorado Springs, CO., Cook Communications Ministries, 2006), p.15.
7. The following is from an interview with a Catholic nun, "Sister" Ann, who worked in Kathmandu, Nepal, with Mother Teresa's organization Missionaries of Charity. The interview was conducted 11/23/84 at the Pashupati Temple.

   Q: Do you believe if they die believing in Shiva or in Ram [Hindu gods] they will go to heaven? A: Yes, that is their faith. My own faith will lead me to God ... So if they have believed in their god very strongly, if they have faith, surely they will be saved. Q: Today it does not seem that the Catholic Church is trying to convert anymore. I know that John Paul II is saying now that those of other religions are saved. You do not believe they are lost anyway, right? A: No, they are not lost. They are saved according to their faith, you know. If they believe whatever they believe, that is their salvation.

8. A. B. Simpson, *The Christ in the Bible Commentary*, Volume Five, p.416.
9. *The Speaker's Bible, The Epistle to the Philippians, The Epistle to the Colossians*, Edward Hastings, ed., (Aberdeen, Scotland, Turnbull & Spears, 1930), p.128.
10. C. S. Lewis, *The Problem of Pain*, (New York, The Macmillan Company, 1962), p.56.
11. G. D. Watson, *A Pot of Oil*, p.61.
12. Ibid., p.62.
13. *The Speaker's Bible, The First Epistle to the Corinthians* Volume II, *The Epistle to Philemon*, James Hastings, ed., (Aberdeen, Scotland, Turnbull & Spears, 1927), p.233.
14. *The Speaker's Bible, The Gospel According to St. Mark Volume II*, James Hastings, ed., (Aberdeen, Scotland, Turnbull & Spears, 1929), p.83.
15. R. C. Sproul, *The Holiness of God*, (Wheaton, Tyndale House Publishers, 1985), pp.121, 122.
16. Soren Kierkegaard, *Purity of Heart*, (New York, Harper and Row, 1956), p.65.
17. A. W. Tozer, *Who Put Jesus on the Cross*, (Harrisburg, Christian Publications, 1975), p.47.
18. Angel Martinez, *Revival at Midnight*, (Grand Rapids, Zondervan, 1956), p.63.
19. David H. C. Read, *Overheard*, (Nashville, Abingdon, 1971), p.74.
20. Blaise Pascal, *Pensees*, (New York, Washington Square Press, 1965), pp.130, 131.
21. *Journal of the American Institute of Criminal Law and Criminology* 18, no. 1 (May 1927) as written in the Minnesota Crime Commission Report of 1926, which was commissioned by then Governor Theodore Christianson.
22. G. D. Watson, *The Seven Overcomeths*, (Salem, Ohio, Schmul Publishing Company, 2007), p.105.
23. Blaise Pascal, *Pensees*, p.147.
24. W. Y. Fullerton, *Charles H. Spurgeon*, (Chicago, Moody Press, 1966), p.23.
25. J. I. Packer, *A Quest for Godliness*, (Wheaton, Crossway

Books, 1990), p.216.

26. Author unknown, *The Power-Filled Christian*, (Grand Rapids, Zondervan, 1984), p.34.
27. The prospect of a person coming to possess a new nature has long been denied. E. Stanley Jones, missionary to India, recalled the Muslim proverb which said that if one hears that a mountain has been moved, he should believe it; but if he hears that a man character has changed, he should not believe it. A Hindu told Dr. Jones, "A man may change his acts, but not his character—that is fixed." *The Speaker's Bible, The Gospel According to St. Mark Volume II*, p.99.
28. Judson Cornwall, *The Best of Judson Cornwall*, (South Plainfield, N. J., Bridge Publishing, 1992), p.1.
29. Brother Lawrence, *The Practice of The Presence of God*, (Old Tappan, Fleming H. Revell, 1958), p.89.
30. Watchman Nee, *Changed into His Likeness*, (Fort Washington, Christian Literature Crusade, 1976), p.85.
31. J. N. D. Anderson, *The Witness of History*, (Wheaton, InterVarsity, 1970), p.46.

Chapter 7— Multiplying the Life of Jesus

1. G. D. Watson, *Our Own God*, p.151.
2. John White, *When the Spirit Comes with Power*, (Wheaton, InterVarsity, 1990), p.152.
3. C. S. Lewis brought focus to the line being crossed between faith and fanaticism when he wrote, "Those who are readiest to die for a cause may become those who are readiest to kill for it." C. S. Lewis, *Reflection on the Psalms*, (New York, Harcourt, Brace and World, Inc., 1958), p.28.
4. Andrew Murray, *In Search of Spiritual Excellence*, (Springdale, Whitaker House, 1984), p.131.
5. Andrew Murray, *The Spirit of Christ*, p.43.
6. Miles J. Stanford, *The Complete Green Letters*, p.65.
7. Elton Trueblood, *The Yoke of Christ*, (Dallas, Word, 1962), p.78.
8. James Hastings pointed out, "Gentleness is a word much misunderstood and not infrequently caricatured." *The Speaker's Bible, Psalms, Volume II*, (Aberdeen, Scotland, G. & W. Fraser, 1925), p.68. According to Alexander Maclaren, "Christianity has altered the perspective of human virtues, has thrown the gentler ones into prominence altogether unknown before ... and has

dimmed the brilliancy of the old heroic type of character ...." *Expositions of Holy Scripture Deuteronomy, Joshua, Judges, Ruth, and First Book of Samuel, Second Samuel, First Kings, and Second Kings* chapters I to VII, Public Domain Books, Kindle Location, p.101.

9. G. D. Watson, *Soul Food*, p.93.
10. Ian Thomas, The *Saving Life of Christ*, (Grand Rapids, Zondervan, 1961), p.82.
11. Andrew Murray, *The Believer's Secret of the Master's Indwelling*, (Minneapolis, Bethany House Publishers, 1977), p.28.
12. Andrew Murray, *The Believer's Absolute Surrender*, (Minneapolis, Bethany House, 1985), p.25.
13. W. Ian Thomas, *If I Perish, I Perish*, (Grand Rapids, MI., Zondervan Publishing House, 1967), p.68.
14. A. W. Tozer, *The Attributes of God*, Volume 2, (Camp Hill, PA., Christian Publications, 2001), p.27.
15. John Tauler, *The Inner Way*, Kindle Locations: 2963-2964.
16. C. S. Lewis, *Mere Christianity*, p.112.
17. A. B. Simpson, *The Fourfold Gospel*, p.117.
18. David C. Needham, *Birthright*, (Portland, Multnomah, 1979), pp.16, 91.
19. A. W. Tozer, *The Warfare of the Spirit*, (Camp Hill, PA., Christian Publications, 1993), p.89.
20. Alexander Maclaren, *Expositions of Holy Scripture, Isaiah and Jeremiah*, Kindle Locations: 1328-1330.
21. One's love for the Master, more than one's commitment to a behavioral standard, is the compelling dynamic of biblical temperance. Stressing this motive, Count Zinzendorf declared, "I have but one enthusiasm; it is he, only he." *The Speaker's Bible, The Epistle to the Philippians, The Epistle to the Colossians*, p.37.
22. A. B. Simpson, *The Fourfold Gospel*, p.130.
23. Wayne DeHoney, an unpublished sermon entitled, "Plumblines and Summerfruit."
24. Ray C. Stedman, *Jesus Teaches on Prayer*, (Waco, Word Books, 1975), p.12.
25. A. B. Simpson, *The Christ in the Bible Commentary*, Volume Five, pp.231, 232.

Chapter 8—Getting Rid of Our Old Man

1. Anthony A. Hoekema writes, "Adam and Eve should have been able to resist the devil's temptations and remain

obedient to God." Anthony A. Hoekema, *Created in God's Image*, p.131.

2. T. Austin Sparks said of sin, "When this happened in Adam's case, death entered; and the nature of death, in the scriptural meaning of the word, is severance in the union of the spirit with God. This does not mean that man no longer had a spirit, but that the ascendency of the spirit was surrendered to the soul." T. Austin Sparks, *What is Man?*, Kindle Edition, 2012: Kindle Locations: 253-255.
3. Jessie Penn Lewis, *Life in the Spirit*, (Parkstone, Poole. Dorset, England, n. d.), p.31.
4. In his book, *Shade of His Hand* (p.124), Oswald Chambers offered this interesting but disputable speculation: "Eve stands for the soul side, the psychic side of the human creation, all her sympathies and affinities are with other creations of God around. Adam stands for the spirit side, the kingly, Godward side. Adam and Eve together are the likeness of God …."
5. James Montgomery Boice, *The Sovereign God*, (Downers Grove, InterVarsity Press, 1978), p.204. In his book, *The King of the Earth*, Erich Sauer contends that the image of God in man was not lost in the fall. "Nevertheless has fallen very far and very grievously. For even if the image of God as a formal endowment, i. e. as the moral substance of personality, persisted, yet the image of God as a real moral possession and an actual state was lost." Erich Sauer, *The King of the Earth*, (Grand Rapids, William. B. Eerdmans Publishing Co., 1967), p.145.
6. Blaise Pascal, *Pensees*, p.163.
7. On page 90 of his book, *God's Eagles*, G. D. Watson wrote, "We will never know how much Adam lost by the fall until we are glorified, and look down from those lofty heights of glorification into the depths of the fall of man."
8. A. W. Tozer, *Gems From Tozer*, p.17.
9. Rollo May, *Love and Will*, p.127.
10. C. S. Lewis, *Surprised by Joy* (New York, NY: Harcourt Brace & Company, 1955), p.226.
11. When speaking of all those born in this condition, Stephen Charnock said it was "… as though iniquity had been their tutor in the womb!" *The Works of Stephen Charnock*, Kindle Locations: 4923-4924.
12. A. W. Tozer, *The Attributes of God*, Volume 1, p.103.
13. Stephen Charnock, *The Works of Stephen Charnock*, Kindle Locations: 3902-3903.

14. G. D. Watson, *White Robes*, p.76.
15. A. B. Simpson, *The Christ in the Bible Commentary*, Volume Six, (Camp Hill, PA., WingSpread Publishers, 2009), p.507.
16. John Haggai, *How to Win over Worry*, (New York, Pirimand, 1969), pp.26, 27.
17. Bruce Larson, *Ask Me to Dance*, (Waco, Word, 1973), p.53.
18. Fenelon, *Let Go*, (Springdale, Whitaker House, 1973), p.19.
19. Erich Sauer, *The King of the Earth*, pp.184, 185.
20. J. I. Packer, *Rediscovering Holiness* (Ann Arbor, MI: Servant Publications, 1992), p.83.
21. John MacArthur, "The Good-Natured Believer," Masterpiece (March–April 1990), p.18.
22. G. D. Watson, *White Robes*, p.24.
23. John Murray, *Principles of Conduct* (Grand Rapids: Eerdmans, 1957), p.218.
24. Miles J. Stanford, *The Complete Green Letters*, p.219.
25. David C. Needham, *Birthright*, p.245.
26. Neil T. Anderson likens a believer to a tree (the old nature) onto which new fruit (the new nature) is grafted. Anderson even says that the roots of the old tree help to nourish this new fruit. This kind of thinking is inevitable whenever the construct of our position in Christ and our identity in Christ are trusted to offer explanations beyond which they can provide. If we don't see that God *actually* put a new nature inside us and *actually* removed the old nature from us, double-talk and messy metaphors will abound. To the question—do we have one nature or two?—Anderson answers, yes and no. Due to this failure to distinguish between imputed righteousness and imparted righteousness, subsequent commentary yields needless confusion.
27. David C. Needham, *Birthright*, p.246.
28. Robert Letham's insight on this point is eloquently expressed: "Union with Christ in his burial is the most triumphant affirmation imaginable. Whatever the process leading up to it, however sad or horrible the ordeal, once we have died the forces of sin and decay are over." (*Union with Christ*, p.123).
29. David C. Needham, *Birthright*, p.79.
30. Anthony Hoekema's comments on this point bear repeating. "This passage contains three infinitives, both in the translation and in the Greek: 'to put off' (*apothesthai*, aorist tense); 'to be made new' (*ananeousthai*, present

tense); and 'to put on' (*endusasthai*, aorist tense). Many English translations as if they were imperatives, as if the apostle were saying: You *must* put off the old self, you *must* be renewed, and you *must* put on the new self. Though occasionally Greek infinitives may be used as imperatives (as, e.g., Rom.12:15), it is not necessary to interpret them as such here. I prefer, with John Murray, to think of these forms as infinitives of result or as explanatory infinitives, depending on the verb you were taught (*eididachthete*, from v. 21 in the Greek), and giving the content of the teaching). This is in fact the way the NIV renders the passage ...." Anthony A. Hoekema, *Created in God's Image*, pp.26-27. The NIV rendering to which Hoekema referred is as follows:
(22) You were taught, with regard to your former way of life, to put off your old self, which is being corrupted by your deceitful desires; (23) to be made new in the attitudes of your minds; (24) and to put on the new self, created to be like God in true righteousness and holiness.

31. Martyn Lloyd-Jones, *Romans, Exposition of Chapter 6, The New Man*, p.82.
32. H. C. G. Moule, *Ephesians Studies*, (Fort Washington, PA., Christian Literature Crusade, 1975), p.225.
33. Oswald Chambers, *Making All Things New*, p.99.
34. A. B. Simpson, *The Cross of Christ*, (Camp Hill, Christian Publications, 1994), pp.16, 17.
35. Charles H. Spurgeon, *Christ's Glorious Achievements*, p.70.
36. F. J. Huegel, *The Cross of Christ, The Throne of God*, (Dixon, MO., Rare Christian Books, n. d.), p.111.
37. Author unknown, *The Glory Christian*, (Grand Rapids, Zondervan, 1987), p.67.
38. H. A. Ironside, *Romans*, (Neptune, New Jersey, Loizeaux Brothers, 1928), p.68.

Chapter 9—The Enemy Within

1. Lloyd John Ogilvie, *You've Got Charisma!*, p.135. Likewise, A. B. Simpson quotes Dublin's nineteenth-century Archbishop, Richard Whately, to have said: "If you ask me to tell you who it is that causes you the greatest trouble, and threatens you with the direst danger, I can only say that if you will look in the glass, you will see an excellent picture of him." A. B. Simpson, *Standing on Faith*, Kindle Edition, 2010, Kindle Locations: 763-765.

Endnotes

2. Lloyd J. Ogilvie, *Life Without Limits*, p.32.
3. Thomas Watson, *The Lord's Prayer*, Kindle Location: 1112.
4. Tony Lane, *Timeless Witness*, pp.251, 252.
5. According to W. E. Vines, *An Expository Dictionary of New Testament Words*, (Westwood, N. J., Fleming H. Revell Company, 1966, Volume 2), p.101, there is a wide range of meaning for the word "flesh" in the New Testament; more so than in the Old Testament. While the word flesh can have the un-regenerated nature as a referent (Romans 7:5), there are other instances when this isn't the case.
6. W. Ian Thomas, *The Saving Life of Christ*, p.91.
7. A. B. Simpson, *The Fourfold Gospel*, p.142.
8. Ibid., p.143.
9. Erich Sauer, *The King of all the Earth*, p.111.
10. Translated and quoted by Anthony A. Hoekema, *Created in God's Image*, p.68.
11. C. S. Lewis, *God in the Dock*, (Grand Rapids, Eerdmans, 1970), pp.216, 217.
12. Debbie Rogers, *Rejoice*, (Little Rock, Revival Press, 1985), p.45.
13. Challenging the assumption which too strongly identifies the physical with evil, A. J. Gordon argued that the physical is compatible with the eternal when he offered this quote on page 195 of his book, *In Christ* (Grand Rapids, MI., Baker Books, 1964): The translation of Enoch, says Dr. Owen, "is a divine testimony that the body itself is capable of eternal life." Extending this thought, A. J. Gordon said, "And so vital is this witness to God's Church, that like Peter's vision it has been thrice repeated before human eyes—in the Patriarchal age by Enoch, in the Prophetic age by Elijah, and in the Gospel age by Christ."
14. John F. MacArthur, Jr., *Romans*, 2 vol. (Chicago, Moody Press, 1991), 1:337.
15. Martyn Lloyd-Jones, *Romans, Exposition of Chapter 6, The New Man*, p.247.
16. Ibid., p.151.
17. It cannot be stressed too strongly that the flesh is not another nature inside the believer. Those who see the believer as having two natures are supported in this argument by the NIV's penchant to interpret the Greek word *sarx* as "sin nature," although other Bible translations render this same word "flesh." Perhaps translation hasn't become interpretation if a further

explanation about that word "nature" is properly provided. By "nature," do we mean the characteristics of sin: its genesis, its strategies, its attributes, its manifestations? If so, this translation is acceptable. But if we mean that which is so deeply rooted in self that it defines part of our being, then this translation is not accurate.

18. George B. Peck, *Throne Life*, (Boston, Mass., The Watchward Publishing Co., 1888), p.28.
19. David C. Needham, *Man Alive*, (Sisters, OR., Multnomah, 1995), p.65.
20. E. M. Bounds, *Winning the Invisible War*, (Springdale, Whitaker House, 1984), p.55.
21. Dr. and Mrs. Taylor, *Hudson Taylor's Spiritual Secret*, p.159.
22. Oswald Chambers, *The Psychology of Redemption*, p.78.
23. Ibid., p.81.
24. Norman P. Grubb, *God Unlimited*, (Blowing Rock, North Carolina, Zerubbabel Press, 2002), p.110.
25. Thomas Watson, *The Great Gain of Godliness*, (Carlisle, PA., The Banner of Truth Trust, 2008), p.49.
26. Oswald Chambers, *Approved unto God*, (Fort Washington, PA., Christian Literature Crusade, 1946), p.17.
27. L. E. Maxwell, *Born Crucified*, p.41.
28. G. D. Watson, *Heavenly Life*, p.12.
29. John Henry Jowett, *The School of Calvary*, Kindle Locations: 233-234.
30. John White, *When the Spirit Comes with Power*, (Wheaton, Intervarsity Press, 1981), pp.182, 183.
31. Oswald Chambers, *Biblical Ethics*, (Fort Washington, PA., Christian Literature Crusade, 1946), p.52.
32. Oswald Chambers, *The Highest Good*, (Grand Rapids, Discovery House Publishers, 1992), p.213.
33. John Owen wrote, "Places there are in the world that have enjoyed the Word at God's appointed season ... but continuing unprofitable under it, what is now their state and condition?" John Owen, *The Ultimate Collected Works of 22 Books*, Kindle Edition, 2011, Kindle Locations: 121145-121146.
34. Of course one cannot minimize the damage inflicted upon the Church by Schleiermacher, Ritcshl, Harnack, and Schweitzer, which was hardly remedied by Brunner, Barth, Tillich, and Bultmann.
35. A. W. Tozer, *The Root of the Righteous*, (Harrisburg, Christian Publications, 1955), p.153.

36. Francis McGaw, *Praying Hyde*, (Minneapolis, Bethany House, 1970), p.67.
37. Dan DeHaan, *The God You Can Know*, (Chicago, Moody Press, 1982), p.19.
38. Bill Gillham, *Lifetime Guarantee*, (Brentwood, Wolgemuth and Hyatt Publishers, 1987), p.9.
39. W. Ian Thomas, *The Mystery of Godliness*, (Grand Rapids, MI., Zondervan Publishing House, 1964), p.35.
40. W. Ian Thomas, *If I Perish, I Perish*, p.84.

Chapter 10— The Foiling of Our Flesh

1. W. Ian Thomas, *If I Perish, I Perish*, p.110.
2. Ray C. Stedman, *Man of Faith*, (Portland, Multnomah Press, 1986), p.91.
3. Andrew Murray, *The Believer's Secret of the Master's Indwelling*, p.32.
4. C. S. Lewis, *The Four Loves*, p.180.
5. A. W. Tozer, *That Incredible Christian*, (Harrisburg, Christian Publications, 1964), p.42.
6. R. C. Sproul, *The Holiness of God*, p.46.
7. Judson Cornwall, *Let Us Worship*, (Plainfield, NJ., Bridge Publishing, 1983), p.76.
8. Hannah Hurnard, *Winged Life*, (Wheaton, Illinois, Tyndale House Publishers, 1985), p.35.
9. A. B. Simpson, *The Christ in the Bible Commentary*, Volume Two, p.259.
10. Ibid., p.260.
11. Andrew Murray, *The Believer's Secret of the Master's Indwelling*, p.24.
12. L. E. Maxwell, *Born Crucified*, p.31.
13. A. W. Tozer, *Gems From Tozer*, pp.43, 44.
14. Roy Hession, *Not I, But Christ*, (Fort Washington, Christian Literature Crusade, 1980), p.6.
15. G. D. Watson, *Soul Food*, p.27.
16. Vance Havner, *Reflections on the Gospels*, (Fort Washington, PA., CLC Publications, 2004), p.193.
17. Thomas Watson, *A Body of Divinity: Contained in Sermons upon the Westminster Assembly's Catechism*, p.192.
18. Ruth Paxson, *Life on the Highest Plane*, (Grand Rapids, Baker Book House, 1928), p.235.
19. F. J. Huegel, *Forever Triumphant*, (Minneapolis, Bethany Fellowship, 1955), pp.37, 38.
20. Ibid., pp.18, 19.

Endnotes

21. Francis Schaeffer conveys an inadequate understanding of reckoning by supposing that justification instead of regeneration is its foundation (Francis Schaeffer, *True Spirituality*, Wheaton, Tyndale House, 1971, p.56). We extend our faith in reckoning based on actual reality, not just judicial reality, based on capacities resident in our new nature that are able to make vital connections with God and effective connections with his promised resources.
22. In the volume, *The Epistle to the Romans, New International Commentary on the New Testament*, (Grand Rapids, Eerdmans, 1996), p.373, Douglas J. Moo contends that the our relationship to the death and resurrection of Christ should be considered in a forensic manner and not in an ontological manner. But in the most profound way our being (the new nature) *actually* experienced the death and resurrection of Jesus. The spirit of him who was on that cross and arose again on that day is now in us and is so constituted that overcoming powers of victory reside within it. What Dr. Moo says in his commendable commentary seriously diminishes this fact.
23. Anthony A. Hoekema, *Created in God's Image*, p.109.
24. F. B. Meyer, *Samuel the Prophet*, (Fort Washington, PA., Christian Literature Crusade, 1978), p.75.
25. J. Oswald Sanders, *Spiritual Problems*, (Chicago, Moody Press, 1971), p.122. Used by permission.
26. J. C. Ryle, *Holiness*, (Grand Rapids, Baker, 1984), p.xxvi.
27. Watchman Nee solves the problem many have with reckoning with this sage insight: "Unfortunately, in presenting the truth of our union with Christ the emphasis has too often been placed upon this second matter of *reckoning* ourselves to be dead, as though that were the starting point, whereas it should rather be upon knowing ourselves to be dead. God's Word makes it clear that 'knowing' is to precede 'reckoning'. "Knowing this ... reckon." That must be the sequence, or we will overload reckoning with a distorted agenda. Watchman Nee, *The Normal Christian Life*, (Fort Washington, PA., Christian Literature Crusade, 1974), p.42.
28. G. D. Watson, *Coals of Fire*, p.82.
29. G. D. Watson, *White Robes*, p.29.
30. A. W. Tozer, *Keys to the Deeper Life*, (Grand Rapids, Zondervan, 1957), pp.23, 24.
31. Jessie Penn-Lewis, *Face to Face*, (Fort Washington, PA., CLC Publications, 1999), p.110.

Endnotes

32. Ibid., p.111.
33. Roy Hession, *My Calvary Road*, (Fern, Rosk-shire, Scotland, Great Britain, 1996), p.84.
34. A. W. Tozer, *Whatever Happened To Worship?*, pp.90, 91.

Chapter 11— The Release of the Spirit

1. John Henry Jowett, *The School of Calvary*, Kindle Edition, 2010, Location: 756.
2. Dorothy L. Sayers, *The Man Born to Be King*, (Grand Rapids, Wm. B. Eerdmans Publishing Company, 1976), p.17.
3. J. Gregory Mantle, *Beyond Humiliation*, (Minneapolis, Bethany Fellowship, 1975), p.15.
4. Andrew Murray, *The Believer's Secret of The Master's Indwelling*, p.142.
5. J. H. Jowett, *The Passion for Souls*, p.84.
6. A. B. Simpson, *The Holy Spirit* Volume 2, (Harrisburg, PA., Christian Publications, n.d.), p.24.
7. Andrew Murray, *The Believer's Secret of the Master's Indwelling*, p.89.
8. Martyn Lloyd-Jones, *Joy Unspeakable*, (Wheaton, Harold Shaw Publishers, 1984), p.52.
9. Leonard Ravenhill, *Why Revival Tarries*, (Minneapolis, Bethany Fellowship, 1959), p.112.
10. G. D. Watson, *White Robes*, p.30.
11. Andrew Murray, *The Believer's Secret of the Master's Indwelling*, p.55.
12. A. B. Simpson, *The Fourfold Gospel*, p.117.
13. Charles G. Trumbull, *Victory in Christ*, (Fort Washington, Christian Literature Crusade, 1959), p.38.
14. Paul E. Billheimer, *Don't Waste Your Sorrows*, (Minneapolis, Bethany House, 1977), p.20.
15. John Henry Jowett, *A Friend on the Road and Other Studies in the Gospels*, Kindle Location: 976.
16. Jack Taylor, *The Key to Triumphant Living*, (Nashville, Broadman, 1973), p.81.
17. A. B. Simpson, *The Fourfold Gospel*, p.156.
18. Ibid., p.160.
19. F. J. Huegel, *John Looks at the Cross*, p.26.
20. A. B. Simpson, *The Larger Christian Life*, (Uhrichsville, OH., Barbour Book, 1988), p.80.
21. Andrew Murray, *The Spirit of Christ*, p.47.
22. A. W. Tozer, *Keys to the Deeper Life*, p.47.
23. Homer Duncan, ed., *Revival Fires*, (Lubbock, TX., MC

International Publications, n.d.), p.45.
24. John Owen, *The Mortification of Sin*, (Feather Trail Press, 2009), p.83.
25. G. D. Watson, *Love Abounding*, p.54.
26. Miles J. Stanford, *The Complete Green Letters*, p.180.
27. G. D. Watson, *Holiness Manual*, (Salem, Ohio, Schmul Publishing Company, 2007), p.79.
28. Clyde E. Fant, Jr. and William M. Pinson, Jr., *20 Centuries of Great Preaching, Volume Nine*, (Waco, Word Books, 1971), p.309.
29. A. B. Simpson, *The Christ in the Bible Commentary*, Volume 6, p.58.
30. A. B. Simpson, *The Fourfold Gospel*, p.159.
31. G. D. Watson, *Soul Food*, p.93.

Chapter 12— Getting God's Grace

1. A. J. Gordon, *In Christ*, (Grand Rapids, MI., Baker Book House, 1964), p.174.
2. Ruth Paxson, *Life on the Highest Plane*, p.377.
3. A. B. Simpson, *The Holy Spirit Volume 2*, p.199.
4. In George D. Watson's book, *The Secret of Spiritual Power*, (Nicholasville, Kentucky, Schmul Publishing Company, 2009), this statement is made on page 22: "We are so frail even after we are sanctified, and although all our depravity is purged away, all our faculties are so weak ...'" It seems that regardless one's view of sanctification, this weakness of the soul's faculties is widely recognized. Therefore, there is a need to daily impact the soul, which involves the usage of realities God furnished the spirit.
5. Alexander Maclaren writes, "Life comes to us pulsation by pulsation, breath by breath, by reason of the continual operation, in the material world, of the present God's present giving. He does not start us, at the beginning of our days, with a fund of physical vitality upon which we thereafter draw, but moment by moment he opens his hand, and lets life and breath and all things flow out to us ...." (*Sermons on 1 & 2 Kings*, Public Domain, Monergism Book, Kindle Locations: 447-451).
6. Stephen Charnock, *The Works of Stephen Charnock*, Kindle Locations: 8086-8087.
7. Andrew Murray, *The Believer's Secret of The Master's Indwelling*, p.45.
8. John E. Hunter, *Limiting God*, (Grand Rapids, Zondervan,

1966), p.19.

9. Stephen Charnock, *The Works of Stephen Charnock*, Kindle Locations: 9662-9663.
10. Watchman Nee, *The Spiritual Man*, (New York, Christian Fellowship Publishers, 1968), p.158.
11. F. B. Meyer, *Meet for the Master's Use*, (Chicago, Moody Press, 1898), pp.58, 59.
12. W. Ian Thomas, *The Mystery of Godliness*, pp.132-133.
13. A. B. Simpson, *The Christ in the Bible Commentary*, Volume Six, (Camp Hill, PA., WingSpread Publishers, 2009), p.279.
14. *The Speaker's Bible, The Second Epistle to the Corinthians*, Edward Hastings, ed., (Turnbull & Spears, Aberdeen, Scotland, 1933), p.223.
15. Ibid., p.92.
16. A. W. Tozer, *Faith Beyond Reason*, p.10.
17. Andrew Murray, *With Christ in the School of Prayer*, (Grand Rapids, Fleming H. Revell, 1963), p.80.
18. James S. Stewart, *River of Life*, p.105.
19. F. B. Meyer, *Meet for the Master's Use*. p.91.
20. Jerry Bridges, *The Discipline of Grace*, (Colorado Springs, CO., Navpress, 1994), p.18.
21. From an unpublished sermon by Wayne DeHoney entitled, "A Talk with Yourself."
22. A. B. Simpson, *When God Steps In*, (Camp Hill, PA., Christian Publications, 1997), p.vii.
23. F. B. Meyer, *Christ in Isaiah*, (Fort Washington, PA., CLC Publications, 2001), p.11.
24. Note the double emphasis in this verse: abounding, abundance—about which Thomas Goodwin speaks "of this great big swelling word ... overflowing, gushed out" to indicate its remarkable extent (*The Works of Thomas Goodwin, Volume I*, p.130).
25. G. D. Watson, *White Robes*, p.70.
26. *The Works of Thomas Goodwin*, Volume 1, p.149.
27. On page 31 of his book, *Humanity and God*, Samuel Chadwick wrote these words about the grace that defeats sin and restores character, "Grace goes over the trail of sin, track its innermost recesses, destroys its power, undoes its mischief, and turns its very weapons to its own destruction."
28. On page 31 of his book, *The Gospel of Healing*, (Camp Hill, PA., WingSpread Publications, 1986), A. B. Simpson wrote: "The natural and the spiritual, the earthly and the

heavenly, the works of man and the grace of God cannot be mixed any more than a person could expect to harness a tortoise with a locomotive. They cannot work together."

29. Martyn Lloyd-Jones, *Romans Exposition of Chapter 6, The New Man*, p.129.
30. F. B. Meyer, *Joshua*, (Fort Washington, PA, Christian Literature Crusade, 1977), p.129.
31. Thomas Goodwin recalls how bitterness can take up the supposed offense of another which never even existed. Goodwin writes: "In the Old Testament, Joshua, though he proved a man of a choice spirit, yet when he was young in years, and but a young beginner in grace, envy rose up in him, for his good master, Moses' sake. Eldad and Medad prophesy, says he, Num. xi. 29; 'but Moses said to him, Enviest thou for my sake?' and so reproved him ...'" Moses never felt that prophesy was solely his privilege among the people. Yet, Joshua took up this perceived offense against Moses, only to hear Moses say, "Would God that all the Lord's people were prophets; and that the Lord would put his Spirit upon them!'" Thomas Goodwin, *Patience and Its Perfect Work*, (Kindle Edition, 2010, Kindle Locations: 285-288).
32. Thomas Watson, *A Body of Divinity: Contained in Sermons upon the Westminster Assembly's Catechism*, p.250.
33. Roy Hession, *When I Saw Him*, (Fort Washington, PA., CLC Publications, 1975), p.50.
34. A. B. Simpson, *The Fourfold Gospel*, p.214.
35. A. B. Simpson, *The Christ Life*, p.50.
36. *The Works of Thomas Goodwin, Volume 1*, p.287.
37. Evan H. Hopkins, *Practical Holiness*, (Fort Washington, PA., CLC Publications, 2003), pp.12, 13.
38. Erich Sauer, *The King of the Earth*, p.123.
39. Ibid., p.123.

Chapter 13—The Renewed Mind

1. G. D. Watson, *White Robes*, p.32.
2. A. W. Tozer, *I Talk Back to the Devil*, (Camp Hill, PA., Christian Publications, 1972), p.101.
3. James Orr, *The Christian View of God and the World*, (Grand Rapids, Eerdmans, 1954), p.21.
4. On page 10 of his book, *Heavenly Life*, G. D. Watson states, "There are four Greek words translated mind—one signifies the apprehending faculty, another the reasoning

faculty, another the judging or determining faculty, and yet another suggests the imaginative faculty ...." Each of these functions of the mind need to be sanctified.

5. Martyn Lloyd-Jones, *Romans Exposition of Chapter 6, The New Man*, p.169.
6. Ibid., p.173.
7. A. B. Simpson, *The Christ in the Bible Commentary*, Volume Six, p.371.
8. *The Speaker's Bible, James*, James Hastings, ed., (Aberdeen, Scotland, G. & W. Fraser, Limited, 1926), p.26.
9. J. H. Jowett pondered this confusion when he wrote: "If two men are at the wheel with opposing notions of direction and destiny, how will it fare with the boat? If an orchestra have two conductors, both wielding their batons at the same time with conflicting conceptions of the score, what will become of the band?" J. H. Jowett, *My Daily Meditation for the Circling Year*, (New York and Chicago, Fleming H. Revell, 1914), p.292.
10. G. D. Watson, *A Pot of Oil*, p.32.
11. A. B. Simpson, *The Christ in the Bible Commentary*, Volume Two, p.75.
12. Ibid. p.93.
13. A. W. Tozer, *Man: the Dwelling Place of God*, (Camp Hill, PA., Christian Publications, 1993), p.168.
14. Ibid., p.162.
15. *The Speaker's Bible, The Second Epistle to the Corinthians*, Edward Hastings, ed., p.147.
16. In his book, *The Tripartite Nature of Man*, John B. Heard observed that in "the generation after Luther popular Lutheranism was as dead in notional theology as Rome was in ceremonial." Whether the form be ideational or ritual, it can have a chilling effect on vibrant faith. John B. Heard, *Bibliotheca Sacra*, "The Tripartite Nature of Man," Volume: BSAC 058:232 (Oct 1901), p.216.
17. A. W. Tozer, *And He Dwelt Among Us*, p.187.
18. After quoting Romans 12:2, Hannah Whitall Smith summarized its intended outcome by saying: "A real work is to be wrought in us and upon us. Besetting sins are to be conquered; evil habits are to be overcome; wrong dispositions and feelings are to be rooted out; and holy tempers and emotions are to be begotten" (*The Christian's Secret of a Happy Life*, p.21).
19. Bill Gillham, *Lifetime Guarantee*, pp.113, 114.
20. Ibid., p. 115.

21. A. B. Simpson, *Wholly Sanctified*, (Camp Hill, PA., Christian Publications, 1991), pp.83, 84.
22. We shouldn't uncritically accept the assertion that those in the inner healing movement and those counseling integrationists who accept psychoanalytic assumptions typically set forth. Their attempts to connect the unconscious with Scripture are not at all persuasive. Saying that the wicked heart which cannot be known (Jeremiah 17:9) refers to the unconscious is an imposition on the text and not a conclusion drawn from it. Yet, writers like Leanne Payne, in her book, *The Healing Presence: Curing the Soul Through Union with Christ*, (Baker Books, 1995, p.136), seek in vain to make this connection with Scripture. Another feeble attempt is made by Larry Crabb in his book, *Inside Out* (Colorado Springs, Co., Navpress, 1988), when Jesus' words to the Pharisees about cleaning the inside of the cup (Matthew 23:25, 26) becomes a justification for psychoanalytic inspection of the unconscious mind. A huge paradigm shift takes place if an interpretation like this is allowed. In Scripture, man is dealt with as a rational being, responsible before God, with each Divine directive appealing to his conscious faculties. The unconscious (in any psychoanalytic sense) is completely bypassed. Scripture never enmeshes spiritual with the unconscious domain psychoanalysts are so determined to investigate. The Scripture-twisting that then ensues from those who take this approach invariably demeans the Word and elevates the psychotherapist.
23. James S. Stewart, *A Man in Christ*, p.159.
24. G. D. Watson, *Spiritual Feasts*, pp.41, 41.
25. David C. Needham, *Birthright*, p.230.
26. G. D. Watson, *Pure Gold*, p.75.
27. Stephen Charnock, *The Works of Stephen Charnock*, Kindle Locations: 3671-3672.

Chapter 14—The Protected Heart

1. Eddie Radice, translator, *In Praise of Folly*, (London, Penguin, 1971) p.87.
2. Connecting emotions to the heart, as the title of this chapter implies, has some biblical justification, even though Gordon Clark is correct in his estimate that less than fifteen percent of biblical references to the heart make reference to emotions. The more frequent attribution to heart is intellect, not emotion. Yet, emotions are rooted in

cognitions, both of which are attributes of the heart.

3. C. S. Lewis said, "I think we all sin by needlessly disobeying the apostolic injunction to "rejoice" as by anything else." C. S. Lewis, *The Problem of Pain*, New York, The Macmillan Company, 1962), p.67.
4. F. B. Meyer, *Israel*, (Fort Washington, PA., CLC Publications, 2002), p.98.
5. A. B. Simpson, *The Fourfold Gospel*, (Alachua, FL., Bridge-Logos, 2007), p.226.
6. Charles G. Trumbull, *Victory in Christ*, p.81.
7. A. B. Simpson, *The Christ in the Bible Commentary*, Volume Five, p.503.
8. Ibid., p.504.
9. Ibid., p.504.
10. Ibid., p.512.
11. Thomas Goodwin, *Patience and Its Perfect Work*, Kindle Locations: 33-34.
12. F. B. Meyer, *Meet for the Mater's Use*, p.73.
13. A. B. Simpson, *The Christ in the Bible Commentary*, Volume Two (Camp Hill, PA.,WingSpread Publishers, 2009), p.313.
14. Mr. and Mrs. Howard Taylor, *Hudson Taylor's Spiritual Secret*, pp.162, 163.
15. F. B. Meyer, *Jeremiah*, (Fort Washington, PA., CLC Publications, 2002), p.67.
16. Jeremiah Burroughs, the seventeenth-century Puritan, points out how Satan lacks peace and therefore is doubly determined to steal it from others so they will become like him. "The Devil is the most discontented creature in the world, he is the proudest creature that is, and the most discontented creature, and the most dejected creature. Now, therefore, so much discontent as you have, so much of the spirit of Satan you have." *The Rare Jewel of Contentment*, (Lafayette, IN., Sovereign Grace Publishers Inc., 2001), p.71.
17. John A. MacMillan, *The Authority of the Believer*, (Camp Hill, PA., WingSpread Publishers, 1982), p.66.
18. *Ibid.*, pp.69, 70.
19. Dietrich Bonhoeffer, *Life Together*, (San Francisco, Harper and Row, 1954), p.112.

Chapter 15—The Surrendered Will

1. See Appendix A.
2. George MacDonald, *Life Essential*, (Wheaton, Harold

Shaw Publishers, 1954), p.17.
3. A. B. Simpson, *Seeing the Invisible*, (Camp Hill, Christian Publications, 1994), p.215.
4. Andrew Murray, *The Secret of the Throne of Grace*, (Fort Washington, PA., CLC Publications, 1998), p.46.
5. Horatius Bonar, *God's Way of Holiness*, p.68.
6. Ruth Paxson, *Life on the Highest Plane*, p.321.
7. A. B. Simpson, *Wholly Sanctified*, (Camp Hill, PA., Christian Publications, 1991), p.89.
8. Jesse-Penn-Lewis, *Communion with God*, (Fort Washington, PA., CLC Publications, 1996). p.10.
9. A. W. Tozer, *Faith Beyond Reason*, (Camp Hill, WingSpread Publishers, 2009), p.57.
10. Jessie Penn-Lewis, *Fruitful Living*, (Fort Washington, PA., CLC Publications, 1998), p.37.
11. Ibid., p.37.
12. Author unknown, *The Power-Filled Christian*, pp.80, 81.
13. George MacDonald, *The Best of George MacDonald*, p.102.
14. Ibid., pp.91, 92.
15. A. W. Tozer, *Whatever Happened to Worship?*, p.124.
16. J. C. Ryle, *Holiness*, p.xv.
17. Jessie Penn-Lewis, *Fruitful Living*, p.42.
18. Charles Spurgeon, *According to Promise*, (Chicago, The Moody Press, 1975), p.85.
19. H. A. Ironside, *Full Assurance*, (Chicago, Moody Press, 1968), pp.96, 97.
20. A. W. Tozer, *The Root of the Righteous*, p.127.
21. Os Guinness, *The Dust of Death*, p.10.
22. Henry Drummond, *The Changed Life*, (Dixon, Mo., Rare Christian Books, n.d.), p.2.
23. Jessie Penn-Lewis, *Life out of Death*, (Fort Washington, PA., CLC Publications, 1991), p.94.
24. William Barclay, *In the Hands of God*, (New York, Harper and Row, 1966), pp.97, 98.
25. C. S. Lewis, *The World's Last Night*, (New York and London, Harcourt Brace Jovanovich, Inc., 1959), p.92.
26. Lloyd J. Ogilvie, *Life Without Limits*, (Waco, Word, 1975), p.76.
27. Jessie Penn-Lewis, *Fruitful Living*, p.17.
28. J. C. Ryle, *Holiness*, p.xii.
29. William Law, *A Serious Call to a Devout and Holy Life*, (Grand Rapids, MI., William B. Eerdmans, 1966), p.17.
30. A. W. Tozer, *That Incredible Christian*, p.64.

31. G. D. Watson, *A Pot of Oil*, p.34.
32. Ibid., p.35.
33. T. Austin Sparks wrote, "If Christ had asserted himself, instead of referring and deferring to the Father, Satan would have triumphed." T. Austin Sparks, *What is Man?*, Kindle Locations: 1009-1010. An over-reliance upon self's will, even if the will's purpose is honorable, is easily defeated by Satan. And therefore T. Austin Sparks wrote, "A forceful, dominating, assertive soul, not under the government of the Holy Spirit, is a terrible menace to the interests of God. Decisions will be made, courses adopted, objectives secured, positions occupied, in the name of devotion to God, which will be Towers of Babel, Pyramids of Egypt, Ishmaels of Abram (not Abraham)." T. Austin Sparks, *What is Man?*, Kindle Locations: 988-990.
34. Roy Hession, *When I Saw Him*, p.27.
35. Miles J. Stanford, *The Complete Green Letters*, p.21.
36. Andrew Murray, *In Search of Spiritual Excellence*, p.78.
37. Andrew Murray, *The Believer's Absolute Surrender*, p.118.
38. Hannah Whitall Smith, *The Christian's Secret of a Happy Life*, p.62.
39. F. J. Huegel, *Bone of His Bone*, p.38.
40. A. W. Tozer, *That Incredible Christian*, p.31.
41. Charles Finney, *How to Experience the Higher Life*, (Kindle Edition, 2010, Locations: 275-276).
42. Samuel Rutherford letter to William Gordon, written February 20, 1637.
43. A. B. Simpson, *The Gospel of Healing*, pp.88-89.
44. Andrew Murray, "God Maintains Your Surrender," located on the website sermonindex.net under Sermon Texts.
45. A. B. Simpson, *The Christ Life*, p.58.
46. A. J. Gordon, *In Christ*, p.144.

Chapter 16—New Nature Benefits

1. In his book, *Behind the Veil* (available for reading on line through the Worthy Christian Library website), A. B. Simpson further addresses the criterion which credentials Christianity by the superior character it produces. He does this by referring to Jesus himself, as well as to those listed in the hall of fame chapter of the Bible, Hebrews chapter 11. Simpson asserts, "The eleventh chapter of Hebrews is a star cluster in the firmament of inspired biography." Simpson then writes: "Just as the character of Jesus Christ is the supreme evidence of the divinity of His teachings, so

these ancient lives bear witness to a source of power and goodness infinitely higher than mere human virtue." There is a dramatic contrast to these lives which Simpson subsequently points out: "Look for a moment at the divinities of heathen religions: the coarse and brutal Ram, the household god of India; the cruel Kali, their Supreme female divinity; or even their venerated Buddha himself, who was but a dreamer. Look at the heroes of Greek and Roman history, Aeneas, Romulus, Achilles, Hercules; or at their fabled deities, the imperious Jupiter, the licentious Venus, or any of the real or ideal figures that loom out of the gray antiquity of the world's traditions" (chapter 6, paragraph 2). What these other religions admired hardly compares with the virtues espoused and lived by followers of the one true God. "By their fruit you shall know them," Jesus said. And indeed one's nature, one's character, does provide strong evidence of the authenticity of the biblical message.

2. A. W. Tozer, *The Set of the Sail*, p.103.
3. A. J. Gordon, *In Christ*, p.11.
4. E. M. Bounds, *Winning the Invisible War*, p.10.
5. From an unpublished sermon by Bruce Wideman, entitled "The Cross."
6. G. D. Watson, *Soul Food*, p.47.
7. Ruth Paxson, *Life on the Highest Plane*, p.233.
8. J. I. Packer, *Keep in Step with the Spirit*, (Grand Rapids, BakerBooks, 2005), pp.103, 99.
9. Like many in the Reformed tradition who share this perspective, many of the Puritans shared it as well. *The Valley of Vision*, which is a book edited by Arthur Bennett, includes Puritan sentiments like these: "Lowest abasement is my due place for I am less than nothing before Thee" (p.88); "I am ... one that has nothing and is nothing" (p.91); "I am less than nothing, a creature worse than nothing" (p.95); "I come before Thee as a sinner condemned by conscience and Thy Word" (p.193).
10. Thomas Watson, *The Doctrine of Repentance*, Kindle Locations: 82-83.
11. E. M. Bounds, *E. M. Bounds on Prayer*, (New Kensington, PA, Whitaker House, 1997), p.158.
12. Andrew Murray, *In Search of Spiritual Excellence*, p.88.
13. *The Christian World Pulpit*, Volume 82, (London, James Clarke and Co., 1912), p.221.

Endnotes

14. By speaking of Paul in this manner, we accommodate his manner of speaking in Romans 7 without conceding the point that in fact Romans 7 may not, as such, be autobiographical and certainly does not represent the dilemma of a regenerate person (see Appendix F).
15. A. B. Simpson, *Apostolic Testimony*, (Worthy Christian Library, Chapter 6, paragraph 3).
16. To talk so much about forgiveness and so little about the new nature is a huge mistake. Steve McVey observed, "Today's brand of evangelism has continued to present forgiveness, but generally ignores the aspect of receiving divine life at salvation" (*Grace Walk*, p.158). This omission seriously deprives the believer from knowing God's best exit plan from sin.
17. Judson Cornwall, *The Best of Judson Cornwall*, p.131.
18. Josh McDowell, *Building Your Self-Image*, (Wheaton, Tyndale House Publishers, 1986), p.26.
19. Jessie Penn Lewis, *Life in the Spirit*, p.56.
20. While there are obvious truths embedded in the theme, knowing our true identity, this motif may mask more than it discloses. This is because the concept of identity is somewhat broad. In normal discourse identity can be discussed in terms of finger prints, genetic code, race, gender, citizenship, career choice, a badge, a license, a credit card number, and other such criteria. Yet, one can have information about all these things and scarcely know the person at all! When it comes to discovering who a person really is, a focus on the new nature is much more revealing than is a discussion of our identity, especially if the identity issue is mostly forensic, going no further than a discussion of imputed righteousness. The same deficits of disclosure, by the way, are also attached to the subject, union with Christ. Somehow, this subject has attracted abstract thinking and a comparison of paradigms offered by different theological schools of thought. Meanwhile, specific and helpful information about our new nature remains almost entirely out of view.
21. A. W. Tozer, *God's Greatest Gift to Man*, (Harrisburg, PA., n.d.), pp.9, 10.
22. Ibid., p.5.
23. There are reality-based counterparts to this fictitious story. In 2004 Russian authorities discovered seven-year old Andrei Tolstyk abandoned by his parents in a remote area of Siberia. For several years the boy's only companion had

been a guard dog. Incapable of speech, the little boy barked and growled when upset and bit people when provoked. He also adopted other canine characteristics, such as walking on all-fours and sniffing his food before he ate. Tolstyk was not the first boy in Russia to have been raised by dogs. In 1998, police found six year-old Ivan Myshukov near Moscow; and when discovered, Ivan functioned as the leader of a pack of dogs. Each boy thought he was a dog and acted as if he were a dog because the image reinforced by environment dictated that impression.

24. Charles Hodge, *Commentary on the Epistle to the Romans*, (Grand Rapids, MI., Wm. B. Eerdmans, reprint, 1955; 1986), p.290.
25. David C. Needham, *Birthright*, p.159.
26. F. B. Meyer, *Jeremiah*, (Fort Washington, PA., CLC Publications, 2002), p.55.
27. While it is true that the two times we see the term "led by the Spirit" in the New Testament are not cited as modalities for information dispensing, it is also true that the leading the Spirit gave to Jesus (Matthew 4:1) and Paul (Acts 16:6, 7) did include information being dispensed.
28. A. B. Simpson, *The Christ in the Bible Commentary*, Volume 5, (Camp Hill, PA., WingSpread Publishers, 2009), p.383.
29. Andrew Murray, *The Spirit of Christ*, p.78.
30. Ibid., p.78.
31. Judson Cornwall, *Let Us Worship*, (South Plainfield, Bridge Publishing, Inc., 1983), p.96.
32. Jessie Penn-Lewis, *Life out of Death*, p.61.
33. Andrew Murray, *The Believer's Absolute Surrender*, p.26.
34. G. D. Watson, *Spiritual Feasts*, p.38.
35. Jessie Penn-Lewis, *Spiritual Warfare*, (Fort Washington, PA., CLC Publications, 2006), pp.73, 74.
36. *The Valley of Visions*, Edited by Arthur Bennett, (Edinburg, UK, The Banner of Truth Trust, 2011), p.51.

Chapter 17—Clarifying Contrasts

1. Stephen Charnock, *The Works of Stephen Charnock*, (Kindle Edition, 2011, Location: 1038).
2. J. N. Darby, *The Collected Writings of J. N. Darby*, (London, G. Morrish, 1914), Volume X, p.53.
3. C. S. Lewis, *Mere Christianity*, p.174.
4. F. J. Huegel, *Forever Triumphant*, p.66.

5. Steven Barabas, *So Great Salvation*, p.87.
6. Alexander Whyte is reported to have said to his church that they will never get out of Romans, chapter 7, as long as he was the minister of the church. Many evangelicals, particularly those who adhere to Augustinian theology, make this same error. Perhaps the most obvious defect in J. I. Packer's book, *Keep in Step with the Spirit*, is his failure to expound Romans 8:2. Packer discusses Romans 7 on 88 pages, but mentions Romans 8:2—without explanation even—in only 2 paragraphs. This is difficult to understand, because Paul's explanation of victory is set forth in Romans 8:2 and not in Romans 7. In Romans 8:2, Paul very specifically connects the victory with the struggle of Romans 7. So why leave this verse out?
7. Paul E. Billheimer, *Destined to Overcome*, (Minneapolis, Bethany House, 1982), p.35.
8. Dr. and Mrs. Taylor, *Hudson Taylor's Spiritual Secret*, p.173.
9. Charles G. Finney, *Principles of Holiness*, (Minneapolis, Bethany House, 1984), p.221.
10. F. B. Meyer, *Elijah and the Secret of His Power*, (Chicago, Moody Press, 1976), p.110.
11. Some of these views resonate with believers today, and do so to an extent people can't imagine why these views should be questioned. Partial explanations for doing so surface in this book but are dealt with more directly and comprehensively in *Pursuing God*, Volume Two.
12. Steven Barabas, *So Great Salvation*, p.97.
13. Ibid., p.97.
14. Charles Finney, *Power from on High*, (Telfair, PA., Worthy Christian Library website, chapter 10).
15. Oswald Chambers, *The Psychology of Redemption*,), p.51.
16. John E. Hunter, *Knowing God's Secrets*, (Grand Rapids, Zondervan, 1974), p.28.
17. John E. Hunter, *Limiting God*, p.23.
18. Norman Grubb, *Rees Howell Intercessor*, (Fort Washington, PA., Christian Literature Crusade, 1952), p.62.

Appendix A—Soul and Spirit

1. R. A. Torrey, "True Christian Union," printed text found on sermonindex.net

Endnotes

2. Charles Hodge, *Systematic Theology, Volume II*, (Grand Rapids, MI; Christian Classics Etheral Library, 2005), p.506.
3. Ibid., p.507.
4. This type of thinking appears to resonate in some respects with Cyril of Alexandria, who construed union with Christ as participating in the energies of Christ. The aversion to seeing an ontological foundation for this union assumes that to grant this premise is to breach the Creator/creature distinction. But this premise is false, since commonality of essence hardly requires identity of functional attributes such as omnipotence. Even the ineffable qualities of God related to being are excluded from our union with Christ in that he is the originator, not we; and all that we are is in its genesis derivative and in its history defective. Nevertheless, in the words of the 14th century theologian Nicholas Cabasallis, union with Christ "is closer than any other union which man can possibly imagine and does not lend itself to any exact comparisons."
5. Samuel Whittlesey Howland wrote, "The earlier Christian fathers, as Irenæus, Justin Martyr, Origen, and others, held a tripartite view as to man's nature, as the most natural interpretation of Scripture." Bibliotheca Sacra, "The Tripartite Nature of Man," Volume: BSAC 058:232 (Oct 1901).
6. Gordon H. Clark, *The Biblical Doctrine of Man*, (Jefferson, MO., The Trinity Foundation, 1984) pp.34, 35.
7. John Laidlaw, *The Bible Doctrine of Man*, (Edinburgh, T. & T. Clark, 1895), p.67. Likewise, Franz Delitzsch cited three errors that proved prejudicial against trichotomy despite the prevailing status of this view during the first two centuries. Besides, the "Apollinarian error, that Christ had body and soul in common with us, but that the eternal Logos had in him usurped the place of the Spirit." Delitzsch was particularly critical of the "The semi-Pelagian error, that the spirit is excepted from the original sin which affected the body and soul ...." This view, Delitzsch said, "probably contributed most of all to make our old dogmatists averse from trichotomy." Franz Delitzsch, *A System of Biblical Psychology* (Edinburgh, T. & T. Clark, 1985), p.106.
8. A. B. Simpson, *The Fourfold Gospel*, p.65.
9. Samuel Chadwick, *The Way to Pentecost*, p.150.

Endnotes

10. Watchman Nee, *The Spiritual Man, Volume 1*, (New York, Christian Fellowship, 1968), p.22.
11. T. Austin Sparks, *What is Man?* (The Online Library of T. Austin Sparks, found under first heading of first chapter).
12. Even Anthony Hoekema, a theologian who correctly recognized the death of our old man, adopted a more monist view, saying "One of the most important aspects to the Christian view of man is that we must see him in his unity, as a whole man ... in Christian circles man has been thought of as consisting of 'body' and 'soul,' or as 'body,' 'soul' and 'spirit.' Both secular scientists and Christian theologians, however, are increasingly recognizing that such an understanding of human beings is wrong, and that man must be seen in his unity." (Anthony A. Hoekema, *Created in God's Image*, p.203.) While Hoekema's statement is objectionable on several levels, the most obvious argument against it is its assumption that recognition of distinct parts of man amounts to a denial of the whole man. This assumption is false. Acknowledging functional differences in man hardly sets aside an integral connection between these differing functional parts. The rhetoric of "unity" and "whole man" certainly appeals to modern minds, and does possess the additional advantage of sounding like truisms. But such a contrived concept must not be allowed to obscure the fact that the locus of the new nature is uniquely the domain of man's spirit. Of course, body and soul should benefit as new nature qualities emerge from the domain of the believer's spirit to impact them. However, body and soul receive; they do not generate. A monist model utterly obscures this point; and if accepted, dooms an understanding of the new nature to the abstract status it has had for so long. It is somewhat ironic that I Thessalonians 5:23 harmonizes the concept of unity and differences by specifically citing each part of man and then speaking of sanctifying us "wholly," or as some translations word it, "entirely." The monist model muddies what Scripture presents clearly.
13. Wayne Grudem, *Systematic Theology*, (Intervarsity Press, 38 De Montforth Street, Leicester LE17GP, Great Britain, and by Zondervan Publishing House, 5300 Patterson Avenue S. E., Grand Rapids, Michigan, USA., 1994), p.481.
14. Ibid, p.481.
15. Ibid,. p.475.
16. A. B. Simpson, *The Fourfold Gospel*, p.153.

Endnotes

17. John Laidlaw, *The Bible Doctrine of Man*, p.94.
18. Ibid., p.94.
19. A. T. Pierson, webpage 6.
20. Jessie Penn-Lewis, *The Story of Job*, p.154.
21. Martin Luther, *A Commentary on St. Paul's Epistle to the Galatians*, ed. Philip S. Watson (Westwood, NJ: Fleming H. Revell, n.d.), p.501.
22. C. H. Lenski, *The Interpretation of St. Paul's Epistles to the Galatians, to the Ephesians, and to the Philippians* (Columbus, OH: Wartburg Press, 1946), p.281.
23. John Calvin, *Calvin's Commentaries: Romans–Galatians*, p.1921.
24. Wayne Grudem, *Systematic Theology*, p.479.
25. Jessie Penn-Lewis, *Life in the Spirit*, p.54.
26. Norman P. Grubb, *God Unlimited*, pp.116-117.
27. On page 49 of George D. Watson's book, *The Secret of Spiritual Power*, there is this helpful soul/spirit distinction set forth regarding the realm impacted by affliction: "If we take the catalogue of all possible affliction, the loss of health, the pinch of poverty, the tongue of slander, the desolation of bereavement, the eclipse of reason, the dungeon of imprisonment, the red scorch of persecution and death itself, they are all on the outer, earthly side of the soul. They cannot penetrate the inner citadel of the spirit, nor break the union of a perfectly loyal heart with its God."
28. Norman Grubb, *The Key to Everything*, (Fort Washington, PA., CLC Publications, 1960), p.42.
29. Jay E. Adams, *More Than Redemption*, (New Jersey, Presbyterian and Reformed, 1979), p.112.
30. W. E. Vine, *An Expository Dictionary of New Testament Words*, (Westwood, NJ., Fleming H. Revell Company, 1966), p.328.
31. F. J. Huegel, *Bone of His Bone*, p.68.
32. John Laidlaw, *The Bible Doctrine of Man*, p.95.
33. In his book, *The Holy Spirit*, Volume 1, A. B. Simpson distinguished the old heart and the old covenant with the new heart and new covenant by saying: "The old covenant gave light and law, but it did not give the power and disposition to obey it. But the new covenant writes it in our inmost being; makes it part of our very nature; incorporates it into our will, our choice, our desires, our very intuitions, so that it becomes second nature to us, our

spontaneous desire, and our deepest life." (Chapter 19, paragraph 42).

34. Appendix F explains why this chapter may not have referred to Paul, but was set forth in a dialogical manner in order to make more vivid the point. In this same manner, I will continue this analysis. Appendix F also explains why most of Romans 7 refers to a pre-converted Jew, but stipulates which verses refer to a born-again believer. Quite obviously, personality functions of the pre-converted have an affinity with those faculty descriptions that are, for purposes of theological classification, placed in the Old Testament bin.

35. On page 51 of his book, *Heavenly Life*, G. D. Watson contends that emotions can be generated from the spirit and not just from the soul and body. Since God is a spirit, this helps to explain how he can experience emotions. The intrusion of Platonic thought isn't the only source of the anthropopathic hypothesis. Dichotomous thinking also contributes to the error.

36. Jessie Penn-Lewis, *Soul and Spirit*, (Fort Washington, PA., CLC Publications, 2005), p.146.

37. Jessie Penn-Lewis, *Soul and Spirit*, p.109.

38. Ibid., p.12.

39. T. Austin Sparks, *The Things of the Spirit*, (Jacksonville, FL., SeedSower Publishing House, reprinted, 2004), p.12.

40. John Laidlaw, *The Bible Doctrine of Man*, p.96.

41. *The Works of Thomas Goodwin, Volume 1*, p.366.

42. British scholar John B. Heard asserts, "The *psyche* is like the flesh, prone to evil, and remains so, yea, even in the regenerate. But the *pneuma* or godlike in man is not prone to evil—indeed it cannot sin." John B. Heard, *The Tripartite Nature of Man*, (Edinburgh, T & T Clark, 1875), p.218.

43. Ibid., p.359.

44. Ibid., p.359.

45. George Eldon Ladd, *A Theology of the New Testament*, (Grand Rapids, Eerdmans, 1974), p.459.

46. A. B. Simpson, *The Holy Spirit, Volume 1*, (Chapter 2, paragraph 14).

47. A. B. Simpson, *Wholly Sanctified*, (Camp Hill, PA., Christian Publications, 1991), p.27.

48. John B. Heard stated succinctly, "Where this mastery of the spirit over the soul, and the soul over the body is

complete, there sanctification is complete also." *The Tripartite Nature of Man*, p.220.

49. This transformation of soul is now possible, T. Austin Sparks declared, because the upsetting of the Divine order in Eden has now been reversed. "In the new creation in Christ, the principles of the true Divine order are re-established. The spirit quickened, raised, indwelt, and united with Christ is set to be the organ of Divine government over the rest of man, soul, and body." T. Austin Sparks, *What is Man?* Kindle Locations: 460-461.
50. G. D. Watson, *Soul Food*, p.76.

Appendix B—Enlightenment Through Our Spirit

1. Jessie-Penn Lewis, *War on the Saints*, (New Kensington, PA, Whitaker House, 1996), p.234.
2. Oswald Chambers, *The Psychology of Redemption*, p.53.
3. The plight of "earnest" Christians brings to mind Faber's brief but blunt retort, "Earnestness is not theology." Frederick W. Faber, *All for Jesus*, (London, Richardson and Son, 1854), p.95. Sincere people can think all sorts of things, but as Faber insisted, "There is but one view of things which is true, and that is God's view of them." (Ibid., p.167).
4. Blaise Pascal, *Pensees*, p.127.
5. G. D. Watson, *Holiness Manual*, p.63.
6. Martyn Lloyd-Jones, *Romans Exposition of Chapter 6, The New Man*, p.247.
7. F. J. Huegel, *Bone of His Bone*, p.49.
8. C. S. Lewis, *Miracles*, (New York, The Macmillan Company, 1973), p.112.
9. David C. K. Watson, *My God Is Real*, (New York, The Seabury Press, 1969), pp.79, 80.
10. Oswald Chambers, *Bringing Sons Unto Glory*, (Grand Rapids, Discovery House Publishers, 1991), p.40.
11. G. D. Watson, *Holiness Manual*, p.83.
12. A. W. Tozer, *The Set of the Sail*, p.66.
13. Andrew Murray, *The School of Obedience*, (Chicago, Moody Press, 1990), p.93.
14. A. W. Tozer, *Gems from Tozer*, p.18.
15. A. B. Simpson, *In Step with the Spirit*, p.41.
16. William Law, *Wholly for God*, (Minneapolis, Bethany House Publishers, 1976), p.33.
17. Martyn Lloyd-Jones, *Joy Unspeakable*, (Wheaton, Harold Shaw Publishers, 1989), p.111.

18. G. D. Watson, *The Seven Overcomeths*, p.100.
19. Martyn Lloyd-Jones, *Joy Unspeakable.*, p.111.
20. Ibid., p.73.
21. Ibid., p.112, 113.
22. Ibid., p.107.
23. A. B. Simpson, *The Fourfold Gospel*, p.254.
24. Ibid., p.139.
25. Ibid., p.139.
26. Ibid., p.139.
27. Oswald Chambers, *The Psychology of Redemption*, p.20.
28. A. W. Tozer, *The Set of the Sail*, p.67.
29. Thomas Watson, The Godly Man's Picture, p.21.
30. Jessie Penn-Lewis, *Power for Service*, (Fort Washington, PA., (CLC Publications, 1998), pp.68, 69.
31. G. D. Watson, *A Pot of Oil*, p.33.
32. G. D. Watson, *Our Own God*, p.159.
33. A. B. Simpson, *The Holy Spirit*, Volume 1, Chapter 2, paragraph 13.
34. J. H. Jowett, *Brooks by the Traveler's Way*, p.44.

Appendix C—Our Spirit and God's Will

1. F. F. Bosworth, *Christ the Healer*, (Old Tappan, NJ., Fleming H. Revell Co., 1973), p.40.
2. It is true that the dynamic of trust will re-emerge during a faith transaction, especially when the waiting is long and the manifestation of answered prayer doesn't yet exist. However, the releasing of trust in this context is appreciably more advanced than the type of trust with which many in the church are too long acquainted.
3. A. B. Simpson, *The Fourfold Gospel*, p.206.
4. On page 84 of his book, *The Psychology of Redemption*, Oswald Chambers said, "The agony of our Lord in Gethsemane is not typical of what we go through, any more than his cross is typical of our cross. We know nothing about Gethsemane in personal experience. Gethsemane and Calvary stand for something unique ...."
5. G. D. Watson, *Love and Duty*, p.13.
6. Ibid., p.14.
7. A. B. Simpson, *The Land of Promise*, (Camp Hill, PA., Christian Publications, 1996), p.26.
8. R. A. Torrey, "True Praying," text found in sermon.index.net
9. E. M. Bounds, *E. M. Bounds on Prayer*, p.602.
10. Jessie Penn-Lewis, *Face to Face*, p.58.

11. A. B. Simpson, *The Fourfold Gospel*, p.205.
12. Andrew Murray, *With Christ in the School of Prayer*, (Westwood, N. J., Fleming H. Revell, 1963), p.81.
13. John A. Macmillan, *The Authority of the Believer*, p.50.
14. When commenting on the three groans in this passage, G. D. Watson interjected a literal groaning of the cosmos when he wrote: "It has been noticed by scientific men that every sound in the natural world is in a minor key. The breaking of the waves, the moaning of the wind, the rippling of the streams, the bleat of cattle, the singing of birds; every single sound in the natural world is in a minor key, as if, in spite of all the charms of nature and the beauties of creation, there is still a curse that pervades every atom of the world about us which is expressed in tones of sadness ...." (*God's Eagles*, p.87).
15. The commentary on this verse from The Speaker's Bible supports this point. "The word 'helpeth' is only used twice in the New Testament, the other passage being in Luke x. 40, where Martha begs the assistance of Mary to help her in the work she is doing—to share with her in serving. It is used a few times in Greek translations of the Old Testament, and always with this same meaning; not to do something in place of another, but to share something with another." *The Speaker's Bible, The Epistle to the Romans*, Volume I, James Hastings, ed., (Aberdeen, Scotland, G. & W. Fraser, 1936), p.155.
16. Norman P. Grubb, *God Unlimited*, p.163.
17. *The Works of Thomas Goodwin*, Volume I, p.134.
18. Jessie Penn-Lewis, *Life in the Spirit*, (10 Marlborough Road, Parkstone, Poole, Dorset BH14 OHJ England, n.d.), p.13.
19. Paul E. Billheimer, *Destined to Overcome*, (Minneapolis, Bethany House Publishers, 1992), p.81.
20. G. D. Watson, *Bridehood of the Saints*, (Hampton, TN. Harvey and Tait Publishers, 1988), p.53.

Appendix D—Getting God's Guidance

1. James Hastings, *The Speaker's Bible, Psalms, Volume II*, (Aberdeen, Scotland, G. & W. Fraser, Limited, 1925), p.127.
2. Os Guinness, *The Dust of Death*, p.148.
3. James Stewart, *Heralds of God*, (Grand Rapids, Baker Book House, 1972), p.210.
4. G. D. Watson, *Love and Duty*, p.44.

5. J. I. Packer, *Knowing God*, (Downers Grove, InterVarsity Press, 1973), pp.213, 214.
6. Jessie Penn-Lewis, *Spiritual Warfare*, p.65.
7. G. D. Watson, *A Pot of Oil*, p.124.
8. Jessie Penn-Lewis, *Spiritual Warfare*, p.63.
9. Alexander Malaren, *Expositions of Holy Scriptures, Isaiah and Jeremiah*, Kindle Location: 157.
10. G. D. Watson, *White Robes*, p.101.
11. In contrast with repeated instructions to a horse or mule, the previous verse (Psalm 32:8) envisions a higher level of communication between God and the believer when it quotes God as saying that he will guide us with his eye. Accomplishing this more sophisticated type of guidance requires considerable understanding gained through intimacy. So to distracted souls lacking this intimacy, Alexander Maclaren writes: "What is the use of the glance of an eye if the man for whom it is meant is half a mile off ... God might look guidance at us for a week, and we should never know that he was doing it ... we are so far away from him that it would need a telescope for us to see his face." Alexander Maclaren, *Expositions of Holy Scripture, Deuteronomy, Joshua, Judges, Ruth, and First Book of Samuel, Second Samuel, First Kings, and Second Kings chapters I to VII*, Public Domain Books, Kindle Location, p.113.
12. A. W. Tozer, *The Set of the Sail*, pp.76, 77.
13. Stephen Charnock, *The Works of Stephen Charnock*, Kindle Locations: 1982-1983).
14. A. B. Simpson, *The Christ in the Bible Commentary*, Volume One, (Camp Hill, PA., WingSpread Publishers, 2009), p.252.
15. A. B. Simpson, *The Christ in the Bible Commentary*, Volume Four, (Camp Hill, PA., WingSpread Publishers, 2009), pp.552, 553.
16. F. B. Meyer, "Canst Thou By Searching Find Out God?" located under Sermon Texts on the website sermonindex.net
17. G. D. Watson, *Holiness Manual*, p.78.
18. James S. Stewart, *Walking with God*, p.66.

Appendix E—Examining Emotions

1. Horatius Bonar, *Rent the Veil*, Public Domain, published 1874, Edinburgh, Pensacola, FL., Mt. Zion Publications, p.8.

Endnotes

2. A. W. Tozer, *The Knowledge of the Holy*, p.107.
3. J. I. Packer, *A Quest for Godliness*, p.252.
4. John Piper, *Desiring God*, (Multnomah, Portland, 1986), p.24.
5. Tony Lane, *Timeless Witness*, p.357.
6. G. D. Watson, *Spiritual Feasts*, p.9.
7. James. S. Stewart, *The Wind of the Spirit*, (Grand Rapids, MI., Baker Book House, 1984), p.190.
8. Stephen Charnock, *The Works of Stephen Charnock*, Kindle Location: 3223.
9. A. W. Tozer, *The Divine Conquest*, (Harrisburg, PA., Christian Publications, 1950), pp.100, 101.
10. *The Speaker's Bible, The Epistle to the Philippians, The Epistle to the Colossians*, ed., Edward Hastings, p.106.
11. *The Speaker's Bible, The Gospel According to St. John, Volume 1*, Edward Hastings, ed., (Aberdeen, Scotland, Turnbull & Spear, 1931), p.77.
12. G. D. Watson, *Spiritual Feasts*, p.37.
13. D. E. Harding, *The Hierarchy of Heaven and Earth*, (New York, Harper and Brothers, 1952), p.128.
14. Samuel Chadwick, *The Way to Pentecost*, (Fort Washington, PA., CLC Publications, 2007), p.127.
15. J. I. Packer, *A Quest for Godliness*, p.321.
16. Ibid., p.322.
17. *The Speaker's Bible, The Gospel According to St. John*, Volume II, Edward Hastings, ed. (Aberdeen, Scotland, Turnbull & Spears, 1931), p.96.
18. A. W. Tozer, *That Incredible Christian*, p.123.
19. G. D. Watson, *A Pot of Oil*, p.120.
20. G. D. Watson , *The Secret of Spiritual Power*, pp.167, 168.
21. Ibid., p.168.
22. A. B. Simpson, *The Christ Life*, p.44.
23. Asa Mahan, *Out of Darkness into Light*, pp.104, 105.
24. A. W. Tozer, *Tozer: The Mystery of the Holy Spirit*, p.144.
25. Thomas Goodwin, the Puritan expositor who received his doctorate from Oxford, wrote, "Now, faith is seated in two faculties, the understanding and the will." (*The Works of Thomas Goodwin, Volume 1*, p.226). According to Goodwin, emotions have a lesser role.
26. Andrew Murray, *An Exciting New Life*, p.152.
27. Jessie Penn-Lewis, *The Awakening in Wales*, (Fort Washington, PA., CLC Publications, 2002), p.21.
28. G. D. Watson, *Soul Food*, p.19.
29. Thomas Watson, *The Lord's Prayer*, Kindle Location:

1475.

30. In his book, *Humanity and God*, Samuel Chadwick writes, "The Spirit-filled man glows, radiates, and burns with the fire of God." (p.167).
31. Wesley L. Duewell, *Heroes of the Holy Life*, (Grand Rapids, Zondervan, 2009), p.43.
32. Ibid., p.187.
33. John Henry Jowett, *The Whole Armor of God*, Kindle Locations:1466-1467.
34. A. W. Tozer, *The Next Chapter After the Last*, Christian Publications, Camp Hill, PA., 1987), p.52.

Appendix F—The Romans 7 Debate

1. Gerd Theissen, *Psychological Aspects of Pauline Theology*, (Philadelphia: Fortress Press, 1983), p.191.
2. James S. Stewart, *A Man in Christ*, p.101.
3. John Laidlaw, *The Bible Doctrine of Man*, p.279.
4. James S. Stewart, *A Man in Christ*, p.99.
5. G. D. Watson, *Soul Food*, pp.32, 33.
6. Ibid., p.43.
7. *Luther's Works, vol. 25: Lectures on Romans*, edited by Hilton C. Oswald (St. Louis: Concordia Publishing House, 1972), p.332.
8. John Calvin, *Commentary upon the Epistle to the Romans*, edited by Henry Beveridge (Edinburgh: Calvin Translation Society, 1844), p.187.
9. On page 218 of *The IVP Dictionary of the New Testament*, (Downers Grove, Ill., InterVarsity Press, 2004), we find this acknowledgment: "The autobiographical character of Romans 7:2-25 is not just disputed; it is the center of a major controversy in Pauline studies." In this same article A. F. Segal's view "that Paul is describing Jewish-Christian experience with the law after conversion" is commended. According to this view, Paul uses "I" as a Jewish Christian for Jewish Christians ... Thus Romans 7:2-25 is the description of the personal struggle by any Jewish Christian who tries to keep the law as a Christian" (pp. 218-219). Of course, the Jewish-Christians in view here were contemporaries of Paul who had not yet transitioned to the gospel understandings set forth in the book of Romans.
10. F. Godet, *Commentary on the Epistle to the Romans* (Grand Rapids, Michigan: Zondervan Publishing House, 1970), p.271.

Endnotes

11. Andrew Murray, *The Believer's Secret of the Masters Indwelling*, p.166.
12. John Murray, *Principles of Conduct*, (Grand Rapids, Eerdmans, 1957), pp.218, 219.
13. Benjamin Warfield, "On the Biblical Notion of Renewal," in *Biblical and Theologica Studies*, (Philadelphia, Presbyterian and Reformed, 1968), p.372.
14. *Dictionary of Paul and His Letters*, Editors: Gerald F. Hawthorne, Ralph P. Martin, Daniel G. Reid, (Downers Grove, InterVarsity Press, 1993), p.909.
15. G. D. Watson, *Love and Duty*, p.20.
16. Donald L. Alexander, *Christian Spirituality*, (Downers Grove, IL., InterVarsity Press, 1988), cited on p.112 by Professor Laurence W. Wood.
17. Horatius Bonar, *God's Way of Holiness*, (Chicago, Moody Press, 1970), p.93.
18. John Murray, *Redemption Accomplished and Applied*, (Grand Rapids, Wm. B. Eerdmans Publishing Company, 1955), p.145.
19. Anthony A. Hoekema, *Created in God's Image*, p.25.
20. Based on Colossians 3:10, which says the new man is being renewed, Dr. Hoekema contends: "If something needs to be renewed, it is not yet perfect" (*Created in God's Image*, p.25). However, this deductive reasoning is just that, deductive reasoning and not a statement credentialed by Scripture. What Professor Hoekema says is flawed and misleading, because the life of Jesus in our re-created spirit is perfect. However, access to that life and appropriation of that life requires ongoing faith and repeated contact with the presence of God. These dynamics intensify through repetition the transmission of new nature virtues. And when checking out the Greek word for "renewed" in Colossians 3:10 (*Anakainoo),* Strong's Concordance says it conveys the ideas of intensity, repetition, and freshness (#303 and 2537). This is a passive form verb, indicating that God does the renewing. In some ways this charging up may be analogous with a battery being recharged so that a perfectly constituted cell phone, not in any way defective, may remain in use.
21. For a discussion of this see, *Dictionary of Paul and His Letters*, Editors: Gerald F. Hawthorne, Ralph P. Martin, Daniel G. Reid, pp.853-855.
22. While the objection that Paul's words in Romans 7 appear to be intensely personal have plausibility on surface, this

objection is undercut by the total absence of biblical information to support this view. By arguing from silence, this view is speculative at best. Of course, there would be no theological problem incurred if evidence showed that Paul experienced Romans 7 defeat prior to salvation.

23. Andrew Murray, "O Wretched Man that I Am," found on the website sermonindex.net under Sermon Texts.
24. James S. Stewart, *A Man in Christ*, p.99.
25. The Greek word for "now' in verse 20 is different, the word, *de*. This word doesn't serve to emphasize a difference in domain between law and grace functions. That difference of domain was already established for these precise words in verse 17.
26. W. E. Vine, *An Expository Dictionary of New Testament Words*, (Westwood, NJ., Fleming H. Revell Company, 1966), Volume 3, p.119.
27. The Greek word for "now" in this verse in the word, *nun*, previously discussed in this appendix. According to Strong's Concordance (#3568), this word may indicate transition (i.e. henceforth, in contrast to what had gone on before).
28. F. J. Huegel, *Bone of His Bone*, p.81.
29. Norman P. Grubb, *God Unlimited*, p.109.
30. Hannah Whitall Smith, *The Christian's Secret of a Happy Life*, p.19.
31. Ibid., p.15.
32. *The Works of Thomas Goodwin, Volume I*, p.361.
33. Ibid., p.381.
34. Ibid., p.361.
35. Ibid., p.35.

The Pursuing with Passion Series

Pursuing A Divine Life
A Study of the New Nature

Pursuing God, *volume one*
Strategies for the Spiritually Stuck

Pursuing God, *volume two*
Strategies for the Spiritually Stuck

Pursuing Fellowship, *volume one*
By Activating the "One Another" Principles

Pursuing Fellowship, *volume two*
By Activating the "One Another" Principles

Pursuing the Vision
How Imagination Affects Daily Life

Pursuing Obedience
How to "Want to" When Your "Wanter" Doesn't Want to

Forthcoming book in this series:

Pursuing the Good Life
While Restoring Its Intrigue

46988159R00282

Made in the USA
San Bernardino, CA
20 March 2017